D0547821

Applied Business

AS

Malcolm Surridge   Tim Chapman   Stuart Merrills

Debbie Cornelius   Glynis Frater

Collins

William Collins' dream of knowledge for all began with the publication of his first book in 1819. A self-educated mill worker, he not only enriched millions of lives, but also founded a flourishing publishing house. Today, staying true to this spirit, Collins books are packed with inspiration, innovation and practical expertise. They place you at the centre of a world of possibility and give you exactly what you need to explore it.

Collins. Do more.

Published by Collins
An imprint of HarperCollinsPublishers
77–85 Fulham Palace Road
Hammersmith
London
W6 8JB

Browse the complete Collins catalogue at
www.collinseducation.com

© HarperCollinsPublishers Limited 2004

10 9 8 7 6 5 4 3 2 1

ISBN 0 00 719738 1

Malcolm Surridge, Tim Chapman, Stuart Merrills, Debbie Cornelius and Glynis Frater assert their moral rights to be identified as the authors of this work

British Library Cataloguing in Publication Data
A Catalogue record for this publication is available from the British Library

Commissioned by Graham Bradbury

Cover Design by Blue Pig

Cover picture courtesy of Getty Images

Page design by Patricia Briggs

Additional design and page layout by Stephen Moulds, DSM Partnership

Project managed by Paul Stirner, DSM Partnership

Series managed by Kay Wright

Picture research by Thelma Gilbert

Production by Sarah Robinson

Printed and bound by Martins the Printer, Berwick upon Tweed

Acknowledgements

The authors and publisher would like to thank the following for permission to reproduce photographs and other material:

Advertising Archives p108, p210, p216

Alamy p44, p71, p80, p104, p106, p122, p144, p134, p212, p213, p220, p240, p252, p267, p300, p302, p328

Anthony Blake Picture Library Joff Lee p299

Cadbury Schweppes p70

Collections p326, p327

Corbis p30, p58, p98, p130, p131, p138, p152, p198, p202, p213, p247

Dell p140

DfES 'Get On' Campaign p282, p284

Empics p3, p37, p131, p196, p239, p248, p286, p288, p291, p303, p305, p306, p310, p317, p322

Everyman Theatre, Cheltenham p228

Holt-Studios p102, p104, p117

Kwik-Fit p73, p204

Leicestershire Constabulary p36

John Lewis Partnership p218

MGA/Vivid p123

Panos Pictures p44

Photofusion p213

Red Cross p115

Rex Features p32, p63, p82, p92, p96, p119, p131, p141, p187, p198, p214, p222, p291, p329

Royal Mail p236, p237, p238

S&A Foods p127, p292

Science Photo Library p39

Roger Scruton p19, p48, p63, p67, p72, p78, p82, p83, p90, p114, p116, p118, p120, p123, p129, p130, p137, p147, p202, p220, p224, p232, p236, p262, p310, p318

Toyota p69

Unilever p10

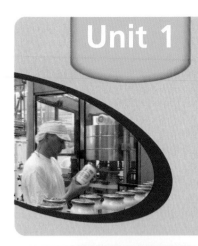

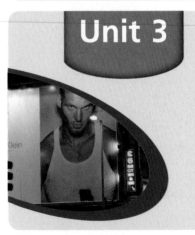
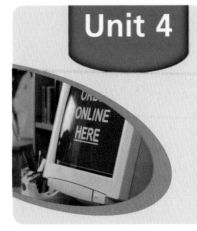
Applied Business AS for Edexcel

Using this book and CD-ROM

Welcome to AS Applied Business. This textbook is written specifically for students taking the Edexcel Applied Business awards, covering everything you will need to know for either the single or double award (see table opposite). If you are taking a single AS-level you will only need to complete Units 1, 2 and 3. To gain a double AS-level, you will need to complete Unit 6 and two units from Units 4, 5 and 7.

Your knowledge and understanding of the different units will be assessed either through:

■ an assignment that is written and marked by your teacher (internal assessment)

■ a written examination lasting one and a half hours that is written and marked by Edexcel, your awarding body (external assessment).

Setting the scene
Real-life case studies and images stimulate your ideas and help you focus on the topic. Many of the scenarios have questions to further engage you with the topic and to stimulate group discussion.

Text
Coverage of each topic is linked closely to the Edexcel specification of the essential knowledge-base you need to understand business.

Key terms
The specialist terminology used in the world of business is explained in simple terms.

Stop and think
These are short activities that can be done individually, in pairs or small groups that will help you to think about the issues raised by the text.

Unit	Title	How is this unit assessed
1	Investigating people at work	External test
2	Investigating business	Internal assessment
3	Investigating marketing	Internal assessment
4	Investigating electronic business	Internal assessment
5	Investigating customer service	Internal assessment
6	Investigating promotion	External test
7	Investigating enterprise	Internal assessment

Single AS-level award

Double AS-level award:
you must study Unit 6 plus two units out of Units 4, 5 and 7

Collins Applied Business AS for Edexcel is divided into seven units and each unit in this book corresponds to a unit of the Edexcel AS-level applied business awards. The units in this book have been divided into topics and each topic provides a manageable chunk of learning covering the subject content of an Edexcel AS-level unit.

● **Knowledge summary**
This provides a quick revision of the key points covered in the text.

● **Quick questions**
Comprehension questions designed to test your understanding of the topic you've just covered. All the answers can be found in the text.

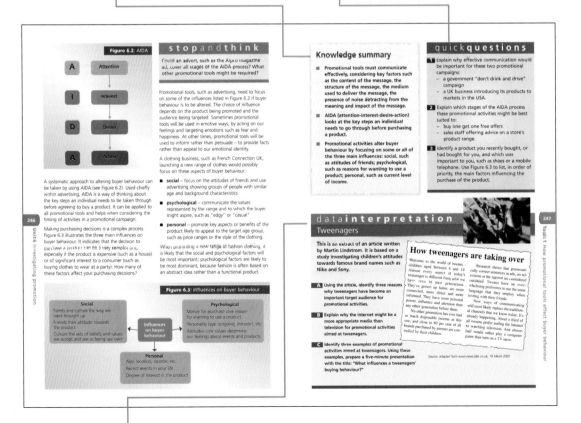

● **Data interpretation**
These activities encourage you to extend your knowledge and skills through a variety of investigative and active learning exercises, which include internet-based research, small-scale research projects and information-gathering activities.

Virtual Business CD-ROM

What's on the Virtual Business CD-ROM?

Studying business should be an active experience that will help you to develop the skills required in the workplace. The Virtual Business CD-ROM attached to this textbook offers you interactive virtual work placement experiences when used alongside your textbook studies.

Unit 1 Investigating people at work:

Hiring a new employee

As a junior manager at a store in a newsagents' chain, you have been asked to hire a junior shop assistant.

Unit 2 Investigating business:

Managing cash flow

In the role of finance manager you must respond to different scenarios that impact on your financial plan (cash flow statement).

Unit 3 Investigating marketing:

Evaluating market research

You are employed as a market researcher for a computer games company. The company has asked you to look at launching a new mass-market computer game with a view to increasing its market share and raising the company profile.

Unit 4 Investigating electronic business:

Commissioning a website

Your company is launching a new website and you are in charge of selecting the most appropriate features to appear on the site to enable your company to make the most of its new web presence.

Unit 5 Investigating customer service:

Providing good customer care

As the manager of a luxury hotel you will be challenged by three different customer care scenarios. You will need to use your skills to deliver good customer care to clients before, during and after their stay at your hotel.

Unit 6 Investigating promotion:

Organising a promotional campaign

You are in charge of making appropriate choices, based on cost and effectiveness, of suitable media channels to promote your organisation.

Unit 7 Investigating enterprise:

Run your own business

The pop business is a cut-throat industry. Make the right decisions and you'll be number 1. Make the wrong ones and you will not do so well.

Operating systems required for installing the CD-ROM

PC

Windows 98SE/2000/XP
Windows: Pentium III 600MHz or equivalent
MPC compatible sound card
800 x 600 minimum size monitor display with
16 bit colour, or higher
64MB available RAM
You will need a minimum of 90MB of free space on your hard drive

Installation instructions:

- Insert the Virtual Business disc into your CD-ROM drive

- Double click on the CD-ROM drive icon inside My Computer

- Double click on the SETUP.EXE icon Follow the onscreen instructions

Mac

MacOS 9.x; Mac OS X
Mac: PowerMac G3, 350 MHz or higher
800 x 600 minimum size monitor display with
16 bit colour, or higher
2 speed CD-ROM
64MB available RAM
You will need a minimum of 90MB of free space on your hard drive

Installation instructions:

- Insert the Virtual Business disc into your CD-ROM drive

- Double click on the CD-ROM drive icon inside My Computer

- Double click on the SETUP.OSX icon Follow the onscreen instructions

Good luck with your GCE AS-level studies. This book and CD-ROM provide you with interesting, supportive and motivating learning materials that we hope will help you to succeed in your applied business course.

THIS UNIT EXAMINES THE KEY ROLE THAT PEOPLE play in helping any business organisation achieve its aims and objectives. It looks at the procedures that businesses use to recruit employees, how they train and motivate their staff to work to high standards and how all businesses must comply with a range of legislation to protect the well-being of employees and to avoid discrimination in the workplace.

This unit is organised into four broad sections which will help you to investigate the role of people at work:

- business aims, objectives and organisation
- how businesses obtain employees
- how businesses motivate employees
- how people are influenced at work.

Investigating people at work

Introducing people at work

Setting the scene: Renault plans its new workforce

In 2005, the French car manufacturer Renault confirmed its expansion plans. One of the company's aims is to expand its sales in international (as opposed to French) markets.

Renault had enjoyed a prosperous period in the run up to this announcement and overall sales had risen by 15 per cent in 2004. In part, this had been due to the launch of some successful new models, as cars like the Renault Mégane helped to revitalise the company's fortunes. But Renault has also benefited from the success of its partnership with the Japanese manufacturer Nissan, in which it holds a 44 per cent stake.

Renault's plans have significant implications for the company's workforce. In order to implement its ambitious expansion, the company plans to hire 14,000 new employees to increase its production capacity.

The company will be seeking to recruit managers, employees with engineering and other technical skills, as well as workers to carry out a range of duties on the company's production lines.

In addition, some 4,000 new employees will work in Renault's chain of car dealers selling cars and providing after-sales service for customers.

A Renault spokesperson admitted that the success of the plan depended on appointing "talented people". This will be crucial if Renault is to thrive in the face of the tough competition that exists in the car manufacturing industry.

KEY TERMS

Aims are the long-term visions or goals of a business.

Objectives are specific, measurable targets that help managers to achieve a business's aims.

Recruitment is the process of finding and appointing new employees.

Motivation examines the factors that influence people to behave in certain ways.

Why are people important to business?

When we think of businesses, many things come to mind. Some businesses have world-famous brands. Coca-Cola is thought to be the second most commonly spoken term in the world – the first is OK! – and is of huge value to the company. Other businesses are famous for the physical assets that they own. For example, Eurotunnel, the Anglo-French company, is completely associated with the Channel Tunnel, its prime asset.

Assets – both physical and intangible – are clearly necessary for any business to operate. However, many managers argue that a business's employees are the most important assets that an enterprise possesses.

There are several reasons why business managers hold this view.

- Employees can be creative. The team working for Microsoft has been endlessly ingenious in designing a range of computer software products that have made the company one of the largest and wealthiest in the world. Microsoft announced in 2005 that its quarterly profits had doubled, boosted by rising sales of its Windows operating system and its Xbox games console.

- Employees can satisfy consumer demands and create a reputation for high-quality products. Lotus, the sports car manufacturer, prides itself on designing innovative and unconventional cars for customers whose passion is driving. To achieve this reputation for excellence, Lotus is heavily reliant on the high-quality design, engineering and assembly skills of its employees.

- For many service businesses – such as banking, restaurants and hairdressing – the staff's skills determine the customers' experience to a great extent. There is no point in locating a restaurant in a beautiful building and staffing it with poorly skilled chefs and shoddy waiting staff. Diners are unlikely to enjoy their experience.

- Employees represent a major knowledge base for most organisations. In recent years, many businesses have attempted to cut costs by slimming down workforces and by cutting numbers of middle-ranking managers in particular. One of the consequences of this downsizing has been a reduction in the pool of knowledge and experience shared by the remaining employees, and this has affected the quality of management decision making in some companies.

- All businesses can only achieve their aims and objectives with the help of their employees. The example of Renault (opposite) illustrates the importance of planning the numbers and types of employees required when taking any major strategic decision. This process is known as workforce planning.

What this unit covers

This unit examines an organisation's aims and objectives and the roles that people can play in helping a business achieve these goals.

Business aims, objectives and organisation

All organisations have varied aims and objectives, but these often differ between different types of business organisations. The unit looks at how the different legal structures that businesses can adopt might influence the ways in which they operate, and discusses the key roles within organisations and the duties and responsibilities associated with these roles.

How businesses obtain employees

Most businesses need to recruit staff at some stage. The unit reviews the elements that make up the recruitment process and the techniques that businesses use to select potential employees from a small group of people who make it through to the final stages of the recruitment process.

How businesses motivate employees

Businesses use a range of financial and non-financial incentives to influence the performance of their employees. The unit examines how businesses choose to motivate staff and sets out how they must comply with a range of legislation designed to protect the well-being of employees.

How people are influenced at work

Business are affected by a range of issues that impact on people at work. These include environmental issues such as pollution and recycling, social and ethical issues, and wider legal issues covering matters such as health and safety, employment protection and consumer protection.

GO TO the accompanying CD-ROM. Choose Unit 1 from the main menu. This will take you to an interactive game about hiring a new employee. It is better to try this game once you have read Unit 1 Topics 3 and 4.

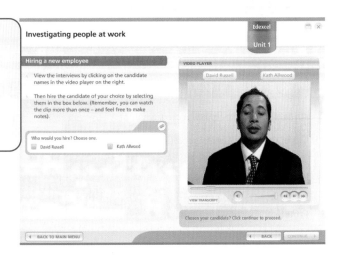

Business aims, objectives and organisation

Setting the scene: business diversity

There are a huge variety of business organisations, varying in size from large global multinationals to small one-person enterprises, and ranging from private sector companies to organisations in the public and voluntary sectors that need to bring a business-like approach to all their activities.

Despite this apparent diversity, every business organisation has a number of common features. Each will have:

- an aim and one or more objectives
- a structure and a form of ownership
- one or more functions.

To begin to appreciate the kind of aims and objectives set by business, consider the two examples presented here.

Next's strategy, set out in its July 2004 interim statement, shows what the company is trying to achieve. Next has been successful in increasing both its sales and profit in the competitive retail market. It aims to drive further growth through delivering quality products for customers and growing both its in-store and mail order trade.

Boots' aim is to be the UK market leader in its sector and to grow the business internationally. That aim will be backed by a number of detailed objectives – and we have just quoted one here to illustrate that, while aims embrace a broad vision, objectives tend to be expressed in terms of very specific targets.

Source: www.boots-plc.com

Boots mission

Boots aims to be the place for health and beauty customers. We want to secure market leadership in the UK and build on our brands' growing success internationally.

One of Boots' objectives

As part of our commitment to meet the objectives of the Disability Discrimination Act, staff in all Boots stores must complete disability awareness training to prepare for the implementation of the new requirements in October.

Next, interim statement July 2004

In his interim statement, David Jones CBE, chairman of Next has announced a 15 per cent increase in turnover and a 30 per cent increase in pre-tax profit. This brings Next's total turnover to £1,293.5 million and the company's profit before tax to £162.7 million.

The company's strategy is "to provide great product ranges for our customers in areas where we can add something to the design of the product; and to improve access and choice through the expansion of retail selling space and the Next Directory".

Source: www.next.co.uk

NEXT

KEY TERMS

Aims are the long-term visions or goals of a business.

Objectives are specific, measurable targets to help to achieve the overall aims of the business.

Structure is the way in which the business activities are grouped or arranged.

Functional areas are distinct operating areas within the business, such as marketing, finance, logistics and sales.

Business aims

The overall aim of an organisation describes its long-term vision or goals – in other words, it purpose for being. Organisations often describe their aims through a vision or mission statement.

Tesco and Coca-Cola are two of the biggest brands in the UK retail sector. Here (opposite) are the published mission statements of these two companies.

- The Coca-Cola Company exists to benefit and refresh everyone who is touched by our business.

- Tesco's core purpose is to create value for customers to earn their lifetime loyalty. We deliver this through our values – no-one tries harder for customers and we treat people how we like to be treated.

Look now at the aims of four very different organisations:

- a local council – to provide a range of services that enhances the quality of life of the population it serves

- a theme park – to provide a piece of magic to everyone who visits, young or old

- a cancer charity – to raise the awareness of this condition and to provide the support to continue a programme of research and education

- a removals company – to provide customers with a worry-free solution to their house move.

These various mission statements show that not all the aims of a business relate to making a profit; non-profit aims and objectives are often equally important in a business.

The language used in a vision or mission statement can also be instructive. Although the mission statement sets out the organisation's reason for being, often, by the way in which the aim is described, the statement also indicates the organisation's values.

Companies do not always express their vision or goals within a single statement. They may have two or three long-term aims set out in separate statements. For example Apple, the computer manufacturer and retailer, has set out its environmental goals in a separate vision statement:

> Environmental protection is a priority for the conservation of precious natural resources. At Apple, we take this reality seriously. From the earliest stages of design, to our recycling initiatives worldwide, we are committed to reducing the environmental impact of the work we do and the products we create.

(Source: www.apple.com/environment/policy)

Business objectives

Aims provide the general direction, the overall goal of the business and give an important focus. However, they are not specific enough on their own to help direct an organisation's effort to be effective.

Objectives (or targets) are required for this purpose. A business will only have one (or a very few) aims, but it is likely to have a number of objectives; and, while its aims are unlikely to vary much over time, its objectives will change frequently.

Objectives relate to specific business outcomes. They come in all shapes and sizes. For example, a newly formed business's objective might simply be 'to survive for the first twelve months in operation'. In general, though, objectives help to define key aspects of operations and will vary across the business organisation. Here, for example, are the objectives Apple has set to meet its environmental aim that we quoted above:

> meet or exceed all applicable environmental, health and safety requirements
>
> support and promote public policy that will enhance environmental quality, health and safety
>
> communicate environmental, health and safety policies and programs to Apple employees and stakeholders.

Organisations express their objectives in a variety of ways. However, to be really useful to the business, objectives should be SMART. This is an acronym; spelt out it means that objectives should be:

- **specific** – explain exactly what is to be achieved

- **measurable** – a form of measurement is essential to establish what has been achieved

- **achievable** – should provide a challenge (to motivate) but should be capable of being delivered

- **realistic** – it should be reasonable to expect that the objective can be met by those responsible for doing so

- **time-bound** – it should have a defined timescale setting out when the objective should be achieved.

You can see that the objective on disability awareness training at Boots (quoted in setting the scene) meets at least some of the SMART criteria: it is specific (staff training to prepare for the new disability legislation), it is measurable (staff in all stores), it is time-bound (the implication is that the training must be delivered by November), though we are not in a position to judge whether it is realistic or achievable.

stop and think

Look back at Tesco's mission statement quoted above, in which the company says its core purpose is 'to create value for customers to earn their lifetime loyalty'.

■ How is Tesco positioning itself in what is a highly saturated grocery market in the UK?

■ What is Tesco doing to stay on top of the competition? What products is Tesco using to beat the competition?

Visit Tesco's website (www.tesco.com) to help you complete this task.

Influence of ownership

The type of ownership impacts on the types of decisions an organisation can make and, to a lesser or greater extent, the types of objectives that it sets. For instance, for a university to operate effectively, it needs to be able to supplement the money it receives through government funding in the form of tuition fees by winning research grants. This need to win additional funding to function as an effective teaching and research organisation shapes both the university's objectives and the way it operates.

Consider now other types of organisation.

■ **Sole traders** and **partnerships** largely use their own capital to set up their businesses. Sole traders and partners are free to set their objectives and have control over all decisions within the business.

■ **Limited companies** are owned by their shareholders, though run by managers and directors. The broad aims of companies will be set (or agreed) by the shareholders, however day-to-day operational decisions and short-term objectives will be decided by managers and directors. These decisions can impact on the share price of the business, and directors usually see their role as to maximise shareholder value.

■ **Public sector organisations**, such as local authorities, central government departments, schools, colleges and hospitals, rely primarily on the government for funding. There has been a trend in recent years to devolve management responsibility away from central government to, say, individual schools and hospitals, but broad objectives and performance targets are still set by government.

■ **Registered charities** are free to set their own objectives providing they are within the legal criteria that defines whether a body qualifies for charitable status. Managers in charities have reasonable freedom to take decisions, but charities' overall activity is constrained by the need to obtain donations to continue to operate.

Figure 1.1: Functional areas in a manufacturing company

Functional area	Tasks
Production	The making of the goods or individual parts. May also relate to the provision of a service.
Sales	Selling the products to the customer.
Marketing	Finding out what the customer wants and the best way of meeting their needs, promoting products to potential customers.
Purchasing	Buying raw materials and components needed in production.
Finance	Keeping financial records, producing annual accounts, keeping accurate records of costs and revenues.
Human resources	Attending to staffing requirements, ensuring correct processes and procedures are in place for the staff.
Health and safety	Ensuring workplace safety and legislation needs are met.
Logistics	Delivering the products to the customers.

Business functions

A business is likely to be performing a number of functions. In all but the smallest businesses, functions and responsibilities are likely to divided between different staff and usually different departments. How this is done varies considerably, not only across different sectors of industry but between companies operating within the same sector and in the same markets. Figure 1.1 illustrates the functional areas you might expect to find in a manufacturing company.

The way functions operate within a business and the way they work together to deliver the business's objectives has a crucial impact on its level of success. Some functions might be front line, others labelled as support functions, but each function will have objectives relevant to their contribution. Functions could not be effective without working with other functions. This calls for an extensive network of processes, procedures and communication channels.

Knowledge summary

- **Business aims set the general direction of an organisation and provide a focus all their activities.**

- **Business objectives provide specific targets that an organisation attempts to achieve through its operations.**

- **The objectives of an organisation will vary according to the type of business and its form of ownership.**

- **The form of ownership shapes both the decision-making process of a business and the ways in which it is funded.**

- **The functions of a business help to contribute towards the achievement of its objectives.**

quick questions

1 Outward Bound successfully runs outdoor activity centres across the UK. Consider what the aims of this business might be.

2 With new outdoor activity centres opening up all the time, what objectives might be most important for Outward Bound as a business? Explain your answer.

3 Compare the objectives of a private sector business, such as The Gillette Company, to those of a non-profit making business, such as Oxfam. Why do the objectives differ?

4 The Body Shop has aims which relate to making a profit and which relate to caring for the environment. Explain why. You may need to visit www.bodyshop.co.uk to research your answer.

data interpretation
Researching aims, objectives and functions

Select two organisations that operate in a similar market, and which operate within the same business sector – that is, your two organisations should either both be in the private sector, or the public sector, or the voluntary sector.

For example, you might choose two private sector transport businesses, such as easyJet and British Airways, or two schools or colleges in the public sector education market, or two charities in the voluntary sector, such as Cafod and Oxfam.

Research both organisations to find out about their aims, objectives, functions and structures. You can get most of this information from the internet and your chosen organisations' websites. Find out:

- what is the aim of each organisation?
- what are their current objectives?
- what functions exist in each organisation?
- how similar or dissimilar are these functions?
- how are the two businesses structured?
- why are they structured in that way?

A Write a short report comparing your chosen two organisations. Identify the key features you have learned from your research.

Business structures and job roles

Setting the scene: looking at company structure

Company A and Company B are both construction businesses operating in the Midlands. They have a similar turnover and both offer the same range of building services.

There are differences between the companies, both in their type of ownership and their organisational structure. Company A is a partnership founded by two ex-school friends; Company B is a limited company. Figure 1.2 shows the organisational charts of the two businesses.

Company A has three members of permanent staff who support the two founding partners. Their specific work responsibilities vary, depending on the requirements of the current jobs

on Company A's books. When the company needs specialists or additional labour, the partners bring in subcontractors to help it fulfil the contract.

Company B has 25 employees. They are organised into three divisions: ground works, construction and painting services. These divisions report to the company secretary, who in turn reports to Company B's director.

Why do you think the owners of Company A and Company B chosen these different structures for their businesses? Can you think of some of the advantages (and any possible disadvantages) of each approach.

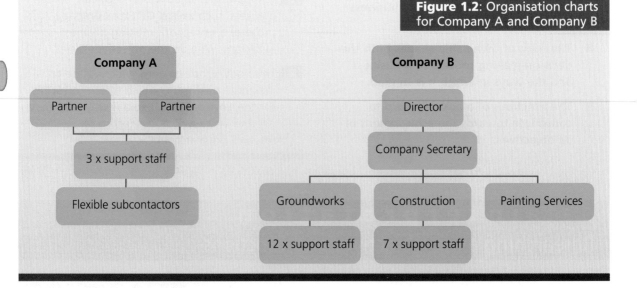

Figure 1.2: Organisation charts for Company A and Company B

KEY TERMS

Managers plan and co-ordinate activities within a business

Supervisors and **team leaders** take day-to-day responsibility for employees within their work area, ensuring they work effectively and dealing with problems as they arise.

Support staff and **other employees** have responsibilities defined in their job role. They provide functional support to the business and essential specialist services to enable the business to work effectively.

Business structures

In Topic 1, we considered the aims and objectives of business and discussed the way most businesses need to undertake a variety of functions. The way an organisation operates in practice will depend in part on the way it is structured. Structure identifies what parts of the organisation exist and the hierarchical nature of the component parts.

Organisation charts are a useful way to illustrate the structure of a business and also the relationship of management roles and reporting lines. Figure 1.2 shows the organisation charts for two construction companies. These charts show us the lines of responsibility – the chain of command; and they indicate the span of control – how many people report to each manager.

Job roles

Each McDonald's restaurant employs a team of 60 or more people. There is a wide range of job roles, including crew members, customer care specialists, party entertainers, maintenance people and trainee business managers. Each job role makes a different contribution to McDonald's overall business.

Similarly, other businesses need to have a range of job roles in order to function effectively. Each job role is different. Our jobs are differentiated through:

- the type of job we do
- the level of responsibility we hold
- the level of authority we have
- the extent to which we make decisions
- the type of work we do.

If a business is to perform successfully, it is essential that it creates an appropriate mix of job roles. The roles that people play within the business are critical to its success. Figure 1.3 shows a simplified set of job roles in a limited company, linked by the chain of command. We will use this categorisation to look at the various job roles that exist in a business and the different responsibilities that are associated with each role.

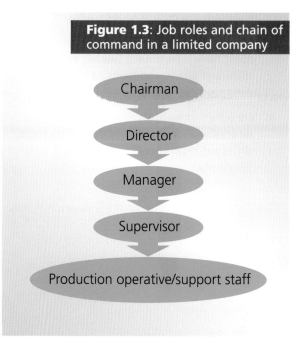

Figure 1.3: Job roles and chain of command in a limited company

Chairman

Director

Manager

Supervisor

Production operative/support staff

1 Directors

Directors are appointed by the shareholders of a business to control and manage the activities and affairs of the business. The directors' role is largely strategic; they have to identify opportunities and set corporate objectives for the business. The board of directors usually appoints one of their members to act as chairman.

2 Managers

A manager has a variety of activities to carry out. As Figure 1.4 shows, these activities can be grouped under four main functional headings: planning, organising, motivating and controlling. These groupings indicate broadly what managers do in practice. They can be applied to supervisory and junior management positions as well as to middle and senior management roles.

Figure 1.4: Four key management activities

Planning

A plan is a design for achieving something. Strategic plans – planning for the long-term – are usually made at higher levels of management. Tactical plans, such as setting budgets or planning a marketing campaign, have more of a short-term focus. Tactical planning is carried out at lower levels in the business, such as middle management or supervisor levels.

Organising

In implementing plans, managers need to decide on the activities that need to be undertaken and they must allocate responsibilities. This involves allocating staff and resources to specific functions and activities in order to carry out tasks and achieve the objectives.

Motivating

In order to achieve the goals and objectives of the business, manager have to gain the commitment and co-operation of employees. Managers need to demonstrate leadership to ensure that employees work towards the business's objectives.

Controlling

Managers have to evaluate the effectiveness of work undertaken by employees for which they are responsible. This requires monitoring performance against required standards and taking corrective action where improvements need to be made.

3 Supervisors

A supervisor provides a link between a manager and the operatives and support staff. They are classed as the first line of management, taking on some management functions through delegation of authority. With the move towards flatter organisational structures, more organisations are passing authority lower down the organisational structure. This process – known as delayering, as it involves stripping away layers of middle management – has resulted in many supervisory and junior managers being given more responsibility and authority.

The responsibilities of a supervisor include:

- controlling the day-to-day work of operational and support staff
- monitoring the work they do to ensure targets are being met
- advising management of any problems that arise in the work of the business
- taking corrective action to get back on target if there are any shortcomings.

4 Operational and support staff

The role of other employees in a company depends on the type of business in which they are working. For example, operational staff may be working on a production line in a manufacturing plant or as retail assistants within a shop. Operational employees have lower levels of authority than a supervisor and the type of work they do is usually routine in nature.

Support staff provide a specialist service to staff at all levels in a business. Examples of support roles include information technology support, administration and secretarial services. Some support work can be highly specialised and technical. The level of decision making and responsibility will depend on the extent and nature of the support role. Similarly, pay rates are likely to vary considerably depending on the type of skills required for each support role.

---

job profile: Kitchen supervisor

As a kitchen supervisor in a hotel or restaurant, you may be in charge of particular areas of the kitchen. For example, you may be a section chef, an under-chef or sous chef.

Kitchen supervisors are trained chefs or cooks who organise and oversee the work done by their team. They make sure that the food is prepared and produced at the right quality, the right price and the right time. They plan menus, order food and keep control of the budget.

Kitchen supervisors and managers decide which tasks are to be done each day and delegate these to members of their team. They produce duty rotas, making sure that enough staff will be on duty at all times. They also deal with health and safety issues and disciplinary matters.

Source: www.learndirect-advice.co.uk

Knowledge summary

- **The structure of a business refers to the way in which the business activities are grouped or arranged.**
- **The roles that people play within the business are critical to its success.**
- **There is a wide variety of job roles in most businesses, each linking to the different levels and parts of the organisation structure.**
- **Directors, managers, supervisors, operational staff and support staff have different responsibilities and job functions.**

data**interpretation**

Two contrasting job roles

job profile: Telesales agent, easyJet

As a telesales agent, you need to be friendly and customer focused, able to remain calm and work efficiently under pressure, be an excellent communicator with people of all ages and of different cultures, and be able to take direction and accept feedback. You will be responsible for driving sales for the business, and work with other members of the telesales team to ensure that all calls are responded to in line with policy guidelines.

You are expected to be fluent in written and spoken French (to A-level standard, or to be a native speaker); to be fluent in written and spoken English; to have a good general standard of education to GCSE level or equivalent, to be prepared to work flexible hours including some weekends and evenings, and to have excellent keyboard skills.

Source: www.easyjet.com

job profile: B&Q Store Manager

B&Q store managers are responsible for managing a group of team leaders who each control their own department in the store. They are responsible for achieving sales targets, staff development and appraisals.

Store managers at B&Q are responsible for managing every aspect of the business. They are accountable for driving sales and exceeding profit targets, developing and implementing business plans, and communicating targets and objectives to their team.

B&Q expects anyone applying for a store manager position to have the ability to handle many tasks at once, and to be able to prioritise effectively and decisively. The ability to mentor and support teams, and sound interpersonal skills are also desirable. Applicants should have previous retail management experience. Store managers at B&Q receive £25–£35,000 plus bonuses and a benefits package.

Source: www.diy.com

A Suggest why easyJet insists on these minimum requirements for the telesales job role.

B Explain how this job role can be classed as a support function.

C Consider a B&Q employee that moves from a part-time customer adviser job to a store manager position. How would their job roles and responsibilities have changed?

D What problems might this switch of job roles have created? Suggest ways that B&Q could overcome these problems.

How businesses obtain employees

Setting the scene: Airbus

Airbus is the world's leading aircraft manufacturer, and the company received a total of 370 firm orders in 2004. Airbus received these new orders for its aircraft from two carriers in June 2004.

Eurofly orders Airbus A319 long-range aircraft

Italian leading charter carrier Eurofly has signed a contract for one A319 long-range aircraft and plans to acquire a second, becoming a new customer for the Airbus Corporate Jetliner (ACJ) family.

JetBlue orders 30 A320s

New York-based low-fare carrier JetBlue Airways has ordered 30 new Airbus A320s. Like the rest of the airline's extensive A320 fleet, they will be powered by International Aero Engines V2500s. Deliveries of the newly contracted aircraft will begin in 2006 and run through 2011. To date, JetBlue orders for Airbus aircraft total 173.

For Airbus, increased demand can mean there is a need to recruit additional staff in order to fulfil new orders. Look at the two press cuttings. What effect will these new orders have on the demand for staff within Airbus? Do you think that this is likely to generate a long-term or short-term need; and how do you think a company like Airbus can effectively recruit the staff it needs without risking long-term overstaffing?

Reasons for recruiting staff

Why do vacancies occur in businesses? There could be several reasons a business needs to recruit more employees. Certainly demand is one factor, as is the case at Airbus. An increase in orders may be linked to other business activities such as a proactive advertising and promotion campaign.

However, businesses have to look closely at other external factors that may affect their demand for staff in the future. There are a range of political, environmental, social and technical influences which might increase (or decrease) the need for staff within a business. For example, if new employment laws limit the number of hours employees can work each week – say, an extension of the European Union's working

hours directive – then a business might need to recruit more staff. Conversely, if more people expect and want to work past the traditional retirement age, a business might need to recruit less staff as its older workers choose to stay on.

KEY TERMS

Recruitment involves looking in the right places to find the best staff for the business.

Selection is the process of choosing the best staff from those who apply.

A **job description** is a document that provides a detailed list of the roles and responsibilities entailed in a job.

A **person specification** identifies the attributes required in the person required to fill a job.

The government is committed to removing age discrimination at work. Find out more about the government's campaign from www.agepositive.gov.uk. In what ways might age discrimination affect young people in the workplace? What do you think will be impact be of anti-age discrimination legislation on (a) a small business employing less than 20 staff and (b) a large, private sector business in the transport sector.

Age on the agenda

Marks & Spencer, Sainsbury and Tesco along with B&Q are actively employing people in their 50s. There's a hard-edged business case for companies to employ older workers. We are actually moving towards full employment as a social trend in the UK and we are moving into a state of almost full employment. Staff involved in recruitment will have to look at stopping discriminating on any grounds, because the pool of available people is getting less and less.

People Management, 17 June 2004

Apart from external factors, vacancies may occur within a business for many reasons. These include:

- a member of staff promoted within the business

- a member of staff resigning

- a member of staff retiring, or a death in service

- new posts being created or new job roles being introduced

- business expansion and/or diversity into new markets.

The recruitment and selection process

The aim of every recruitment and selection process should be to ensure that the right person is chosen for the job. Failing to do so can have huge adverse implications in terms of organisational effectiveness, staff and individual morale, and staff turnover. Add this to the cost of the recruitment process itself and getting recruitment wrong represents a huge drain on a business's finance. Getting recruitment right represents a worthwhile investment.

A robust, systematic recruitment and selection process is vital to ensure that the right person is found for the job, and unsuccessful applicants are left with a good image of the business and feeling that they have been dealt with fairly throughout. The aim is to:

- recruit high-quality staff, with appropriate skills and experience

- appoint staff on an appropriate contract of employment

- ensure equal opportunities are respected

- ensure that the process is fair, efficient and cost-effective

- encourage recruiters to follow structured guidelines

- monitor and review the process regularly

- maintain quality, robust methods which adequately meet the business needs.

Although each business will have its own procedures, Figure 1.5 shows the stages that make up a robust and fair recruitment and selection process.

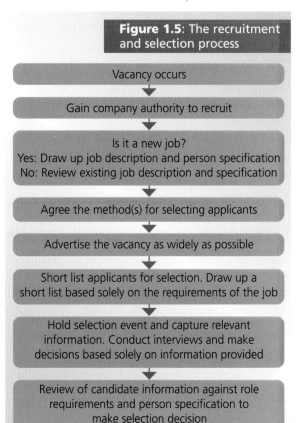

Figure 1.5: The recruitment and selection process

Vacancy occurs

Gain company authority to recruit

Is it a new job?
Yes: Draw up job description and person specification
No: Review existing job description and specification

Agree the method(s) for selecting applicants

Advertise the vacancy as widely as possible

Short list applicants for selection. Draw up a short list based solely on the requirements of the job

Hold selection event and capture relevant information. Conduct interviews and make decisions based solely on information provided

Review of candidate information against role requirements and person specification to make selection decision

23

Topic 3 How businesses obtain employees

In the rest of this topic, we are going to focus on the top part of Figure 1.5 – on job descriptions, person specifications and advertising job vacancies. In Topic 4, we look at depth at the rest of the selection process, that is how to choose between applicants.

1 Job descriptions

A job description should be created for every job role. This document should set out the overall purpose of the job and the key tasks and responsibilities of the post. Figure 1.6 shows the five main components of a job description.

Figure 1.6: Structure and components of a job description

Component	Function
Job title	This should be a short descriptive title that explains the nature of the job, such as customer service assistant or senior team leader.
Purpose	Usually a one sentence summary of why the role exists: for example, to provide customer service support to the retail sales team.
Key tasks	These should be specific activities and described clearly using action words; for example, to co-ordinate, calculate and produce sales reports.
Scope of the role	Gives the boundary of responsibility: that is, who the job holder is responsible to (who they are managed by) and who they are responsible for (who they manage). This section should also list any budgetary responsibilities.
Special requirements	Specific requirements such as shift or flexible work patterns, travelling requirements, essential languages and professional qualifications.

2 Person specifications

An accurate person specification is an essential part of an effective recruitment process. It sets out the criteria needed for effective performance in the job role. It allows selectors to make accurate comparisons between candidates against the specific requirements of the person needed to fill the job role.

There are three essential components to a person specification:

- essential requirements – requirements without which an applicant could not be considered for the job

- desirable requirements – it would be good if candidates had these attributes, though they are not required in order to start the job (and they could be subsequently developed through training)

- contra-indicators – criteria or features which would make any applicant immediately unsuitable for the job; for example, unspent criminal convictions for theft or fraud are contra-indicators for any post that involves handling cash.

3 Job advertising

All job advertisements should be consistent with the job description and the person specification. They should be worded to attract suitable candidates who match the essential job and person criteria and should provide a positive public image of the business.

A business needs to make sure it attracts a sufficient number of suitably qualified applicants to apply for the job. So it needs to advertise in the right places. One of the key decisions a business needs to make is whether to restrict the job to internal candidates or to invite applications from people outside the company. There are benefits in keeping recruitment in-house: it is cheaper, it can be good for staff morale and all applicants will already be familiar with the business. However, by looking for external applicants, companies will be able to draw from a much wider pool of talent and, obviously, all businesses need fresh blood at some stage. Figure 1.7 shows the options for advertising vacancies.

Figure 1.7: Means of advertising job vacancies

Internal advertisements	External advertisements
On company noticeboards	Newspapers – local or national
In a company newsletter	Contact with schools, colleges and universities
In an internal vacancy bulletin	Specialist magazines
On the premises in the form of a poster	Job centres
E-mail to all (or selected) staff	Internet – company websites
	Recruitment agencies
	Recruitment or job fairs
	Radio and television advertisements

Knowledge summary

■ The aim of every recruitment and selection process should be to ensure the right person is chosen for the job.

■ A robust, systematic recruitment and selection process is vital to ensure that the right person is found for the job.

■ External factors can affect the number of staff needed by a business. A business has to monitor the political, social, environmental and technical factors that may affect its future demand for staff.

■ All businesses should draw up (or revise existing) job descriptions and person specifications for any vacancy.

data interpretation
Royal Mail

The Royal Mail often advertises for casual staff to cover the Christmas period. It has sent a mailshot to individual homes in the form of a Christmas card offering "seasons greetings" with a job advertisement on the reverse of the card. It has also placed this advert on its website (www.royalmail.co.uk).

Want to earn extra cash this Christmas?

Our job of delivering millions of letters and packages becomes even bigger at Christmas. At the height of the season, we handle over 130 million mail items a day.

To make sure we deliver all this mail, and all our customer promises, at this busy time of year, we need teams of seasonal workers to help out our mail centres from the end of November through to Christmas. We are looking for people who will be enthusiastic about working as postmen and postwomen, sorters, customer advisers and drivers.

You could be out delivering mail, working indoors in a mail centre or driving a van. And your tasks could include:

■ sorting mail to correct address order ready for delivery
■ carrying bags of mail for delivery on foot or by bike
■ collecting mail from post boxes and businesses
■ transporting mail by road between mail centres, stations and airports
■ advising and talking to customers.

You do not need any experience. You just need to be 16 or over, conscientious, reliable, a team player and flexible enough to work a variety of shifts.

A Why does the Royal Mail need additional staff during the Christmas period?

B Look at the job advert that appeared on its website. What would you expect to see in the job description for this role?

C Give three reasons why the Royal Mail might use a mailshot as well as advertising on its internet site.

D How might the mailshot increase the effectiveness of the staff recruitment process for the Christmas period?

E Suggest other ways in which the Royal Mail might advertise for these posts. Explain why you think these are appropriate. You may wish to consider where you have seen other businesses advertise for Christmas staff. Would any of these be appropriate for the Royal Mail to use?

The selection process

Setting the scene: compiling a CV

Some job advertisements ask you to apply in writing. In these cases, you will need to send both a curriculum vitae (CV) and a covering letter.

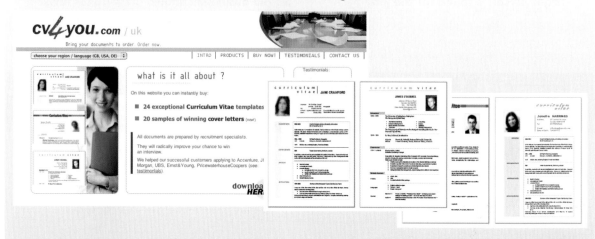

Your CV should give any potential employer a profile about you. It should include your qualifications, where you were educated, any work experience you may have had and any interests you may have as well as, in chronological order, details of your working career to date.

There are many resources that provide advice on writing a CV. For example, if you visit the BBC onelife website (www.bbc.co.uk/radio1/onelife), you can find comprehensive advice about CVs by first clicking on "work" and then on "CVs". This

site gives you hints and tips on how to complete your CV.

Use the aims and content section of the onelife CV pages to prepare your own CV ready to use in future job applications. Look at the sample job description page of this site. This will advise you on how to pick out key details about the job for which you are applying that you can focus on when preparing your CV and writing a covering application letter.

Getting a short list

In Topic 3, we reviewed the first stages in the recruitment and selection process: drawing up job descriptions and person specifications and deciding where and how to advertise the job vacancy. The next step is deciding on a short list of applicants, with the required qualities, from which a business can select a preferred candidate.

There are many different methods used by businesses to compile a short list of candidates. Most typically, applicants are asked to return either a curriculum vitae (CV), a competed application form or a letter of application. Sometimes they are asked to supply two, and occasionally all three, of these different means of job application.

These applications are then used to assess the strengths and weaknesses of applicants, which allows the business to draw up a short list to go through to the final stage of the selection process.

KEY TERMS

Curriculum vitae (CV) a document outlining a person's educational and professional history, which is often submitted with their job application.

Interviewing conversing with and questioning of an individual for different reasons, such as a job interview.

Short-listing involves compiling a list of suitable applicants for a job, from which the successful candidate will be selected.

Let's now consider the advantages and disadvantages of each of the main methods of inviting applications.

Application forms

A well-designed application form will not only capture the personal details of each applicant but it allows the business to ask key questions that are particularly relevant to the job. An application form is also a useful public relations tool; it can portray the image of the business and be used to provide background information to potential applicants. Application forms also work well online. However, forms can put off some applicants: some get discouraged if the form is too long and detailed, and sometimes poor form design does not give sufficient space for respondents to provide an in-depth profile.

Letter of applications

By inviting letters of application, businesses allow applicants to set out their reasons why they should be considered for the job and to give an in-depth profile of themselves. However, it is very difficult to use letters of applications to make any rigorous comparison between applicants as structure and information contained in each letter will vary widely.

CVs

CVs will provide employers with the basic facts about applicants' qualifications, school and college record and work history. However, CVs may miss out information that the employer needs to know. It can also be difficult to compare one candidate's application to another, because the information given on a CV is not laid out in a standard way.

> ## stopandthink
>
> Compile a list of essential questions that you believe should be included on an application form for any job.

Choosing a successful candidate

The most common way of choosing the person to fill a vacancy is to invite the candidates on the short list to an interview. Before we look at interviews, let's look at two other methods – which can be used on their own or in combination with an interview – that are used to assess job applicants.

1 Psychometric tests

Employers are often interested in knowing about the personality and character of applicants as well as their abilities. A psychometric test can assess an individual's ability, personality and interest type. These tests ask questions about how a person typically behaves in given situations.

One particular form of psychometric test is the personality test. Usually presented in the form of a questionnaire, the personality test does not contain questions with any "right or wrong" answers. Instead the test is structured to try and get a picture of how a person will behave in particular circumstances.

Some businesses use psychometric tests to help them draw up a short list, by removing applicants who do not match the criteria for the post. Others use them in the final selection process as they feel that the tests provide them with a more accurate picture of the applicant. More recruiters are using these tests to help them to get a better understanding of candidates rather than relying totally on the interview.

> ## stopandthink
>
> In what way do you think a personality questionnaire will help to improve the recruitment process?

2 Aptitude tests

Aptitude tests are suitable for jobs which demand specific skills. They are aimed at testing whether candidates have these specific skills; for example, they can be used to test whether applicants have the aptitude to learn computer programming, or whether they can actually speak a particular foreign language.

There are many "off-the-shelf" ability and aptitude tests available to employers, including tests for computer programming, manual dexterity (the ability to handle and place very small items such as electronic components with ease), word processing aptitude, and verbal, spatial and numerical tests.

3 Job interviews

The job interview is by far the most common form of assessment. Interviews consist of questions to applicants, providing information about their attitude to, and knowledge of, the job role. They also provide an opportunity for applicants to ask their prospective new employer questions about the job.

To ensure as much objectivity as possible, open questions should be prepared before the interview and addressed to all applicants, probing further as required. Questions should be based on the person specification. It is essential that there is no discrimination in the interview process – as in all stages of recruitment. (Topic 6 looks at the legal obligations of employers in recruitment.)

Interviewers should know appropriate techniques to use in interviewing. The key skills are effective questioning, active listening and summarising accurately.

Careful questioning is of little use if the interviewer(s) does not listen to the answers given by the candidate. Active listening is an important skill – this involves not just listening carefully but demonstrating that the interviewer has taken in the candidate's answers by:

- maintaining eye contact
- nodding
- gesturing
- keeping an 'open' posture
- linking questions to interviewees' previous answers
- making summaries of the interviewee's replies.

The interview can be a poor method of selection if the people involved in the process are not trained or are not aware of the pitfalls that may occur and lack the skill to avoid making mistakes. Some of the common pitfalls are:

- thinking ahead to the next question, instead of listening to the answers
- interrupting or answering the question instead of allowing the candidate to talk
- being selective about what you want to hear.

Some interviewers place more importance on negative impressions than on any positive evidence they encounter during the interview – almost as if they are looking for a reason to reject a candidate. Some come with a set of preconceptions before they even meet the candidates, forming impressions from looking at the CVs, application forms and covering letters.

4 Other interviews

Interviews are not only used within the selection process. This form of one-to-one questioning is also used in staff appraisal. The same open-type questioning techniques need to be used, in order to conduct an effective appraisal which highlights the strengths and weaknesses of the employee.

Some companies also conduct exit interviews to establish the reasons why a member of staff has chosen to leave the business. Aimed at being very open and non-confrontational, they help the business to establish any problems that exist which have caused an issue, giving them the opportunity to put this right and prevent any other member of staff choosing to leave. According to i-resign.com, you might be asked these questions at an exit interview:

- what factors have led you to decide to leave?
- what are your views on the management?
- were you given enough support in your job?
- what did you most like about the company and what did you like the least?
- what are your views on the way we treat our staff?
- how could we improve effectiveness and morale?
- is there any way we could improve the business?

stop and think

Give two reasons why a business might consider the use of exit interviews. Explain why an exit questionnaire may be offered as an alternative to attending an exit interview in person or over the phone.

Evaluating recruitment and selection

One indicator of good recruitment and selection practice in a business is low labour turnover: if you select the right staff, they are likely to stay with the company; if there is high staff turnover, the business may be appointing the wrong people and it should try to gather information on the impact of the recruitment and selection process from exit interviews.

Other key issues to address when evaluating the effectiveness of the recruitment and selection process are cost and efficiency, legal compliance and employee performance.

Cost

Recruitment isn't a cheap process. It includes advertising expenses and the cost of accompanying documentation, staff time taken to administrate the process, and the time and expenses of interviewing and testing applicants.

Legal compliance

Employers should ensure that their recruitment and selection procedures meet legal requirements. They should monitor the number of complaints or grievances that are received as a result of the recruitment and selection process, review the number and type of any formal discrimination claims against the company, and check that all documentation and criteria used in the selection process conform with equal opportunities good practice.

Employee performance

Monitoring how well an employee performs once appointed is perhaps the best way of determining how successful the process has been. Looking at how the new staff member is performing will show whether the "right" person post has been selected. This can be assessed through reports from the employee's line manager, appraisals, feedback received from customers, and the level of support and the training needs of the new employee.

Knowledge summary

- **Businesses use different methods to draw up a short list of candidates for final selection, including asking for completed application forms, curriculum vitae (CV) and letters of application.**

- **Interviewing is the most common method of making the final selection. Other methods include personality and aptitude tests, sometimes in combination with a job interview.**

quick questions

1. When interviewing for jobs it is important that personal views and prejudices do not interfere with the process of objective and fair selection. How do you establish which information can be used as part of the selection decision?

2. Explain how each of the three key issues of cost, legislation and monitoring performance can be used to evaluate the effectiveness of the recruitment and selection process.

data interpretation
Recruitment for Disneyland Resort Paris

Disneyland Resort Paris employs over 10,000 cast members. It wants people who bring dynamism to the company and who can "use their professional skills and enthusiasm to work magic". Disneyland's website (www.disneylandparis.com) includes details of job vacancies plus online application forms. Find out more about working at Disneyland Paris by visiting the website. This is an extract from the jobs section of the website:

Disney.co.uk   CLICK HERE FOR MORE DISNEY MAGIC!

needmagic?

DISNEYLAND RESORT PARIS

parks
hotels
more magic
quote & book

Employment

Find a fresh new way of working, see your job differently, and discover a world of work outside the norm in a multicultural environment.

That's what putting magic in your CV means. Every year, Disneyland® Resort Paris makes dreams come true for more than 13 million visitors. It's a world that keeps dreams alive, where we suggest you take part in the magic, too!

A How much information is provided about the job vacancies on the Disneyland Paris website?

B What do the company mean by "putting magic in your CV"?

C What are the benefits to the company of inviting both online or postal applications?

D How would Disneyland Paris measure the effectiveness of its recruitment and selection procedures?

Setting the scene: reasons for training

Why do many businesses put money into training programmes? Why do they invest in staff development? What methods and approaches do they use?

These are questions that we will consider in this topic. But first note that not all businesses place a high priority on training. As the news clipping shows, many people think that companies do not take enough responsibility for training their staff.

As we shall see, the government has schemes which encourage businesses to train their staff, but successive governments have preferred voluntary approaches rather than making training mandatory.

So why does a business train its staff? There are many reasons why a business should train and develop its workforce:

- to ensure staff are fully able to meet the needs of the job role
- to ensure staff are motivated to deliver the business's objectives
- to adapt and respond to change
- to avoid the costs of lost business opportunities
- to reduce wastage and re-work costs
- to be able to maintain competitive advantage in the market

Source: news.bbc.co.uk, 16 November 2004

Firms 'must train or face fines'

Most people in Britain agree that employers who do not train their workers properly should be fined by the government, a survey suggests.

Some 59 per cent think companies cannot be relied upon to take responsibility for improving skills, the Association of Colleges says. Of the 2,045 people interviewed in England, Wales and Scotland, 74 per cent were in favour of fines.

- to help staff to meet their potential
- to raise staff morale – people prefer to be creative, innovative, adaptable and productive
- to retain staff.

Training methods

There are many methods available to develop and train individuals and teams. A business needs to decide which methods best suit its specific purposes, taking into account cost, convenience and the fact that some methods are better suited to particular training needs or circumstances. In all cases, however, one of the first decisions a business needs to take is whether to provide on-the-job or off-the-job training, or a combination of the two approaches.

On-the-job training, as the name suggests, uses the workplace as the learning tool. Methods like coaching, mentoring and work shadowing can be delivered on the job. Training tends to be practically focused – centred, for example, on learning a skill or

a procedure – and trainees benefit from be able to learn from experienced work colleagues. Figure 1.8 shows the rich variety of ways in which work-based learning can be delivered.

KEY TERMS

Training is the process of imparting new skills.

Development is the process of consolidating new skills and building them to greater levels.

On-the-job training takes place in the normal work environment.

Off-the-job training takes place away from the normal work environment.

Induction training is given to new employees.

Figure 1.8: Forms of on-the-job training

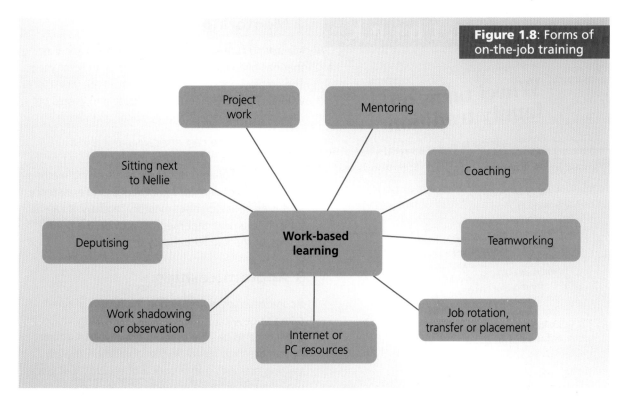

Off-the-job approaches allow individuals time away from the workplace to undertake development or training. Workshops, project work and technology-based learning are often delivered in this way.

Off-the-job training can be delivered in-house, by the company's own trainers or by consultants training staff in a room or centre on the company's premises, or externally, by attending a course, for instance, run by an external provider such as a local college or a training company.

Some types of training like apprenticeships use a mixture of on-the-job and off-the-job training. They learn on the job, through practical skill application, and off the job, perhaps at a local college. Figure 1.9 shows some of the advantages and disadvantages of on-the-job and off-the-job training.

Figure 1.9: Advantages and disadvantages of on-the-job and off-the-job training

	Advantages	Disadvantages
On-the-job training	■ easy to organise ■ job specific ■ relatively inexpensive ■ adaptable to meet the needs of the trainee	■ disruptive in the work environment ■ reliant on the trainer having specialist skills and knowledge to pass on to the trainee
Off-the-job training	■ run by a specialist trainer ■ training is intensive and focused ■ no workplace distractions ■ new theories and ideas can be considered ■ trainee exposed to new people	■ relevance of the training back at work ■ may be difficult to apply training in the workplace ■ costly ■ disruptive, removes employee from their normal place of work

stop and think

Wheel turns on family tradition

Renewed interest in rural crafts could mean the industry overtakes farming as the biggest contributor to the rural economy within 15 years, a study by the government's Countryside Agency suggests.

Philip Gregson, 21, is one person working in rural crafts as he continues a family tradition of wheelwrighting. His great-grandfather, grandfather, father and uncles were all wheelwrights.

He is one of 30,000 rural craftspeople working today. After taking a one-year training course at Herefordshire College of Technology when he was 19, he has set up his own business.

Source: Adapted from news.bbc.co.uk, 17 November 2004

Philip attended an external training course to learn the skills he needed to become a wheelwright. What are the benefits of attending an external training course? What are the disadvantages of this type of training? Consider any on-the-job methods of training that could have been used to train Philip effectively in these skills. What are the potential benefits of training on the job?

1 Coaching

Coaching is an on-the-job method of training that involves regular informal meetings between the manager and the employee. Discussion of performance takes place, allowing the manager to identify any strengths or weaknesses in the employee's performance at work. This will highlight the employee's potential for promotion, and any skill gaps that may be met through further training and development opportunities.

2 Mentoring

Mentoring formalises a method of on-the-job training that has been used in a more informal way for years. The employee is allocated a mentor in the workplace, who acts as adviser to the employee and passes on their own experiences and personal knowledge.

Mentoring can be cost effective and it is less disruptive than off-the-job as it takes place while the employee is working. However, as a training method it relies on each mentor's knowledge and experience so it is essential to select mentors carefully. It can be difficult to ensure that mentors provide the right quality of training required by the employee.

3 Apprenticeships

Apprenticeships acknowledge the length of time taken to develop sufficient skills, knowledge and experience to be able to work effectively in a trade. Apprenticeships blend on-the-job and off-the-job training activities over a period of typically 2–4 years, providing time for an apprentice to receive a wide range of practical experiences and a vocational qualification.

The government backs an apprenticeship scheme (called modern apprenticeships until May 2004) that provides young people with the opportunity to learn on the job while working towards nationally recognised qualifications.

These government-backed apprenticeships are open to young people in England. They are designed to provide young people with vocational training options beyond the traditional educational routes. Apprentices undertake on-the-job training with a suitable employer while studying for nationally recognised qualifications such as National Vocational Qualifications (NVQs).

In 2004, the government introduced a new family of apprenticeships. These include:

- a young apprenticeship for 14–16 year olds still in full-time schooling

- pre-apprenticeship for young people who are not yet ready or able to enter an a full apprenticeship

- the apprenticeship – leading to level 2 qualifications and involving 12 months training with an employer

- the advanced apprenticeship – involving full-time employment and leading to a level 3 qualification.

There are over 180 different types of apprenticeship on the government-backed programme, available in 80 industry sectors from business administration and customer service, to specialist areas such as engineering. Although the scheme is supported by the government, each apprentice is taken on by an individual employer and the relevant training is designed by business.

The scheme's website (www.realworkrealpay.info/employer) sets out the business benefits of employers taking on apprentices:

- Apprentices make a contribution to the business from day one; they learn while they work so their knowledge is up to date. And because their training is on the job, the practical skills they gain are the ones that are right for the business.

- Apprenticeships can help businesses. Apprenticeships are established qualification that can be trusted. Unlike many training courses, apprenticeships ensure that young people have the practical skills to do the job.

4 Induction training

The purpose of the induction training is to help a new employee settle down quickly into the job by becoming familiar with the people, the surroundings and the business. Without this training, it has been proved that new recruits tend to leave the business earlier, and overall employee retention rates are significantly lower than in a business that provides an effective induction course.

According to Businessballs.com, the free online development resource for people and organisations:

> Induction training is more than skills training. It's about the basics that seasoned employees all take for granted: what the shifts are; where the noticeboard is; what's the routine for holidays, sickness; where's the canteen; what's the dress code; where are the toilets. New employees also need to understand the organisation's mission, goals and philosophy; personnel practices, health and safety rules, and of course the job they're required to do, with clear methods, timescales and expectations.
> (source: www.businessballs.com/traindev.htm)

National training initiatives

Though businesses are of course free to develop their own training programmes, they can benefit from working within nationally determined training structures and take advantage of government training initiatives. We have already considered the national apprenticeship scheme (see above): here are three more initiatives that impact on business training.

1 National vocational qualifications (NVQs)

Employees gain these occupational qualifications by demonstrating that they are competent in carrying out a range of tasks connected with their occupation. Assessment is based on evidence that an employee collects from their place of work rather than through test or exercises in a classroom or laboratory.

Ranging from NVQ level 1 through to 5, they are nationally recognised awards and developed to meet the needs of all groups of employees, from operator, through to supervisor and senior manager.

2 Investors in People

Investors in People uses a powerful model as the basis of a process that helps organisations link staff development to meeting the needs of their business. The Investors in People standard is a tried and tested framework that helps companies succeed and compete through improved people performance.

Over 30,000 organisations have formally achieved the standard. These organisations employ over a quarter of the UK workforce and range from companies employing anything from two people upwards, stretching across all sectors of the UK economy.

The Investors in People website lists four principle benefits that organisations gain from achieving the standard:

- business development – by providing the infrastructure to enhance organisational performance and guide growth

- management – by helping organisations focus on developing management capabilities and strengthening internal systems

- employee development – by providing guidance on how to structure and manage learning strategies to help employees achieve their potential

- communication – by highlighting the importance of employee involvement and ownership in progress towards business goals.

You can get more information about Investors in People from its website www.investorsinpeople.co.uk.

3 National Skills Strategy

The National Skills Strategy aims to provide unskilled or low-skilled adults with the skills they need for sustained and productive employment. Examples of what is offered through the strategy (which may vary regionally) include:

- free tuition for a first full NVQ level 2 qualification

- adult learning grant for adults on low incomes

- employer training pilots – help for improving skills at work

- free information and advice, covering courses and qualifications

- learner support funds – extra help with costs of things like transport and childcare

- business support services for small and medium-sized enterprises.

Knowledge summary

- **There are many reasons why businesses train and develop their workforces. These include being able to ensure staff are able to meet the needs of their job role, reduction of wastage, maintaining competitive advantage in the market and helping to retain staff.**

- **There is a rich variety of approaches that businesses may use to train their staff, including both internal on-the-job and external off-the-job methods.**

- **There are a number of nationally recognised training structures that may influence a business's approach to training its staff, including apprenticeships and Investors in People.**

Clarkson Evans is a Gloucestershire-based electrical contracting firm. It has contracts with almost all of the UK's premier house builders. The company employs a workforce of nearly 200 and each year turns over in excess of £7.5 million.

The company takes on around 30 new apprentices each year. Training takes place in-house, using a purpose-built, modern training centre at the company's headquarters in Gloucester.

Gerald Crittle, a director of Clarkson Evans, explains why the company has chosen this route: "To meet customer demand, we needed to expand our workforce, but as there weren't enough qualified electricians available, we decided to train people ourselves.

"Having a highly trained, quality workforce undoubtedly has major business benefits. There are high levels of satisfaction and confidence in both our workmanship and customer service, and increased skills help minimise wastage of electrical materials."

The company has identified several advantages to using an apprenticeship scheme:

■ training can be tailor-made to meet specific business needs

■ it can monitor individual progress and provide extra tuition where required

■ it achieves very high staff retention and apprenticeship completion rates.

Clarkson Evans won a government-backed National Training Award in 2001 and has received other accolades for its training programme. This has helped enhance business reputation as a good employer, helping attract applicants for jobs and allowing the company to be highly selective in its recruitment, as well as helping it to win extra business.

Adapted from: www.apprenticeships.org.uk

35

A Why did the business set up their own in-house training centre? What advantages have Clarkson Evans found from using on-the-job training?

B Suggest reasons why Clarkson Evans has managed to maintain a "very high staff retention and apprenticeship completion rate".

C What are the major business benefits from the company's training programme?

D Do you think that the apprenticeship scheme is a good or bad way to train employees in a business? Explain your view.

E Explain how a business such as Clarkson Evans might benefit from using the Investors in People standard.

F Use appropriate software to design an advertisement to encourage other businesses to take up an apprenticeship programme.

Topic 5 Training and development

Employment legislation

Setting the scene: drive to recruit ethnic officers

New efforts are being made to increase the percentage of black and ethnic minority officers in Leicestershire's police force.

The county is currently top of the national league table with 5 per cent of the force coming from black and ethnic minority communities, but the Home Office target is 15 per cent.

Chief Constable Matt Baggott officially launched the Breaking Through campaign. He said that the Constabulary "was committed to achieving a workforce that fully reflects the ethnicity and cultural mix of Leicester, Leicestershire and Rutland".

The poster campaign will feature serving Leicestershire police officers. The police force has also planned a number of recruitment events across the county.

Source: adapted from news.bbc.co.uk, 11 October 2004

Do you think that it is legal to encourage more applications from minority ethnic communities?

Preventing discrimination at work

Discrimination involves treating a person unfavourably because of their race, sex, disability, age, sexual orientation or religious belief. There is a considerable amount of legislation designed to protect people from discrimination at work or in the labour market.

This includes legislation relating to sex discrimination, employment equality (religion or belief, and sexual orientation) regulations, race relations, national minimum wage, equal pay, disability discrimination, holiday entitlement, maternity and paternity leave regulations, maximum hours of work legislation and employment protection.

A business must ensure that it follows its legal and ethical responsibilities relating to discrimination and equal opportunities when recruiting staff. This includes job advertisements. Once appointed, the business must continue to abide by the legislation.

Source: timesonline.co.uk, 27 Feb 2005

Move to give women parity

Companies are likely to be forced to carry out equal pay reviews for female staff. A woman's right to earn the same as a man may be enforced by "equality police" in the office with firms being forced to carry out equal pay reviews.

A draft copy of the Women and Work Commission's paper says companies could be made to carry out compulsory pay reviews to force them to narrow the pay gap between men and women.

It argues that radical measures are needed to plug this pay differential, more than 40 per cent for part-time workers and 18 per cent for full-time employees.

stop and think

Cherie Blair, the employment lawyer, has privately argued in favour of "naming and shaming" firms that fail to respect equal pay law. What might be the impact of this policy? Is it likely to change a firm's behaviour?

In short, this means that employers have legal as well as ethical responsibilities both to prevent discrimination in the work place as well as to apply equal opportunities policies in the recruitment and selection process. This does not mean that organisations are unable to apply some positive discrimination measures in certain circumstances. For example, the recruitment campaign by Leicestershire police (featured above) is, perhaps not surprisingly, lawful. Organisations can run positive recruitment campaigns where there is a low proportion of a particular group employed by the business.

Figure 1.10 shows the range of anti-discrimination legislation now in place in the UK. If businesses fail to comply with this legislation, they face both the legal consequences – fines and compensation to victim – as well as possible claims for civil damages. In addition, they can receive extremely negative press coverage, which can damage their public image and have an impact on their trade.

Though most businesses' first response may be that they need to uphold the law to avoid the financial and other negative consequences of non compliance, they should realise that equal opportunities good practice also brings benefits, including a positive impact on the motivation, retention and recruitment of staff.

Businesses need to be aware that the law is frequently being updated and changed. For example, the UK government has pledged to bring in legislation to tackle age discrimination in employment by 2006, and in 2004 new regulations came into effect to strengthen the law preventing discrimination against disabled people.

From October 2004, it has been unlawful for any employer to discriminate against a disabled person when choosing someone for a job, considering people for promotion, transfer, training, dismissal or redundancy. A disabled person should not be treated less fairly than other workers, or subject to harassment.

Figure 1.10: Key anti-discrimination legislation

Legislation	Purpose
Sex Discrimination Act 1975 (amended)	Sex discrimination covers all aspects of employment, from recruitment to pay, and training to contract termination. Employers should not discriminate on the grounds of sex, marriage or because someone intends to undergo, is undergoing or has undergone reassignment.
Employment Equality (Religion or Belief) Regulations 2003	Designed to protect employees from discrimination on the grounds of all religions and beliefs. All businesses must treat everyone fairly regardless of their religion or belief.
Employment Equality (Sexual Orientation) Regulations 2003	Designed to protect employees on grounds connected with sexual orientation. All businesses must treat everyone fairly regardless of their sexual orientation.
Race Relations Act 1976	Makes it unlawful to discriminate in employment against men or women on the grounds of race, colour or ethnic background.
Equal Pay Act 1970	All businesses must treat employees of both sexes equally; a woman doing the same or comparable job as a man must receive the same pay and have similar working conditions.
Disability Discrimination Act 1995	Makes it illegal for an employer to treat a disabled person less favourably than other staff. Employers are required to make reasonable adjustments to the working environment so that disabled people can be employed or access training opportunities.

In fact, the disability legislation expects businesses to make changes as far as is reasonably practicable to do so. In this instance, it may be possible for the shop owner to be able to adapt the premises for wheelchair usage at a reasonable cost, therefore the owner would be expected to do so.

Many small employers find these type of changes in the law difficult. But disability is more common than many think, and it is important that small businesses such as the newsagent realise that disability does not automatically mean a wheelchair user. For example, there are many people who are hearing impaired, and with an induction loop they would easily be able to work in a shop. There are many types of disability, you cannot always tell just by looking at someone whether they are disabled.

Protecting employees' well-being

Legislation also exists to protect the well-being of employees. This includes a number of measures to prevent businesses over-exploiting the staff. There are regulations by such as restricting the number of hours they work in a week, the minimum wages that can be paid to employees and regulations with regard to leave arrangements.

1 Minimum wage rates

Under the National Minimum Wage Act 1998, employers must cannot pay below fixed wage rates as defined in the Act. The legislation covers part-time and temporary workers as well as full-time employees, and rules have been tightened to offer protection to people who work from home. The full rate applies to workers aged 22 and over, with a sliding decreasing scale for those aged 18–21 and aged 16–17. In 2004, the minimum wage was raised to £4.85 an hour for adults (22+), with rates of £4.10 an hour for 18–21 year olds and £3.00 for 16–17 year olds.

2 Holiday entitlement

Employees are entitled to four weeks paid leave per year if they work full time. There are exceptions to this regulation. Excluded groups include members of the armed forces, trainee doctors and the police.

3 Maternity and paternity leave

Women are entitled to 26 weeks ordinary maternity leave regardless of how long they have worked for their employer; at the end of the 26-week maternity leave period, a woman is entitled to return to her old job. Both parents can take 13 weeks unpaid parental leave until the child's fifth birthday. Expectant fathers can get two weeks statutory paid paternity leave.

4 Maximum hours of work

The regulation on working hours is aimed at limiting the working week to a maximum of 48 hours. All employees, regardless of their age, are also entitled to rest breaks while working.

The maximum hours legislation also places special restrictions on the working hours of people aged under 18. They are not allowed to:

- work before 7am or after 7pm
- work for more than two hours on a school day or for more than one hour before school
- work for more than eight hours on Saturdays or holidays, or two hours on Sundays
- work for more than 35 hours a week during the holidays.

Knowledge summary

- All employers have to comply with legislation protecting employees in their work. Failure to comply can result in fines, compensation costs and bad publicity. Compliance also avoids disputes in the work place.

- Legislation also prevents discrimination in respect of recruitment and selection of staff.

- Respecting equal opportunities and other employment legislation can help to keep staff happy and motivated, and improve staff retention and recruitment.

quick questions

1 Why is it important for a business to want to ensure that it complies with employment legislation and protects the well-being of its employees through this legislation?

2 Some groups of workers, such as junior doctors, members of the armed forces, au pairs and those working in transport, are not covered by the maximum hours legislation. What effect might this have on these groups of employees? How might it effect their motivation?

3 Should people under the age of 18 have special restrictions placed on their hours of work? Justify your response.

data interpretation
NHS staffing crisis

The NHS is on the verge of a major staffing crisis, members of the House of Lords have warned. In a report, they say new European Union rules on how long junior doctors can work could create serious problems for hospitals.

Junior doctors had not been covered by the EU working time directive, which limits the working week of most workers to 48 hours. Any attempt to immediately limit junior doctors' working week to 48 hours would cripple many hospitals.

To allow hospitals to cope with the change, there is a two-step plan to reduce junior doctor hours, reducing them first to 58 hours, then to 48 hours per week by 2009.

However, there has now been a ruling that time doctors spend on call must be counted as time worked. This will have a massive effect, the equivalent of losing 3,700 junior doctors if the changes in working hours is followed.

Adapted from news.bbc.co.uk, 8 April, 2004

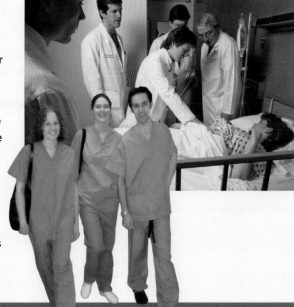

A The working hours directive has the effect of protecting staff in their work and ensuring their well-being. What benefits are there to a business of complying with this legislation?

B The NHS is a service industry in which staff face heavy demand. How might compliance with the working hours directive help the service?

C Consider the effect of the working hours directive on junior doctors. In what ways will they benefit from this change?

D Discuss the impact the change in working hours might have on the motivation of employees throughout the NHS.

How businesses motivate employees

Setting the scene: Argos

Argos recognises that motivated employees perform better, benefiting not only the individuals concerned but the company as a whole. Argos believes that a well thought-out staff incentive programme can help to reduce staff turnover by making staff feel valued.

Argos' business solutions service offer advice on developing motivational programmes for other businesses. Its business-to-business website (www.argos-b2b.co.uk) claims that: "whether your staff are in field sales or call centres, we have flexible and tailored solutions that will enable them to choose their own reward from thousands of top branded products."

Rewards offered range from gift vouchers, through to a fully managed online reward management programme called the Hive – an online programme which other businesses can buy into and Argos will manage on their behalf – taking out the time-consuming administration associated with running such a benefits scheme.

Why do you think that businesses would want to buy in services such as the Hive? What benefits do companies hope to gain for their business from such schemes?

Adapted from www.argos-b2b.co.uk.

The importance of motivation

Consider what happens if people are unhappy in their work: they are unlikely to perform as well as they might, and they are more likely to want to leave, to join a business that offers them a more satisfactory working environment. In contrast, keeping employees happy in their work can help to retain the staff, improve performance levels and create the environment that attracts potential new recruits.

Businesses therefore need to ensure that their employees are motivated and there is good morale, otherwise they potentially can suffer the twin penalties of poor performance and high staff turnover rates. Poor performance can lose business; high staff turnover is extremely costly – the business loses the money invested in staff training and development, it faces loss of performance and disruption if it is short staffed or lacks people with the right experience, and it must meet the cost of having to recruit new people to fill vacant posts.

Motivational factors

The challenge for companies therefore is to find ways of motivating their staff to stay in the business and to perform to the best of their ability. Motivation of people in work can be affected by many different factors, from the way they are managed, to the environment they work in.

How can we improve the chances that people will feel motivated in their jobs? One key factor affecting motivation and staff retention is the way that people are managed: people don't leave their jobs, they leave their managers.

To become an employer of choice, one that people want to work for and stay with, begins with the way that the business recruits its staff and continues with the way in which they treat their employees once they are working in the business.

KEY TERMS

Motivation is the desire, interest or drive to want to work.

Staff retention measures a business's ability to retain its staff.

Delegation involves giving authority to lower levels of management so they have the power to use the business's resources to produce and deliver goods and services.

Of course, it is important to offer the right incentives, and businesses use a variety of financial and non-financial motivators to create a benefits package. They can offer a variety of financial motivators on top of (or as an alternative to) basic pay:

■ piece rate – payment given per item produced that meets a defined standard

■ commission – an additional payment made based on a targeted level of sales being achieved or exceeded

■ bonuses – flexible in when and how they are paid to staff, aimed at motivating staff to work harder to achieve the bonus offered.

Companies can also offer a range of non-financial motivators such as:

■ fringe benefits – company car, cheap travel, holidays, vouchers

■ good conditions of work – hours of work, holidays, flexibility

■ prospects – opportunities for development, promotion and interest in the job.

But, as we suggest above, motivating staff isn't just about incentives, it has much to do with the way employers treat and manage staff. Figure 1.11 suggests methods of treating and managing staff to encourage motivation.

stop and think

How could a shop manager use the ideas presented in Figure 1.11 to help manage and motivate the shop assistants?

Figure 1.11: Ways on encouraging staff

Give your staff	Purpose
Responsibility	Empower staff to carry out decision making within the job role. Delegate control and responsibility to your team leaders or supervisors for managing their team.
Goals	Provide your staff with clear goals, that are both challenging and achievable.
Resources	Ensure you provide your staff with the resources they need to carry out their work effectively.
Support	Provide support for your staff, including training and guidance with open and frank communication.
Variety	The very spice of life! Give your staff some element of variety to avoid boredom in their work.
Fairness	Always be seen to be fair. You gain a lot more respect that way and staff will feel valued.
Regular talk time	Through talking on a regular basis, you will soon be alerted to any issues that may affect your staff's short-term performance – and it shows you care!
Encouragement	Encourage your staff to give you feedback and put forward their suggestions. Enable your staff to feel that you trust them and value their opinions.

Motivational theories

Industrial psychologist Frederick Hertzberg has identified two sets of factors that he believes influence job satisfaction: motivators and hygiene factors (see Figure 1.12). He set out the ideas behind his two factor theory in 1987.

The motivators are factors that managers must focus on if they want their employees to experience job satisfaction and be motivated to work. The hygiene factors are not in themselves sufficient to motivate employees, but are necessary factors to be met in order to prevent dissatisfaction of people in work.

In other words, true motivation comes from the motivators, providing the hygiene factors have been addressed. The hygiene factors do not motivate us directly; but they will cause dissatisfaction at work if they are not right.

Another way of understanding motivation can be found in Abraham Maslow's hierarchy of needs. Maslow suggested that people are motivated by a range of needs which he presented as a hierarchy. He assumed that employees will try to move from one level of need to the next, only moving up the hierarchy to meet higher-order needs once their lower-level needs had been satisfied.

Figure 1.12: Hertzberg's two-factor theory

Motivators	Hygiene (or maintenance) factors
Achievement – completing a challenging project	Status
Recognition – praise for doing a job well	Job security – length and stability of the employment contract
The work – variety, creativity and chance to do complete tasks	Relationship with subordinates
Responsibility – accountability, responsibility within job role	Personal life/relationship with peers
Advancement – opportunities for development and promotion	Salary – any financial rewards that are offered
Salary – can be a positive feature	Work conditions – and company policy and administration
	Supervision and relationship with supervisor

Working from the bottom up, Maslow defined the five levels as:

- physiological needs – basic life needs, air, food, drink, shelter, warmth, sleep; key employment factors here are pay, conditions of work

- safety needs – includes the need to seek order during times of change; in work, this means protection, security, order, stability of employment

- belonging and social needs – group or team work, relationships at work

- self esteem/ego – confidence, achievement, status, prestige, recognition, status (job title, job perk such as a plush office) reputation, responsibility

- self-actualisation – job satisfaction, personal development through growth and fulfilment, control over the work, promotion.

Maslow's theory suggests individuals seek to satisfy unmet needs, but they will only seek to satisfy the next level of needs once the needs below it have been satisfied. The lower-level needs match Hertzberg's hygiene factors. The higher-level needs match the motivators discussed by Hertzberg. By looking at each level of need, it is possible for a manager to identify what needs are being met, and how others may be met. By addressing these factors, the motivation of the workforce should improve.

If we look at Hertzberg's theory, we see a range of factors that affect people's attitudes to their work. Hertzberg concluded that hygiene factors do not actually motivate people. Taking the England football team as an example (see below) their high salaries did not motivate them to perform better as a team. Whether Sven-Göran Eriksson can find the motivators to take the team to another level remains to be seen.

case study: Management and motivation

How do managers such as Sven-Göran Eriksson motivate their staff? Eriksson managed to motivate the England team to qualify both for the 2002 World Cup and Euro 2004. How did he manage to motivate his players to play as a team?

If we look at Maslow's hierarchy of needs (see Figure 1.13), we can learn what factors may be contributing to the lack of motivation of any team. Between 1990 and 2001, six managers had managed England's national team. Not one of these appointments lasted longer than four years. With such inconsistency, it is hardly surprising that the team's lower-order needs of 'safety, security and order' were not being met.

Sven-Göran Eriksson began by taking an active interest in his team. Through in-depth research of

the performance of the team, he brought in younger talent, tried out new players and encouraged innovative ideas. From the start, Sven set out to bring out the best of the outstanding individual talents his team had.

By securing the lower-order needs within the team, Sven had effectively ensured that the players were no longer feeling dissatisfied, which is a key cause of demotivation. As the team has grown, players have felt a sense of pride and purpose in playing for England, which meets with Maslow's status and esteem needs. Being encouraged to play to their own strengths meets the higher-order self-actualisation need.

Adapted from "Sven's men", Business Review, September 2002

Kingfisher is Europe's leading home improvement retailer. In the UK, it owns the B&Q chain and Screwfix Direct. It also has stores throughout France and in other countries.

Benefits offered by the Kingfisher Group to reward its managers and their teams include:

- competitive salary
- extensive bonus scheme
- pension scheme
- BUPA cover
- sharesave scheme
- five weeks' paid holiday

- discount card for use in company's stores
- discounts on selected major products such as motor insurance, cars, holidays
- fast track internal management development programme
- wide-ranging promotional opportunities.

Why does Kingfisher offer this wide range of benefits to its staff? To what extent do you feel it is in the company's interest to do so?

Why is it important to businesses to compete on the range of benefits they offer their staff? What aspects of Hertzberg's two-factor theory can you identify in the Kingfisher package?

data interpretation
Unilever in the UK

Unilever is proud of its reputation of being among the UK's best places to work. It is committed to enabling its employees to achieve their full potential.

Unilever has developed a comprehensive and highly competitive employee benefits package including an excellent company pension plan, a sharesave scheme and private medical cover.

The company's commitment extends outside of the workplace, through its provision of flexible working policies, career break schemes and progressive maternity policies.

Unilever UK is committed to embracing diversity in the workplace, bringing together a rich mix of people with differing perspectives and backgrounds, and placing value on those differences.

> People deliver their best when they feel valued and when their opinions are welcomed, respected and acted upon. This means everyone in Unilever UK knows they can realise their full potential, which in turn helps us to foster an enterprising and diverse culture within which the very best people want to come and work, making us a magnet for talent.

> All of this not only makes people proud to work for an organisation, it also leads directly to higher performance and the creation of a special buzz which helps everyone to raise their game, deliver exceptional performance and enjoy doing so.

Source: www.unilever.co.uk/careers

A Describe the ways in which Unilever UK has provided an environment that motivates their staff. (You may need to get more information from the company's website www.unilever.co.uk.)

B Using Maslow's hierarchy, explain how Unilever UK is meeting the needs of its employees.

C Using Hertzberg's two-factor theory, identify which key motivators Unilever UK is committed to providing for its staff.

D Evaluate how the provision of motivators might be different in another type of workplace, such as a restaurant chain.

Setting the scene: money isn't everything

Jobseekers are increasingly refusing to accept work with firms that have no ethical or environment policies, a survey suggests.

Research for recruitment website totaljobs.com showed material perks such as company cars were becoming less important. A survey of 5,000 job hunters showed that 43 per cent would not work for a firm which had no ethical or environmental policies – even if they were offered £10,000 a year more.

But younger job seekers were less principled than older people, according to the survey. Two out of three under-18-year-olds said they would accept a job offer from a company without a sense of corporate social responsibility.

Keith Robinson, of totaljobs.com, said companies needed to realise they could no longer tempt recruits using financial incentives alone: "A new breed of job seeker is placing ethical issues above financial incentives when considering a job offer. Future job packages need to reflect this new-found ethical consciousness among job seekers."

If people are prepared to reject higher-paid jobs with companies that lack good environmental or ethical policies, then what effect do you think this may have on businesses?

Source: news.bbc.co.uk, 12 Sept 2003

KEY TERMS

Pollution is contamination of the environment.

Recycling is the process of reusing or reclaiming products for further use.

Global warming is the widely accepted theory that the greenhouse gas effect is causing an increase in average temperature worldwide.

Ethical codes are the moral principles and values held by a business, identified through its culture, behaviour and codes of practice.

Stakeholders are people or groups having an interest in the operations of a business.

Pressure groups seek to influence others in order to promote their own ideas or agendas.

Environmental awareness

All businesses operate within society. This means not just that businesses face the same challenges and pressures experienced by wider society, but that they have a social responsibility to the people and communities which are affected by their activities and operations.

Increasingly, businesses are being challenged by employees, pressure groups and other stakeholders to demonstrate greater social responsibility and to set higher ethical standards. In this topic we look at the business impact of environmental issues, such as pollution, recycling and global warming, as well as consider some of the wider social and ethical concerns.

The environment is perhaps the most pressing challenge facing businesses. According to Fujio Cho, president of the car manufacturer Toyota, "in the past, being an environmentally conscious company was a luxury...but if automakers don't reduce smog-forming emissions, greenhouse gases and the need for petroleum, I believe we won't be in business".

1 Pollution

Concern for the environment has caused businesses to examine the impact of their practices in many areas. Pollution is obviously one major concern, and businesses have a legal and morale responsibility to ensure that their processes don't pollute the environment.

If a business does cause environmental pollution, the consequences can be costly. The polluter faces financial penalties: for example, Kronospan, a North Wales firm that makes woodchip products, was fined £60,000 in November 2004 after pleading guilty to pollution offences including oil leakages into the River Dee. But companies also suffer damage to their reputation and public image, which can also be expensive even if difficult to quantify.

However, as the cutting above shows, environmental compliance also comes with a price. Huge amounts of additional investment may be required by the business. This can impact on a profitability, and businesses may be forced to seek cuts in other costs such as wages.

2 Recycling

Recycling is a more proactive approach to reducing environmental damage. A business may recycle its waste products because it wants to be environmentally responsible and sees a benefit in terms of an enhanced corporate image. In parading its green credentials, a business may generate good publicity, gain more customers and appear more attractive to potential recruits.

Equally, many businesses are recycling for more financial and commercial reasons. There is money to be made from recycling waste products – businesses can reducing their waste handling and disposal costs and potentially lower their material costs.

Some new businesses have started up simple to recycle domestic and industrial waste products. The

stop and think

Toyota's website (www.toyota.com) has set out some of the steps it is taking to become more environmentally responsible.

Toyota is looking at both lowering emissions and improving fuel economy in its vehicles, and also reducing landfill wastage at its manufacturing plants. In the US, four of Toyota's engine and parts plants are at zero landfill status, and energy use at Toyota's North American plants is down 17 per cent since 2000.

Toyota's "green" complex in California has one of the largest commercial solar panel systems in North America, conserving more than 11 million gallons of drinking water annually through special pipelines that supply recycled water for cooling and landscaping.

Why do businesses such as Toyota believe that it is essential to be environmentally conscious in order to stay in business? What impact does this have on the people who work within the business?

recycling industry is a fast-growing sector, creating jobs and wealth. This is having a positive impact on the environment, as well as demonstrating that it makes good business and economic sense to recycle products.

3 Global warming

The Kyoto Protocol on fighting climate change became a legally binding treaty in 2005. The protocol commits industrialised nations to making significant cuts in the emission of gases such as carbon dioxide by the year 2012. In all, 141 countries have ratified the treaty, although the United States (the country that produces the most emissions) has not signed up to the accord. Each country has been set emission targets, and countries in Europe will need to take action if they are to meet their targets.

Why should businesses be interested in global warming? Businesses are aware that they are likely to come under increasing pressure from governments, pressure groups and the general public to reduce or control greenhouse gas emissions generated by their operations and products. Regulation or taxation – such as carbon taxes – may force them to modify their activities.

Some businesses might also see increasing public concern about global warming as an opportunity. A business that can demonstrate a genuine concern for global warming – through introducing green products and processes – is going to receive a level of public support. This positive public image may generate greater demand for their products, making them more competitive, as well as making the company a more attractive employer, helping it to recruit high-quality staff.

Ethical behaviour and codes of practice

Many businesses are now developing codes of practice after pressure from consumers and pressure groups about the way they are behaving. These codes of practice take in far more than the environment, covering a range of issues that impact on a business's stakeholders, including customers, local communities and suppliers.

For example, the UK supermarkets, such as Sainsbury, Waitrose and Tesco, have introduced codes of practice to try and respond to growing consumer concern about food production methods and their impact on poor people and the environment. These codes cover issues such as food quality, the social impact of the supermarket's operations and environmentally friendly production.

Ethical policies have an impact on a business's operations. It is not sufficient to simply publicise the fact that the business operates ethically. They have to be seen to deliver on the commitments. This can mean anything from changing their contractual relationships with suppliers to investing in training of staff to make them aware of (and deliver) the business's ethical policies.

This would give them a better public image, and make them more competitive as they are responding to consumer pressure. Therefore, they need to identify ways of communicating this information to key stakeholders of the business, such as through their web sites, through corporate literature (Annual Reports), and through other methods of publicity such as company magazines and the national press.

stop and think

Sometimes it is not easy to reconcile the demands of a business's different stakeholders. Take the case of airport expansion. The government want to press ahead with moves to build new runways at airports in south-east England to cope with growing demand for flights.

The airport authorities are in favour of the plan. Their direct customers (the airlines) want more capacity, the indirect customers (air passengers) would also benefit from more flights and airport development would bring more jobs for local communities.

Yet pressure groups are preparing to oppose any proposals to expand what are already some of the country's largest airports. And the opposition isn't just coming from environmental groups, as householders and local residents forming campaign groups to fight the proposals.

Why are so many people concerned about airport expansion plans? Who are the key stakeholders in the development? Draw up a list of costs and benefits of the airport development. How do the airport authorities and their employees gain? Who suffers the most?

Knowledge summary

■ Growing environment concern has caused many businesses to examine and modify their practices and operations. They are increasingly aware of the need to meet environmental standards.

■ Businesses may need to make further investment to comply with new environmental protection law, which might force cutbacks in other areas.

■ Good environmental and ethical practice can bring commercial benefits. Businesses that demonstrate a real commitment to meeting public concerns may gain a competitive advantage.

quick questions

1 Give one reason why a firm might be interested in recycling.

2 Apart from being fined by the courts, explain one other impact on a business if it is seen to cause pollution.

3 Describe the possible impact of ethical issues on recruitment in a business. Explain how this might affect the competitiveness of the business.

data interpretation
Tesco's ethical trading policy

Tesco is a founder member of the Ethical Trading Initiative (ETI). The company has an ethical trading policy and it aims to act responsibly in its commercial and trading activities.

Although Tesco says, reasonably enough, that it does not have all the answers to complex ethical or social issues, it claims that it does do all it can to ensure that the labour standards of people working for its suppliers meet relevant international standards.

Friends of the Earth, as the article below illustrates, takes a different view and has attacked Tesco's unethical practices. Tesco responded to this attack by noting that it was disappointed by Friends of the Earth's comments and saying that it had written to the group rejecting each of its "misleading claims".

A Why is the pressure group Friends of the Earth keen to make its views known to the public? What impact may this have on Tesco?

B Look at Tesco's economic, environmental and social codes of practice. These are on the company's website (www.tesco.com). What impression does this give you, in comparison to the article by Friends of the Earth?

FoE says Tesco being unethical

Friends of the Earth has launched a blistering attack on Tesco, accusing the supermarket giant of "unfair and unethical trading practices".

"Tesco claims that it supports local communities and creates jobs for local people, but it does not say how many other jobs in local communities may be lost as a result of its new superstores opening as local shops close down," FoE said.

FoE wants a limit on the floor space of supermarket superstores and it is putting pressure on local authorities to consider more carefully the impact of out-of-town developments on businesses in town centres before granting planning permission.

The pressure group also claims that Tesco is failing to protect the livelihoods of workers on farms and plantations supplying the supermarket with produce from overseas.

"Tesco's success has made it immensely powerful - a position that it is clearly abusing by putting small traders out of business and killing off local high streets, bullying suppliers, and damaging the environment through its never-ending demand for cheap food," said Sandra Bell, the group's food and farming campaigner.

news.bbc.co.uk, 17 June 2004

C Use the website to explain what standards Tesco applies to its suppliers under the Ethical Trading Initiative.

D In what way does Tesco consider its social responsibilities in provision of its services to the public? How might the employees in the business be affected?

Consumer and employee protection

Setting the scene: Competition Commission

Governments want to ensure that there is fair competition in all markets. If one company completely dominates a market, it would be able to use its monopoly position to set trading terms, prices and employment conditions to the detriment of consumers, other businesses and its own employees.

In the UK, the Competition Commission is part of the regulatory framework that exists to protect the interests of the consumer by maintaining competition in markets. The aim is that no business should be allowed to grow so large that it dominates and controls a particular market sector.

Cases are often referred to the Competition Commission when companies are proposing mergers and acquisitions. For example, in 2003 some of the large supermarkets were proposing to buy the chain of Safeway stores. There were fears that if a deal was allowed to go ahead, the successful bidder for Safeway could exert a dominant position in the supermarket industry. The case was referred to the Competition Commission.

In this case, the Competition Commission ruled that the proposed acquisition of Safeway plc by either Asda, Sainsbury or Tesco might be expected to operate against the public interest, but that the acquisition of Safeway by Morrisons could go ahead, subject to certain conditions being met where local competition concerns may arise.

In March 2004, Morrisons completed the takeover of Safeway, creating the UK's fourth largest supermarket group with more than 400 stores across the country.

More information on the work of the Competition Commission can be found on its website www.competition-commission.org.uk

Consumer protection

Over the years, successive governments have passed a wide range of legislation to ensure that consumers and customers get a fair and reasonable service from businesses. This legislation has had two main thrusts:

- consumer protection law – regulations which govern the description and labelling of products, trade terms and credit agreements

- competition law – regulations that ensure fair competition in markets, and so benefiting consumers by prohibiting restrictive practices and preventing monopoly situations.

Figure 1.14 shows some of the main Acts of Parliament which have been passed in the last 40 years to provide greater consumer protect and to ensure competitive markets. All businesses need to comply with this wide-ranging legislation, which imposes a cost that some companies, particularly smaller firms, can find hard to meet. However, failure to comply risks fines and legal sanctions as well as damage to a business's reputation.

KEY TERMS

Consumer protection laws aim to safeguard the consumer from unfair business practices.

Competition law is designed to ensure fair competition between businesses, and that firms act in the best interests of customers.

Employment protection laws are legal safeguards to prevent employees from being harmed or mistreated in some way at work.

Figure 1.14: Major consumer protection and competition law

Consumer protection law	Competition law
Consumer Credit Acts 1974 and 2005	Competition Act 1998
Consumer Protection Act 1987	Restrictive Practices Act 1976
Trade Descriptions Act 1968	Resale Prices Act 1976
Fair Trading Act 1973	
Sale of Goods and Services Act 1982	
Weights and Measures Act 1985	

1 Labelling, packaging and trade description

Laws relating to product labelling and description are designed to ensure that businesses do not try to encourage trade by providing misleading information. Consumers have a right to know what they are buying before a sale is transacted.

The law on labelling and packaging relates to all goods, including food products and other retail products. For example, food labelling regulations include strict regulations regarding date marking: most packaged foods are required to be date marked with an indication of their durability (a "best by" or "consume by" date).

Sun creams fail tests

The Trading Standards Institute (TSI) is warning that some children's sunscreens do not offer the level of protection that they claim on the packaging. Following spot checks the TSI found that seven out of eight sun cream products specifically marketed at children and babies did not live up to their sun protection branding.

Tighter regulations are required, both on the labelling of these sunscreen products and on the way that SPF and UVA ratings are determined, which the TSI would like to see carried out only by approved laboratories.

Adapted from news.bbc.co.uk, 22 June 2004

2 Office of Fair Trading

The Office of Fair Trading (OFT) has the power to investigate business practices to ensure fairness for the consumer. The OFT can examine the terms of trade. For example, the OFT has examined the terms used in holiday caravan agreements to make sure that they are fair and clear. It recommended that suppliers use standard contract terms and has ruled that some contracts should be revised to comply with the consumer protection regulations.

Another area that can be examined by the Office of Fair Trading is pricing. For example, the OFT has warned holiday tour operators about unclear pricing. It has ruled that under the Fair Trading Act 1973 (superseded by the Enterprise Act 2002) tour operators must include aviation security charges (ASC) in basic holiday prices. They cannot hit customers with a hefty surcharge after they have booked their holiday. The OFT has warned that failure to advertise brochure prices fairly will result in enforcement action.

3 Consumer credit

There is far more credit available to consumers today. In 1971, there was only one type of credit card available – now there are about 1300 credit cards on the market. There is also a thriving loans industry. In addition, many businesses offer credit terms to customers with a range of hire purchase and other "buy now, pay later" deals.

Regulations are needed to protect consumers against unfair credit practices. There is concern that consumers are not always aware of the interest rates charged on credit deals. Loan deals can often tie people in for the long term, and include penalties for early repayment. The government is also concerned that some lenders are acting irresponsibly by failing to make sure consumers can afford the cost of credit.

The Consumer Credit Act 2005 was the first big shake-up of UK consumer credit laws for more than 30 years, and was introduced amid concern about the levels of personal debt. It places stricter controls on lenders and offers greater consumer protection.

stop and think

Investigate the role of the Trading Standards Institute by visiting its website (www.trading standards.gov.uk). Who has it been set up to protect? Does it have any legal powers?

Suppose sunscreen products are subject to tighter regulations. What impact do you think this would have on the businesses that produce and sell these products? What would be the implications of tighter regulations for consumers of sunscreen products?

4 Regulatory bodies

Bodies such as the Office of Fair Trading and the Competition Commission have a remit which allows them to investigate any industry. In some industries, however, there are also separate regulatory authorities which control competition within specific sectors. These regulatory bodies tend to be in sectors such as telecommunications, rail transport, water and energy supply that until relatively recently were served by nationalised industries.

These regulatory bodies can intervene to ensure fair competition and pricing. For example Ofcom, the regulatory body in the communications sector, investigated the prices BT charged other broadband providers for using its network to deliver their services to residential customers. Ofcom suggested that BT was breaking competition law, and BT was forced to review its pricing strategies for these services to enable other businesses to compete in the market on a more equal footing.

Employment protection

Topic 6 reviewed the laws that are designed to prevent discrimination at work and in the labour market and which govern conditions of employment, such minimum pay, holiday entitlement and maternity leave. Businesses also have additional statutory responsibilities to their employees, including a duty to prevent victimisation and bullying in the workplace, as well as to ensure the health and safety of all staff.

All work activities are covered by health and safety laws, and there is a government body, the Health and Safety Executive (www.hse.gov.uk), which ensures that this legislation is enforced. The main regulations governing health and safety are:

- the Health and Safety at Work Act 1974 – regulations made under this Act such as the Control of Substances Hazardous to Health Regulations (COSHH) and the Workplace (Health, Safety and Welfare) Regulations apply to all work situations

- Food and Environmental Protection Act, Control of Pesticides Regulations

- laws that cover health and safety in specific industries such as mining, nuclear energy, railways, and offshore oil and gas

- older laws that pre-date the Health and Safety at Work Act such as the Factories Act – these cover a range of industries, but not all workplaces, and most of these laws are gradually being modernised.

Given the wide range of legislation that covers health and safety, every business has to invest a lot of money and time in making sure that it complies with the requirements. The costs can be extremely high. It is not sufficient to provide a safe working environment – all staff have to be made aware of safe ways of working and how to avoid hazards within their workplace. This often means that a business needs to run health and safety training programmes, which have to be constantly updated as regulations change. Employers must also appoint a person or persons responsible for monitoring health and safety in the business. They have to conduct risk assessments to identify any potential risks and hazards.

Trade unions

Though the law safeguards individual employee's rights, including the right to work in safe environment, many workers feel that they need additional protection at work. Trade unions exist to protect their members' working conditions, employment rights and welfare. Trade unions work in the interests of employees by:

- campaigning against unfair practices by employers

- demanding that businesses respect employees' statutory rights under existing employment legislation

- working for improvements in conditions of employment, such as hours of work, holidays, rates of pay

- representing members in cases of discipline, grievance, dismissal or redundancy.

Trade unions work for their members by negotiating on their behalf with employers and, in some circumstances, providing members with additional financial help and legal advice. For example, trade unions can try and protect their members against unfair dismissal. Under the terms of the Employment Protection (Consolidation) Act 1978, every employee has the right not to be unfairly dismissed. Employers have to follow specified procedures before they can sack employees or make staff redundant.

Trade unions can have an influence on business decisions by ensuring that managers are aware of (and respect) employment legislation and that they take account of the views of employees in planning any changes. The relationship between trade unions and businesses can be confrontational – and industrial disputes can lead to strike action – but there are benefits from giving employees representation. Certainly, trade unions can help employees feel confident that their employer will not be able to abuse their position of power and influence in the workplace, enabling them to continue with their day-to-day work effectively.

stop and think

Following the announcement that Ford planned to close its Jaguar plant in Coventry, the Transport and General Workers' Union warned it might urge the workforce of all Ford's UK plants to take industrial action. The union has accused Ford of failing to honour agreements about the security of the factory.

Unions rally resistance

Unions in Jaguar are currently holding a series of meetings with the workforce to oppose the end of car production at the company's Browns Lane factory. Jaguar's parent company, Ford, has announced plans to stop production at its Coventry plant. Trade union officials at the plant say strike action could be possible.

news.bbc.co.uk, 27 September 2004

The union is taking up the case of the hundreds of workers that might be affected by the proposals. Under the plans, there will be:

- 400 voluntary redundancies in manufacturing at Browns Lane

- 750 white-collar jobs lost in Coventry and across the company

- 310 staff remaining at Browns Lane

- 425 staff transferring to Castle Bromwich

- 300 new jobs created at the Aston Martin factory in Gaydon.

The Transport and General Workers' Union claims that the company is trying to satisfy its US shareholders by looking for cutbacks in its operations.

The union is acting to protect their members, and to ensure that their conditions and prospect are not worsened. This is a good example of a social issue affecting people in business.

What effect do you think that any proposed industrial action may have on Jaguar's business?

If you were an employee of the company, what benefits do you feel you might gain through joining a trade union?

Knowledge summary

- Competition law is designed to ensure fair competition in markets and to prevent businesses from exploiting consumers through achieving a dominant market position.

- Consumer protection law is designed to protect consumers from unfair trading practices of businesses such as the false or misleading description of goods and services.

- The Office of Fair Trading and the Competition Commission have powers to investigate cases of unfair competitive practice, and can prohibit unfair pricing strategies and prevent mergers and acquisitions that are not in the public interest.

- Employment protection laws are designed to ensure fairness and safety in the workplace. All businesses must comply with health and safety legislation and take active steps to protect the welfare of their employees.

- Trade unions aim to protect (and improve) members' working conditions, employment rights and welfare at work.

quick questions

1. Name three examples of consumer protection law. Explain the impact that these laws may have on businesses.

2. Why is it important for a business to protect its employees? What legislation exists to protect the employee in the workplace?

3. Look on the internet to find the names of three trade unions. Why do you think so many different trade unions exist?

4. How might the work of a trade union impact on a business?

Borrowers to get fair deal

The first big shake-up of UK consumer credit laws for more than 30 years has been unveiled amid growing concern about the levels of personal debt.

Existing rules come under the Consumer Credit Act 1974, but there is far more credit available to consumers today. In 1971, there was only one type of credit card available. Now there are about 1,300 credit cards on the market.

Consumer groups are concerned with the complexity and lack of transparency of some financial products. They make it difficult for consumers to pick the right product for their needs.

Loans often tie people in for the long term, and include penalties for early repayment.

There is also concern that lenders are acting irresponsibly by failing to make sure consumers can afford the cost of credit.

The measures in the new credit card bill include:

■ creation of an "unfair credit" test, making it easier for people to take lenders to court if they feel they are paying an unnecessarily high level of interest or charges

■ consumers to be given free access to the financial ombudsman service to resolve disputes over credit agreements with lenders

■ lenders to provide annual statements to borrowers outlining in full the amount owed

■ Office of Fair Trading (OFT) to be given new powers to fine rogue lenders – at present, the only sanction the OFT has is the removal of a lender's credit licence.

Several changes have already been made.

■ The APR, which refers to the costs of the loan, must be more prominent than all other financial information.

■ It will become an offence to conceal the true cost of a loan in the terms and conditions. Companies that flout the rules could lose their consumer credit licence.

■ In addition, charges for paying off a loan early will be limited to interest for one month and 28 days (at present, lenders can charge two months and 28 days interest).

■ The industry has also acted to put its own house in order, incorporating a so-called "honesty box" in their credit card statements which outlines the costs of the loan and any additional charges.

Some consumer groups, such as Which? (formerly the Consumers' Association) say the charges don't go far enough. They have called for a ceiling to be imposed on lenders' interest rates.

The Department of Trade and Industry (DTI) decided not to impose a cap on the grounds that it could make it hard for low-income consumers to get credit. Lenders often charge a high interest rate to cover themselves against the potentially high risk of certain borrowers.

Source: adapted from news.bbc.co.uk, 23 November 2004

A **Why is it necessary for consumer groups such as Which? to work on behalf of the consumer?**

B **What impact will the stricter controls in the revised Consumer Credit Act have on businesses offering credit?**

C **How might this affect the employees within the consumer credit industry?**

D **Do you think that consumers will be better protected with the revised Credit Act? Explain why you think this is the case.**

Business in practice: Boots Group plc

Boots is one of the best-known retail names in the UK, selling health and beauty products and employing around 75,000 people. Its products are sold in 130 countries worldwide. In addition to retailing, it has international sales and marketing operations, and it also develops and manufactures its own products.

Figure 1.15 shows the 2003/4 sales and profit figures for the group's three main businesses. The UK and Ireland retail operations generate the bulk of the group's sales but Boots Retail International and Boots Healthcare International are showing strong growth.

Figure 1.16 shows the organisational structure of the Boots Group.

Figure 1.15: The Boots Group financials, 2003/4			
Business area	Sales £m	Increase %	Profit £m
Boots The Chemist	4,475.7	4.5	531.1
Boots Healthcare International	504.6	7.8	80.6
Boots Retail International	43.0	20.8	(10.4)

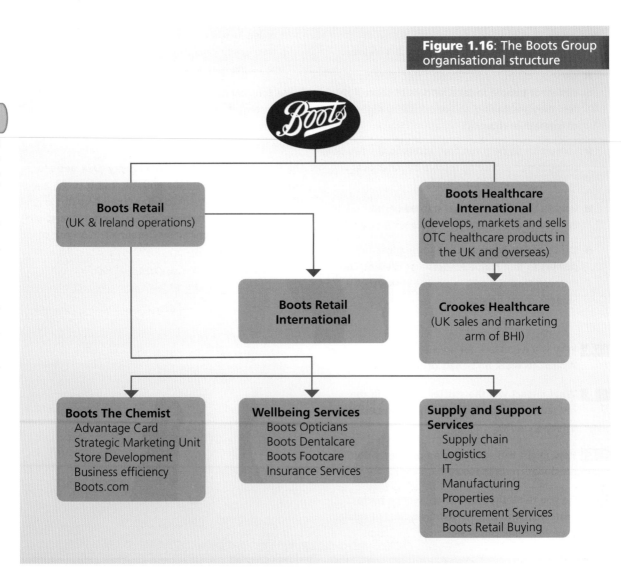

Figure 1.16: The Boots Group organisational structure

Business aims and objectives

The company's aim is to make Boots a more modern, competitive and efficient retail business in order to deliver value for shareholders.

It has three key objectives:

- modernising the business, providing customers with stores where they want them, meeting their needs in being able to shop and pay quickly, and presenting the right customer offer

- making Boots more competitive, through expert people, differentiation of products and improving value for money

- making Boots a more efficient operation in order to make more profits.

Environmental policy

Boots has a code of conduct for ethical trading. It aims to implement a policy of no animal testing of any kind to be undertaken by the company. Its environmental policy is an integral part of its values.

Effect of legislation

To illustrate how legislation can impact on the Boots Group, consider the company's response to the Disability Discrimination Act (DDA). This legislation affected the provision of all Boots Group goods, facilities and services in the UK. As a company Boots gives high priority to helping the Disability Rights Commission achieve its aim of "a society where all disabled people can participate fully as equal citizens", and it has implemented many changes to meet the new legislative requirements. These include:

- top-level commitment given, with a statement of intent published in the company accounts

- service to disabled customers to form an integral part of Boots goods, facilities and service standards

- a new executive director with direct accountability for DDA compliance appointed

- market research to understand disabled customers' preferences and requirements

- review of accessibility of all goods and services to disabled people

- accredited audits to the physical aspects of Boots in-store goods and services, to take all reasonable steps to ensure that the physical environment does not prevent disabled people from shopping at Boots

- staff training and disability awareness, to communicate new service standards to all employees throughout the group

- a variety of formats of communication with customers to be used, including advertising and other brand imagery to reflect a diverse customer base

- influencing other organisations to adopt a similar policy (suppliers, contractors, peer companies, etc.)

- increased involvement with the wider community, to consult with disabled people and local disability groups and organisations

- monitoring of performance at executive level.

Staff motivation

Boots believes it is essential to gain the commitment of its employees:

"A business will only thrive when it builds on the skills and retains the commitment of the people who work within it. It's a key part of our corporate responsibility to achieve this by the way we reward our employees, develop and train them, and earn their trust. Our focus on well-being should be reflected in our management style as well as our customer offer."

Careers in Boots

There are many different career paths and opportunities within the company. For example, there are many retail opportunities available through local Boots store; there are opportunities for opticians and pharmacists – Boots is the UK's largest pharmacy chain, employing over 3000 pharmacists and the group provided pre-registration training to a third of all graduates from UK schools of pharmacy.

Benefits offered to staff within the Boots Group plc include:

- discounts for staff purchases

- family-friendly practices, flexible working

- employee share scheme

- pension plan

- bonus.

In addition, the company encourages and supports employee participation through training programmes. It offers training in new skills, with investment in training to meet the changes taking place in the business and commitment to ongoing staff development.

Boots aims to create an environment where every member of staff feels respected and value. The company encourages staff to be involved in its Community Investment Programme, offering a Certificate of Recognition as a Community Associate to add to the CV of those who volunteer.

This seasonal advertisement was placed on Boots' website.

It's a good job – it's Christmas

Christmas has always been a special time at Boots. And we believe nobody does it better. But it's not just about great products. It's also about having a great team who all pull together to provide the very best in customer service.

In over 1400 stores across the country, we welcome more than three million customers each day. But Christmas is certainly our busiest time. And even when the pressure's on, we need to maintain the standards people expect from a trusted and well-loved name like ours. Which is why we need people like you.

Santa won't be the only one with a hardworking team this Christmas

Sales Assistants & Operations Assistants

Temporary and permanent, full and part-time opportunities.

As one of our friendly and fun-loving store team, you'll be working together to create a great customer experience this Christmas.

From welcoming people into the store to helping them find the products they're looking for, you'll provide valuable advice as one of our experts in customer care.

Just like any retail environment, there's also an element of selling involved and, if you join us as an Operations Assistant, you'll be ensuring our shelves are always full of fantastic products too.

And don't forget, as you'll be with us at one of the busiest times of the year, it's going to be hard work and you'll be on your feet for most of the day. But you're sure to get a great deal of satisfaction from knowing you've made the customer experience the best it can be.

If you're to be a big hit this Christmas, you'll need to be friendly and outgoing with lots of energy, resilience and enthusiasm for when things get really busy. Above all, you must share our passion for people and the products we sell.

Have yourself a merry little Christmas

In addition to a competitive salary, you can look forward to some great benefits for the contribution you make, including:

- generous discounts – 22% on Boots products, 12.5% on non-Boots products
- free uniform
- pension plan
- bonus
- employee share plan
- special offers from other companies
- choice of flexible working operations.

If you join us on a permanent basis, you'll also benefit from our commitment to your ongoing development through many opportunities for training and career progression.

activities

1 Explain how Boots' aims and objectives are influenced by the fact that it is a public limited company?

2 How might the structure of Boots help to contribute to it working effectively as a successful business?

3 What effect does Boots environmental policy have on it business? You may need to look on the Boots website (www.boots-plc.com) for details of the impact this policy has on their company.

4 Recruitment in Boots is mainly through three methods: direct application to their stores, through internet applications, and through the use of a recruitment agency. Explain why Boots might use these three methods for staff recruitment throughout the company.

5 Boots Christmas advertisement (which we have reproduced here) was placed online. Explain why the company may have selected this method of advertising for staff. How might this encourage applicants?

6 Explain how Boots motivates its workforce.

7 Prepare a draft job description and person specification for one of the positions advertised in the Boots Christmas recruitment campaign (reproduced here).

8 Explain the impact that legislative changes on disability discrimination have had on the business. Explain the impact this may have had on the staff working within the Boots Group.

THE WORD BUSINESS COMES FROM THE IDEA of "busy-ness", which is appropriate as businesses are busy organisations. Running a business involves a wide range of activities including managing resources, selling products, marketing and promotional activities, and managing staff.

The focus in this unit is on the management of a business's finances and its use of resources. The unit covers:
- business planning
- monitoring performance
- financial management
- using software to aid decision making.

In studying this unit, you will learn the crucial importance of planning in running a successful business and how financial management is the key tool in the effective planning and evaluation of a business.

Unit 2

Investigating business

Introducing financial planning

Setting the scene: financial planning at Fiat

Fiat, the Italian car manufacturer, is facing troubled times. In 2005 the company ended its partnership with the huge American car maker GM. This relationship had existed since 2000 and had seen the companies involved in a number of joint ventures. Although Fiat will continue to manufacture GM's diesel engines, it will no longer work with GM on other projects.

The end of the partnership with GM has highlighted Fiat's financial problems. Fiat's debts are reported to be in the region of £5600 million and it must make regular heavy interest payments. In the short term these have been eased by a payment of £1100 million from GM to buy itself out of the partnership deal. However, the payment from GM is not enough to resolve Fiat's serious underlying financial problems.

Further difficulties for the company are that its sales of cars are declining and it is losing market share in its home market; once the company had a 60 per cent share of the Italian car market, latterly it has fallen to 25 per cent. Fiat's overall sales fell by 9 per cent in 2004.

The challenge facing the company's managers is to find ways of ensuring that the company is able to survive in financial terms in the medium term. GM's money will help in the short term, but unless Fiat can increase sales and revenues, its bankers may become nervous about the company's ability to pay its debts as they become due.

A key element of the company's financial planning will be to consider ways in which the company can reduce its costs over the next few years. The company's managers are reported to be seeking a new partnership with another car manufacturer as a means of cutting costs. The other important issue for Fiat will be to manage its cash effectively. The company is facing falling sales and will need to invest in new models to improve its market standing. This may stretch the company's limited reserves of cash.

KEY TERMS

Financial management is the process of producing and interpreting accounts that record a business's expected or actual costs, revenues and profits. This helps managers to take good decisions.

A **budget** is a financial plan for the future operations of the business. Budgets are used to set targets to monitor performance and control operations.

A **business plan** is a detailed statement setting out the proposals for a new business or describing the ways in which an existing business will be developed.

Cash flow is a measure of the amount of money moving into and out of a business over a particular time period.

What is financial planning?

Financial planning is the drawing up of forecasts or estimates of future costs, revenues and profits (or losses) to help managers to make decisions. Financial plans come in a number of different forms.

Businesses estimate their likely sales and the revenue or income they expect to earn from these sales. In 2004 Fujitsu, the Japanese electronics firm, reported that its sales were significantly below forecasts mainly because consumers were purchasing fewer technological products.

Businesses also estimate costs of production. These are not always easy to forecast. For example, in 2004 many airlines faced unexpected rises in their operating costs because of a sharp increase in fuel prices.

By putting together expected or budgeted costs and revenues, businesses are able to estimate future profits or losses. In 2005 Barclays Bank reported profits of £9,400 million roughly in line with its forecasts.

Businesses also forecast cash flows. This is an important part of financial management because if a business runs out of cash, it may be unable to pay its bills. Drawing up a forecast of cash outflows and inflows for the year ahead is an important part of financial planning. Cash flow problems are a very common cause of business failure.

Banks pull the plug on Courts

Courts, the furniture retailer chain, disappeared from UK high streets in 2005 because of cash flow problems. The company was forced to cease trading and go into administration because it had insufficient cash to pay the interest due on its loans.

GO TO the accompanying CD-ROM. Choose Unit 2 from the main menu. This will take you to an interactive game about managing cash flow. It is better to try this game once you have read Unit 2 Topics 1, 4, 5, 6 and 7.

What this unit covers

This unit examines how businesses manage and review their finances and other resources. You will investigate a number of issues relating to the management of resources.

Business planning

All businesses should engage in planning. It is vital for a new business as a means of assessing the viability of the venture, but planning is equally important for an existing firm intending to engage in a major new project. The section on business planning considers sources of finance available to businesses, the value to be gained from business plans, as well as the key elements that a business should include in its plans.

Managing business activities

Business managers should monitor the performance of their enterprises to assess whether they are achieving their planned level of performance. The business plan offers a series of targets to help managers monitor performance. This monitoring will include assessing the performance of the workforce, the use of the business's physical resources (factories, machinery, etc.) and its finances.

Financial management

The financial performance of a business can be judged in a number of ways. This unit introduces the two main financial statements – the balance sheet and the profit and loss account. It also considers the importance of forecasting and monitoring a business's cash reserves. Other financial techniques such as breakeven analysis and budgeting are included in a wide-ranging coverage of the techniques of financial management.

Using software in decision-making

The use of information and communications technology (ICT) can enhance the efficiency of a business. Topic 9 investigates the uses of spreadsheets within businesses and the main legal issues that need to be considered in the use of ICT in business.

Setting the scene: Energy & Vision

By the age of 22 Paul McCabe had reached rock bottom. Following a period of drug addiction and crime which culminated in armed robbery, he was sent to prison. Yet seven years later Paul is happily married and running his own business.

Paul manages Energy & Vision. His business gives advice to schoolchildren, parole and police officers and government agencies on the best way to overcome problems associated with drug addiction. Paul got the idea when was invited into a local school to talk to students about the dangers of using drugs.

Paul had to draw up a business plan to attract financial support before he could start his business. He did this with the help of a fellow ex-addict and was lent £13 000 by Lloyds TSB. His

plan included proposals to gain qualifications in management and counselling (which Paul has done) and to establish an office as well as employing staff.

Energy & Vision is now a highly successful business. It has 10 staff and advises the Home Office on training police officers as well as visiting schools. In 2001, Energy & Vision won a Prince's Trust Business of the Year award.

Why do you think it was essential for Paul to plan his business before starting Energy & Vision?

Source: Adapted from www.news.bbc.co.uk, 7 September 2004

What is a business plan?

A business plan is a detailed statement setting out the proposals for a new business or explaining the ways in which an existing business might be developed. Business planning involves researching and collecting information, and analysing and presenting this information in such a way as to aid decision-making.

A good business plan contains background information and comprehensive details on the proposals.

- An initial summary outlining the key features of the proposal.

- A statement of the business's aims and objectives.

- A description of the business to be started or the nature of the development of an existing business.

- Market research data relating to the proposal, which can be used to make and support sales forecasts.

- Details on the operations and/or production requirements, including premises, machinery, facilities for production and IT systems.

- Details of all other resources required (finance, staff, etc.) to carry out the proposal.

- Some information about the manager or management team of the business.

- Financial forecasts showing the expected profit or loss for the first year or two, as well as estimated inflows and outflows of cash.

Business planning is not a static, one-off process. A business plan should be updated to allow for new information or any unexpected changes that may occur. For example, plans may need to be revised if a new competitor enters the market; financial forecasts would need to change if the price of energy rises sharply, thereby increasing the business's costs. The aim is set out clear plans supported by accurate forecasts.

Every year about 500 000 businesses are started up. Only around 300 000 (or 60 per cent) will survive their first three years of trading. A major reason for failure of newly established businesses is poor initial planning. Even established businesses still need to plan very carefully when expanding or implementing a new strategy for the company.

stop and think

Eurotunnel operates the Channel Tunnel between Kent and northern France. The company borrowed heavily to build the tunnel. In its early planning, Eurotunnel forecast that 17 million passengers would use the Channel Tunnel in 2003. In fact, the actual figure was 7 million. Why do you think this forecast was wrong? Why does it matter?

Financial planning

Arguably, the financial forecasts and statements are the most important elements of a business plan. The financial plans normally contain three elements.

1 Statement of sources of finance

Most new businesses require capital. Some businesses – or new business ventures – may require vehicles, machinery and buildings. Others may simply need the working capital to meet their running and living costs before they start to receive income from sales. A vital part of financial planning is to detail how the business will pay for its capital expenses. The plan will state whether the money is to be borrowed, raised by selling shares (in the case of companies) or obtained from other sources such as retained profits, redundancy pay or savings.

2 Forecasting cash flows

Cash flow is a measure of the amount of money moving into and out of a business over time. Businesses often experience cash flow problems when expanding or starting trading. This means that cash (from sales) does not flow into the business in time to allow expenses to be paid promptly. If suppliers are not paid, they might become anxious – especially if they are dealing with a new business – and they can force the business to close down. Any potential

lenders will want to see a cash flow plan or forecast to show that major cash problems are not expected or, if they are, plans are in hand to deal with them.

3 Forecasting profits

Potential lenders will also be interested to see when the project is expected to make a profit. This aspect of financial planning will be of particular interest to anyone buying shares in the business, as shareholders will expect to receive a return on their investment in the form of dividends financed out of profits.

stop and think

In 2004, Philip Duxbury opened a bookshop in a small town in Norfolk. In the first year of trading Philip suffered from a shortage of cash. Why might this have occurred? What could Philip do about it?

Topic 1 Business plans and planning

The importance of business planning

Planning is important because it helps the business's stakeholders to make decisions. Crucially, a business plan will help managers and owners decide whether to proceed with the proposal and it will help investors decide whether to invest money in the venture.

1 The business's owners

The process of planning helps entrepreneurs to think in depth about their business proposals in an analytical way. Without proper planning, the reasons for starting or expanding a business may remain unclear or incomplete. Producing a business plan concentrates the mind of managers and entrepreneurs, especially where financial matters are concerned. The planning process might indicate the project, although apparently a good idea, would not be profitable. On the other hand, planning may suggest the project will be extremely profitable.

The planning process is useful for anyone staring their own business in that it makes them consider whether they have the skills and knowledge necessary to run an enterprise successfully. Many of the UK's banks produce materials to assist entrepreneurs plan a new business. These materials often contain a questionnaire that helps people assess whether they have necessary qualities to manage a business.

Business plans are also vital documents for the management of the business. The plan can be used to monitor progress and to see whether the business is performing as expected. If something is going wrong – if, say, sales are lower than forecast – managers receive an early warning if they are monitoring progress against the business plan and this will provide an opportunity to take corrective action.

2 Banks and other investors

One of the most important reasons for any business to prepare a business plan is to raise money. Most businesses, even large prosperous ones, are likely to need external finance when implementing important new proposals. It is imperative that they provide banks and other potential lenders with detailed information. Lenders are likely to especially interested in:

- the market for the product and forecasts of sales
- the cash flow associated with the product – will the business receive a steady inflow of cash?
- profitability over the first year or two.

Banks and other potential lenders are taking a risk by investing money into a new enterprise. They will expect to see a thorough and well prepared business plan. For example, they are more likely to respond positively to any request for finance if they can see that careful financial forecasts have been made and that the business is likely to be able to repay the loan over time.

stop and think

Why do banks offer so much support (advice leaflets and software to assist with business planning) to people who want to start up a new business?

Business planning and objectives

Setting objectives is an important part of managing a business. Business objectives are the targets or goals of the entire organisation, and these objectives will influence the business planning process. Any business plan should be drawn up to help a business achieve its overall objectives.

The overall objective of Amazon, the online bookshop, is growth. Its business plans will be developed to assist it in achieving this objective: so, for example, it may propose expanding by operating websites in new countries or selling a wider range of products (such as toys and wine). In contrast, Boots, the high street retailer, has set itself the objective of improving profitability (its profits fell by 50 per cent in 2004). Boots' plans have centred on selling off some of the less profitable elements of the business, including the company's dentistry and laser eye treatment ventures.

Knowledge summary

- Businesses normally draw up business plans before they first start trading, when they are expanding or when they are implementing a new strategy.

- Financial planning is particularly important. Financial plans should detail sources of finance and forecast cash flow and profits.

- Business plans can be used by managers as an early warning system (by monitoring progress against planned targets) and have a vital role to play in raising finance.

- Business plans should assist the organisation in achieving its objectives.

data interpretation
SpeedDater: a successful new business

Speed dating is designed for single young people. It offers participants the opportunity to meet up to 30 potential partners in a single evening. Speed dating allows two people the chance to chat briefly before each moves on to meet someone else. If a couple "click", they can exchange details and meet up later.

SpeedDater was founded by Simon Prockter and Ben Tisdall in 2002. Simon had tried internet dating. After experiencing a couple of blind dates going wrong, he heard about speed dating. Simon loved the concept and SpeedDater was launched to offer speed dating in a non-pressurised environment to the kind of people who probably wouldn't consider contacting a dating agency.

SpeedDater uses upmarket bars to host events for professional single people. By the end of 2004, SpeedDater was running more events in more cities than any other company, and had quickly become Europe's leading speed dating company and a commercial success. SpeedDater charges between £20 and £25 to each person attending one of its events. There are more than 30,000 people registered with the company. More information can be found at www.speeddater.co.uk.

A Explain two benefits Simon Prockter and Ben Tisdall might have gained from drawing up a business plan for their new business.

B Explain three items of information that the two entrepreneurs should have included in their business plan.

C Imagine you are considering starting a speed dating company. Use the internet to research and answer the questions below. Sources include BBC News, Google and newspaper websites as well as the SpeedDater website.

Which companies currently offer speed dating in the UK? Is there a gap in the market?

What prices do companies in the market charge? What price might your company charge?

What might be the profile your customers?

Setting the scene: business advice websites

The internet has transformed the market for business advice, making it much easier for budding entrepreneurs to find help and support.

In the past, anyone wanting advice on starting or expanding a business would have to make an appointment with an adviser from a bank or the local council, or arrange to meet their accountant or solicitor. Today, they just need to turn on their computer to find a range of online resources.

BizHelp24 is one of these new resources. Its website (www.bizhelp24.com) offers individuals and small businesses with information, news, help and services. As well as informing and educating on many key areas of business, BizHelp24 also recommends quality UK business and finance service providers.

BizHelp24 provides information and services on a variety of business and financial issues, raging from credit policy, cash flow control and business loans to bankruptcy, home working and business accounting.

BizHelp24 promotes itself as the UK's premier small business advice website. However, if you conduct a search on the internet you will find many other websites offering business advice.

What are the possible advantages of getting business advice from a website? Can you think of any disadvantages? Visit www.bizhelp24.com to help you reflect on these questions.

Enterprise

Enterprise is the willingness to take risks in a business venture in the hope of making money. Many individuals and companies have a reputation for being enterprising. This means they have a flair for business, that they can see a business opportunity and are prepared to take a risk in the hope of turning that business opportunity into profits.

KEY TERMS

A **business plan** is a detailed statement setting out the proposals for a new business or describing the ways in which an existing business will be developed.

Enterprise is the willingness to take risks in a business venture in the hope of making money.

Innovation is the process of introducing novel ideas to develop new products or new methods of production.

There are many types of enterprising business.

- Truancy Call won the most enterprising business category in the 2004 Orange small business awards. Stephen Clarke established Truancy Call in 2000 and it supplies the technology to enable schools to contact parents by phone, text and email on the first day of a pupil being absent. It has helped to reduce truancy.

- The Arcadia Group, which includes well-known high street stores such as BHS, is flourishing under the ownership of self-made billionaire Philip Green. The company has expanded in recent years – it even launched a bid to take over Marks & Spencer in 2004 – and has increased its profits.

Enterprise is seen as vital to the future economic welfare of the UK. The government has launched several initiatives to create a more enterprising society and it actively encourages new and budding entrepreneurs.

What benefits does Apple Computers receive from its investment in innovative products such as the iPod? How does researching and producing innovative products affect the company's finances in the short and long term?

Apple unveils photo-display iPod

Apple has unveiled an iPod with a photo-display function aimed at maintaining the company's lead in the market for compact digital music players.

The new iPod comes in two versions, including a 60-gigabyte model capable of storing 25,000 colour photographs, which retails at $599 in the US.

The device is intended to meet demand for convenient ways of storing pictures in the age of digital photography. "We think music plus photos is the next big thing," said Apple boss Steve Jobs.

Source: news.bbc.co.uk, 27 October 2004

One scheme that recognises achievement in business is The Queen's Awards for Enterprise (www.queens awards.org.uk). These awards are made annually to businesses and individuals who have been particularly enterprising.

If you visit the website, you can look at the lists of recent winners of The Queen's Awards for Enterprise. Which business impressed you as the most enterprising? Why?

Innovation requires the practical application of new ideas as the basis for enhanced processes or new products. Regular innovation resulting in new products and processes is the cornerstone of a competitive business, but it requires heavy expenditure on research and development if it is to succeed. Businesses in industries such as pharmaceuticals and computer manufacture rely heavily upon innovation to stay ahead of their competitors.

Legal implications

The Law is the rules which govern our society are established by Acts of Parliament and by the courts. If businesses do not work within the law, they risk their reputations as well as facing fines and other legal penalties. Figure 2.1 below summarises some of the legal issues and regulations that govern businesses.

One key issue is limited liability. If a business trades as a company (shown by the letters Ltd or plc after its name) then the financial liability of the owners to any debts incurred by the business is limited to the amount of money they have invested. This means that shareholders do not risk their entire personal wealth by investing in a business. Other types of businesses, such as sole traders and partnerships, do not benefit from this privilege of limited liability, and owners can potentially lose all they own, including their homes, if the business incurs huge debts.

Figure 2.1: Legislation impacting on business

Business activity	Issues covered by legislation	Examples of legislation
Starting a business	The name of the business, meetings and voting rights, the rights and responsibilities of partners in a business, the responsibility of the business's owners for its debts.	Business Names Act, 1985 Partnership Act, 1890 Limited Liability Partnerships Act, 2000
Consumer protection	The description of goods and services in adverts, the quality and quantities of products sold, the terms under which a consumer is offered credit by a seller.	Trades Descriptions Act, 1968 & 1972 Consumer Protection Act, 1987 Consumer Credit Acts, 1974 & 2005
The environment	The prevention of air and water pollution, the safe disposal of waste products, the efficient use of energy and the restoration of land when businesses no longer use it.	Clean Air Acts, 1956 & 1993 Environmental Protection Act, 1991 Pollution Control and Prevention Act, 2000
Employing workers	The avoidance of discrimination on the grounds of sex, race and disability. Minimum wage rates, trade unions (especially relating to strikes and whether employers have to negotiate with trade unions), and health and safety.	Disability Discrimination Act, 1995 National Minimum Wage Act, 1998 Employment Relations Act, 1999 Health and Safety at Work Act, 1974

Source of advice used	Apr 2000 (%)	Nov 2001 (%)	Nov 2002 (%)
Accountant	37	41	42
Bank	35	38	32
Business Link	6	6	8
Trade association	6	6	6
Chamber of commerce	4	4	4
Solicitor or lawyer	3	3	3
Colleagues or other business people	3	6	4
Local business adviser or consultant	5	1	3
Financial adviser	1	4	2
Local authority, council or government	1	2	2

Source: Adapted from www.euro.gov.uk/surveys

Business advice

There are a number of organisations that can help an entrepreneur when starting a new business or offer advice and support to established organisations.

Professional advisers

Accountants are experts in providing financial advice particularly in respect of matters such as keeping financial records and business taxation. Similarly, solicitors can provide information on a range of legal issues relating to the establishment and operation of a business. Banks can also provide a wide range of advice for budding entrepreneurs and experienced managers. For example, banks can offer support with business planning and may be able to advise on whether a business is entitled to financial support from the UK government or the European Union.

Business Links

Business Links offer a variety of help to small and medium-sized businesses. This includes:

- seminars and workshops on business issues
- advice on UK government and EU grants
- factsheets on key business management issues
- tailored advice, support and information service.

Most areas of the UK have a local Business Link. Visit www.businesslink4london.com to find about one of the UK's largest Business Links, or search for your local Business Link on www.businesslink.gov.uk.

Chambers of commerce

Chambers of commerce support businesses as well as trying to influence governments to implement business-friendly policies. You can find out more at www.chambersonline.co.uk.

Trade associations

Trade organisations provide a service to specific industries and, as such, they are able to give highly specialised advice to businesses trading in that industry. For example, the Association of British Travel Agents (ABTA) and the Booksellers Association are the trade associations in the travel retail sector and the bookshops business respectively.

Business planning

All aspects of planning a business are important, but two are essential if the business is to prosper.

First, marketing is vital in business planning. If a business has insufficient customers, it will not succeed. It is important to research a market before launching a new business or expanding an existing enterprise. This research will help managers decide whether enough customers are interested in purchasing the proposed product at the offered price to make it financially viable, and will provide some of the data needed to construct accurate forecasts. Businesses will also have to budget in their plans for any marketing expenditure necessary to promote the product. Marketing is considered in detail in Unit 3.

Second, financial planning. Many businesses require capital to buy or lease machinery, buildings and vehicles as well as to pay for other business expenses such as marketing. An essential ingredient of the business plan is to identify the source of this capital (bank loan, savings, loan from friends and family, for example) and to make sure that the repayments are affordable. Another key issue in financial planning is cash flow. A business's finances must be planned so that bills can be paid as they fall due. This means ensuring that the business has sufficient cash at all times. This can be tricky when establishing a business.

Knowledge summary

- Sources of business advice include websites, Business Link and chambers of commerce, but the most widely consulted are banks and accountants.

- Enterprise is the willingness to take business risks, and innovation is the process of using new ideas as the basis for processes or new products.

- There are several government initiatives that support enterprise and innovation.

- All businesses are subject to laws covering their structure, employee rights and consumer protection.

quick questions

1 Describe two ways in which the government has attempted to create a more enterprising society. Why does the government want to achieve this aim?

2 Imagine you are setting up a bookshop as a sole trader. Identify and describe three laws that you might need to observe during your first few months of trading.

3 What single source of business advice would you use before starting your business as a bookseller? Explain your choice.

data interpretation
Innovation in car design

A Outline the planning Toyota would have had to carried out prior to starting the project to manufacture and sell robotic pods.

B Why is this project a risky venture for Toyota? Explain your answer fully.

C Discuss the case for and against Toyota being the first company to sell robotic pods.

Toyota's robotic pods challenge traditional car design

A new breed of wearable robotic vehicles that envelop drivers are being developed by Japanese car giant Toyota.

The company's vision for the single passenger in the 21st century involves the driver cruising by in a four-wheeled leaf-like device or strolling along encased in an egg-shaped cocoon that walks upright on two feet.

The models are being positioned as so-called personal mobility devices, which have few limits.

Both these prototypes will be demonstrated, along with other concept vehicles and helper robots, at the Toyota stand at Expo 2005 in Aichi, Japan.

Also on display at the show will be the egg-shaped "i-foot". This is a two-legged mountable robot-like device that can be controlled with a joystick.

Standing at a height of well over seven feet (2.1 metres), the unit can walk along at a speed of about 1.35km/h (0.83mph) and navigate

Source: adapted from news.bbc.co.uk, 10 December 2004

Topic 2 More issues in business planning

Setting the scene: all doesn't go to plan at Cadbury

In autumn 2003, Cadbury Schweppes, the confectionery and soft drinks manufacturer announced that it was planning to cut 10 per cent of its 55 000 strong workforce.

As a part of this rationalisation programme, the company planned to shut 20 per cent of its factories around the world. Already, Cadbury Schweppes has revealed that it will close two UK factories (in Manchester and Chesterfield), with 550 jobs being lost as a consequence.

The rationalisation programme is designed to cut the company's costs by an estimated £400 million each year. Cadbury Schweppes intends to use some of the savings to market its products more effectively. For example, it hopes to sell more chewing gum in the UK, a market in which it has not been successful in the past.

And why has the company decided upon this drastic action? Because the company has not been performing to expectations. In the six months prior to the announcement, the company made a £294 million profit, one-third less than in the same period in the previous year and well below the forecast (or budgeted) figure. Cadbury's managers decided that the company's costs were too high and took action to reduce its cost base.

Making effective use of resources

1 Human resources

A business's human resources are all the people that work for the organisation, including office staff, operational and shop floor employees, and managers. A well managed business seeks to employ the minimum number of employees necessary to provide goods and services at an appropriate level of quality.

This helps to control costs and can boost profits.

Some managers will try to control labour costs by paying low wages. They may be prepared to accept the fact that some staff may leave the business after a short period of employment because they get better paid jobs elsewhere. Some companies even move operations to regions or countries with lower labour costs. For example, some companies in the banking and insurance sectors have opted to transfer some jobs abroad to countries such as India where wages are much lower than in the UK.

KEY TERMS

Human resources are all the people that work within an organisation, including office staff, operational and shop floor employees, and managers.

Quality control is a system for checking completed products to ensure they meet agreed standards.

Quality assurance is a continuous system used by businesses to make sure their products match specified standards.

Total quality management (TQM) is a management philosophy that encourages all employees within an organisation to take responsibility for producing and delivering high-quality goods and services.

Other firms seek to manage their human resources effectively by developing a long-term relationship with their staff. These companies aim to develop the skills of their staff as much as possible. This entails investment in training but can result in improved output as well-motivated and highly skilled staff ensure better quality products and enhanced customer satisfaction. Businesses that adopt this approach aim to recruit employees with the potential to perform to a high standard.

2 Physical resources

All businesses, even internet-based firms, require some physical resources including a space to work and the equipment needed to produce and deliver goods and service. Many companies will have substantial physical assets such as high-tech equipment, buildings, vehicles and stocks of raw materials and components. It is important to manage these resources as efficiently as possible to minimise costs. Keeping costs to a minimum allows managers to reduce prices or to make higher profits. For example, manufacturers want to utilise their factories as fully as possible, so that the costs of owning and running the building are spread over as many units of output as possible.

3 Financial resources

Most businesses aim to make a profit. For this reason, it is vital that a business's finances are carefully managed. Costs should be minimised; revenues and income should be increased as much as possible. To help manage a business's finances, managers draw up budgets – financial plans setting out expected costs and revenues. If costs are higher than expected – or revenues lower than anticipated – it is important that remedial action is taken. Failure to meet its financial targets is what prompted Cadbury Schweppes to embark on a cost-cutting exercise (as we highlighted insetting the scene at the start of this topic). Budgets are discussed more fully in Topic 6 (*see page* 82).

The importance of quality

A quality product is one that meets the needs of the business's customers. This is important because satisfied customers are likely to become repeat customers – making furthers purchases in the future, thereby boosting a business's revenues and profits. Businesses therefore need to monitor the quality of their products (goods or services) to make sure that customers are satisfied and not tempted to go elsewhere.

There are various systems and approaches that businesses can use to monitor and control quality. However, underpinning all approaches is an underlying ethos that quality is an ongoing issue that businesses must monitor continuously.

1 Quality control

Quality control is a system for checking completed products to ensure they meet agreed standards. Quality control normally takes place after the

production process is complete to establish that products are of sufficient quality to meet the needs of consumers. Some companies also ensure that all stocks of raw materials and components bought from other businesses also undergo a quality control check.

Quality control is widely used in manufacturing; typically teams of inspectors check the quality of products, though some firms encourage all employees to take responsibility for checking that quality standards are met. Kellogg's, the global manufacturer of breakfast cereals, checks both the quality of ingredients as they arrive at the factory and the standard of the finished product.

stopandthink

In addition to carrying out quality control in its factories, Kellogg's monitors its product quality by collecting samples from stores throughout the world and sending them back to its quality department for analysis. What benefits might Kellogg's receive from testing the quality of its products in this way?

2 Quality assurance

Systems of quality control assume that defects are inevitable: the quality system focuses on the detection of sub-standard products. Quality assurance, in contrast, is about prevention: the focus is on ensuring that all products meet specified quality standards.

Quality assurance is about making sure that employees at each stage of production meet quality standards so that the final product satisfies the needs of its consumers. This philosophy emphasises the importance of employees producing goods and services that conform to standards every time, thus minimising the number of defective or sub-quality products. Some quality assurance systems place importance on employees checking their own work to avoid sub-standard products slipping through. This requires a well-trained and committed workforce.

A feature of quality assurance is that products should be designed to meet consumers' needs as fully as possible. This means that quality assurance is as relevant for businesses supplying services as well as for manufacturers. For example, hotels strive to provide clean rooms and the full range of services that guests require including minibars, hairdryers and internet connections.

3 Total quality management

Total quality management (TQM) develops and extends the quality assurance approach by instilling a quality culture within the entire workforce. Under TQM, each area of the business is encouraged to regard other employees within the business as customers and to ensure that they receive good quality products. For example, within an insurance company the IT department would ensure that it maintained the IT equipment of other departments within the company to agreed standards – it might, say, agree to deal with complaints within six hours.

TQM extends further. Total quality businesses encourage employees to suggest ways in which quality can be improved through the use of quality circles. These are regular meetings of employees drawn from all levels in the business with the aim of developing more effective ways of improving quality.

Quality should be paramount to all aspects of the business's operations. So, for example, businesses adopting a TQM approach also focus on meeting customers' needs after a sale has taken place by operating an efficient after-sales service.

Monitoring business performance

Successful businesses don't rest on their laurels. As with quality, the process of monitoring all aspects of a business's performance should be ongoing. Managers can assess performance in several ways.

Liquidity

Liquidity refers to the amount of cash within a business. Cash is vital to all businesses, enabling them to pay wages and other expenses. Assessing liquidity is a key part of monitoring the performance of a business. This issue is considered in depth in Topic 7.

Profitability

Most businesses exist to make profits. Declining levels of profitability can provide a clear indicator that action is needed. Equally, a business might regard rising profit levels as an indicator of success.

Meeting legal requirements

Businesses should operate within the law to avoid fines and other penalties. It is also important because any illegal action can result in damaging publicity which may reduce sales and profitability.

Knowledge summary

■ Businesses that manage their human, physical and financial resources effectively increase their chances of success.

■ Using quality control or quality assurance systems to ensure that customers' needs are met is an important element of managing a business efficiently.

■ Managers need to monitor the performance of businesses continuously to make sure that standards do not decline.

quick **questions**

1 Explain the benefits that a national chain of travel agents might gain by providing regular training to its employees.

2 Using examples, explain the difference between quality assurance and quality control.

3 Describe two ways in which a manager might assess the performance of a business.

data **interpretation**
Kwik-Fit and customer delight

Created by Sir Tom Farmer CBE in 1971, Kwik-Fit has grown to become one of the world's leading automotive parts, repair and replacement specialists. The company sells and fits tyres, exhausts and batteries to private motorists.

Kwik-Fit invests heavily in marketing and operates more than 2,400 outlets throughout Europe. As market leader, the Kwik-Fit brand is distinctive and well known. Despite fierce competition, Kwik-Fit has remained the dominant force in the market sector and it services are used by more than seven million motorists a year.

The company has grown rapidly and has worked hard to develop an image of being convenient, friendly, helpful, fast, affordable and operating according to professional values. The Kwik-Fit fitter has become the emblem of the brand and is used to help to reinforce the now famous proposition: you can't get better than a Kwik-Fit fitter. This is all part of the company's aim, not just to satisfy customers, but to give 100 per cent customer delight.

A What is meant by the term customer delight?

B Kwik-Fit has grown rapidly over recent years. How might its focus on quality have assisted it to expand its operations?

C "Kwik-Fit's policy of 100 per cent customer delight has only been of use in relation to its marketing." Do you agree with this statement? Justify your view.

Why should individuals and companies commit time and resources to a business? For many, it is because businesses have the potential to make a profit. After all, it is the profit motive that drives many people towards starting out in business in the first place.

Profit is one of the most important business goals. Business owners want to know how successful they've been and profit is one of the main ways a business monitors its success or failure. Other stakeholders in a business also have an interest in its profitability, which is why companies have a legal obligation to report their profit levels each year. These stakeholders include the business's employees, suppliers, competitors and government.

Take time to consider why each of these groups would be interested in a business's profitability.

Profit and loss accounts

A profit and loss account is the way an organisation determines and sets out the level of profits it has made. As profit is so important to many different stakeholder groups, it is vital that it is calculated accurately; therefore, businesses must follow guidelines – as set out in the Companies Acts and as issued by professional accountancy bodies – which detail how a profit and loss account should be calculated. The idea is that it shouldn't matter who prepares the profit and loss account, they should arrive at the same answer.

There are five stages to calculating the profit (or loss) made by a business:

- determining turnover
- accounting for cost of sales
- calculating gross profit
- accounting for expenses
- calculating net profit.

1 Turnover

A profit is made if a business generates more revenue than its costs. Usually this revenue comes from selling goods and services. The sales revenue earned by a company is calculated by considering the number of items sold and at what price:

sales revenue = quantity sold x price per unit

However, some customers may have subsequently returned goods. These returns must be taken off sales revenue to reflect the fact that some of the company's sales revenue over the period would have been refunded. So, sales less returns is called turnover:

turnover = sales revenue – returns

2 Cost of sales

We next need to calculate how much it cost to buy or produce the goods or services that have been sold; this is called the cost of sales. For example, the cost of sales for a bookshop is the total amount that it pays to publishers for all the books that the shop sells. For a car manufacturer, the cost of sales is the cost of all the raw materials, components and direct labour used in each car that the manufacturer sells.

KEY TERMS

Profitability is a measure of a business's ability to generate more revenue from its activities than it actually costs to undertake those activities.

A **profit and loss account** is a statement that shows a firm's revenue generated over a trading period and all the relevant costs incurred in earning that revenue.

Revenue is the total income made from selling goods and services over a period of time.

Expenses are costs incurred by a business in its day-to-day running, including employees' wages, utility bills (light, heat, water) and administration costs such as stationery.

Profit arises when a firm's revenue is greater than its total costs.

Gross profit is the difference between revenue generated by sales and the cost of the products which have been sold. It measures profit made on buying and selling activities.

Net profit is the actual amount left after all other costs associated with running the business are taken into account, such as expenses like marketing costs or electricity.

A **loss** occurs when revenue is less than a firm's total costs.

Note that in each case the cost of sales comprises the cost of any goods and raw materials that the business has bought and then used, and subsequently sold to customers. The cost of sales does not include the cost of any raw material or stock that has not been sold on to customers. The reason that cost of sales is calculated in this way is that if a business has raw materials and stock that it has not sold, then no profit can have been made on these items. So any unsold items are not counted in the cost of sales calculation.

3 Calculating gross profit

Gross profit is a measure of how much profit has been made on buying and selling; it is a measure of how good a business is at trading. Gross profit is calculated by deducting the cost of sales from turnover:

gross profit = turnover − cost of sales

Gross profit is calculated and presented in a formal layout called a trading account. An example of a trading account is shown in the top half of Figure 2.3.

4 Accounting for expenses

There is more to running businesses than just buying goods and raw materials and selling them to customers. The costs of all the other aspects of the business need to be considered so the final amount of profit can be found. These additional costs are called expenses. They are the overheads or indirect costs

that a company incurs that are not the direct material costs involved in production, buying and selling.

Expenses are characterised as items which the business has paid for and "used up" in conducting its activities. Typical expenses are staff wages and salaries, rent and rates, utility bills (electricity, gas, water), marketing expenses including advertising and promotions, motor expenses, distribution and warehouse costs, depreciation, administration expenses and finance costs. These expenses can be presented in the trading account in different ways. Usually, large companies divide expenses into two categories, administration costs and distribution costs, as in Figure 2.3. It is not necessary for every category of expenses to be present, as some categories will not apply to all businesses.

5 Calculating net profit

Expenses are added to the formal trading account layout after the gross profit line. At this stage, it is then possible to calculate the net profit for the period. Net profit is calculated by deducting the total expenses from the gross profit figure obtained earlier. This is shown in the bottom part of Figure 2.3.

Net profit is the second and final calculation of profit. It measures how much overall profit the business has made after taking into account all the costs that have been incurred.

Figure 2.3: A full formal trading profit and loss account with net profit calculation

Trading account for Johnston Ltd. Year ending 31-12-200x		
	£000s	£000s
Sales	87,200	
Less **Returns in**	(3,210)	
Turnover		83,990
Less **Cost of sales**		(40,840)
Gross profit		34,222
Less expenses		
Administration expenses Wages and salaries; advertising and marketing; rent; utilities; finance costs	8,288	
Distribution costs Motor expenses; warehousing; wages and salaries; depreciation	1,760	10,048
Net profit/(loss)		24,174

Public limited companies

Limited companies are required by law to publish accounts. These accounts can be analysed by directors, shareholders and potential investors (banks, building societies, anyone considering buying shares) but they can also be seen by competitors.

A profit and loss account drawn up for internal company use – for directors and management – will look very similar that in Figure 2.3. However, published accounts are likely to contain less information. The Companies Act 1985 sets out the minimum information that must be included in a published profit and loss account and the layout in which it should be shown.

Figure 2.4 shows an extract taken from mmO$_2$ plc's published accounts. You can see that this external account provides much less information than the internal one. Companies can choose to include more information in their published accounts than the minimum standard, but not less.

Figure 2.4: Profit and loss account for mmO$_2$

mmO$_2$ plc	2004 £m
Group turnover	5,694
Net operating expenses	(5,536)
Group operating profit	158

Source: www.mmo2.com/

Many companies do not include more information in their published accounts than that required by law so that they do not give potentially useful or sensitive financial information to their competitors. Imagine, for example, that you are in business and you could tell from one of your competitor's financial accounts that it was struggling badly: what might you do? What actions would you advise your company to take that might allow it to capitalise on this situation?

Knowledge summary

■ **The function of accounting is to provide information to business owners, managers, potential and actual investors and others on how a business has performed over a given period.**

■ **The profit and loss account is a formal statement that shows a firm's sales revenue and all the relevant costs incurred in generating that revenue over a trading period.**

■ **Gross profit is the excess of turnover over the cost of the goods sold in the period. Net profit is what is left of gross profit after all other expenses have been deducted.**

■ **Profit and loss accounts can be very detailed and provide important information for directors and managers to make decisions. However, published accounts are often summaries that conform to the minimum legal requirements.**

quick questions

1 What are the implications for a business if it calculates profits incorrectly? Consider this question from two aspects: first, what if profits are calculated as being higher than they actually are; second, what if they had been reported lower.

2 Use this information on Marler's Ltd's costs and revenues in the year to 31 December 2004 to construct a formal profit and loss account in as much detail as possible.

Item	£
Advertising	2,500
Turnover	480,000
Rent	6,000
Administration salaries	71,000
Utilities	2,000
Cost of sales	300,240
Depreciation	8,400
Distribution wages	40,000
Warehouse expenses	8,500
Finance costs	4,000
Motor expenses	7,500

3 Make an assessment of Marler's Ltd for a client who is thinking of investing some money in the company. What else would you want to know about Marler's, other than how much profit it is making?

Sunny Departures plc is a successful travel company. It operates as an intermediary for UK and overseas tour operators. Its main area of operations is to source quality hotels in the Far East and Asia and block book rooms (at a substantial discount) for the main UK holiday periods and then resell the bookings in smaller units to independent travel agents in the UK.

Due to recent falling profits, Sunny Departures is contemplating setting up operations as a high street travel agent in its own right. However, recent surveys report a decline in high street bookings and a trend toward consumers booking more holidays and flights individually through online travel companies. This has given the directors some concerns about whether this is the right way for their company to proceed.

Figure 2.5 presents information on Sunny Departures' recent profitability as well as summary profit and loss accounts for two rivals: Skyways Travel Ltd, a competitor based in the same market as Sunny Departures, and Takemeaway.co.uk, a company that allows individuals to book overseas rooms direct online.

Figure 2.5: Summary profit and loss accounts for three travel businesses

	Sunny Departures		Skyways Travel Ltd		Takemeaway.co.uk	
	2005 £m	2004 £m	2005 £m	2004 £m	2005 £m	2004 £m
Turnover	189	240	154	165	47	23
Cost of sales	(113)	(144)	(80)	(99)	(19)	(10)
Gross profit	76	96	74	66	28	13
Total expenses	(33)	(32)	(29)	(27)	(21)	(17)
Net profit/(loss)	43	64	45	39	6	(4)

A Analyse the profit and loss accounts of Sunny Departures and Skyways Travel Ltd. What information can you gain from these profit and loss accounts that you can use to advise the directors of Sunny Departures about what they should do?

B Now look at the profit and loss account information for Takemeaway.co.uk. Does this information, taken together with your findings for task A, support Sunny Departures' intended project or not?

C Prepare either a five-minute presentation or a short report advising the directors of Sunny Departures plc of your findings. Include any relevant data, facts and figures you have drawn from the profit and loss accounts.

The balance sheet shows what the business has achieved during its entire existence. It values all the assets that have been built up over time – that is, it accounts for what the company actually owns – and set out where the money came from to purchase these assets.

A balance sheet helps you assess the strength of a business. By studying how much a company owns and comparing it with how much it owes, you can establish an idea of what that business is worth. It's like looking at the squad of players for a football club: you can see what players they have, how good they are and which ones are own by the club and which are on loan from other clubs.

Many stakeholders use the information contained on balance sheets to make important decisions. For example, a supplier might look at the balance sheet before deciding whether to supply goods on credit. Suppliers want reassuring that a business is financially sound and that they will get paid; and a bank will certainly assess the balance sheet before deciding whether to lend money to a business.

Balance sheets

A balance sheet is a formal document that states in detail the asset, liability and capital structure of a business. Figure 2.6 shows a typical balance sheet. There are six main parts to a balance sheet and we shall now consider the elements that make up each part of the balance sheet in turn.

1 Fixed assets

This is a list showing the value of items owned by the business that have a long-term use such as vehicles or machinery. These are assets the business plans to keep and use. It shows anybody looking at the accounts what the business actually possesses.

Though all the fixed assets in our example are tangible assets, a business may have intangible assets. These items also have a value, but not a physical presence. A good example of an intangible fixed would be a brand name.

stop and think

The Virgin group of companies operates in many different sectors. List all the different Virgin products that come to mind. How does a brand name like Virgin add value to a product and to the Virgin group as a whole?

2 Current assets

This section tells us how much money the business currently has got or will be able to access soon. These current assets are available to the business to fund its everyday operations, for example by providing the cash to pay staff wages and suppliers.

KEY TERMS

Liquidity is an assessment of a business's ability to meet its short-term debts. It is a measure of whether the business has enough cash available to pay bills and invoices as they come due for payment.

A **balance sheet** is a statement that sets out an organisation's assets and liabilities. It is a statement of the business's position on a stated day, that in effect states what the business owns and how it finances its activities.

Assets are resources owned by an organisation that have a monetary value.

Liabilities are debts owed to other parties. Liabilities are sources of finance and provide the means for an organisation to acquire some of its assets.

Share capital is the money that has been invested by the owners into the business. This is used by the business to purchase assets and help finance operations. It is called share capital as owners invest money by buying shares.

Shareholders' funds are made up of reserves that have been accumulated by the business over the years it has been operating. This retained profit actually belongs to the shareholders but is reinvested to help the business grow and become stronger.

Figure **2.6**: Example of a balance sheet

Johnston Ltd Balance sheet, 31 December 2004			
	£	£	£
Fixed assets: tangible			
Land and buildings	600,000		
Machinery and equipment	245,000		
Fixtures, fittings and furniture	47,000		
Vehicles	98,000		= 990,000
Current assets			
Stock	84,000		
Debtors	40,700		
Bank	24,320		
Cash in hand	3,340	= 152,360	
Current liabilities: debts due within one year			
Creditors	64,300		
Short-term loans or overdrafts	9,000	= 63,300	
Net current assets			89,060
Net assets employed			1,079,060
Long-term liabilities: debts due after one year			
Loans	50,000		
Debentures	98,000		
Mortgages	310,000		= 458,000
Capital and reserves			
Share capital	500,000		
Reserves	90,000		
Retained profit	31,060		= 621,060
			1,079,060

Current assets are listed by convention in ascending order of liquidity. Liquidity is a measure of how easy it is to turn assets into cash, and the balance sheet lists the most illiquid current assets first. For example, stock can only be turned into cash once it has been sold and the sales income recouped from customers. Debtors refers to customers who owe money to the business but perhaps are given 30 days or so to settle their bills.

3 Current liabilities

In this section, the balance sheet totals the debts, bills and invoices the company has to pay within the next 12 months. These are the liabilities that a business will have to pay with its current assets. Note that creditors are the business's suppliers, such as companies that raw materials or components to the business. Many

suppliers will offer credit terms to their business customers, giving them, say, 30 days or so to pay their bills.

4 Net current assets

This is the first measure of the financial strength of a company. Here, you can determine the liquidity of the business – that is, its ability to pay its short-term debts. Net current assets are calculated by simply subtracting the business's total current liabilities from its current assets.

This resulting figure is often called working capital as it shows the finance available for day-to-day operations after all short-term debts have been met. In other words, it shows how much finance a company has available to work with.

5 Long-term liabilities

The next section provides information regarding the company's long-term debts, loans or mortgages. Again, we can make an assessment of the company's financial strength by comparing the value of the assets owned to the amount borrowed. Obviously, a company that has not borrowed too much money but has significant assets is in a position of substantial financial strength.

The long-term liabilities section of the balance sheet allows you to see how much money the company actually owes to other parties. By comparing a business's long-term liabilities with its total fixed assets, you can determine how much of the fixed assets actually belong to the business.

6 Capital and reserves

The final section shows the share capital invested and the shareholders' funds. This part of the balance sheet shows how much of a company's resources or asset strength has actually been financed by investment rather than borrowing. This is the difference between share and loan capital, as loan capital (long-term liabilities) has to be paid back (usually with interest as well) and share capital and shareholder funds do not.

Note, finally, that the balance sheet actually balances. It shows how the company's total assets (the sum of its fixed assets and net current assets) have been financed (the sum of its long-term liabilities plus capital and reserves).

Public limited companies

All public limited companies are required by law to publish their balance sheets. Examples of published balance sheets can be found on the websites of most public limited companies.

As with the profit and loss accounts (see Topic 4), the published version usually does not provide as much information as the balance sheet constructed for internal use. Published balance sheets generally only show the total figures for each section rather than give a breakdown by the various individual categories. This minimises the amount of potentially sensitive information that competitors might be able to obtain from their rivals' accounts.

Knowledge summary

- The balance sheet is a formal statement that shows the total value of assets owned by a company, together with detail of where and how the company raised the finance to obtain those assets.

- Net current assets is an assessment of a company's liquidity position and its ability to pay its short-term debts. It is a measure of financial stability.

- A company's long-term prospects can be assessed by examining how it financed its asset base. Does it actually own the majority of its assets?

quick questions

1 Describe two external users of financial information and give reasons why they might analyse a balance sheet.

2 Why is liquidity an important measure of a company's financial strength?

3 What is the main advantage to a company from raising finance from its shareholders?

data interpretation

Jacksons seeks new suppliers

Jacksons is a small limited company that manufactures professional sports equipment. It is well-known, with a reputation for expensive but high-quality goods. The business has been in operation for over 40 years and the company is regarded as being one of the leading manufacturers of high performance rackets for sports such as squash, badminton and tennis.

Recently Jacksons has been experiencing problems with one of its suppliers. Jacksons wants to upgrade its own processes and its current supplier is unwilling or unable to meet its new production requirements.

Jacksons has therefore looked for alternative suppliers. It has approached Micromesh plc, a company that produces high-quality plastic mesh which is suitable for use squash and badminton rackets. Jacksons wishes to place a £35,700 order with Micromesh plc, but it wants two months credit before paying for the goods.

These are some of the financial figures from Jacksons' latest balance sheet:

Cash	£7,000
Bank overdraft	£13,000
Creditors	£44,000
Debtors	£26,000
Loan (1 years)	£200,000
Stock	£43,000

A Calculate Jacksons' current working capital.

B What stakeholder groups would be interested in the company's working capital position? Choose three stakeholders and explain what they might be looking for.

C From the perspective of Micromesh's financial adviser, write a memo to the managing director of Micromesh advising whether to accept the order.

Budgeting and variance analysis

Setting the scene: the purpose of budgets and forecasts

Most businesses have an aim or mission statement. The mission statement can be used to underpin a business's goals, objectives and targets.

A good example of a mission statement is Coca-Cola's aim to "get people to drink more Coca-Cola than water". Coca-Cola's objectives and targets must be co-ordinated so that the whole company is working in the same direction at the same time to achieve this mission.

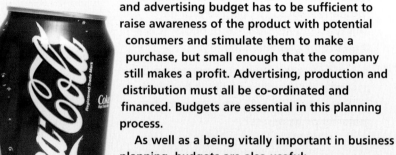

A business as large as Coca-Cola needs to ensure that it has the available resources and finances needed to achieve its planned objectives. This is where businesses use budgets: they provide a plan of future activity, the finances available to fund that activity and set targets to be achieved – in short, they help employees stay focused on achieving the company's objectives.

The financial proposals and targets contained within budgets are often challenging. Given unlimited funds, most people could organise a successful marketing campaign to raise sales and therefore achieved their target. However, can they do the same within a specified budget and time period?

Think of the launch of a new games console like the PlayStation 2: the marketing

and advertising budget has to be sufficient to raise awareness of the product with potential consumers and stimulate them to make a purchase, but small enough that the company still makes a profit. Advertising, production and distribution must all be co-ordinated and financed. Budgets are essential in this planning process.

As well as a being vitally important in business planning, budgets are also useful:

■ to aid communication throughout a business

■ to motivate staff

■ to help persuade potential lenders to invest money.

All businesses can benefit from budgets. But, do you think it is as important for a small local business like a newsagent to budget as it is for a multinational public limited company like Cadbury Schweppes? Would each type of business receive the same level of benefit from budgetary activities?

Unit 2 Investigating business

KEY TERMS

A **budget** is a financial plan for the future operations of the business. Budgets are used to set targets to monitor performance and control operations.

Variance analysis is one of the methods used to monitor company performance. It is the comparison of what actually happened with what the business budgeted (planned to happen).

An **adverse variance** occurs when the business's actual results are worse than those anticipated and planned for in the budget.

A **favourable variance** occurs when the actual results are better than those anticipated and planned for in the budget.

The main types of budget

As budgets are so valuable, they can actually be drawn up for any individual person, project or department. However, the main budgets and forecasts focus on key areas of business activity.

1 Sales budgets

This is the key budget, as the amount a business sells determines the amount it needs to produce, which in turn has implications for the number and type of staff that are employed. Sales are also the main area of generating cash inflows, so it is also a key indicator of how much money a business expects to receive.

Sales budgets are difficult to forecast as the amount a company will sell in future is affected by consumer tastes and fashions as well by the actions of competitors. Companies therefore use combinations of historical data, trend analysis and market research to try and forecast sales. One problem for multi-product companies is the forecast sales may be different for each product, so they may draw up a separate forecast and budget for each product they sell.

Notice that the example sales budget in Figure 2.7 shows forecasted sales value and units; this is so there is an estimate both of how much income will be received from sales and how many units the company needs to satisfy demand.

2 Production budgets

A production budget sets out how many units need to be made. This is important because if too few goods are produced, a company could lose customers, sales and profits. If it makes too many goods, then it risks either making goods which cannot be sold – this is especially the case for perishable items like food products – or incurs potentially high storage costs; storing products costs money in terms of space, wages and insurance, incurring costs which reduce a company's profitability. The production budget needs to take into account that there may be seasonal fluctuations in the availability of raw materials.

> ### stop and think
>
> Many companies carry buffer stocks. Why do they do this? Think of three reasons why the actual production of a breakfast cereal manufacturer may differ from the forecast production budget.

> ### stop and think
>
> If a business overestimates its future sales, this would impact on other areas of activity. How would a firework manufacturer's profits be affected if it overestimated its future sales? Similarly, what problems might occur if it underestimated its future sales?

Figure 2.7: An example of a sales budget

	Actual sales			Forecast sales			
	Jan	Feb	Mar	Apr	May	June	July
Sales value (£)	125,000	125,400	126,000	126,300	126,700	127,300	127,200
Sales (units)	5,000	5,080	5,200	5,260	5,340	5,460	5,440

3 Purchases and labour budgets

Once it has decided how much it needs to produce, a company needs to ensure that it has enough raw materials, components and employees to be able to deliver that level of production. Figure 2.8 gives an example of a purchases and labour budget.

The purchase budget sets out the material requirements that will be needed to produce the budgeted amount of finished products. Often, the purchase of materials must take place before employees need them to allow time for delivery. This budget should ensure that resources are bought and ready at the right place and time.

Each product may have its own raw materials and component requirements, so budgets for each individual product might be produced. A budget could be drawn for any department, project or individual product. It is possible a purchases or expenditure budget could be constructed, which forecasts each area of expenditure separately and in detail.

The labour budget allows managers to plan how many, and what type of, employees they need. Managers need to know if they currently have too many employees or, more importantly, too few. The aspect of planning is crucial so that a business can make sure it has sufficient employees to produce its budgeted level of output, but not so many that some stand around idle. If a company gets this aspect of budgeting right, it will be optimising potential profits by not losing sales (by not making enough products) or wasting money on unproductive staff.

4 Capital expenditure budgets

Businesses must also make sure that they have enough capital for their employees to use. By capital, we mean plant, equipment, machinery, vehicles and premises. If a business is planning increases in sales and production, it may need more machinery to increase productive capacity or it may need additional delivery vehicles to service its planned greater customer base. Figure 2.9 shows an example of a

Figure 2.8: An example of a purchases and labour budget

	March	Apr	May	June	July
Forecast production		5,260	5,340	5,460	5,440
Forecast materials needed:					
Raw materials 2 kg per unit at 20p per kg		10,520kg	10,680kg	10,720kg	10,880kg
Raw material cost purchased one month in advance (£)	2,104	2,136	2,144	2,176	
Components 5 per unit at 10p each		26,300	26,700	27,300	27,200
Raw material cost purchased one month in advance (£)	2,630	2,670	2,730	2,720	
Forecast labour needed:					
Skilled labour costs costed @ £8 per unit		42,080	42,720	43,680	43,520
Semi-skilled costs costed @ £5 per unit		26,300	26,700	27,300	27,200

Figure 2.9: An example of a capital expenditure budget for the next financial quarter

Capital item	Existing availability	Forecast requirement	Cost of existing capacity (£)	Additional capital needed (£)
Premises	60,000 sq m	54,000 sq m	40,000	none
Machinery	12,000 hours	12,300 hours	32,000	11,600
Production equipment	20,000 hours	17,200 hours	8,700	none
Vehicles	6 cars	6 cars	13,500	none
			Total cost	£105,800

capital expenditure budget. The budget shows the cost of capital for the budget period: it includes cost of using the existing plant and equipment plus the cost of any purchase of new equipment.

The capital expenditure budget is vital to the smooth running of the company. The business must plan when to purchase new assets if it faces a shortfall in capacity, as without them the workforce would not be able to produce the required goods. However, buying new assets is often expensive and the business needs to plan for large capital outflows so it doesn't dangerously drain its financial resources.

5 Master budgets

Businesses often create a master budget (a forecasted profit and loss account) compiled from the individual budgets. This allows owners and managers to get an idea of how the cumulative affect of the budget decisions is likely to impact on profitability.

stopandthink

It is likely that at some point that a company's employees will want a pay rise. How will the calculation and drawing up of budgets help managers make decisions on pay?

In particular, how would the compilation of a master budget help to inform the level of any pay rise offered?

Variance analysis

Variance analysis compares actual performance with forecast performance. The purpose of this exercise is to pinpoint and highlight areas of good and poor performance. This allows managers to build on areas of strength and remedy or remove areas of weakness.

A favourable variance occurs when results are better than expected, and an adverse variance occurs when results are worse than budget. Figure 2.10 (on page 86) shows an example of variance analysis.

Managers use variance analysis to ask why differences between actual performance and forecast budget occurred. Don't assume an adverse variance is necessarily bad, or a favourable variance is necessarily good. In the example in Figure 2.10, wages are lower than expected mainly because employees have not produced as much output as forecasted. Here, the company may have spent less of labour costs, but at the cost of failing to meet production targets,

Even an adverse variance doesn't mean things have gone wrong; a business may get an adverse variance for the cost of labour, but this may mean it hired more skilled employees who did a better quality job.

stopandthink

Using Figure 2.10 try to give one reason why the company appears to have made less units than expected, used less labour than expected, but at the same time used more materials?

Figure 2.10: An example of variance analysis

	Budgeted amount	Actual amount	Variance
Wages	£42,000	£37,200	£4,800 favourable
Materials	£27,000	£29,400	£2,400 adverse
Output	14,000 units	12,900 units	1,100 units adverse

Knowledge summary

- Budget forecasts provide a method by which managers can plan and co-ordinate business activities. They make managers think about how to achieve goals.

- Budget forecasts provide managers and employees with targets. They allow managers to monitor the performance of the business against the plan, and thereby identify possible areas of strength and weakness.

- Through planning, a business can ensure it has the right resources in place at the right time. The aim is to prevent the waste of resources without missing out on potential sales.

- Variance analysis allows an assessment of budget accuracy and identification of problem areas. It enables informed decisions to be taken to improve business performance.

quick**questions**

1 Why is it so important for businesses to accurately predict future sales levels?

2 Forecasts and budgets are an important method of financial planning. How might the drawing up of budgets also act as a motivational tool?

3 Basenthwaites makes traditional hardwood kitchen units. The production manager has identified an adverse variance for the amount time it took his workforce to produce a set of custom-built units. Explain to the production manager why this adverse variance may not necessarily be a bad result.

Muncaster Conservatories produces a range of UPVC conservatories for retail through large DIY superstores. The company prides itself on having a highly skilled workforce that produces conservatories of an exemplary standard.

Although Muncaster's approach is a more expensive than other forms of production, the company believes that customers will pay extra for the guarantee that they are getting a high-quality conservatory. Customers can then choose either to erect the conservatory themselves, to contact Muncaster and hire its team of skilled specialised fitters, or to hire a local firm of builders to fit it for them.

Recently Muncaster's sales have been falling and it appears that the company faces rising costs to produce each conservatory: profits are starting to decline. Muncaster uses a series of budgets to determine how much it should cost to produce each of its standard conservatory models. Managers have conducted a variance analysis exercise for the Edwardian model. The findings are given in Figure 2.11. During the exercise, there have been no changes in wage rates paid to employees nor have there been any price rises for supplies of raw materials.

Figure 2.11: Labour and purchases budget for Edwardian conservatories

	Budget (£)	Actual (£)	Variance
Labour			
Skilled	700	610	
Semi-skilled	420	530	
Manual	200	270	
Materials			
UPVC	2,300	2,475	
Glass	1,300	1,420	
Fittings	120	124	
Total			

A Complete Figure 2.11 by calculating the variances for each item and calculate the total variance for the whole job.

B Using your findings, draft a short report for the management of Muncaster Conservatories suggesting where you believe the major problems have occurred.

C Include, as a final section in your report, some recommendations explaining how Muncaster could solve its problems. Describe the impact your recommendations may hopefully have on the company's falling sales and why.

Cash flow forecasting

Setting the scene: the purpose of cash flow forecasts

Pro Game Retail was set up in 2002 by a group of business graduates to sell games consoles, games and peripherals. The company was successful and profitable, but in late 2004 it began to run out of cash and was in danger of danger of closure.

Cash flow problems arise because in the usual course of business activity companies have to spend money on buying stock and machinery and paying employees before they are in a position to sell products to customers. In other words, companies must meet the costs of bringing products to the market before they can receive income through sales.

Pro Game's problems happened for exactly this reason. As the company expanded by opening more stores, it had to order more stock, buy fixtures and employ extra staff. Each new shop incurs costs but it takes time for customers to become aware of the new outlet and start using it, especially in such a competitive marketplace.

Cash flow is not just a problem for small businesses. Companies like Vodafone, Orange and mm0$_2$ have had to spend large sums to set up their mobile networks and secure licences for the right to operate 3G services. They had to meet these upfront costs before customers were able to use any of their services.

A major benefit of cash flow forecasting is that it enables managers to anticipate periods when cash flows may be high or low, thereby indicating periods when cash might be available for spending and investment or, more importantly, periods when cash is likely to be tight.

Consider why is it important that managers can identify periods of poor cash flow. For example, what might be the consequences for a business like Pro Game Retail that has insufficient cash to pay its employees wages or utility bills? If a business had forecast this cash flow difficulty in advance, what help could it have arranged with the bank to prevent problems occurring?

KEY TERMS

Cash flow is the money that enters and leaves a business as it makes and receives payments.

Cash flow forecasts are detailed estimates of when and how cash is expected to flow into and out of a business.

Cash inflows are money received by a business from sales, investments or loans.

Cash outflows are money that leaves a business through paying for wages, materials, marketing, fixed assets, etc.

Trade credit is an arrangement in which suppliers allow customers a period of time (usually one or two months) to pay their bills. The offering of goods for sale and purchase on payment terms.

Working capital is the excess of current assets over current liabilities.

In Topic 6, you saw how businesses use budgets to plan their future operations. Once a budget has been determined and agreed, a business needs to ensure that it actually has the finances in place to execute its plans. A cash flow forecast is a detailed examination of a company's expected future cash inflows and outflows over a future period (such as one year ahead). They are usually calculated on a monthly basis and, by keep a running total of the business's anticipated bank balance, managers can highlight times when cash difficulties may arise.

Even if a business does not draw up a formal budget – many small businesses don't have the expertise or time to prepare budgets – a business is still likely to prepare a cash flow forecast. All businesses are aware that the delay between the outlay on materials, stock and wages and the receipt of sales income that can cause difficulties. In fact, many businesses to fail because they run out of cash rather than because they are inherently unprofitable. Monitoring cash flows helps a business maintain its working capital so that sufficient funds are available to finance its day-to-day operations.

Benefits of cash flow forecasts

Cash flow forecasting is not just a defensive activity. It brings a number of positive benefits for a business:

- ensuring liquid assets are available to meet payments and maintain working capital

- identifying periods of cash shortfall so remedial action like overdrafts can be arranged

- identifying periods of cash surplus so high-cost items can be purchased at little risk

- highlighting periods when large expenditure is not possible, so businesses may have to spread payments for fixed assets over monthly instalments

- limiting borrowing and minimising interest payments, as a cash flow forecast should enable a business to only borrow the sum that it needs

- highlighting cash surpluses that can be more profitably invested elsewhere

- supporting applications to lenders by demonstrating that funds would be available to meet interest and capital repayments on loans.

Constructing forecasts

Cash flow forecasts are constructed using historical information (past company data) and the forecasts contained in the budgets. They have three sections:

- **cash inflows** – money received by the business from sales and other sources

- **cash outflows** – money paid out by the business on wages, materials and other expenditures

- **the running balance** – a calculation of the net effect of the cash inflows and outflows on the business's bank balance on a monthly basis.

Figure 2.12: An example cash flow forecast

	April	May	June	July
Cash inflows				
Sales	126,300	126,700	127,300	127,200
Loans	30,000	nil	nil	nil
Capital introduced	nil	10,000	nil	nil
(1) Total cash inflow	156,300	136,700	117,300	117,200
Cash outflows				
Purchases	20,136	20,144	20,176	20,700
Wages and salaries	42,080	42.720	43,680	43,520
Heat and light	800	800	800	800
Water	500	500	500	500
Telephone	1,120	1,120	1,120	1,120
Advertising	28,700	5,000	3,000	3,000
Administration expenses	19,240	19,870	20,100	20,000
Distribution expenses	6,400	6,550	6,720	6,680
Capital expenditure	nil	60,000	nil	16,200
(2) Total cash outflow	118,976	155,606	94,998	112,520
(3) Opening bank balance	(14,300)	23,024	4,118	26,420
(4) Net cash flow (1 – 2)	37,234	(18,906)	22,302	4,680
(5) Closing bank balance (3 + 4)	23,024	4,118	26,420	31,100

In appearance, cash flow forecasts are similar to the other budgets. Figure 2.12 shows a simple cash flow forecast. However, many will contain more detail – with more categories of expenditure, for example – due to the key importance of the forecast to the business's financial health.

A cash flow forecast like Figure 2.12 would be compiled by taking information and forecasts from the budgets and by using historical data. The calculations are made in the lines numbered 1–5. Lines 1 and 2 are simply the respective totals of the cash inflows and outflows. Lines 3–5 are the calculation of the running balance: the business's closing bank balance at the end of each month is forecast by adding the net cash flow (which might be a negative number of course) to its starting bank balance.

Banks encourage their business account holders to draw up cash flow forecasts. Banks produce a range of information and material to help their customers with forecasting; some, for example, provide templates that allow firms to compile cash flow forecasts online.

Improving cash flow

The key reason for drawing up a cash flow forecast is to prevent a business from running out of cash and not being able to meet its day-to-day running costs. This raises the obvious question of how can businesses improve their situation when in difficulties.

One solution is to arrange an overdraft in advance as soon as difficulties are anticipated, although this may not address the underlying reasons for the situation. However, an overdraft as with other loan deals may improve the short-term cash position, it will require making regular interest payments so it does have implications for cash outflows.

There are other solutions to improve a firm's cash position which do not necessarily add to cash outflows (in the short or long term). These include:

- buying and holding fewer stocks, perhaps adopting a just-in-time approach

- improving credit control, by allowing less time for customers to settle their bills

- improving inflows by stimulating sales

- selling fixed assets, such as machinery and vehicles, to gain a cash injection.

Knowledge summary

- **Forecasts provide a method by which businesses can plan and co-ordinate activities. Budgets and forecasts set targets for managers and employees.**

- **By budgeting, a business aims to have the right level of resources in place at the right time, so preventing waste and not missing out on potential sales.**

- **It is vital that businesses plan cash inflows and outflows to ensure that they have enough working capital to meet their day-to-day running costs and maintain financial stability.**

quick questions

1 Why do banks encourage businesses to use cash flow forecasts?

2 Name three actions a business could take to tackle short-term cash flow problems.

3 Why might a small business not compile a full set of budgets but still draw up a cash flow forecast?

Willcox Web Designs

Robbie Willcox runs a website design company. Until recently he has had a team of designers working for him, but now he is left with only one modern apprenticeship trainee. The problem seems to be that although Robbie's company is receiving more and more orders, he doesn't seem to have the resources to be able to pay his workforce on time, despite taking out a loan in May to help him meet his commitments and buy new equipment and software applications. Figure 2.13 shows data from Robbie's actual cash flow for the last four months.

Figure 2.13: Willcox Web Design cash flow

	April	May	June	July
Cash inflows				
Sales	21,300	11,700	7,300	7,200
Loans received		10,000		
(1) Total cash inflow				
Cash outflows				
Wages and salaries	11,000	6,140	4,700	3,890
Purchases	5,200	4,200	2,400	2,400
Heat and light	90	90	90	90
Water	110	110	110	110
Office rent	3,000	nil	nil	3,000
Rates (for the year)	1,200	n/a	n/a	n/a
Telephone	200	230	190	185
Advertising	150	150	150	150
Loan payments	nil	nil	345	345
Insurance	300	300	300	300
Motor expenses	570	480	390	410
Capital expenditure (new equipment)		8,000		
(2) Total cash outflow				
(3) Opening bank balance	1,427			
(4) Net cash flow (1 – 2)				
(5) Closing bank balance **(3 + 4)**				

A Compile the finished cash flow from the information given.

B What difficulties has Robbie encountered over the last few months.

C Using the information given, and any ideas of your own, draft a letter to Robbie advising him of what steps you would recommend he take to try and improve his situation.

Imagine you are setting up a business or launching a product. It is important you know how much your product costs. This information will help you decide:

- how much to charge

- how many you need to sell to make an acceptable profit

- how much you can afford to drop prices, or let costs to rise, before you start losing money

- how many products you have to sell to cover costs and avoid making a loss.

Breakeven analysis is a simple and valuable forecasting technique. Businesses can use breakeven analysis to:

- estimate the output they need to produce and sell

- assess the impact of price changes on profit and the output needed to break even

- assess how changes in costs impact on profits and breakeven output

- determine their margin of safety and what changes in levels of demand they can survive.

Costs and revenue

All businesses need to manage their costs, and it is important to understand the difference between fixed costs and variable costs.

Fixed costs are costs that do not vary with the level of output. They are linked to a time base rather than level of activity. Fixed costs exist even if a business is not producing any goods or services. Businesses have to pay rent on premises they hire irrespective of their actual activity. The rent does not vary according to how much an office or factory is used; if, for example, a manufacturer doubles output by using the factory space more intensively, the rent does not alter. Other examples of fixed costs include rates, management salaries, interest charges and depreciation.

In working through this topic, we are going to consider breakeven in relation to a manufacturer of trainers. Lets suppose the fixed costs of the factory that manufactures trainers is, say, £20,000 a month – this cost has to be paid regardless of the level of production or sales.

stop and think

Suppose you are about to open a nightclub and are currently looking for suitable premises; you have written a business plan and conducted market research. By using breakeven analysis, you can model how many customers paying on the door and drink sales you need each night before you make any profit. Why might it be valuable to know this information before setting up the business?

KEY TERMS

Breakeven is the point at which a business sells exactly the right number of products so that its sales revenue equals its costs. In other words, at breakeven the business makes no profit but also incurs no loss.

Fixed costs are costs that do not vary with the level of output. Fixed costs exist even if a business is not producing any goods or services.

Variable costs vary directly with output. They include labour, fuel and raw materials. If a manufacturer increases output, then these costs rise in proportion.

Total cost is the sum of the fixed and variable costs.

Margin of safety is the amount current output exceeds the amount necessary to break even.

Variable costs are costs that are dependant on the production level. If production increases, then costs like wages and raw materials also increase. The variable cost per unit is the cost of producing one unit of a good or service. So, if the cost of producing 1000 pairs of trainers is £7,500, the variable cost is £7.50 per pair.

Total costs are the sum of the fixed and variable costs. So, in the case of our example of the trainer manufacturer, if the factory produces 1000 pairs of trainers a month, its total monthly cost is £27,500 (that is, £7,500 + £20,000). The total cost of producing each pair is £27,500/1000; that is, each costs £27.50 to produce.

Revenue is the income that a business receives from selling goods or services. If each pair of trainers sells at £32.50, the total revenue received each month by the manufacturer is £32,500 (assuming all 1000 pairs of the monthly output are sold).

stop and think

Suppose the trainer manufacturer manages to double output while holding its fixed costs constant. What happens to the total cost of each unit?

Calculating breakeven

Breakeven is calculated by using the formula:

$$\text{breakeven point} = \frac{\text{total fixed costs}}{\text{selling price} - \text{variable cost per unit}}$$

Applying the formula to our trainer manufacturer example:

$$\text{breakeven point} = \frac{20,000}{(32.50 - 7.50)} = 800 \text{ units}$$

So, in order to break even, the factory must make and sell 800 pairs of trainers each month. Obviously by making 1000 pairs a month, factory output is currently above the breakeven point. There is a simple relationship between breakeven and profit:

- if total output and sales are greater than breakeven, then revenue is greater than cost: the business makes a profit

- if total output and sales are equal to breakeven, then revenue equals total costs: the business breaks even

- if total output and sales are less than breakeven, then revenue is less than total cost: the business makes a loss.

The breakeven point can also be represented by a chart. This is useful as diagrammatic representation makes it easier for non-mathematical people to understand. A breakeven chart is compiled from plotting costs and revenue information on a graph.

Step 1: fixed costs

These remain the same no matter how much output is produced; so fixed constants are represented by a horizontal line.

Step 2: variable costs

These rise in direct relationship to production. If there is no output, variable costs equal zero, but variable costs increase in direct proportion to output. So the variable cost line is shown sloping upwards from left to right, with the slope of the graph representing the corresponding rise in cost as output rises.

Step 3: total costs

This is plotted by adding the fixed cost and variable cost lines together. At zero output there are no variable costs, but still fixed costs. So the total costs line starts at the fixed cost level and rises, with output, in the same relationship as variable costs.

Step 4: revenue

Revenue is the income from sales. If there are no sales, revenue is also nil. But as sales rise so does revenue. So the revenue line slopes upwards from left to right, with the slope of the graph representing the corresponding rise in revenue as sales increase.

Figure 2.14 shows the breakeven chart for our trainer manufacturer. It shows the profit (or loss) made at each level of production. The amount of profit or loss at any level of production is shown by the vertical distance between the total cost and revenue lines.

If actual production and sales levels are below breakeven output, the business will be making a loss; if production and sales levels are above breakeven, the business will be in profit. The margin of safety is the difference between breakeven output and the current level of output. It represents the number of units by which production and sales can fall before the business starts to make a loss.

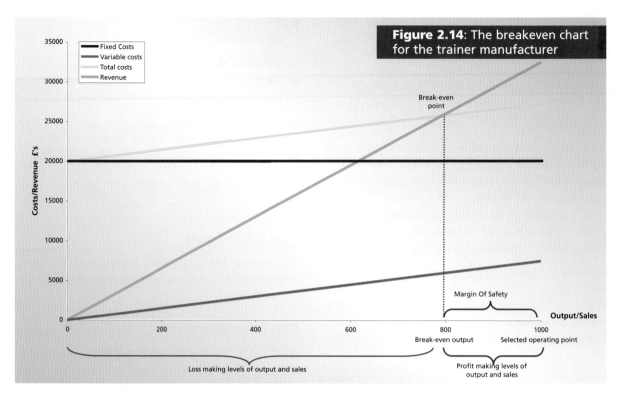

Figure 2.14: The breakeven chart for the trainer manufacturer

(Legend) Fixed Costs / Variable costs / Total costs / Revenue

Break-even point

Margin Of Safety

Output/Sales

Break-even output — Selected operating point

Loss making levels of output and sales

Profit making levels of output and sales

stop and think

What would be the profit (or loss) if the manufacturer produced and sold 950 pairs of trainers each month. Try finding the answer by using the chart in Figure 2.14

Uses and limitations

Few business situations remain constant. Changes in the economy, markets, tastes and fashions affect costs and revenues. The breakeven point will change if a business's costs or prices change. Figure 2.15 summarises the effect that some price and cost changes will have on a company's breakeven position.

By using breakeven analysis, businesses can model what the impact of changes in their cost or price structure. For example, a business could examine whether to invest in new machinery; this may help it reduce variable costs – the machine might be more efficient or need less labour to operate – but would also raise fixed costs. Redrawing the breakeven chart to reflect these proposed changes in cost could help the business reach an informed decision.

Although a simple and easy tool, breakeven analysis has drawbacks:

- fixed costs are unlikely to stay constant in the long run, and are likely to change as productive capacity changes

- variable costs and sales revenue are also unlikely to be straight lines – factors like discounts, bulk buying and overtime cause constant fluctuations

- breakeven analysis makes the assumption that the business sells its entire output – in reality, a business is rarely able to sell all it produces.

Finally, it is worth noting that any information gained from breakeven charts or calculations is only as accurate as the information it was based upon. Collecting accurate information is expensive and time consuming, and while breakeven analysis is useful, any time a single price or cost factor changes, breakeven has to be redrawn or calculated.

Figure 2.15: Factors affecting breakeven

Change	Impact on breakeven
Fixed or variable costs rise	Total costs rise, so more units have to be sold to cover costs. The number of units needed to break even increases.
Fixed or variable costs fall	Total costs also fall, so less units have to be sold to cover costs. The number of units needed to break even falls.
Sales price rises	Each unit produces more revenue, so costs are covered more quickly. The breakeven number of units decreases.
Sales price falls	Each unit sold earns less revenue, so it takes more units to cover costs. The breakeven point increases.

Knowledge summary

■ Breakeven is an easy way to measure the impact on profits (or losses) as levels of business activity change.

■ Breakeven can be used to examine "what if" situations – it allows a business to analyse the effect if certain situations occur.

■ Increases in costs make it more difficult to break even; falling costs mean less sales are needed to break even.

quickquestions

1 Explain the term breakeven. Why is the determination of the breakeven point important?

2 Explain two ways in which breakeven charts can help managers make decisions.

3 Why might calculating breakeven be more useful than drawing breakeven charts? Conversely, when might drawing a chart prove helpful?

datainterpretation
Beasty Burgers

Beasty Burgers was set up by John and Nick Amis following a trip to the United States. They decided that the burgers in the UK were poor in comparison to US versions. Although slightly more expensive than many competitors, Beasty Burgers' reputation for quality and size has helped John and Nick establish a successful business. Figure 2.16 has data on Beasty Burgers' average costs and prices for its last financial year.

Figure 2.16: Beasty Burgers costs and prices

Annual sales/ output of burgers	Total variable cost (at £2.00 each)	Annual fixed cost	Total cost	Total revenue (Selling price of £3.00)
0	0	40,000		0
16,000	32,000			48,000
32,000	64,000			
48,000				
64,000				
80,000				

A Complete Figure 2.16 by calculating total cost and sales revenue at each level of production.

B Using your findings construct a breakeven chart and calculate the profit or loss made at 30,000, 50,000 and 70,000 units of output.

C Beasty Burgers expects its variable costs to rise by 10 per cent next year and its rent to go up by £1000 per month. John is unworried; he says they can just raise prices by 10 per cent. Work out Beasty Burgers' new breakeven point should these changes take place. Draft a memo advising John and Nick of any other factors they should take into account while considering a price rise.

The use of software to aid decision making

Setting the scene: efficiency in business

Businesses need to be competitive. They need to supply products at attractive prices to customers and they need to control their costs by operating efficiently.

A CD mail order company, for example, needs to offer CDs at the right price to attract customers and to deliver them cost effectively and efficiently. Part of this challenge involves information management; in carrying out its business, the CD mail order company needs to find information, store it, manipulate it and use the results to deliver customer satisfaction.

Computer software applications can help businesses improve their efficiency. Software can address a wide range of tasks. Some businesses may just use simple applications for keeping data on customers, such as names and addresses; others will have sophisticated and integrated management information systems to manage all the company's financial, stock, production and sales records.

Consider how software applications could be used to improve the operational efficiency of the CD mail order company. Would this company, and other mail order businesses, be able to compete with online suppliers without using IT?

Information is a key business resource. Many websites ask you to register by completing a questionnaire when you first log on. Why would a business ask you to register when you first visit its website? How does this help it to operate more efficiently?

KEY TERMS

Spreadsheets are software applications that facilitate the manipulation of numerical data.

Databases are applications that store collections of information, allowing them to be accessed and interrogated to aid decision making and other business functions.

Word processing packages allow the input, manipulation and formatting of text-based operations.

The **internet** is a global network of computers. It enables information to be widely accessed and shared.

E-commerce is the buying and selling of goods, information products and services through an electronic medium such as the internet.

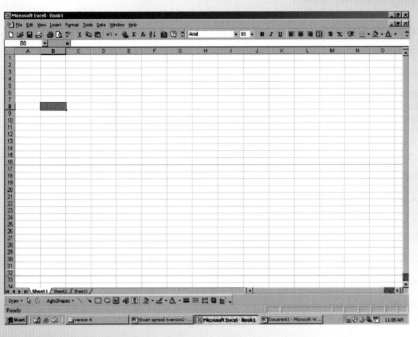

Figure 2.17: A blank spreadsheet

Spreadsheets

Spreadsheet packages allow users to create worksheets that can manipulate data. A spreadsheet is divided into vertical columns and horizontal rows to form a reference grid. Each cell within the grid is referred to by its coordinate. So the highlighted cell in Figure 2.17 – at column B, row 8 – is B8.

Numerical data can be entered into the cells, and a set of cells can be linked by mathematical formulas enabling the worksheet to carry out automatic routines such as adding up or calculating percentages.

Spreadsheets can be used for many purposes. For example, the mail order company (featured in setting the scene at the beginning of this topic) may use one to record its sales, its stock purchase (that is, its cost of sales) and its expenses so that it can easily calculate its current level of profitability.

1 Spreadsheets and budgets

Spreadsheets are particularly useful when setting and monitoring budgets. They can be used to set up the original budgets and, by entering the actual figures as they occur, spreadsheets can be set up to automatically calculate variances. This allows managers to see which areas are performing above or below expectations and to take actions to improve efficiency before problems become too great. By linking budget worksheets together, a business can also create a master budget (a forecast profit and loss account) which enables managers to assess quickly the overall effect of any transaction or change in circumstance.

2 Spreadsheets and cash flow

One of the main uses of spreadsheets in business is in cash flow forecasting. By setting up a cash flow forecast on a spreadsheet, a business is able to monitor its cash position continuously.

Spreadsheets also enable a business to assess easily the impact of any changes in cash inflows and outflows or any planned spending decisions on its bank balance. Managers can model alternative courses of action, and use the results to choose the option which minimises the risk to its cash position. This helps prevent the business from incurring any cash flow problems.

Figure 2.18 shows a spreadsheet that has been set up with formulas to calculate a cash flow forecast. The formulas entered in the cells highlighted in colour instruct the spreadsheet to perform the necessary routines. So, for example, Cell B7 is adding up the total cash inflows for January. The advantage is that once a spreadsheet is set up in this way, a business can model any "what if" scenario immediately and automatically.

Figure 2.18: A spreadsheet set up to calculate a cash flow forecast

	A	B	C	D	E
1		**January**	**February**	**March**	**April**
2	**Cash inflows**				
3	Sales cash				
4	Sales credit				
5	Bank loan				
6					
7	**Total Cash Inflow**	=B3+B4+B5	=C3+C4+C5	=D3+D4+D5	=E3+E4+E5
8					
9	**Cash Outflows**				
10	Purchases				
11	Wages				
12	Utilities				
13	Capital				
14	Expenses				
15					
16	**Total Cash Outflows**	=B10+B11+B12+B14	=C10+C11+C12	=D10+D11+D12+D1◄	=E10+E11+E12+E
17					
18	**Net Cash Inflow/(Outflow)**	=B7-B16	=C7-C16	=D7-D16	=E7-E16
19					
20	**Opening bank balance**		=B21	=C21	=D21
21	**Closing Bank Balance**	=B20+B18	=C20+C18	=D20+D18	=E20+E18
22					

stop and think

How might a spreadsheet application be useful in other areas of business operation? Consider how might a spreadsheet for a retailer like Game (www.gamegroup.plc.uk) be used to help monitor stock?

3 Spreadsheets and breakeven

In Topic 8, you saw that one main drawback of breakeven analysis was that as soon as one factor altered – a change, say, in a company's costs or its price structure – then the whole analysis needed to be undertaken again. Producing revised breakeven charts and calculations could be time consuming and expensive. However, by using a spreadsheet application and by setting up an automatic routine, this problem is overcome. As Figure 2.19 shows, the spreadsheet can be set up to perform the breakeven calculations and to plot and draw breakeven charts. Again, this makes it much easier to model "what if"

situations, and allows breakeven analysis to become a much more useful tool in the management decision-making process.

Word processors and specialist applications

There are several other software packages that are commonly used to increase business efficiency. These include word processing and database applications, as well as a range of specialist task-specific software.

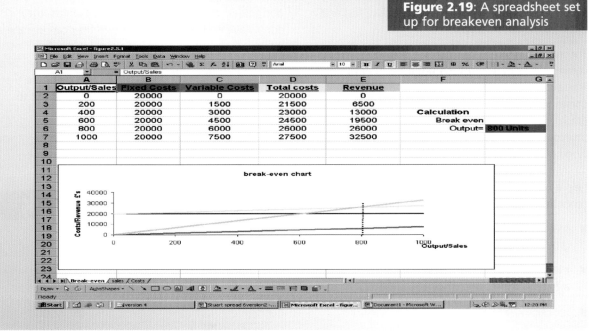

Figure 2.19: A spreadsheet set up for breakeven analysis

The main applications of word processing are:

■ creation of letters, reports and documents

■ automatic spelling and grammar checks

■ importing of pictures, graphics and charts

■ creation of publicity and advertising materials

■ editing, storing, formating and printing documents

Databases allow businesses to manage and utilise large amounts of data. For example, a business could use a database application to:

■ keep a record of customer information, such as names, addresses and profiles

■ manage stock, by holding files recording each stock item's description, quantity and reorder level

■ operate an efficient booking system.

Database and word processing applications can be effectively combined – using a mail merge facility – to create "personalised" letters to individual customers and suppliers.

Although database (and spreadsheet) software applications can be set up to carry out defined operations, they are general packages and many businesses may not have the time or expertise to program them to undertake their specific requirements. Specialised packages can be bought or adapted to perform the exact functions the business needs. In particular, many businesses use specialist software to carry out accounting and payroll functions and stock control operations.

Large organisations may choose to develop their own software – either written by in-house specialists or hired IT consultants – to automate and manage their systems. In principle, programs can be written to support any business function, from a booking system for hotel rooms to a scheduling system to control the flow of work in a modern car plant.

The internet, e-mail and e-commerce

The internet has opened up new opportunities for business. It is both a global marketplace and a vast information resource which can be tapped to improve business efficiency. The internet allows businesses to access information quickly, easily and relatively cost effectively. It provides:

■ access to archives, libraries and news services

■ route planning and logistics

■ easy supplier search facilities

■ information on share prices and market performance

■ access to business information and advice websites

■ discussion forums and usenet groups

■ information on competitor activity and prices

■ access to government sites listing legal information, statistics and contacts.

One particular advantage of the internet is that it enhances a company's ability to undertake fast and effective market research.

The internet also has transformed business communications. One of the key aspects of business efficiency is communications. Fast and effective communications are necessary to ensure that all employees are working towards the business's objectives and to co-ordinate all business activities. Good communications can improve employee motivation, assist management decision making and help a business meet customer needs. E-mail has brought tremendous advances, enabling:

- messages to be sent at low cost to individuals or groups worldwide

- messages to be transmitted in minutes (or at most a few hours)

- messages to be saved and stored for future reference

- electronic transmission of text, graphics, pictures, video and sound.

E-mails enhance both a business's internal and external communications. In particular, e-mail enables many employees to work from remote locations, such as at home, abroad or while visiting clients, as they can maintain frequent contact with (and receive accurate communications from) their office.

> ## stop and think
>
> Norfolk-based Masset Engineering has been contracted to construct specialist pipe systems for an oil rig off the remote north coast of Russia. Jim Clarke, chief engineer, is unsure of some measurements on the technical drawings. Without using e-mail how would Jim obtain copies of the original drawings to check the information? List three benefits that e-mail provides in this situation.

The internet has opened up new trading opportunities for many businesses. By trading on the internet, businesses can benefit from:

- exposure to customers – the internet is a virtual showroom open 24 hours a day

- cost-effective transaction costs

- low overheads compared to retail outlets

- comparatively low-cost advertising

- access to a worldwide customer base.

Most businesses now have a website, and even if they don't trade on the internet – in other words, they don't have a full e-commerce site – they can use the internet to support their marketing activity. For example, by requiring users to register when they first visit the website, a business can build a database that holds the profile of potential customers and use to target individuals with tailored special offers.

Unit 4 (*see page* 152) investigates electronic marketing and other aspects of e-business and e-commerce in depth.

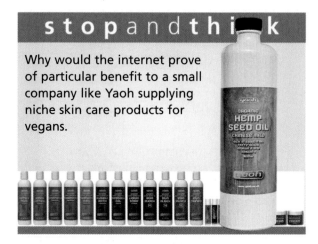

> ## stop and think
>
> Why would the internet prove of particular benefit to a small company like Yaoh supplying niche skin care products for vegans.

Legal issues

Businesses have an obligation to use any information they obtain in the course of their activities correctly and lawfully. Businesses are classed as "data users" and they have legal obligations to "data subjects" – the general public, customers and clients.

A key responsibility is to respect client confidentiality; many businesses have access to client information, such as each customer's name, address, marital status, income, credit history and so on. Businesses must have a policy on client confidentiality and must take steps to prevent any employee misusing or passing on confidential information to other agencies or parties.

Due to the increasing amount of information held by businesses – much of which is now stored electronically – and the growing number of employees that work in IT, successive governments have passed laws to regulate the use of information on customers and to govern IT use in business.

All businesses must understand and respect the provisions of the Data Protection Act 1984. This is designed to ensure that:

- any information held must be securely stored and protected

- private, personal and other data held must be accurate

- data should not be misused – information should not be used for a purpose other than that for which it was collected.

For further information on the principles that underpin the Data Protection Act see Figure 4.12 (*see* *page* 182).

Businesses must also protect the welfare of all employees that use IT in their work. Under the Health and Safety at Work Act 1972, which now incorporates the 1992 Display Screen Equipment Regulations, employees using IT must have:

- the opportunity to take regular breaks

- suitable furniture available

- flicker-free screens.

Knowledge summary

- Spreadsheet applications can help a business perform routine calculations and can be set up to model budgets, cash flow forecasts and breakeven analysis.

- Databases help improve efficiency by acting as large stores of information that can be manipulated and processed to provide data for decision making.

- Word processing applications and e-mail help a business produce documents and communicate quickly and efficiently, both externally and internally.

- The internet has provided business with many new trading opportunities and is a massive information resource.

- Legal constraints exist to ensure that businesses do not misuse information collected on clients.

quick questions

1 Consider three ways a business could use a spreadsheet application to help management decision making.

2 What information might a business keep on a client database? What legal issues must the business consider regarding the use of this information.

3 List three advantages of e-commerce

Business in practice: The Big Outdoors

In 2001, Rachel White received a letter from a firm of solicitors which asked her to make an appointment to visit its offices. There she was told that she had a legacy of £500 000. Rachel decided to quit her job as the manager of a clothes shop and started to realise her life's dream.

Throughout her life, Rachel had enjoyed outdoor activities. She loved walking, riding, climbing and orienteering, and she spent most weekends and all her holidays in what she always called "the big outdoors". After mulling over the possibilities, Rachel decided to see if she could use her legacy to open an outdoor pursuits centre on Dartmoor in Devon.

Rachel started the process of establishing her business by spending two days undertaking some basic initial market research. This involved:

- finding out from the Yellow Pages and other sources if there were many other outdoor activity businesses already operating on Dartmoor

- discovering the cost of suitable premises on Dartmoor from estate agents in Devon

- conducting a quick survey of 20 friends about the kind of activities they would expect and want an outdoor centre to offer and the prices they would be willing to pay.

Rachel decided it would be easier to establish and run the outdoor pursuits centre if she found a business partner to join her in the project. A partner might be able to introduce some finance – reducing the need to start out with a big loan – and would also reduce the pressure on Rachel once the business was operational.

Figure 2.20: Initial financial capital of The Big Outdoors

Source of capital	Investment	Company shares
Rachel White	£450,000	4,500
John Blackmore	£450,000	4,500
John's father	£100,000	1,000

By coincidence, one of Rachel's friends, John Blackmore was also seeking a business opportunity. John came from a wealthy family and had just finished travelling around the world for a year after graduating from university. Rachel and John agreed to form a private limited company holding equal amounts of shares. Between them, they were able to raise £1 million – with John's father taking a minority shareholding with a £100,000 investment – which allowed Rachel and John to:

Figure 2.21: The Big Outdoors cash flow forecast

Income/expenditure	January	February	March	April	May	June
Cash sales	6,200	6,400	7,500	8,850	9,795	12,080
Credit sales	0	0	3,250	4,100	5,250	7,500
Total cash inflow	6,200	6,400	10,750	12,950	15,045	19,580
Wages & salaries	3,450	4,450	5,600	6,600	7,600	8,750
Raw materials	1,850	2,400	2,050	2,150	2,600	3,550
Rates & other costs	500	500	500	500	500	500
Marketing costs	1,500	1,200	2,000	1,800	1,900	2,140
Total cash outflow	7,300	8,550	10,200	11,050	12,600	14,940
Net cash flow	(1,100)	(2,150)	550	1,900	2,445	4,640
Opening balance	(9,400)	(10,500)	(12,650)	(12,100)	(10,200)	(7,755)
Closing balance	(10,500)	(12,650)	(12,100)	(10,200)	(7,755)	(3,115)

- purchase suitable premises
- buy essential equipment and machinery
- undertake initial marketing to publicise the new business
- have some surplus cash to avoid liquidity problems.

It was agreed that John would take responsibility for managing staff and marketing, and Rachel would control financial and physical resources. John recruited and trained four staff to help them run the business.

Rachel and John were surprised at the amount of work that was necessary before trading could start. The farm they had purchased needed some alterations and the builders were slow to complete the work.

Learning the hard way

After six months' trading, The Big Outdoors Ltd was in financial trouble. The company had encountered financial problems from the very start. The building work had proved more expensive than Rachel had imagined and John had not managed to attract as many customers as the business had needed.

Things came to a head when the company's bank refused to pay a cheque that Rachel had written out to one of the business's suppliers. John feared that

the company would be forced to close, but a friend who was experienced in business advised that they go and talk to their bank.

Rachel and John arranged an interview with their bank manager for the next day. The bank manager was scathing about their business planning. She agreed that the business appeared to have potential, but was amazed at the lack of financial planning. She asked the partners to prepare a cash flow forecast for the next six months and also a profit budget for the next year. She asked them to calculate how many customers they needed each month to break even, "so that you have a useful yardstick for monitoring your performance".

John and Rachel worked hard, with some help from a friend who was an experienced entrepreneur, to produce the figures the bank manager required. Figure 2.21 shows the cash flow forecast that they prepared.

The business takes off

Six months later the business looked more secure. John's marketing had attracted increasing numbers of customers. As well as selling to tourists and other individuals, John began to win corporate clients – providing a service for businesses that wanted to offer their customers and staff the chance to enjoy The Big Outdoors experience. However, he had to offer two months' trade credit to attract this type of customer.

As word of mouth spread that The Big Outdoors was a great place to spend time, sales began to rise steadily. The partners had been fortunate in employing experienced staff and the superb location on Dartmoor was a winner too. By the end of June, the company's financial position looked much brighter. The cash position began to ease, and Rachel was able to compare the actual financial position of the business against the cash flow forecast and budgets (in Figure 2.21). Figure 2.22 shows the company's actual cash inflows, and wages and salaries bill for the January to June period.

Rachel was more confident. "I have worked out our breakeven position," she told John. "Fixed costs each month are £3,850. A typical customer pays £125 and the variable costs for that customer are £90. Last month we attracted over 150 customers, so we are doing really well. The next stage is that I am going to have to produce a balance sheet and profit and loss account as our first year of trading is nearly over."

Figure 2.22: Actual cash inflows and wages and salaries bill

	January	February	March	April	May	June
Total cash inflow	5,800	6,200	10,700	13,100	15,250	19,600
Wages & salaries	3,250	4,400	5,700	6,550	7,450	8,600

activities

1 How might Rachel and John have improved their planning process for The Big Outdoors Ltd?

2 Rachel's cash flow forecast proved remarkably accurate. All the figures in Figure 2.21 turned out to be accurate with the exception of the total cash inflows and the wages and salaries bill. The actuals are given in Figure 2.22. Use this information to calculate:
- the company's actual cash flow for the six months
- the total variances for the six months for cash inflow, cash outflow and net cash flow.

3 List the main assets and liabilities that The Big Outdoors Ltd might have had once it started trading.

4 Explain why it is important for Rachel to construct a balance sheet and a profit and loss account for The Big Outdoors Ltd.

5 What benefits might The Big Outdoors Ltd have gained from drawing up its cash flow forecast for the six months January to June?

6 Explain, with the use of a breakeven calculation, why Rachel felt that the business's financial position was so strong in June.

7 How useful might Rachel find breakeven analysis as a tool for monitoring the performance of The Big Outdoors Ltd over future months?

8 Advise Rachel on the potential benefits of using ICT to assist her in managing the financial affairs of The Big Outdoors Ltd.

SUCCESSFUL BUSINESSES ARE GOOD AT MARKETING. They are able to discover and meet the needs of their customers. They are good at getting the right product to the right place at the right time.

This unit provides an introduction to marketing. You will discover why it is important for a business to set objectives for its marketing and consider some of the different objectives that a business might pursue. You will investigate why businesses normally develop products for particular groups of customers and how they target different groups of consumers.

Knowing what customers want is an essential ingredient of business success. This unit introduces you to the ways in which a firm can research its market. It explains the benefits of undertaking market research and the pitfalls that may be encountered.

Every business needs a strategy to sell its products. The marketing mix is a combination of factors which a business can control to meet the needs of the customers that it is targeting. This unit looks at the elements that comprise the marketing mix – the design of the product itself, the price at which the product is to be sold, where it is to be sold and how the product will be promoted. You will see how a business can alter its marketing mix to meet different market conditions.

Investigating marketing

Setting the scene: Microsoft's marketing

In 1975, Microsoft was just an idea in the head of Bill Gates, the company's founder. Yet despite having over 75,000 competitors worldwide, in the 30 years since it was founded, Microsoft has grown rapidly to become one of the largest companies in the world.

Today, Microsoft's products are sold globally and used on over 90 per cent of computers worldwide. The company now employs some 57,000 workers and its annual profits in 2003/4 exceeded £3 billion.

One of the major reasons for the company's astonishing success is its marketing. Microsoft has a clear vision on which to base all its marketing decisions. That vision is Microsoft software on every desktop PC. Microsoft continually monitors its competition to ensure that it stays ahead. The company spends heavily on developing new products, researching customers' opinions and promoting its products. These are the vital elements of marketing that we will consider in this unit.

What is marketing?

Marketing involves all businesses, large and small, in a series of important activities.

- Deciding on what the business is trying to achieve through marketing – for example, is it aiming to introduce new products or to increase sales?

KEY TERMS

Marketing involves discovering and meeting the needs of customers. It allows a business to give customer satisfaction while fulfilling its own objectives.

A **market** is where buyers and sellers come together to trade products and information. It might be a specific location such as a street market or a means of communication such as the eBay website on the internet.

- Investigating what customers want. There is little point in supplying goods or services that customers are not willing to buy. Any investigation of customers' needs is likely to include an assessment of competitors' products.

- Understanding the business's customers. Very few products can be sold to all types of customers. A business needs to understand who its customers are: young or old, rich or poor, men or women?

- Deciding on the precise specification of the product to be sold, the price at which it will be sold and where it will be sold. The results of the investigation into customers' needs will be very helpful in taking these decisions.

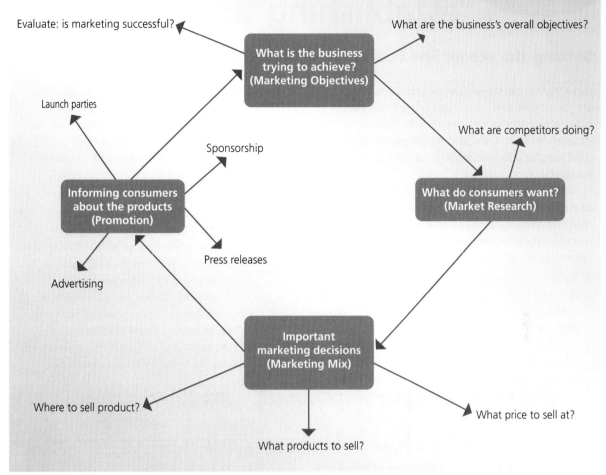

Evaluate: is marketing successful?

What are the business's overall objectives?

What is the business trying to achieve? (Marketing Objectives)

Launch parties

Sponsorship

What are competitors doing?

Informing consumers about the products (Promotion)

What do consumers want? (Market Research)

Press releases

Advertising

Important marketing decisions (Marketing Mix)

Where to sell product?

What price to sell at?

What products to sell?

- Letting consumers know about the products. If customers are not aware of a business's products, they will not buy them. Advertising is the most common way of informing consumers about products, but it is not the only technique that a business can use.

Successful businesses are good at these activities. They know who their customers are, what customers want, what price customers will pay for a product and why customers buy particular goods or services.

Marketing plays a vital role in satisfying customers. High-quality marketing enables a business to understand its customers, and helps it to provide customers with the products they require at an acceptable price and a convenient location. The business benefits from effective marketing. Satisfied customers will buy more of the business's products and they may be willing to pay a higher price for a product that exactly meets their needs. Successful marketing, therefore, can significantly increase profits.

David Packard, the founder of the Packard computer company (now part of the giant Hewlett Packard organisation) has said that "marketing is too important to be left to the marketing department". He argues that everybody within a business should take some responsibility for marketing. All employees who have any contact with customers or competitors are able to gain information that might be of value to the business. Similarly, it is possible for many different employees to publicise the company's products.

GO TO the accompanying CD-ROM. Choose Unit 3 from the main menu. This will take you to an interactive game about evaluating market research. It is better to try this game once you have read Unit 3 Topics 3 to 8.

Topic 1 Marketing objectives: establishing the business

Setting the scene: The Feel Good Drinks Company

Dave Wallwork, Steve Cooper and Chris Wright are all in their early 30s. They have other things in common: until the autumn of 2001 they all worked for Coca-Cola, and then they gave up their jobs to jointly establish The Feel Good Drinks Company.

The trio spent the first nine months planning their business. Part of the planning process involved setting themselves some marketing objectives.

■ **To meet consumers' needs**. The three co-owners used focus groups (groups of potential consumers) as well as friends and family to taste the products they were developing. This provided considerable feedback and helped them to ensure that their products would meet with consumer approval.

■ **To develop thirst-quenching, great-tasting drinks**. The team thought that many of the soft drinks available on the market failed this simple test. To meet what they see as a gap in the market, Feel Good is initially producing a range of five different fruit drinks.

■ **To develop a brand image**. The trio wanted to create a brand that was different: it had to be fun and designed to make consumers (and others associated with the company) feel good. One way in which it has tried to build this feel-good factor is by agreeing to donate 10p to a cancer charity for each customer registering with the company through its website.

■ **To achieve sales of £2.5 million within 18 months of starting trading**. The company comfortably met this target and The Feel Good Drinks Company is on track to achieve annual sales in excess of £10 million within its first three years.

These marketing objectives are not unusual for a newly established company seeking to gain a foothold in a market. The Feel Good Drinks Company is operating in a very competitive market containing major players such as Cadbury Schweppes and Coca-Cola. Attaining these marketing objectives will assist the company in surviving and growing during its testing first few years of trading.

This is the home page of The Feel Good Drinks Company's website. How might the company have used its website to help it to achieve its marketing objectives? (Have a look at the website to help answer this question.)

KEY TERMS

Marketing objectives are the goals that a business attempts to achieve through its marketing activities.

Corporate objectives are the goals of the entire organisation.

A **brand** is a name, symbol, sign or design used by a business to differentiate its products from those produced by its competitors.

Why set marketing objectives?

Marketing is just one of the functions that make up a business's activities. Marketing decisions should complement decisions taken in other functional areas of the business and help the business to achieve its overall (or corporate) objectives. (We looked at corporate objectives in Unit 1, *see pages* 15–16.)

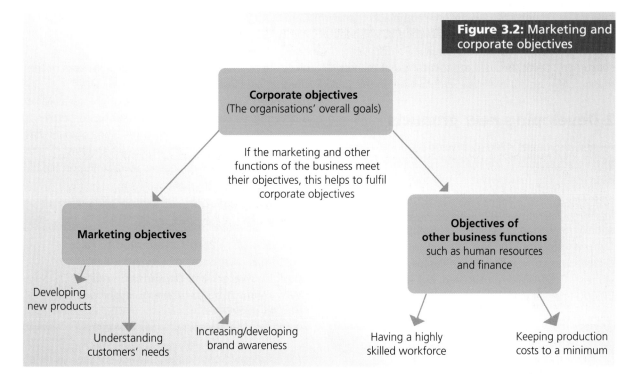

Corporate objectives
(The organisations' overall goals)

If the marketing and other functions of the business meet their objectives, this helps to fulfil corporate objectives

Marketing objectives

Developing new products

Understanding customers' needs

Increasing/developing brand awareness

Objectives of other business functions
such as human resources and finance

Having a highly skilled workforce

Keeping production costs to a minimum

An obvious starting point in marketing is for managers to decide what they are trying to achieve. Without setting objectives, managers cannot know whether or not their marketing activities have been successful. A business's marketing objectives will have a major influence on its marketing activities. A firm that is trying to increase its sales may lower its prices, while one that aims to make more consumers aware of its brand may increase advertising.

Marketing objectives to establish a business

Marketing objectives will vary according to the type of business. A large pharmaceutical company such as GlaxoSmithKline may wish to develop new products and win sales at the expense of rivals, whereas the marketing objectives of a small new company may be more concerned with establishing the business. In this section, you will look at some of the marketing objectives that a new business might pursue. Note, however, that these objectives can also be followed by businesses that have been trading for many years.

1 Understanding customer needs

It is vital for all businesses, small and large, service or manufacturing, to know their customers' needs as fully as possible. A well-managed business finds out what customers want and attempts to supply goods and services that meet these needs. It is also important for the business to be able to anticipate trends and developments which could influence customers' buying habits in the future.

In 2003, the fast-food giant McDonald's announced that it had made a loss of over £200 million on its worldwide operations during the last three months of 2002. A major cause of the company's poor financial performance was falling sales. The market for fast food has changed over the last couple of years, with consumers becoming more health conscious and worried that fast food contributes to the growing problem of obesity, and these changes caught even a huge business such as McDonald's unaware.

A new business, such as The Feel Good Drinks Company, must also understand its customers. In its case, the marketing process began before the company even started trading. To make sure that their idea for healthy fruit drinks was viable, the three entrepreneurs carried out market research into consumer needs as they were planning the business. This is one factor that has contributed to The Feel Good Drinks Company's rapidly rising sales and resulted in it being shortlisted for the Orange award for the best marketing campaign for a small business in 2003.

Businesses cannot afford to become complacent, and a good objective for new and established businesses alike is to monitor markets continually. To discover consumers' needs, businesses must carry out market research. We look at this topic in detail later in this unit.

2 Developing new products

All new businesses need to develop products in order to gain a foothold in the market. For some new businesses, this may involve simply copying an existing idea that is on the market. Other new businesses may be more innovative and introduce customers to an entirely new good or service. For example, in 1994 Cyberia introduced the first internet café in the UK. Cyberia was co-founded by Eva Pascoe, a Polish student. Cyberia did not succeed, but today over 20,000 internet cafés operate around the world.

Established businesses also develop new products to meet the changing needs of the marketplace or to reflect advances in technology. For example, global consumer technology businesses such as Sony have developed minidiscs to replace tapes and CDs, and supermarkets such as Sainsbury have introduced new ranges of foods to cater for customers wanting a healthier diet.

Successful product development requires a full understanding of customers' needs. This need not be a costly exercise. If a business understands its customers and if it is only refining and improving an existing product, then product development can be relatively inexpensive. However, new product development can involve substantial expenditure on research and development.

3 Increasing brand awareness

A new business needs to reach potential customers if it is to generate sales. An important marketing objective, therefore, for any new firm is to raise consumers' awareness of the business and its products. This may be done through advertising, by giving away free samples and by attempting to get television or newspaper coverage of the new business.

Cardiff Ad Bikes is a new company set up by Mike Parfitt, a 32-year-old entrepreneur, that offers a pedal-powered taxi service. The futuristic-looking bikes are pollution free, and can travel in areas of the city that are closed to ordinary taxis. Initially, passengers can use the service free of charge as Mike is covering his company's costs by selling corporate advertising on the side of the bikes. The company has a website (www.cardiffadbikes.co.uk) and has attracted a number of sponsors to raise the profile of this new brand of transport.

Well-established companies may equally seek to raise the profile of their business and their existing products and brands. Some businesses, for example, use the strength of their existing brand names to develop and market new products. Virgin is an example of a company that uses brand proliferation as a marketing strategy. Richard Branson founded Virgin in 1970 as a mail order record company. Since then, Virgin has expanded into other areas, including air travel, mobile phones and financial services by using its strong brand name to enter new markets. By operating in several different markets, the company is not reliant on generating sales from a single market sector.

4 Sales and revenue targets

Most businesses set sales and revenue targets. A new business might set targets for its first year of trading, and thereafter set annual targets. It is important to understand the difference between a revenue target and a sales target. A revenue target sets out the income a firm expects to receive over a period of time. A sales target states the number of items a business hopes to sell, or the number of customers it hopes to attract, over some period, often a month, quarter or year.

For a new business like Cardiff Ad Bikes, Mike Parfitt may set revenue targets as well as passenger targets. The revenue targets would provide an estimate of the income the business hopes to generate, which initially comes solely from selling advertising on the company's pedal-powered taxis. These targets will take into account the costs the company is likely to face and any profit targets it may wish to achieve.

Knowledge summary

- Marketing objectives are the goals that a business attempts to achieve through its marketing activities.

- Marketing objectives vary according to the type of business.

- New businesses normally try to understand what customers want, to develop new products (or copy existing ones) and to raise awareness of their brands.

- Most businesses, including newly established ones, set marketing targets for sales and revenue.

quick questions

1 At the start of this topic, we looked at The Feel Good Drinks Company. Why might the managers of the company benefit from setting marketing objectives? Try to give two reasons.

2 Can you think of two other groups of people associated with the business (known as stakeholders) who might be interested in The Feel Good Drinks Company's marketing objectives? In each case, say why they might be interested.

3 Adventure Ltd is a new business that plans to offer expensive activity holidays in exotic locations for wealthy customers. What marketing objectives might be important for this company? Explain your answer.

data interpretation

Coastdigital's success

Coastdigital designs websites for other businesses and offers advice and support on internet marketing. The company's customers include legal firms, estate agents and a business selling home security products

Though only formed in 2002, the company has won increasing recognition for its work, including the Essex countrywide New Business of the Year award. James Frost, Coastdigital's managing director, says that the enthusiasm and innovation of the team is an important reason for its success. He recognises that the company's continued success depends upon meeting customers' needs and ensuring that they are satisfied with the service they receive.

A Visit Coastdigital's website (www.coastdigital.co.uk) and find out more about the company. Design a webpage (on paper) setting out the company's likely marketing objectives.

B Write a memo to James Frost, Coastdigital's managing director, explaining why the company should set clear marketing objectives, and the benefits the company might gain from including these objectives on its website.

Marketing objectives: expanding the business

Setting the scene: SMART objectives

By setting clearly defined marketing objectives, it becomes much easier for managers to judge the success of marketing strategies. Many marketing managers set SMART objectives. SMART is an acronym, which stands for specific, measurable, achievable, realistic and timely.

Specific
Objectives should clearly specify what they want to achieve.

Measurable
A business should be able to measure whether it is meeting its marketing objectives or not; it may help to include a numerical target.

Achievable
A business should be able to achieve its marketing objectives. A specialist luxury car manufacturer such as Lotus would not set high volume sales targets; it would not expect to sell as many cars as a mainstream manufacturer like Ford.

Realistic
A business should have the resources to achieve its marketing objectives. To achieve a large increase in sales, for example, might require the finance for a major advertising campaign.

Timely
The objective should include a date by which it should be attained. This will normally be expressed in terms of years.

Consider the marketing objectives for a supermarket. A poorly defined objective would be to aim "to increase sales during the year". A SMART objective might be "to increase sales of own-brand products by 10 per cent within 12 months".

In 2004, the supermarket giant Tesco announced its first business venture in China with the purchase of a 50 per cent stake in a 25-strong hypermarket chain for £140 million. Tesco will have set a number of marketing objectives for this new venture. Write down one SMART objective the company might set for its China operation.

Marketing objectives to assist with expansion

In the previous topic, we looked at some of the marketing objectives a company might set to establish the business. Now we consider some marketing objectives designed to expand the business.

KEY TERMS

Marketing objectives are the goals that a business attempts to achieve through its marketing activities.

Market share is the percentage or proportion of the total sales in a market achieved by one business.

Diversification is an approach under which a business produces a broad range of unrelated goods or services.

1 Improving profitability

Profits are the surplus of revenues earned by a business over its costs. Many businesses have a corporate objective to maximise profits. It follows, therefore, that many businesses have improving profitability as a marketing objective. Indeed, a number of other marketing objectives are pursued with this aim in mind.

Businesses attempt to improve profitability in many ways. In marketing terms, a business may decide to invest more in advertising in order to increase product sales and profitability. The bakery chain Greggs spent £1.3 million on an advertising campaign in 2004 which contributed to a 10.6 per cent increase in profits to £13.6 million. The advertising campaign helped the company meet its profits objective.

Another approach a business might adopt could be to try and alter customers' perceptions of its product. By presenting the product as a more luxurious and prestigious item or service, it may be possible to charge higher prices without reducing sales. This will increase the business's profitability.

s t o p a n d t h i n k

Not all organisations have improving profitability as a corporate or a marketing objective. For example, the British Red Cross, which provides emergency aid to people in distress anywhere in the world, is not motivated by profit. What do you think might be the marketing objectives of the British Red Cross?

2 Improving market share

Market share is the percentage or proportion of the total sales in a market achieved by one business. Unless the overall market is growing significantly, a business can only increase its market share at the expense of its competitors. Setting an improvement in market share as a marketing objective means,

therefore, that a business aims to outperform its competitors. This is a very aggressive marketing objective and is likely to provoke a response from rival businesses. Competitors might decide to reduce their prices or to launch major advertising campaigns to hold on to their share of the market.

Improving market share is a difficult marketing objective to achieve. It is likely to require significant spending on marketing activities such as advertising, special offers and price cuts. For example, in September 2004, Nintendo announced that it was cutting the price of its GameBoy portable console in the US and Japan with similar price cuts in Europe to follow. This decision was taken in an attempt to boost Nintendo's market share of the portable gaming market, even though the company already has 95 per cent of this market!

3 Diversification

Businesses diversify when they move into new market sectors by producing an increased range of unrelated goods and services. Mars, the international confectionery manufacturer, has recently diversified its product range by making ice creams as well as its more established range of chocolate and snack bars. This move should allow Mars to increase its overall sales during the summer months. Diversification as a marketing objective usually supports a corporate objective of business growth.

Many businesses are attracted to diversification because it allows them to spread risk. If a product in one market becomes unfashionable or obsolete, a company's financial position will not be threatened if its products in other markets continue to sell well. By receiving income from its successful products, the company will have the time and resources to develop replacement products in the market where its

s t o p a n d t h i n k

Microsoft's Windows operating system is used on 90 per cent of personal computers worldwide. Microsoft's overall market share has fallen slightly in recent years. However, despite this fall, the company has achieved rising sales. How has this been possible?

How does having a strong corporate brand image (such as Virgin, for example) help to persuade a business to adopt diversification as a marketing objective?

products had become unfashionable. However, diversification can be risky. By moving into new unfamiliar markets, a business can be producing and selling products of which it has little experience.

In August 2004, Stelios Haji-Ioannou, the founder of the budget airline easyJet, announced that he was to launch a cut-price UK mobile phone network. This new venture is intended to complement his other enterprises such as easyCar, the low-price car rental service. Stelios Haji-Ioannou recognises that his new business will take time to succeed. He will set sales targets, but acknowledges that it will be some time before the business generates profits. A key part of Stelios Haji-Ioannou's marketing strategy is to diversify by introducing basic low-cost products into new markets. The easyGroup's marketing mix also includes a focus on place, by offering customers new ways of accessing products, as well as advertising and other promotional activity.

4 Product relaunches

In 2003, Cadbury Schweppes plc took the decision to relaunch one of its most famous brands, Cadbury's Dairy Milk. The company decided to do this in an attempt to improve its sales in the increasingly competitive confectionery market. It decided to brand more of its products as Dairy Milk and to package them in Cadbury's eye-catching purple wrapping. This move proved successful for the company as, in the six months following the relaunch, its sales rose by over 13 per cent compared to the same period in the previous year.

Product relaunches are used to boost sales of flagging brands or products. It is a common strategy in the confectionery industry and it is also used by businesses producing washing power and household cleaning products. Companies might also use a

relaunch to reposition a product in the market. The aim might be to make the product appear more luxurious and prestigious to consumers. If this type of relaunch is successful, it can allow the business to charge a premium price for its product. For example, Lucozade, which had been marketed as a drink for people who were unwell, has been successfully repositioned as an energy drink to refresh people after exercise. It is now the market leader in the energy drinks market.

A business that is relaunching a product normally arranges a series of public relations events and other publicity to raise the awareness of retailers and consumers of the new product. Cadbury Schweppes made sure that retailers knew about the relaunch of Dairy Milk and were aware that the new products that would be sold under the brand name. The company targeted retailers to ensure that its new products would have sufficient shelf space in shops.

Why might a company such as Cadbury Schweppes decide to relaunch an existing product rather than introduce an entirely new one to the market?

Knowledge summary

- ■ Increasing profitability is an important marketing objective for many businesses. Some other marketing objectives are also intended to achieve this aim.

- ■ An improvement in market share is likely to be achieved at the expense of competitors. Rival companies are likely to respond to any business that is seeking to gain a bigger market share with their own marketing activity.

- ■ Diversification may be adopted as a marketing objective by companies that wish to reduce risk. As a strategy, it is particularly appropriate for a business with a strong brand image.

- ■ Relaunching a product can improve the sales of a declining product, but it requires an effective publicity campaign if it is to be successful.

quick **questions**

1 Greggs (the bakery chain with over 1300 shops) spent more than £1 million on an advertising campaign to improve its profitability. Why might this approach have proved unsuccessful, especially in the short run?

2 In the first three months of 2004, global sales of mobile phones rose by 25 per cent while Nokia's sales rose by only 19 per cent. Did Nokia's market share rise or fall in that period? Did this mean that the company's profits must have fallen? Explain your answers.

3 Some UK companies that supply water have diversified into other businesses such as hotels and transport. Why might diversification prove to be a risky marketing objective for these companies?

data **interpretation**
Farms need new direction

Small farms in the UK are facing tough times. Britain's farmers are finding it difficult because they can only get low prices for most of their products. Over the past few years, prices for crops and livestock have fallen because of increased supply and greater competition from overseas.

David and Sally Wilson are unable to make a living from their farm in south Devon. The couple have a large flock of sheep and dairy cattle (for milk) on their hill farm in a particularly attractive area of Devon, as well as two holiday cottages that they try to rent out. However, they have struggled to generate sufficient profit to make a living. The couple do not want to sell the farm as the price of agricultural land is low and they enjoy the lifestyle. Other local farms have introduced new crops and livestock such as deer.

In discussions with an adviser, David and Sally have decided that marketing of their current and future produce might be the key to their future. Your task is to prepare a presentation that will set out what they need to do. Working in groups, prepare your presentation by completing these tasks.

A Describe the steps that David and Sally should take in planning the marketing of their business.

B Explain why is it so important for David and Sally to set marketing objectives for their business.

C Prepare some marketing objectives that might be appropriate for David and Sally in their particular circumstances. Explain your choices.

Setting the scene: information technology and segmentation

Most businesses aim their products at particular groups of consumers. Some are very obviously targeting particular groups of people. Club 18–30 organises lively holidays for adults aged 30 or under. Waitrose, one of the UK's leading supermarket chains, targets better-off consumers. Virago is a publisher that produces books for women.

Businesses often want to target particular groups of consumers, and they increasingly use information technology to help them do this. For example, most supermarkets have issued loyalty cards for some years. These cards encourage customers to spend more with the issuing supermarket as they receive points for each purchase which can be exchanged for products or gifts at a later date. However, by issuing loyalty cards, supermarkets find out about their customers' spending patterns. This makes it easier to identify the tastes and attitudes of groups of customers, and to target them using special offers and direct mail.

Sainsbury operates its Nectar Card scheme as a joint venture with a number of other businesses including BP and Vodafone. The scheme was launched in 2002 and within a year some 13 million UK consumers had signed up for a card. The company running the Nectar scheme on behalf of the participating companies admits that by having some personal information about cardholders, such as age, marital status and family size, and by knowing what products customers purchase, it is much easier to segment markets and to target specific groups of consumers with offers.

Most of the UK's leading supermarkets operate loyalty card schemes. Why do you think this is the case?

Unit 3 Investigating marketing

KEY TERMS

A **market** is where buyers and sellers come together to trade products and information. It might be a specific location such as a street market or a means of communication such as the eBay website on the internet.

Market segmentation is the division of potential consumers into groups with similar characteristics.

A **mass market** is a large market with many consumers buying similar products.

A **niche market** is a small but separate part of a larger market.

Direct mail is promotional material posted to the homes of potential customers. It is sometimes called junk mail.

Social grade	Description of occupation	Example
A	Higher managerial and professional	Company director
B	Lower managerial and supervisory	Middle manager
C1	Non-manual	Bank clerk
C2	Skilled manual	Electrician
D	Semi-skilled and unskilled manual	Labourer
E	Those receiving no income from employment	Unemployed

How markets are segmented

Market segmentation is the division of potential consumers into groups with similar characteristics. Businesses can segment markets in a number of ways.

1 By age

The demand for some products is clearly linked to age, and so it is important for some businesses to segment their market in this way. The holiday industry is a classic example of a sector which segments part of its market by the age of the customers. As its name suggests, Club 18–30 aims its holidays at young people; Saga sells its holidays (and other products) exclusively to customers aged 50 and over.

2 By social class

Another way of segmenting the market is by social class and income. This is usually done by considering the occupation of the head of each household and ignoring second or subsequent wage earners. For example, the UK market research industry uses the socioeconomic scale described in Figure 3.3 to provide standardised social groupings. Figure 3.3 illustrates just one method of segmentation according to social class. There are many other classifications, some of which are much more complex with many more subdivisions.

3 By gender

Some businesses aim their products specifically at one gender, producing a range of products for women, and a separate range for men. This type of segmentation is common in the clothing, cosmetics and magazine industries. Some businesses that have traditionally only produced products for one gender are attempting to increase sales by developing products that are targeted at the other gender. For example, many cosmetics' companies now have ranges of products designed for men.

4 By lifestyle

This method of segmentation attempts to classify consumers according to their individual patterns of expenditure. For example, businesses might classify a family's lifestyle according to how they make their purchases: do they buy products on the internet, make purchases using credit or debit cards, or shop in discount stores? By segmenting the market in this way, businesses can target particular groups with offers that may be appealing. For example, a supermarket like Tesco may want to offer busy and internet connected people the chance to purchase goods and services online and take advantage of its home delivery service. Tesco does not want to waste resources by trying to sell this service to customers that don't have internet access or who prefer to do their shopping in the stores.

119

Topic 3 Targeting the market

stop and think

The increase in the number of women in the labour force means that many households have two or more workers. Does this mean that segmenting households by the occupation of one of those working is no longer appropriate?

Some markets are segmented according to more than one classification. This is not unusual as it allows more accurate targeting of consumers. The market for Loaded magazine, for example, is segmented by age and gender: the magazine is targeted at young men.

When next in your local newsagents, identify magazines with target markets defined by each of the methods of segmentation we have considered here: age, social class, gender and lifestyle. Can you find some magazines that are segmented by more than one of these classifications.

5 Geodemographic segmentation

Geodemographic segmentation groups consumers by using a combination of several geographic and economic factors, such as where a customer lives, the size of their family, the type of house in which they live, and so on. This way of segmenting the market is particularly relevant for businesses planning the location and development of hospitality and tourism operations such as pubs, restaurants and leisure facilities.

One way of applying geodemographic segmentation is to use the ACORN (A Classification Of Residential Neighbourhoods) categorisation. Based on geographic, cultural, socioeconomic and other factors, ACORN identifies 38 different types of residential neighbourhood according to the most common type of housing within that neighbourhood. It allows the country to be divided up into a series of neighbourhoods, each consisting of about 150 homes and defined using postcodes. Businesses in many industries use this system, including banks and other financial institutions, gas and electricity companies and credit card operators. Businesses using ACORN believe that they can make judgements about consumers and their spending habits from the types of houses in which they live.

6 Niche and mass markets

Some businesses target niche markets rather than the entire market. This approach to marketing allows companies to identify and meet the needs of relatively small segments of the market. Niche marketing enables small businesses to operate profitably in markets that are dominated by large firms. Examples of businesses that operate in niche markets include Tie Rack and the radio station Classic FM.

In mass marketing, businesses aim their products at most of the available market and normally try to sell a range of similar products to all consumers. This means that the business is not segmenting the market. Mass marketing is only possible if the products are popular and purchased by many different types of people. Groceries and consumer durables such as washing machines, for example, are well suited to being sold in mass markets.

Businesses must be able to produce on a large scale if they are to sell successfully in a mass market. This may mean that a company has to invest heavily in resources such as buildings, machinery and vehicles. Usually, firms have to be price competitive to flourish in mass markets.

Why do businesses segment their markets?

Businesses segment their markets to help them achieve their marketing objectives. There are two main benefits of this market segmentation.

■ **To help launch new products.**
Market segmentation can help to identify the potential demand for new products. Many businesses producing foodstuffs have identified groups of consumers who prefer organic alternatives and have supplied this segment of the market profitably.

■ **To assist in marketing the product.**
Knowing the characteristics and behaviour of potential consumers can aid businesses in planning their marketing activities. For example, if a product's target market is young males, then it might be cost effective to advertise it on the web or through magazines such as Loaded.

Knowledge summary

- Market segmentation is the division of potential consumers into groups with similar characteristics.

- Segmenting a market enables businesses to reach their customers more easily and cost effectively.

- Businesses can segment markets by customers' age, social class, gender and lifestyles.

- Many businesses also segment their markets using geodemographic classifications which take a number of geographic, cultural and socioeconomic factors into account.

- Some businesses elect to sell their products in niche markets, which are small segments of a larger market.

quickquestions

1 Consider each of these industries in turn:
- motor car manufacture
- sporting and leisure activities
- chart music
- DIY products
- children's toys.

For each industry, identify one or more methods of market segmentation that businesses might employ. In each case, justify your choice or choices.

2 In 2003, Matalan moved from selling in the discount clothing market (a niche market) to compete with retailers such as BHS and Marks & Spencer in the mass market. The company has upgraded its stores and has advertised its new position in the market. Imagine you are responsible for marketing at Matalan. Would you approve this change of strategy or not? Explain your decision.

3 Global Ltd imports exotic plants from around the world for UK citizens to grow in their greenhouses and conservatories. How might this company segment its market to make its marketing more effective?

datainterpretation
Up My Street website

Log on to the Up My Street website (www.upmystreet.com). Type in your postcode and view the relevant pages before attempting these tasks.

A List six types of information available on these pages that would be useful to a business.

B Look at the ACORN information on the website. Identify three businesses that might be able to make use of this information. In each case, explain in what ways the information may prove useful.

C Is the information on the website accurate? How useful overall do you consider it to be.

Topic 4 Why businesses carry out market research

Setting the scene: market-oriented and product-oriented businesses

Product-oriented businesses focus on product quality. Essentially they create products and then try to sell them. They assume that consumers will want the product that they are producing. This is a fallacy. Consumers want products that meet their needs as fully as possible and the highest quality product may not be what they want.

Concorde, the supersonic airliner, is a classic example of the weakness of the product-oriented approach. Launched in the 1970s, Concorde was hailed as the future of air travel. It was very advanced in technological terms, offering luxury and high-speed travel, but failed to be a commercial success. Airlines preferred to use subsonic planes in an era when many consumers were seeking low-cost air travel. Concorde was taken out of service in 2003. Perhaps you can

think of any other high technology products that have not proved popular with consumers?

Any business that develops and performs its production and marketing activities with the needs and ultimate satisfaction of the consumer firmly in mind is market oriented. Market-oriented businesses attempt to discover the wants and needs of consumers and then design products to meet these needs and wants. A truly marketing-oriented business places the needs of consumers at the heart of all its decisions, not just those relating to marketing. The car manufacturer Ford researches its new markets thoroughly and uses the information it gains to help in designing the styling of the company's new models. This may be one of the reasons why the Ford Focus was the best-selling car in the UK in 2003.

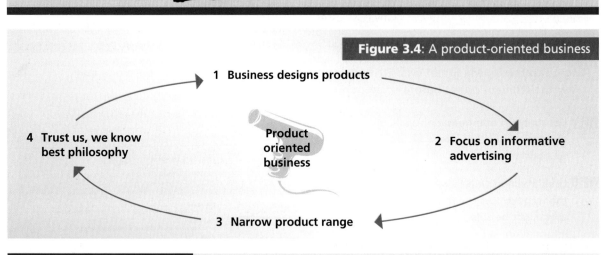

Figure 3.4: A product-oriented business

1 Business designs products

4 Trust us, we know best philosophy

Product oriented business

2 Focus on informative advertising

3 Narrow product range

KEY TERMS

Market research is the systematic collection and analysis of data to enable a business to make better marketing decisions.

Target markets are particular parts or segments of a market at which a business aims its products.

Market-oriented businesses attempt to discover the wants and needs of consumers, and then design products to meet these needs and wants.

Market size is the total sales achieved by all firms in a market. This can be measured by monetary value or by the number of sales.

Market share is the percentage of total sales in a market achieved by a particular business.

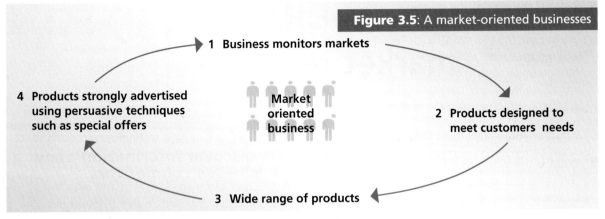

Figure 3.5: A market-oriented businesses

1 Business monitors markets

Market oriented business

2 Products designed to meet customers needs

3 Wide range of products

4 Products strongly advertised using persuasive techniques such as special offers

stopandthink

Some fashion designers such as Gucci might be considered to be product oriented. Do you agree with this view? Does it mean that businesses such as Gucci do not meet the needs of their customers?

The purpose of market research

Market research is the systematic collection and analysis of data to enable a business to take better quality marketing decisions. In simple terms, market research allows businesses to find out what customers want. There are a number of reasons why businesses invest in market research.

1 To identify target markets

Most products are only likely to be purchased by particular groups of customers: the market of young working class males, for example, is very different to that of middle-aged, wealthy couples. Market research can assist a firm in identifying which segments of the market are most likely to buy its products.

It is vital for a business to know who its customers are. This allows the business to:

■ design products to best meet the needs of these customers

■ target advertising and special offers at these groups

■ conduct further in-depth research with specific market segments to uncover their needs as fully as possible.

In 2001, Bratz fashion dolls were released in the UK. Designed by Isaac Larian, an Iranian who has settled in the USA, Bratz dolls are aimed at a target market of girls aged between seven and 12. Having such a clear target market makes it easy in some ways to research the market for the dolls. MGA Entertainment, which owns the Bratz brand, researches this market carefully. The company finds out the views of more than 900 girls across the USA before launching new products.

Bratz is a marketing success story. By 2004, Bratz dolls had recorded over 80 million sales globally. In the same year, Bratz overtook Barbie as the best-selling doll in the UK, achieving a 130 per cent increase in sales compared with the previous year. The dolls sell for an average price of £22.

stopandthink

Many Bratz dolls are bought by adults for children, yet the children are the consumers of the product. How might MGA Entertainment advertise its Bratz dolls when they are purchased and used by different target groups? What problems do you think the company might experience in attempting to discover the views of girls aged between seven and 12?

2 To find out about the market for a product

Businesses need to know what is happening in the market. To be able to plan its product and marketing effectively, a business needs to address three key questions.

123

Topic 4 Why businesses carry out market research

What is the size of the market?

In the UK, the fashion doll market is worth approximately £100 million each year. This is the total value of sales achieved by all businesses selling fashion dolls in the UK. Another way of measuring the size of the market is to consider the volume (or number) of sales made by all businesses selling fashion dolls. In 2003, about five million fashion dolls were sold in the UK.

What is the structure of the market?

This means discovering the number and size of businesses that make up a market. Are there, for example, a few large firms, or many small firms, or a mixture of large and small firms? If a business is in competition with large firms, it may decide to avoid competing on price terms as larger firms may be able to produce their products more cheaply. In the UK, there are three major companies selling fashion dolls: MGA Entertainment (Bratz dolls), Mattel (Barbie) and Robert Tonner Dolls.

Is the market growing or shrinking?

Market research can reveal what is happening to a market over time. A firm may feel more confident about entering a market which is growing, as it is easier to win sales when some customers are not yet loyal to particular brands. The market for fashion dolls in the UK has grown recently.

stop and think

Sales of real ales in the UK are declining. How might market research help a brewery trying to adapt to these market conditions?

3 To discover information about a business's competitors

Market research can provide businesses with information about the number of competitors they may face in a particular market as well as more detailed information about the products that these firms sell. Businesses may also use market research to discover the strengths and weaknesses of competitors and their products as well as to identify where a gap may exist in the market.

Before Isaac Larian launched his Bratz dolls, he researched the fashion doll market carefully. He would have paid considerable attention to the market leader. This was the Barbie doll. Produced by Mattel, Barbie was first sold in 1959. Larian thought that Barbie was outdated and there was room in the market for a new type of doll. Larian's idea was to introduce a range of more contemporary dolls with the slogan: the girls with a passion for fashion.

Knowledge summary

- Market research is the systematic collection and analysis of data to enable a business to take better quality marketing decisions.

- Market-oriented businesses design products to meet the needs of their customers. They research these needs carefully.

- Businesses research markets to discover information about the target groups who will purchase their products.

- Market research can also uncover details about the market, such as its size and whether it is growing.

- Market research can be a valuable source of information about competitors.

quick questions

1 Club 18–30 and 2wentys (a brand of First Choice holidays) aim to sell their holidays to a particular segment of the market. How does this help them to carry out market research?

2 In September 2004, India's first low-cost airline, Air Deccan, began operating a service between Bangalore and Delhi. The company's fares are 30 per cent below those offered by its rivals on the same route. Why would market research have been an essential part of Air Deccan's planning?

3 The Smart car is a tiny two-seater produced by DaimlerChrysler. In 2006, the company is planning to launch the Smart car in the giant US market. What information on the US market would the company want to collect through market research before planning its marketing activities?

In the second quarter of 2004, sales of mobile phone handsets throughout the world rose by 35 per cent compared with the same three months in 2003. All regions of the world saw rising demand, and total sales reached 156 million handsets. The increase in sales was highest in emerging markets such as South America. As at August 2004, Nokia's share of the mobile phone handset market had fallen to 29.7 per cent, while the market shares of Motorola and Samsung had risen to 15.8 per cent and 12.1 per cent respectively (see Figure 3.7 for 2003 figures).

Figure 3.6: Forecast of mobile phone service subscribers, selected countries, (figures in millions)

Subscribers	2001	2005	2010
UK	45.7	50.2	50.9
US	125.6	181.7	226.8
Brazil	27.8	53.9	76.7
Poland	9.6	18.6	23.5
China	133.9	326.1	575.1

Source: Baskerville

Working as part of a group, use the statistics in Figures 3.6 and 3.7 and any up-to-date information you can obtain from the internet (you may want to look at www.mobileisgood.com/statistics), to write a report that addresses these issues.

A Why Nokia should spend money on market research.

B Current and expected trends in the global market for mobile phone handsets.

C How the data presented in Figures 3.6 and 3.7, and the information gained from your own research might help the management team at Nokia plan its future marketing activities.

Figure 3.7: Market share of mobile phone handset market

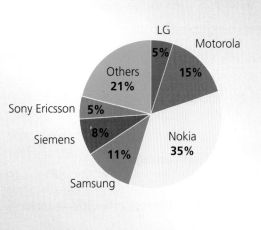

Source: www.mobileisgood.com/statistics

Topic 5 How businesses carry out market research

Setting the scene: primary and secondary market research

There are two main ways of carrying out market research. These are primary research and secondary research, and Figure 3.8 shows the advantages and disadvantages of each approach.

Primary research entails direct contact with potential customers within a target market to gather information about their precise needs. It may involve gathering data through interviews or questionnaires and often businesses use a market research agency to act on the their behalf.

Secondary research, sometimes called desk research, involves the use of data that already exists in reference books, government reports and, increasingly, from sources on the internet.

Figure 3.8: The advantages and disadvantages of primary and secondary research

	Primary research	Secondary research
Advantages	■ Provides up-to-date information on the target market ■ Meets the information needs of the business exactly ■ Helps businesses to under customers' behaviour	■ Can be undertaken quickly allowing earlier decisions ■ Is often a relatively cheap form of market research ■ Can provide information on an entire market including overseas customers
Disadvantages	■ Can be time consuming to collect and analyse data ■ Can be an expensive form of market research ■ May produce biased results if research is not carefully planned with clear objectives	■ The information may be outdated and of limited value ■ Secondary data may not meet the precise needs of the business ■ Some business reports containing secondary data are expensive (£5000 per report).

In 2004, Sainsbury, one of the UK's leading supermarket chains, conducted market research into demand for organic products. The organic market is growing twice as quickly as that for ordinary groceries and is set to become more important in the future. Sainsbury wanted to know more about this market. The company chose to use primary market research methods as it wanted in-depth information about the reasons why consumers are increasingly buying organic fruit and vegetables.

Explain why it would not have been appropriate for Sainsbury to use secondary research to investigate the market for organic foodstuffs.

Types of market research

Before it undertakes market research, a business needs to consider which type of research is likely to provide the most cost-effective means of producing the answers it requires.

1 Primary market research

Primary market research is the gathering of information directly from customers within the target market. This can be carried out in a number of ways.

Surveys

One way of finding out more about customers' wants and needs is to ask them directly through a survey. Surveys may be conducted through face-to-face interviews using a questionnaire, often in the high street or a shop, or carried out by telephone or post. Surveys are a very common form of primary research.

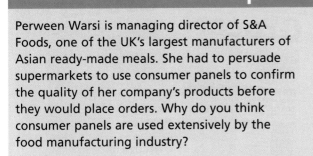

stopandthink

Why might a firm decide to use a postal survey to investigate a particular market, rather than relying on street interviews? In what circumstances might a street interview be more appropriate?

Observation

Businesses can learn much by watching consumers in different situations. Observation can provide market researchers with information on how consumers react to in-store displays, prices or the location of products. Supermarkets make considerable use of observation as a research technique.

Focus groups

In focus groups, researchers bring together a small number of consumers to ask them detailed questions about products. Focus groups are frequently used to discover consumers' attitudes to new products and can provide in-depth information about consumers' habits and opinions.

Consumer panels

Similar to focus groups, consumer panels comprise a number of people from the target market who meet regularly to provide a business with market research data. They are frequently involved in testing new products.

Test marketing

An expensive form of market research, test marketing involves trialling a new product on a part of the market to discover consumers' views prior to a full-scale launch. Often products are tested in one television region, supported by advertising, before a decision is taken on a national launch.

stopandthin

Perween Warsi is managing director of S&A Foods, one of the UK's largest manufacturers of Asian ready-made meals. She had to persuade supermarkets to use consumer panels to confirm the quality of her company's products before they would place orders. Why do you think consumer panels are used extensively by the food manufacturing industry?

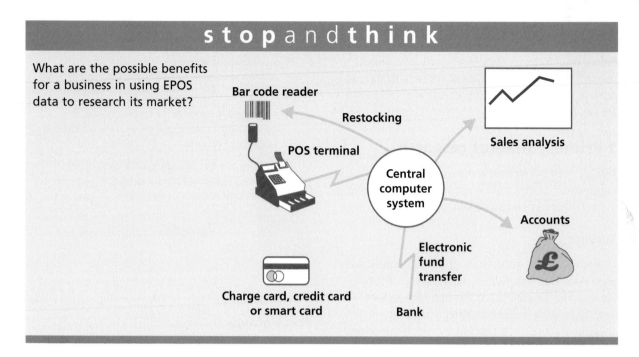

What are the possible benefits for a business in using EPOS data to research its market?

(Diagram labels: Bar code reader, Restocking, Sales analysis, POS terminal, Central computer system, Accounts, Charge card, credit card or smart card, Electronic fund transfer, Bank)

Trade audits

Trade audits are surveys of wholesalers and retailers to gain up-to-date information on consumers' buying habits. Trade audits are usually compiled using electronic point of sale (EPOS) data. EPOS systems collect information about retail transactions from the electronics tills used in supermarkets and many shops. This data is then collated and analysed as part of the trade audit.

2 Secondary market research

Secondary market research relies on information from already published data. This secondary data can be obtained from a variety of sources.

Government statistics

The government and its agencies, such as the Department of Trade and Industry, produce vast amounts of detailed information that can be useful

for businesses. Key publications include the *Annual Abstract of Statistics* and *Social Trends*.

Trade journals

Trade journals contain detailed information on developments in the specific industries that they cover. For example, magazines such as *Construction News* and *The Grocer* regularly feature information on firms in the respective industries that they report on as well as consumer behaviour in those industries.

Commercial research reports

Several companies publish research reports that contain information on market size (by volume and value), the market share held by leading businesses, recent trends in the market, forecasts of future sales and market segments. These research reports are very expensive, but some can be found in larger libraries. Mintel and Keynotes are two of the best-known publishers of market intelligence reports.

What sort of businesses might use *The Grocer* as a source of secondary data? Why might this be a popular source of market research information?

stop and think

One of Mintel's reports revealed that champagne sales in the UK rose by 25 per cent between 2002 and 2004. Champagne consumption is forecast to rise further by 2007. Explain why this might be important information for supermarkets such as Tesco and Waitrose.

The media

Newspapers regularly run articles containing a wealth of useful market information. *The Economist* and the *Financial Times* both publish regular special reports looking at particular markets or countries and these contain valuable data. For example, in September 2004 the *Financial Times* published a special report on the global chemical industry detailing worldwide developments in the sector as well as providing forecasts of future production and sales.

Knowledge summary

■ **Primary market research gathers new data, while secondary market research uses information previously compiled for other purposes.**

■ **Primary data can be more expensive to collect, but is usually more focused and up to date than secondary research data.**

■ **Primary data is collected through direct contact with customers, either through written questionnaires or telephone surveys or by meeting with small groups of consumers.**

■ **Secondary data can be gleaned from government sources, from the press and from reports written by specialist market intelligence businesses.**

The business's own data

Most businesses have data on their customers and sales patterns over recent years. Developments in information technology have allowed businesses to collect and analyse vast amounts of information using techniques such as customer loyalty cards. Loyalty cards and other methods of capturing sales data can provide businesses with detailed information on customers and the types of products that they buy (*see pages 224–227*).

quick questions

1 Read these scenarios and then identify an appropriate method of market research for each scenario. In each case, you should justify your choice.

■ Nestlé is considering launching a new chocolate bar.
■ An entrepreneur wants to investigate the market for a new DVD and computer games rental shop in a small town near Norwich.
■ Asda wants to research the impact of using new packaging on some of its own-brand products.
■ A high street clothing store wants ongoing information about consumers' spending patterns and the types of consumers purchasing its products.
■ A UK-based brewer is contemplating supplying beer to the eastern European market.

2 Adam Lawrence is planning to start a business as a mobile car mechanic in his home town. He does not have much capital to start up his business and has approached his bank for a loan. The bank has asked him to carry out some market research. Write him a business letter explaining the methods of market research that are available to him.

3 Explain why market research is a vital activity for a market-oriented business.

Britain's leading retailer, Tesco, is seeking to expand its activities in the UK. The company has three main options.

- It can open more stores on similar lines to its current supermarkets, selling groceries, clothing, etc.

- It can move into new areas of business, possibly selling other types of products.

- It can move into overseas markets and try and establish the Tesco brand abroad.

Look at the data in Figures 3.9–3.12 and research any terms with which you are unfamiliar. You will need to analyse this data to complete the tasks.

Figure 3.9: Household expenditure, UK

Indices (1971 = 100)	'71	'81	'91	'01	'02	£ billion (current prices) 2002
Housing, water and fuel	100	117	138	152	154	118.4
Transport	100	128	181	242	251	98.3
Recreation and culture	100	161	283	545	570	79.5
Restaurants and hotels	100	126	167	194	199	76.6
Food and non-alcoholic drink	100	105	117	137	138	60.8
Household goods and services	100	117	160	268	296	43.3
Clothing and footwear	100	120	187	340	371	37.8
Alcohol and tobacco	100	99	92	89	91	26.3
Communication	100	190	306	790	828	15.0
Health	100	125	182	175	179	10.1
Education	100	160	199	250	218	8.4
Miscellaneous	100	119	230	280	290	82.0
Less expenditure by foreign tourists, etc.	100	152	187	210	219	-14.3
Household expenditure abroad	100	193	298	669	715	24.6
All household expenditure	100	122	167	227	235	666.9

Source: Office for National Statistics

Figure 3.10: Projected UK population change, 2002–201

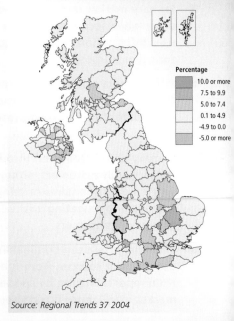

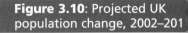

Percentage
- 10.0 or more
- 7.5 to 9.9
- 5.0 to 7.4
- 0.1 to 4.9
- -4.9 to 0.0
- -5.0 or more

Source: Regional Trends 37 2004

A Advise Tesco's managers on:

which regions of the UK might be favoured for new supermarkets

what other products might Tesco consider selling

which other UK markets Tesco might consider entering.

B How useful is the data in Figures 3.9–3.12 to Tesco's strategic planners? What weaknesses might it have, and what other data would be useful to help with strategic planning at Tesco?

Figure 3.11: Households by size, Great Britain

	Precentages				
	1971	1981	1991	2001	2003
One person	18	22	27	29	29
Two people	32	32	34	35	35
Three people	19	17	16	16	15
Four people	17	18	16	14	14
Five people	8	7	5	5	5
Six or more people	6	4	2	2	2
All households (=100%) (millions)	18.6	20.2	22.4	24.2	24.5
Average household size (number of people)	2.9	2.7	2.5	2.4	2.4

Source: Census, Labour Force Survey, Office for National Statistics

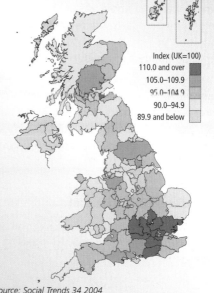

Figure 3.12: Household disposable income per head, by area, 1997–1999

Index (UK=100)
110.0 and over
105.0–109.9
95.0–104.9
90.0–94.9
89.9 and below

Source: Social Trends 34 2004

The value of market research

Setting the scene: sampling

Few businesses can collect information from all their potential customers. This would be too expensive and time-consuming. Therefore if businesses want to get information about the needs and wants of their customers, they need to select a sample which is representative of the whole target market (called the population).

Sampling allows businesses to find out about the views of customers without having to question everyone. At the heart of sampling is a trade-off between cost and accuracy. A larger sample is more likely to represent the views of all consumers more accurately. However, conducting market research on a small sample is likely be cheaper.

Businesses can use a number of techniques for sampling.

- **Random sampling** means that each customer in the target population has an equal chance of being investigated. This is an appropriate approach when a business is researching a product which is consumed by a large target population.

- **Stratified random sampling** is used when a business is interested in the opinions of a particular market segment. If, for example, a business wants to know about the opinions of women in their 40s, it will restrict the target population to women aged 40–49 and then sample randomly from within that group.

- **Quota sampling** splits the population into a number of groups (or segments), each having common characteristics. For example, a business might want to find out the views of players of a new computer game. The research might

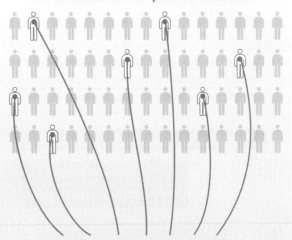

Figure 3.13: The sampling process

The whole market: all possible customers

Sampling selects a small group to represent the views of all customers

want to discover the opinions of different types of players; perhaps the business wants to know if the game has a particular appeal for different ages groups or for men and women. So the overall population of players will be split into several subsections. Researchers will be asked to contact a certain number of people in each subgroup.

- **Convenience sampling** is frequently used by entrepreneurs who have limited funds to finance research. Convenience sampling restricts the survey to those consumers that can be contacted easily. This type of research is susceptible to sampling bias.

KEY TERMS

Market research is the systematic collection and analysis of data to enable a business to make better marketing decisions.

Qualitative data is non-numerical data. For example, market researchers obtain qualitative data on the in-depth attitudes and opinions of consumers.

Quantitative data is numerical data. Businesses want quantitative data about the size of markets, the number of potential customers for their products, etc.

Sampling is the process of selecting a representative group of consumers from a larger population.

Sampling bias occurs when the results gained from the sample do not accurately reflect the views (or attributes) of the larger population.

Qualitative and quantitative research

Qualitative market research uncovers the reasons behind customers' purchasing decisions. In contrast, quantitative market research is designed to collect information on customers that can be analysed statistically and expressed in a numerical form.

Figure 3.14: The difference between qualitative and quantitative research

	Qualitative market research	Quantitative market research
Explanation	This type of research asks the question "why". It is designed to find out why customers prefer certain products, why they make particular choices..	This form of market research obtains numerical information about customers' intentions and helps with sales forecasts and pricing decisions.
How it is gathered	The views of small groups of consumers are researched using focus groups and consumer panels. Detailed information is gathered.	The opinions of large numbers of potential customers are sought using techniques such as questionnaires, telephone surveys and street interviews.
Typical questions	■ Why do you prefer Cadbury's Dairy Milk to rival products? ■ What factors influence your choice when purchasing a new pair of jeans? ■ Does the packaging of food products affect your purchasing decisions? If so, why?	■ How many bottles of wine do you buy each month? ■ Which of the following Virgin brands do you recognise (Virgin Mobile, Virgin Rail, etc.)? ■ What is the most you would be prepared to pay for a night's hotel accommodation in central London?
Benefits	■ Gives detailed information, helping firms to design products to meet consumers' needs precisely. ■ May lead to ideas for new products or improvements to existing ones.	■ Can provide information about conditions in a range of different markets. ■ May help to identify new target markets.

133

Topic 6 The value of market research

The uses and limitations of market research

Market research costs money, and it is not practicable to commission research to support every decision that a business needs to make. A business has to make a judgement about whether market research would be of value in each case. For example, in 2004 Marks & Spencer launched a range of chilled meals based on recipes from several Eastern European countries to mark their entry into the European Union. The company would not have taken this decision without some research into the potential market for the new product range. In contrast, it would not normally require research before taking a decision to reduce its prices for a short period of time.

Increasingly, however, it is unusual for businesses to take any significant decisions without using market research data. In part, this is because so much market research data is now available to managers. Technology has made it so much simpler to collect and analyse information on consumers. Commercial radio stations use new technology to collect detailed information on audience figures, finding out which programmes people listen to and for how long. This data is used by the radio stations to help them sell advertising. Radio stations can tell potential advertisers what kind of people listen to their programmes, allowing companies to target their radio advertising more effectively.

The internet has also made it simpler and cheaper for businesses to collect information on customers and to find out more about their purchasing habits. For example, Smile, the Co-operative Bank's internet banking enterprise, regularly runs an online survey to get information from customers about their views on the bank's financial services.

Managers know that market research has the potential to be of great value, but the research only serves its purpose if it accurately reflects the views of customers and the state of the market. A number of factors contribute to the accuracy, and therefore the value of, market research.

- **The size of the sample**
  It is not possible for market research to be 100 per cent accurate. To achieve total accuracy, everyone in the target market (or population) would have to be questioned. Most market research is carried out with the objective of achieving 95 per cent accuracy. In other words, the results of the market research will be correct 19 times out of 20. This level of accuracy is known as a 95 per cent confidence level. Larger samples are more likely to provide higher confidence levels.

- **The diversity of the market**
  If businesses are selling to a very diverse market, it can be difficult to obtain accurate market research. The target market may have to be divided into several subgroups. Complex systems of quota sampling may be required in such circumstances, and larger samples may be needed.

- **Lack of bias in the questions**
  It is remarkably difficult to write a series of questions that are completely unbiased and do not mislead the person being questioned in some way. Some questions may lead the interviewees towards a particular answer; some may encourage interviewees to provide the answers that they think the interview wants to receive. There is a danger that a badly constructed market research exercise simply provides a business with the answers it expects rather than reveals the true opinions of consumers.

- **The volatility of the market**
  Some markets experience rapid change. For example, the fashion clothing and computer software markets both experience a quick turnaround of products. Gaining accurate data on consumers' preferences can be difficult in markets in which there is a fast rate of change. Perversely, it is often more important for businesses to collect market research data in this type of market if they are to keep informed about consumers' tastes and preferences.

Knowledge summary

- Businesses cannot consult every potential customer before they make marketing decisions. For this reason, they carry out market research on a sample of people from their target markets.

- There are a number of ways in which a business can construct samples to obtain the views of its customers.

- Businesses collect qualitative and quantitative information on their customers and the markets in which they trade.

- Market research is vital when businesses are taking major marketing decisions, but the results should be treated with caution.

quick **questions**

1 Look at these four scenarios in which companies are faced with a marketing decision. For each scenario, decide whether qualitative or quantitative market research would be the best way of getting the information to help make an informed decision. In each case, explain your choice.

(a) The management team of a company producing soft drinks is experimenting with new flavours and bottle designs.
(b) A pet food company wants to forecast future sales of a well-known brand.
(c) A high street bank wants to know if it would be profitable to continue to offer travel insurance to its customers.
(d) British Bakeries (the company that makes Hovis) is experimenting with new types of soft brown bread and wonders which recipes to continue developing.

2 (a) List four pieces of information that a retailer such as Burger King might expect to get through market research.
(b) Why might Burger King treat market research results with caution?

3 Why might market research be vital for an entrepreneur planning to open a vegetarian café in a town centre location?

data **interpretation**
The value of market research for Uniq plc

Ian Martin, the former chairman of Unigate plc (now called Uniq), believes in the value of market research but only to a certain extent. A highly experienced senior business manager, Ian Martin says that he would not take a major decision without market research data but would not take a decision solely on the basis of market research.

Uniq plc, Ian Martin's former company, sells a range of chilled food products throughout Europe. The company sells to other businesses as well as to final consumers. The company manufactures its products in the UK, France, Germany, Poland, Denmark, the Netherlands, Belgium and Spain.

To complete the set tasks, you should visit Uniq's website (www.uniqplc.com) and you may also want to find out recent news relating to the company using the BBC News website (news.bbc.co.uk) and other sources.

A Find out some more about Uniq. What products does it sell? Where does it sell its products? Who are its consumers? Which market segments does it operate in? What are the company's objectives (and marketing objectives)?

B Why is market research of value to a company like Uniq? How does it help the managers of this company?

C Discuss why Uniq's board of directors should treat market research results with caution?

The marketing mix: product and price

Setting the scene: the product life cycle

All products have a finite lifespan. Some last for many years; Cadbury's Dairy Milk was launched in 1905 and is still going strong. Other products, especially those in the fashion, entertainment and technology industries often only have a short lifespan. The pop group Hear'Say lasted for about two years.

As Figure 3.15 shows products pass through four stages during their life cycles.

- **Introduction**
  Most new ideas for products never actually reach the market. Marketing plays a key role in determining which ideas actually get turned into products. Market research helps a business to determine the specification, look and packaging of any new product which is introduced to the market. During the introduction stage, the company will be using marketing to raise both consumer and retailer awareness of the product. Unless retailers agree to stock the product, and give it some exposure in their stores, it is unlikely to succeed. Heavy expenditure will be required to promote the product during its introduction stage. For example, Sony has committed considerable resources to launch its new PlayStation Portable (PSP) games console.

- **Growth**
  If the product is accepted by customers, sales and revenue should begin to rise. The results of ongoing market research will guide managers on the marketing actions that are necessary. Customers will become more aware of the product and marketing may be used to extend product awareness to new target markets. Apple's iPod is a growth product. In a three month period in 2004, Apple sold more than two million iPods, an increase of 150 per cent on the previous quarter. With competitors such as Sony introducing rival products, Apple will have to work hard to maintain this level of sales growth, and it has already responded by launching a new iPod model promising a larger memory and longer battery life.

- **Maturity**
  During this stage, sales level off and the product should be profitable. Marketing activities may concentrate on reminder advertising and producing improved versions of the product to continue attracting new customers. Coca-Cola is a classic mature product, which has seen relatively steady sales over a long period of time. Coca-Cola uses a combination of advertising and sponsorship of high-profile events and sports competitions to maintain brand awareness.

- **Decline**
  Eventually sales will decline for a product. Businesses may decide to try and stimulate sales for a little longer by producing revamped versions of the product or by reducing prices. At some point, a business will have to decide to stop selling the product. For example, few businesses now produce pipes and pipe tobacco; this market is in a definite decline. Well-managed businesses introduce new products long before their established ones reach the decline stage of the product life cycle.

KEY TERMS

The **marketing mix** is the four marketing tools (product, price, promotion and place) used by businesses to inflence consumers' buying decisions.

Product is a general term for the goods and services supplied by a business.

Price is the amount charged by a business for its goods or services.

Place is another term for distribution. It covers the range of activities necessary to ensure that goods and services are available to customers.

Promotion is a series of marketing activities designed to make consumers aware of products and to persuade them to buy those products.

Market share is the percentage of total sales in a market achieved by one business.

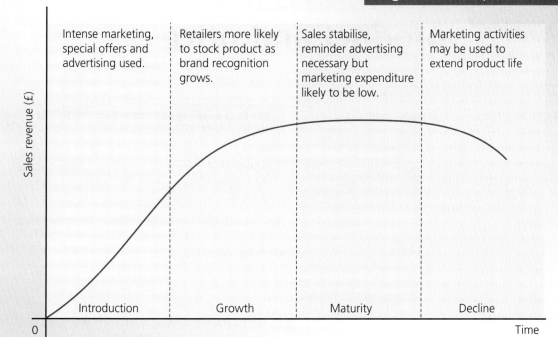

Figure 3.15: The product life cycle

Intense marketing, special offers and advertising used.

Retailers more likely to stock product as brand recognition grows.

Sales stabilise, reminder advertising necessary but marketing expenditure likely to be low.

Marketing activities may be used to extend product life

Sales revenue (£)

Introduction | Growth | Maturity | Decline

0

Time

The marketing mix

The marketing mix refers to the main variables comprising a firm's marketing strategy. The four main elements of the mix are:

- product (including the range of products, their design and pack sizes)

- price (pricing methods and tactics)

- promotion (advertising, sponsorship of sports and cultural events)

- place (the way product is distributed to the consumer, the choice of retail outlets).

stop and think

The product life cycle goes through four stages: introduction, growth, maturity, decline. Identify two examples of well-known brands in each of these stages.

These elements are sometimes referred to as the four Ps. Some writers identify more than four Ps, including factors such as packaging and people. However, we shall concentrate on the four main elements of the mix: product, price, promotion and place. In this section, you will consider product and price. The other two Ps, promotion and place, are dealt with in Topic 8.

Product

This term product covers services (health care, for example) as well as goods, such as cars and houses. Many marketing managers believe that the product is the most important element of the marketing mix.

A successful product needs a number of features. Its design must appeal to the consumer. The needs of the customer should have been identified through market research. Businesses look to include features that appeal to customers, offering products that are:

- fashionable

- safe

- reliable

- durable

- convenient.

137

Topic 7 The marketing mix: product and price

A business should consider offering a range of products to meet the needs of different consumers. For example, Ford, the global car manufacturer, produces cars for large families (the Galaxy), for women drivers (the Ka), for those who love fast cars (the Probe) and for those running small businesses (the Transit van).

Firms should try to develop strong product brands. The Virgin group has been very successful at building its brand. Richard Branson's company has developed a range of products that are offered through the Virgin brand, including air and rail travel, mobile phones, soft drinks, music and financial services. Launching a new product under a familiar brand name is less risky: consumers recognise the brand and may identify it with certain qualities such as being fashionable.

Price

Price is the amount charged by a business for its goods or services. Businesses can employ two broad strategies when deciding what price to charge for their products.

■ **Price penetration**
Businesses using a price penetration strategy charge low prices. By charging low prices in comparison to their competitors, businesses aim to increase sales and perhaps win greater market share. This strategy is frequently used by businesses that are new to a particular market. For example, Stelios Haji-Ioannou, the founder of

easyJet, announced in November 2003 that he was to launch a coach company to rival National Express. His easyBus company is charging low prices to win customers from rivals. Price penetration is more effective if the market is price sensitive, so that a lower price generates significantly higher sales.

■ **Price skimming**
Price skimming entails charging a high price to gain the maximum profit possible on each sale. This pricing strategy is often used by businesses selling new products which have few rivals or for products which are highly fashionable or are technologically superior to the competition. This can be a risky strategy as competitors can enter the market quite quickly with lower prices and win market share.

Having decided upon a strategy, businesses can employ a number of short-term tactics to try and boost sales. Some businesses use loss leaders. This involves lowering the prices of a number of key products to attract customers to their stores. Businesses hope that customers will buy products that provide them with better profit margins as well as purchasing the loss leaders. This tactic is often used by supermarkets such as Asda. Other businesses use psychological pricing: they market products at prices intended to make customers think that they are a bargain or that they are within their price range. For example, by pricing a product at £49.99 instead of £50, a business encourages customers to think that it is "less than £50".

Knowledge summary

■ The marketing mix describes the decisions a business takes about the product, its price, how it is promoted and how it will be distributed and sold.

■ All products pass through a life cycle of four stages. Marketing activities are very different in each stage of a product's life cycle.

■ Product is arguably the most important element of the marketing mix. Firms seek to produce well-designed products to meet consumers' needs as fully as possible.

quick questions

1 Many companies have launched rivals to Apple's hugely successful iPod. What features would a rival product need to give it a good chance of being successful?

2 Explain why the prices of flat screen digital televisions were very high when the products were first launched but have fallen over time.

3 Ryanair has successfully used a strategy of price penetration. In 2003, Ryanair's profits exceeded £100 million. How can it generate such high profits? How might the policy of price penetration affect the service offered by Ryanair?

data interpretation
The games console market

Games are big business. Hit games like Grand Theft Auto sell millions of copies. There are three big players competing to sell games consoles, the platforms on which many games are played. These are Sony, with its PlayStation console, Nintendo and Microsoft, with the Xbox. Figure 3.16 shows the actual and forecast revenue earned by Sony from sales of PlayStation in 2002/7, and Figure 3.17 the actual and forecast shipments of games consoles over the same period.

Figure 3.16: PlayStation revenue forecast ($million)

	2002	2003	2004	2005	2006	2007
PlayStation 1	350	216	83	0	0	0
PlayStation 2	5642	4236	2982	1609	1103	476
PlayStation 3	0	0	0	2275	4095	5400

Source: In-Stat/MDR

A Estimate the likely sales revenue from the three PlayStation products in 2008. Justify your answer.

B What evidence is there that Sony has managed its product development well?

C PlayStation faces tough competition from Nintendo and Microsoft's Xbox. Using all the evidence available to you:

(a) explain the pricing policy that Sony should adopt for its PlayStation 3

(b) discuss the other marketing activities that Sony might undertake in the next three years in relation to its PlayStation products.

Figure 3.17: Games console shipment forecast (units in millions)

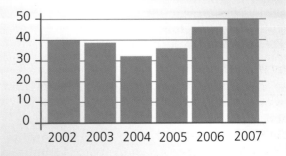

Source: In-Stat/MDR

Topic 8 | The marketing mix: promotion and place

Setting the scene: Dell's marketing mix

Michael Dell founded the Dell company in 1984 while he was still a student. He built his company by making and supplying computers directly to customers rather than through shops. Dell has been highly successful over recent years. The company's growth has been astonishing, with sales increasing from £700 million in 1992 to more than £30 billion in 2003. The company made profits in excess of £1 billion during the first six months of the 2004/5 financial year. This was 29 per cent higher than in the previous year.

Dell has employed a highly individual marketing mix to achieve higher profits than all of its rivals in the computing industry. The company has adapted this mix to meet the changing demands of the businesses and individuals who buy its products across the globe.

- **Product** – Dell has broadened its product range from computers to include printers, cash registers and a digital music player to rival Apple's iPod.

- **Place** – Dell distributes its products directly to consumers. Customers can order its products from Dell's website or from its call centres.

- **Price** – Since 2003, Dell has pursued a policy of price cutting at every opportunity. In August 2003, the company announced that it was slashing its prices by up to 22 per cent.

- **Promotion** – Because Dell's products are not available in shops, the company invests heavily in placing inserts into magazines and newspapers. These leaflets promote its products and special offers, and they tell customers how they can order products through Dell's website and customer service call centres.

This combination of the four Ps has been highly successful for Dell. Not only has the company achieved high sales growth, but it has also gained an increased share of the fiercely competitive computer market. You can find out more about Dell by visiting its website (www.dell.com).

One of the reasons for Dell's success has been its policy of selling its computers direct to customers rather than through retail outlets. What do you think are the advantages of this policy for Dell and what are the benefits for customers?

KEY TERMS

The **marketing mix** is the four marketing tools (price, promotion, product and place) used by businesses to inflence consumers' buying decisions.

Place is another term for distribution. It covers the range of activities necessary to ensure that goods and services are available to customers.

Promotion is a series of marketing activities designed to make consumers aware of products and to persuade them to buy those products.

Advertising is a means by which businesses pay for communication with actual and potential customers through newspapers, television, radio, the internet and other media.

A **brand** is a name, symbol, sign or design used by a business to differentiate its products from those produced by its competitors.

Promotion

Promotion is a series of marketing activities designed to make consumers aware of products. The ultimate aim, of course, is to persuade them to buy those products. Promotion is an important part of the marketing mix and businesses can use a variety of different types of promotion.

1 Advertising

Advertising is a means by which businesses pay for communication with actual and potential customers through newspapers, television, radio, the internet and other media. It can be expensive but advertising is often highly successful in inflencing consumers' purchasing decisions.

Advertising can be informative, by setting out to increase consumer awareness of a product. This type of advertising is based on facts rather than images. On the other hand, persuasive advertising attempts to convince consumers to purchase a particular product. Persuasive advertising aims to persuade that the product being advertised is better than the competition.

2 Branding

A brand is a sign, symbol, design or name used to distinguish a product or business from its competitors. Many businesses, and especially larger ones, attempt to create a strong image for a product, group of products or the entire business by developing a recognisable brand. Creating a successful brand can help boost sales and profits by encouraging customers to make repeat purchases. This is called brand loyalty.

s t o p a n d **t h i n k**

What benefits has the Virgin group received from its strong brand image? What other types of promotion has Richard Branson employed to publicise the Virgin group?

3 Merchandising

The term merchandising covers a range of tactics used by businesses at the point of sale (the location at which products are actually purchased) to achieve higher sales figures.

Merchandising tactics include:

- offering retailers special display stands to encourage them to place the business's products in a more prominent position within stores
- ensuring that the product is available at extra locations (in sufficient quantities) during periods of high demand
- supplying point-of-sale advertisements to display in retail outlets.

Merchandising can be important when:

- consumers make decisions at the point of sale
- competitors make extensive use of merchandising
- a variety of rival products are on display in stores
- rival products have only minor differences.

4 Public relations

Public relations are activities carried out by businesses with the intention of improving their standing in the eyes of consumers and other interested groups. Modern businesses seek positive publicity and most larger organisations have their own public relations departments. Businesses may engage in a variety of public relations exercises. These include:

- making donations to charities – for example, McDonald's collects small change from customers to give to a range of charities
- sponsoring sporting and cultural activities – for example, Cadbury Schweppes plc gains publicity by sponsoring ITV's famous soap *Coronation Street*
- allowing visits to the business by members of the public – for example, many car manufacturers allow the public to visit their factories.

Public relations can be a very expensive form of promotion and it can be difficult for businesses to assess the effect of public relations on sales.

s t o p a n d **t h i n k**

Lotus, the sports car manufacturer, allows the public to visit its factory in Norfolk. This takes up some of the employees' time and may disrupt production. Why is this an important part of Lotus's marketing mix? Why might this activity be more important to Lotus than to a larger car manufacturer such as Ford?

Place

Place is another term for distribution. It covers the range of activities necessary to ensure that goods and services are available to customers. Deciding on the right place involves businesses in taking a range of decisions.

1 Selecting a distribution channel

Figure 3.18 summarises the options available to a business. When deciding whether to use the services of a wholesaler and retailers, a business needs to consider the most cost-effective way of getting its products and service to the final customers. It needs to consider whether it has the ability to supply large numbers of retailers or final customers with relatively small quantities of its products. It needs to look at the implications for its profit margins of each means of distribution.

The growth in use of the internet has encouraged even small businesses to sell products directly to consumers. It allows businesses to use websites to sell their products to what can be a global market. This can be a highly cost-effective means of reaching a wide target audience, but is not suitable for all businesses and all products. We look more fully at the use of websites in Unit 4 (*see pages 152–195*).

(see pages 152–195)

stop and think

A wholesaler buys products in bulk from manufacturers and breaks them up into smaller units to supply retailers. Why does the UK supermarket industry make little or no use of wholesalers?

2 Choosing the right outlets

Some manufacturers aim to persuade the maximum number of outlets to stock their products. For example, chocolate manufacturer Nestlé will achieve its desired high levels of sales if its products are stocked in as many supermarkets, garages, cinemas and newsagents as possible. This is an appropriate strategy because Nestlé's products are purchased by large numbers of people and many sales are impulse purchases; it makes sense for Nestlé to ensure that its products are available at any place where people might want something to eat.

Chocolate and other confectionery products are bought by a wide cross-section of the public. In contrast, some products are only purchased by a small minority of the population. These products are only available through limited, and often exclusive, outlets. Gucci, famous for making a range of luxury goods including clothes, handbags and sunglasses, restricts the number of outlets that can sell its goods. This is part of its strategy to position itself as an upmarket luxury brand, enabling the company to charge high prices for its products.

3 Getting the right mix

Place is the final element of the marketing mix. Businesses seek to design marketing mixes that are complementary and work together to benefit the business and to maximise sales. For example, Lidl promotes its supermarket chain to its target audience on the basis that it offers the lowest possible prices. Place is important to Lidl, and the company locates stores in areas where income levels are relatively low and its low-price foodstuffs are attractive to many local residents. Product is relatively unimportant within Lidl's marketing mix.

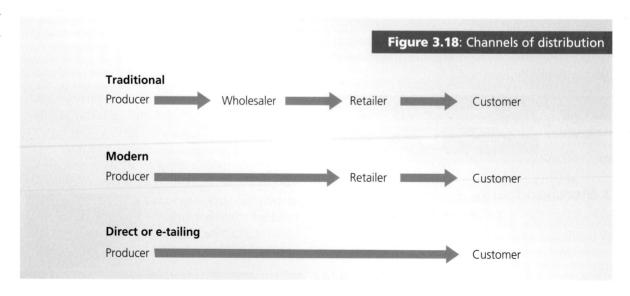

Figure 3.18: Channels of distribution

Traditional

Producer ➡ Wholesaler ➡ Retailer ➡ Customer

Modern

Producer ➡ Retailer ➡ Customer

Direct or e-tailing

Producer ➡ Customer

Knowledge summary

■ **Promotion is designed to increase consumer awareness of a product as well as to increase sales.**

■ **Methods of promotion include advertising, merchandising, public relations and branding.**

■ **Place is the means by which products are made available to consumers. This part of the marketing mix includes selection of outlets as well as channels of distribution.**

quick**questions**

1 Since 2002, most tobacco advertising has been banned in the UK. How might a tobacco company such as BAT adapt its marketing mix to overcome this development?

2 Explain why merchandising (part of promotion) and place are particularly important elements of the marketing mix for Mars, the confectionery manufacturer.

3 Paula Reeves is a watercolour artist, based in a rural part of Devon. Recently she has started selling her pictures through a website she designed herself. Draw up as list explaining the advantages and disadvantages to Paula of being able to sell her paintings via the internet.

data**interpretation**
Nokia sees mobile market shrink

The world's biggest mobile phone maker, Nokia, has seen its market share shrink in 2004. Its sales were down 5 per cent on 2003 to £4.4 billion. The Finnish firm said it estimated its market share in the May to June 2004 period was 31 per cent, down from 32 per cent in the first quarter of 2004 and 39 per cent a year ago.

Nokia has been cutting prices in order to remain competitive. "During the second quarter, we employed pricing selectively with certain products to stabilise our ... market share," said Jorma Ollila, chairman and CEO. Prices have been cut by up to 25 per cent on some phones.

Nokia also warned that profit margins would remain under pressure. The news came on the same day as rival Sony Ericsson posted a 34 per cent rise in second quarter profits.

Figure 3.19: Mobile phone manufacturers, global market share

Manufacturer	2000	2001	2002	2003	2004
Nokia	33.9	34.8	34.7	36.0	29.0
Motorola	12.7	14.8	15.5	14.1	15.4
Samsung	4.8	6.9	9.6	10.5	14.5

Source: www3.gartner.com

A Explain, with the aid of an example, what is meant by market share.

B Price is an important part of Nokia's marketing mix. Explain possible reasons why the company cut its prices selectively rather than cutting the prices of all its products.

C Nokia competes with other major manufacturers in the mobile phone handset market. Discuss how the company might design its marketing mix to compete effectively over the next few years.

The influences on the marketing mix

Setting the scene: the airline industry

The airline industry has changed radically in recent years. Two external factors – the threat of terrorism and the emergence of low-cost, no frills airlines – have radically reshaped the industry.

These external factors have been largely beyond the control of the established airlines. The threat of terrorism has become particularly acute following the hijacking and deliberate destruction of planes in New York and Washington on 11 September 2001. In the immediate aftermath of 9/11, air passenger numbers declined. Most airlines suffered, but those operating long-haul flights were particularly affected.

In the same period, the rise of easyJet, Ryanair and other low-cost airlines has taken market share on short-haul flights from established airlines such as British Airways and SAS (Scandinavian Airways). The combined result is that many of the world's best-known airlines have experienced falling sales and loss of profits.

The established airlines have responded in many ways. The airline industry has witnessed several mergers and takeovers, for example. However, a common reaction has been for the established airlines to adjust their marketing mixes to deal with these twin threats of terrorism and the low-cost airlines.

- **British Airways** has adjusted its prices on selected routes to compete with the low-cost airlines, while maintaining higher fares for other routes and market segments. This has led to the company cutting jobs and cancelling some routes to bring lower prices into effect.

- **Iberia Airlines** has lowered its prices and adjusted its product to compete with low-cost airlines (it does not serve food to economy class passengers). The airline's product has been altered further in response to the perceived threat of terrorism, but Iberia is not prepared to reveal the precise nature of these changes.

- **SAS**, the Scandinavian airline, has positioned its service at a different market. It is attempting to attract more business class passengers and it has raised its prices. It has reduced its capacity to carry passengers by 12 per cent as a consequence of its new marketing mix.

How has technological change affected the "place" for the airline industry? For airlines, place is how and where they sell flights to customers.

KEY TERMS

The **marketing mix** is the four marketing tools (product, price, promotion and place) used by businesses to influence consumers' buying decisions.

Market research is the systematic collection and analysis of data to enable a business to make better quality marketing decisions.

Factors affecting a business's marketing mix

All businesses have a marketing mix, whether they are aware of it or not: they offer products, they make these available at particular places for specific prices, and they choose whether to back the product with various kinds of promotional activity. Better managed businesses actively plan their marketing mix, and they take several factors into account in determining precise nature of the marketing mix for each product.

1 Corporate objectives

If a business's objective is growth, then its marketing mix is likely to place considerable emphasis on price in the marketing mix. A business needs to set very competitive prices to attract new customers, especially if it is operating in an established market.

Jeff Bezos, the founder and chief executive of Amazon, the internet bookshop, has publicly stated that his prime aim for the business is growth. He has pursued this objective relentlessly and Amazon's marketing mix has been distinctive. Key features of Amazon's marketing mix are:

- low prices – the company has reduced prices whenever possible, which has meant that it has struggled to make profits

- heavy promotion – Amazon is noted for offers such as free postage and tailored offers for customers based on their previous purchases

- extending the product range – Amazon sells a wide range of products, including not just new books but toys, CDs, wine and second-hand books.

2 Market research

Well-managed businesses use market research, and especially primary research results, to help shape their marketing mixes. Market research is commonly used to discover aspects of the mix that are important to consumers. If, for example, the research tells a business that low prices are important to customers in the market in it is operating, then it may opt to stress price competitiveness as a major element of the marketing mix.

Market research can also reveal new or unexploited target markets which the marketing mix can then be deployed to meet. In 2004, Mintel, the market research company, published a report showing that British women are less likely to use anti-wrinkle and anti-ageing creams than women in other western European countries. Only 36 per cent of British women used these creams, compared with about a half of French women and Spaniards, and two-thirds of Germans. Manufacturers are likely to use this information to plan marketing mixes that include promotional campaigns to encourage greater usage of anti-wrinkle and anti-ageing products by British women.

3 Internal constraints

Businesses need to consider the financial and practical implications of any marketing mix that they want to implement. Very few businesses are able to operate a marketing mix without first considering the costs involved. Typically, costs can limit a business's marketing mix in several ways.

- **Price** – a business may not be able to set a really competitive price and still make a profit. Obviously, if a business sets its prices too low then it would incur losses. Many of the older established airlines are struggling to compete on price terms with easyJet and Ryanair because they have higher costs. The established airlines have significantly more employees than their low-cost competitors and, perhaps inevitably, they have been shedding staff to cut costs so that they can introduce more flexible, competitive pricing policies.

- **The product** – some businesses are unable to develop the products they would like to sell because the research, development and production costs are too high. In this situation, a business might find that it could only recoup its costs by setting a price that would be too high for many consumers.

- **Promotion** – advertising, public relations and other promotional activities can be very expensive. Some businesses are able to run expensive promotional campaigns because they are able to afford the high costs involved. For example in 2004 McDonald's launched a campaign, fronted by Justin Timberlake, which allowed customers to download music. Many smaller businesses could not consider implementing this type of campaign because of the high costs required.

stop and think

In January 2004, British Airways announced that it was planning to cut costs by £300 million over the next two years. The move was expected to lead to 3000 job losses, though operational staff (such as cabin crew) were expected to be relatively unaffected, and the company was not planning to cut any routes. How might this publicity have affected British Airway's decisions on the other elements of its marketing mix?

4 External constraints

A range of factors outside the control of businesses also shapes their marketing mixes.

Legal factors

Perhaps the best example of legal constraints on the marketing mix is the restrictions placed around advertising some types of product. In the UK, tobacco advertising is banned in newspapers and magazines, on billboards and through direct mail. Some tobacco advertising is still permitted on the internet and at the point of sale (where tobacco product are bought).

Food is another area in which legislation is likely to be introduced to limit advertising. Health campaigners are calling for restrictions to be placed on adverts for fast food, on the grounds that it is contributing to the problem of obesity.

Environment and ecological factors

Many businesses have changed the design of their products to make them more environmentally friendly. For example, manufacturers have removed CFCs (chlorofluorocarbons) from aerosol sprays and other products, they are using more recyclable material in product packaging, and they are introducing more eco-friendly products such as new energy-efficient fridges and washing machines.

Political and economic factors

The marketing mix chosen by a business is likely to be affected by the state of the economy. Typically, firms reduce their prices during a recession when jobs are scarcer and incomes may be lower. They may also produce cheaper, basic products that are more likely to appeal to consumers during lean times. Conversely, in a boom a company might focus its marketing on more luxurious products and place less emphasis on keeping prices low.

Some businesses, particularly those that were formerly in the public sector, must operate within constraints imposed by the government. They must meet guidelines on pricing and product quality, which constrains their freedom to determine their marketing mix. For example, the water companies and electricity supply companies cannot raise prices beyond limits imposed by the government-appointed regulators for the respective industries. The Royal Mail has to operate under significant pressure to limit the cost of postal services and to ensure that remote rural areas still receive a top-quality service.

stop and think

Pilkington, the glass manufacturer, has developed a special coating for its glass that virtually removes any need for cleaning. This new glass should help to reduce the use of detergents which can be harmful to the environment. By improving its product through the development of the eco-friendly glass, Pilkington is altering its marketing mix. How might the company adjust the other elements of the marketing mix, particularly the price charged for the new glass and the way it is promoted?

Knowledge summary

- The design of a company's marketing mix is strongly influenced by its business objectives as well as by the results of any market research it may have commissioned.

- The costs faced by a business will have an important impact on its marketing mix, constraining the types of products it can develop, the prices it charges and the promotional activities it can afford to undertake.

- A range of external factors impact upon a business's marketing mix. These include legal, political, economic and environmental factors.

quick questions

1 The sports goods retailer JJB Sports has admitted that it is facing ever-tougher competition in the market from rival companies. How might JJB Sports adjust its marketing mix to respond to these changing circumstances?

2 Farley Ltd operates a chain of newsagents throughout the north of England. The company has recently switched its key marketing objective from increasing brand awareness to increasing profitability. How might this development affect the company's marketing mix?

3 Hitching Travel sells expensive holidays in exotic locations across the globe. Why is it likely to have to adjust its marketing mix as a consequence of external factors?

data interpretation
Teflon in trouble

It's on saucepans, clothing, even buildings, but now Teflon – the famed non-stick chemical coating – is at the centre of a controversy about cancer and birth defects. Environmentalists have called for the withdrawal of a chemical which is a key ingredient in the manufacture of Teflon because of growing health fears.

Perfluorooctanoic acid, PFOA for short, is a synthetic chemical used in the manufacture of advanced plastics including Teflon. But campaigners allege that PFOA can be linked to birth defects and other hazards. Unlike all new synthetic chemicals which must undergo rigorous testing to be marketed in Europe, PFOA is one of 100,000 or so chemicals which avoided the test because they were invented before 1981.

Teflon was invented in the 1930s by DuPont, the US firm which uses it today to make non-stick cookware, and also markets it as a coating for clothes and carpets as it pursues a policy of growth. The company recently agreed to an out-of-court settlement to a class action lawsuit brought by around 50,000 residents living near its West Virginia plant who claimed that the local water supplies had been contaminated with PFOA. In settling the case, DuPont did not accept liability and the company maintains that PFOA does not pose any public health danger.

Source: Adapted from www.news.bbc.co.uk, 7 October 2004.

A Prior to the adverse publicity, what would you consider to be the most important element of Teflon's marketing mix? Explain your answer.

B To what extent might DuPont's objective of growth have influenced the marketing mix it used until the problems associated with PFOA became public?

C How should DuPont adjust its marketing mix in the light of the difficulties outlined in the article? Do you think that adjusting the marketing mix will enable DuPont to overcome its problems?

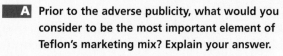

147

Topic 9 The influences on the marketing mix

Business in practice: Tesco's story

Since the takeover of Safeway by William Morrison in 2004, the UK market for groceries has been dominated by four large companies. As Figure 3.20 shows, the four major supermarket chains have over 70 per cent of the market. However, overall, the grocery market in the UK is growing slowly. This means that a company like Tesco can only achieve substantial rates of growth in food sales by taking customers from rivals such as Sainsbury.

Supermarket	Employees	Number of stores	Market share 2003	Market share 2004
Tesco	200,000	775	26.8%	28.0%
Asda	117,000	258	17.0%	16.9%
Sainsbury	174,000	517	15.9%	15.3%
Morrisons*	138,000	599	14.5%**	13.6%*

Figure 3.20: The major players in the UK grocery market

* Including Safeway following the takeover   ** Combined Morrisons & Safeway figure.

Sources: Adapted from www.news.bbc.co.uk and www.corporatewatch.org.uk

Tesco's current position

Tesco has steadily increased its market share – the percentage of the market that it holds – at the expense of rivals, and this trend shows no sign of stopping. As a result of this growth, Tesco has become the UK's largest retailer. During 2004, the company's sales rose by 8.3 per cent compared with the previous year. Its profits for the financial year 2004/5 are expected to exceed £2 billion (that is £2,000 million). Tesco receives one pound in every 12 spent in UK shops.

In 2004, the company opened 64 new stores and expanded the range of retail outlets it operates. Tesco does not just rely on sales through it stores: it is the world's largest internet retailer and its e-business is operational in a number of countries throughout the world.

The company has performed well in food sales, but recently has begun to enjoy strong sales growth in non-food items such as clothing. The company has also entered new markets by:

■ becoming an internet service provider (ISP)

■ operating a mobile phone service

■ issuing credit cards

■ selling online music.

The company carries out all its activities under the Tesco brand. The company believes that this brand is trusted and that consumers recognise that it represents value for money.

Figure 3.21 illustrates the substantial growth achieved by the company in the first years of the 21st century, and Figure 3.22 shows the extent to which the

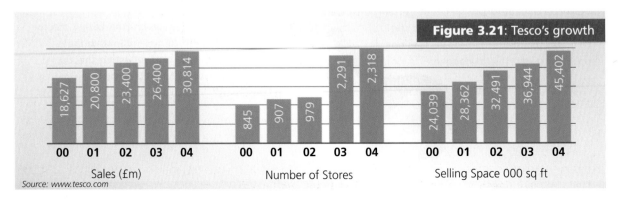

Figure 3.21: Tesco's growth

Sales (£m): 00 — 18,627; 01 — 20,800; 02 — 23,400; 03 — 26,400; 04 — 30,814

Number of Stores: 00 — 845; 01 — 907; 02 — 979; 03 — 2,291; 04 — 2,318

Selling Space 000 sq ft: 00 — 24,039; 01 — 28,362; 02 — 32,491; 03 — 36,944; 04 — 45,402

Source: www.tesco.com

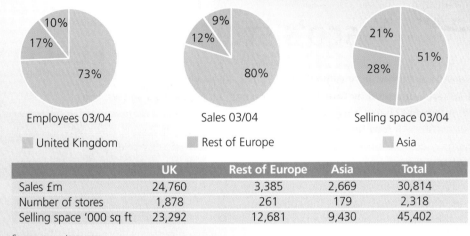

Figure 3.22: Tesco's emergence in non-UK markets

Employees 03/04 — 10%, 17%, 73%

Sales 03/04 — 9%, 12%, 80%

Selling space 03/04 — 21%, 28%, 51%

■ United Kingdom   ■ Rest of Europe   ■ Asia

	UK	Rest of Europe	Asia	Total
Sales £m	24,760	3,385	2,669	30,814
Number of stores	1,878	261	179	2,318
Selling space '000 sq ft	23,292	12,681	9,430	45,402

Source: www. tesco.com

company has developed its business outside its traditional UK base.

Tesco's marketing objectives

Tesco's overall corporate objective is long-term growth. The company's management team intends to expand the business globally over the next few years. From this main corporate objective, Tesco is able to establish key marketing objectives. These are likely to include:

- increasing the company's market share in the UK and overseas

- gaining consumers' lifelong loyalty

- understanding customers' needs better than its competitors

- offering customers unbeatable value for money

- being innovative, and the first to offer customers new goods and services.

Tesco's marketing strategy

Tesco operates in a number of different markets. These can be segmented both by geography (the different regions in which it operates) and by product (the different products and services that the company offers). Tesco has developed appropriate marketing strategies for each of these market segments. All of these strategies combine to help the company achieve its corporate objectives.

1 Expand in overseas markets

As well as operating in the UK, by 2004 Tesco had stores in six other countries in Europe: the Republic of Ireland, Hungary, Czech Republic, Slovakia, Turkey and Poland. The company has a total of 261 stores across Europe and this year it became the leading hypermarket retailer in Central Europe. Its European stores enable it to reach over 175 million people. Tesco plans to open more stores in this region.

In 2002, Tesco opened its first stores in Malaysia. The company plans to increase its operations in the developing markets of Thailand, South Korea, Taiwan and Malaysia, giving it access to a population of approximately 155 million people.

In March 2004, Tesco revealed that the company had bought a 50 per cent stake in Ting Hsin International, a Chinese retail food group. China has a population of 1.3 billion and in 2004 its economy was growing at 10 per cent a year. Tesco is clearly attracted by the huge scale and potential of the Chinese market, although it faces competition from other global retailers such as Wal-Mart and Carrefour that already have a trading presence in China.

2 Selling new products

Since 1998, Tesco has steadily expanded the range of products that it sells. The company has opened a number of stores with larger floor areas to enable it to stock clothes, household products and electrical goods. This has increased the company's sales significantly and has been one of the factors behind the spectacular increase in turnover.

The company has become a highly successful retailer of clothes rivalling established businesses such as Marks & Spencer in this market. It has also enjoyed some success in providing financial products to its customers. Tesco offers car and house insurance, loans and credit cards, and has marketed these products relentlessly.

In September 2003, Tesco announced that it was entering the telephone service market. The company will take on British Telecom in providing a range of packages to UK consumers for their landline telephones. Tesco claims that its packages could cut the cost of calls for residential consumers by up to 30 per cent.

In 2004, the company announced that it was branching out into another new market by launching an online music service which it hopes will rival Apple's iTunes. Tesco says its digital music will sell at 79 pence per song and it intends to offer more than 500,000 tracks with improved sound quality.

3 Opening different types of stores

In 2005, the *Sunday Times* revealed that Tesco was planning to open its first non-food store. The new store was expected to sell a range of products including domestic electrical products such as TVs and DVD players, clothing for children and adults, and music. If the new non-food shop is a success, Tesco is expected to open more non-food stores in locations across the UK. This is a natural development for the company which has seen its non-food sales rise strongly over the last few years.

The UK's major retailers have encountered increasing difficulty in obtaining planning permission for new out-of-town superstores. In response, there has been a move to open smaller stores in traditional high

street sites in an attempt to keep increasing sales turnover. Tesco has been at the forefront of this development, opening its Metro and Express stores in high streets across the country.

This move into local stores continues. In 2004, Tesco bought 45 small stores in the London area for £54 million. The shops were sold by the Adminstore Group and Tesco plans to convert them into its Express brand by February 2005. This move attracted criticism from several of Tesco's rivals. Iceland, for example, claimed that it may not be in the best long-term interests of consumers as the Tesco brand was becoming too dominant, thereby offering less choice to consumers.

4 Offering customers value for money

Tesco aims to offer customers in the UK and overseas markets exceptional value for money. This means that the company has to buy its products as cheaply as possible and to offer the lowest possible prices to its customers. In the UK, Tesco and Asda are keen rivals in terms of price competitiveness.

According to The Grocer magazine, in 2004, an average shop at Tesco cost £167.84 compared with £168.51 at Asda. The equivalent figure at Sainsbury was £175.30. Tesco has based much of its promotion on its competitive price levels.

Reducing its prices below those of its fierce rival Asda is a victory for Tesco. Tesco has been steadily closing the gap on Asda and a 2.7 per cent price cut in 2004 enabled it to achieve price leadership. This is the first time that The Grocer's survey has shown Tesco's prices to be below those of Asda since 1997.

activities

1 Explain how the marketing objectives identified in the case above may have helped Tesco to achieve its overall corporate aim of growth.

2(a) Tesco sells groceries, online music and credit card services. Identify the likely target markets in the UK for each of these products.

2(b) How does having a clearly defined target market help Tesco to sell its products?

3 Explain in detail how Tesco uses the marketing mix to help it achieve its marketing objectives. (Visiting Tesco's website at www.tesco.com might help you to answer this question.)

4 Do you think that Tesco uses the best possible marketing mix given its marketing objectives? Explain and justify your views.

Topic 10 Business in practice: Tesco's story

ELECTRONIC BUSINESS, OR E-BUSINESS, IS RAPIDLY becoming an essential part of our daily lives. Every time you turn on a computer and use the web browser to surf the internet, you become a potential e-business customer.

This unit helps you to understand three aspects of e-business:

- why a business might be interested in the opportunities presented by e-business
- what a business should think about before establishing a website and other related aspects of e-business
- what it takes to develop, produce and launch a business website.

This unit does not attempt to cover all the issues and technologies that fall within the world of e-business, but it will help you to consider how the businesses you investigate might go about developing their use of e-business technologies. In addition, you will learn how to create simple websites and get them onto the internet.

Investigating electronic business

Setting the scene: the market for cars

Before the internet and the age of easily accessible websites, buying a second-hand car wasn't always simple. It was difficult to find the right car at the best possible price. Television programmes could give you a general idea about the types of cars available. Magazines and newspapers could provide you with information about the prices of various models. But you still had to rely on the information given to you by the retailer.

Today you can search the internet to find most of the information you need before parting with your money. The Car Shop is one example of how the internet has changed the market for cars. Using The Car Shop website (www.carshop.co.uk), you can search a detailed database of thousands of second-hand cars. Within a matter of seconds you can find the car you want, complete with photograph, price and mileage. You are also provided with a list of similar cars in the same price bracket.

The freedom of the internet means you can also quickly search alternative websites such as www.autotrader.co.uk. On this website you can use a simple search box to find the car you want.

Given the ease with which information can be accessed on the internet, second-hand car retailers who ignore even the most basic elements of e-business are likely to face a decline in sales and profits. The internet is also impacting on the market for new cars, and manufacturers and car dealers need to develop websites that provide genuinely useful information and meet the needs of individual customers.

Welcome to The Car Shop, the UK's leading Car Supermarket Group.

The Car Shop opened in 1999 and now covers three locations in **Northampton**, **Manchester** and **Cardiff**.

When you buy a car from The Car Shop you get lots of things you don't usually find with a used car.

For a start, you will find prices that are not just low, but guaranteed to be the

KEY TERMS

E-commerce is the buying and selling of goods, information products and services through an electronic medium such as the internet.

Electronic business or **e-business** is the use of internet technologies to carry out business functions. Increasingly companies are using the internet not just for buying and selling but for customer service, marketing, advertising, research and development, human resources and finance.

The **internet** is the global network of computers accessed with the aid of a modem. The internet includes websites and e-mail.

E-mail or **electronic mail** are messages sent across the internet. E-mail is also the act of transferring messages between computers, mobile phones or other devices attached to the internet.

A **website** is a collection of web pages stored on a computer connected to the internet. A web page is an electronic document viewed through a web browser.

Web browsers are computer programs which allow you to view **web pages** and navigate through websites. Examples include Internet Explorer, Opera, Netscape, Safari and Mozilla.

What is electronic business?

Electronic business is the use of the internet by businesses to carry out their day-to-day activities, including:

- buying and selling products

- communicating with suppliers, employees and customers

- finding out about competitors and trends in customer behaviour

- recording and distributing information about the performance of the business.

Electronic business can be carried out on many different levels. For some businesses, simply having an e-mail address is as far as they need to go. They might simply communicate by e-mail with some customers and suppliers. For other businesses, e-business is at the centre of everything they do.

Amazon, the internet retailer, does not have any high street retail stores and communicates with its customers entirely through the internet, by using its website www.amazon.co.uk. Amazon uses e-business technology to communicate with its suppliers to ensure that stocks are kept to a minimum. The company is a good example of a business that makes the most of e-commerce, both buying (from its suppliers) and selling (to consumers) online through the internet.

Figure 4.1 illustrates the steps a company might take as it climbs the e-commerce ladder. Amazon has reached the top rung of the ladder – it exemplifies advanced e-commerce. Your local book store, however, is likely to be somewhere on the bottom three rungs of the e-commerce ladder.

Why is electronic business important?

The arrival of the internet in the 1990s provided another way for people to find out about the world they live in. You have probably used the internet on many occasions to help with school homework or to get information on people or activities you are interested in. It's easy, fast and relatively inexpensive.

For many businesses, the internet is a threat. Before the internet, businesses had more freedom over the prices they set for their products and the type of products they offered to their customers. With the arrival of the internet, customers could quickly find out what other businesses had to offer and what prices these businesses charged for their products. The internet gave customers power.

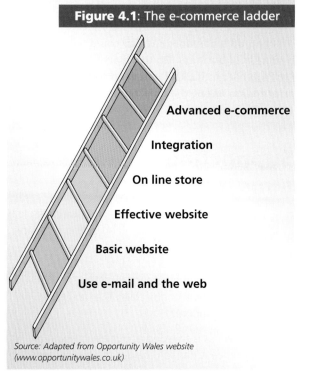

Figure 4.1: The e-commerce ladder

Advanced e-commerce

Integration

On line store

Effective website

Basic website

Use e-mail and the web

Source: Adapted from Opportunity Wales website (www.opportunitywales.co.uk)

GO TO the accompanying CD-ROM. Choose Unit 4 from the main menu. This will take you to an interactive game about commissioning a website. It is better to try this game once you have read Unit 4 Topics 1, 2, 4 and 5.

Topic 1 What businesses hope to achieve online

Setting the scene: Amazon UK's homepage

Amazon, the Internet retailer, is a good example of a business with a successful online presence. Its UK homepage – www.amazon.co.uk – provides a clear illustration of just why Amazon is successful.

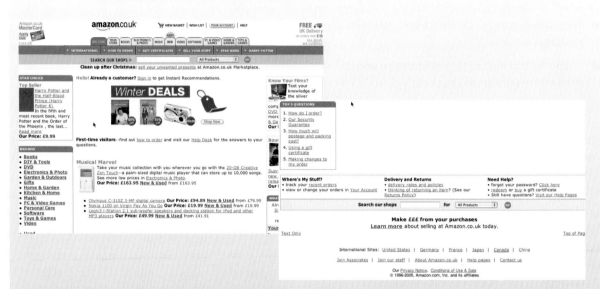

Amazon has thought about how its homepage and its website will help it to be a successful business. At the top of the page, you can quickly appreciate the range of goods on offer – from books to travel – and you can find any particular item by using the "search our shops" facility.

At the bottom of the page, links to additional information are provided. Perhaps you might be interested in working for Amazon? No problem – **just click on the "join our staff" link. Worried about buying online? Find out what happens to the information you provide Amazon by clicking on the "privacy notice" link.**

Identify and explain four other features of Amazon UK's homepage which could help it to be a successful business. Go to Amazon UK's website (www.amazon.co.uk) if you need to find out more information about the links on its homepage.

KEY TERMS

Online presence involves establishing a website to communicate and carry out transactions with customers, partners and other stakeholders.

Search engines are websites that store and index links to various pages on the internet. A **meta search engine** is computer software that searches multiple search engines, producing a wider range of results.

Products in **electronic** or **downloadable format** are capable of being accessed across the internet. Examples in software, music (in MP3 format, for example) and books (in pdf format).

Cookies are files written to a computer's hard disk by a web browser to store information that can be accessed to identify users and customise interactions with them.

Supporting business aims and objectives

Unit 1 looked at the range of aims and objectives that businesses set. In general, having an online presence can help to achieve a wide range of aims and objectives. Figure 4.2 sets out some of the objectives that can be achieved by an online presence. Can you identify other aims and objectives that an online presence could support?

When a business is thinking about establishing an online presence it has to consider the real reasons for doing so. Does it want to provide information to potential customers? Is it having problems with international competitors? Does it want to appeal to a

Figure 4.2: Business objectives supported by an online presence

- Appealing to a global market
- Profit maximisation
- Improving customer service
- Cutting costs
- **Aims of an online presence**
- Attracting new staff
- Increasing sales
- Strengthening business relationships

global market? Perhaps it wants to sell directly to customers? Each business will have a different set of reasons for wanting to establish an online presence.

1 Increasing sales

Achieving a sale is a complex process. An online presence can help a business reach its customers. However, to be effective, a business's website needs to be visited. A business's website can get more exposure if it is listed on the search engines used by people when they search for products on the internet. Search engines, such as Lycos (www.lycos.co.uk) and Google (www.google.co.uk), and meta search engines, such as Copernic Meta (www.copernic.com), are online directories that help users track down all useful information stored on the internet.

The website needs to provide clear and accessible information on the features, prices and performance of the business's products. Some businesses will provide information that compares their goods to competitors' products. This allows the business to pick out features in which it believes it excels. For example, on Tesco's website (www.tesco.com/pricecheck), Tesco compares its prices with those of major competitors such as Asda.

An e-commerce website needs to provide simple and effective ways for customers to buy products. This used to be difficult for a small business but the arrival of online purchasing systems, such as PayPal and World Pay, have made this much easier. These systems will be covered in Topic 6 of this unit.

stop a n d **think**

How easy is it for a business to set up an online purchasing system? Find out by visiting PayPal's website (www.paypal.com).

2 Cutting costs

Establishing an online presence can reduce business costs by increasing the efficiency of the business. This means that a business uses fewer resources to create the same amount of sales.

The software industry was one of the first industries to create an online presence and establish successful online retailing systems. As software products are already in an electronic format, it is relatively easy to sell software directly to customers over the internet. Most antivirus software, such as Norton and Kaspersky, can be bought over the internet and downloaded directly onto your computer. As sales staff are not involved – and postage and packaging costs are zero – business costs are instantly reduced. Travel companies can also reduce their sales teams by using sophisticated online booking websites.

stop a n d **think**

Identify two other industries that could have reduced their costs by establishing an online presence. How might websites have been used by firms in these industries to reduce costs?

3 Maximising profits

If an online presence can increase sales and reduce costs, then it is clear that profits can also be increased. Maximising profits is a very bold aim: it requires a plan of action, and an online presence is likely to be just one part of that plan. It requires responding to competition, and a business might be forced to establish an online presence because of the action of its competitors. In general, a business that is aiming to maximise profits needs to keep a careful watch on its costs as it strives to meet the needs of its customers.

4 Improving customer service

In a competitive market, in which many businesses are competing for customers, an online presence is essential. Customers need to feel special and one way of achieving this is to establish good customer service. At the heart of good customer service is the ability to anticipate and meet customer expectations.

Figure 4.3: Customer expectations

- Personalised care and attention
- After-sales service
- Good value
- Customer expectations
- Quick response to enquiries
- Clear product information
- Information about suitability of products

Many websites use cookies to monitor the interest shown by individual customers in particular goods and services. Cookies are small files stored on a customer's computer by the web browser. These cookies work in conjunction with data stored on the business's central database. Amazon, for example, makes extensive use of cookies to track your past purchases and offer information and products tailored to your interests.

In addition to cookies, business websites try to provide customer service in other ways. Many have pages giving answers to frequently asked questions (FAQs) and some specifically invite customer feedback.

5 Appealing to a global market

As soon as a business establishes an online presence it has entered the global market. A website can be accessed by anyone in the world who has a computer, a web browser and a connection to the internet.

However, as most customers are likely to find a website by using a search engine, a business needs to ensure that its website is listed by a relevant foreign search engine to attract potential overseas customers. The website www.searchengines.com lists a wide range of search engines that are used in different countries.

The website needs to be translated into an appropriate foreign language and it needs to take into account cultural preferences. The use of colour is also crucial. For example, in India positive colours are bold ones such as green and red; in Europe, white and blue are generally perceived as positive.

stop and **think**

What other issues does a business need to consider when establishing an online presence in foreign countries?

6 Attracting new staff

Recruiting staff is an expensive process. A business website can go some way to reducing the recruitment costs. Most business websites have a jobs section, where you can view details of current vacancies. For example, the fashion retailer Next has details of job opportunities on its website and lets you download an application form. Some websites also provide a facility to apply online: you can enter details about yourself on an online form and upload your CV.

7 Strengthening relationships

One of the major potential benefits of an online presence is the way in which it can improve the relationship a business has with its suppliers and retailers. Instead of just focusing on customers, an effective business website will also assist in attracting potential suppliers and retailers by detailing product requirements and sales opportunities.

Many business websites have separate sections for general customers and wholesalers. The wholesaler section usually lists prices for bulk orders and provides information about new products. A sophisticated business website will have a log-in page for suppliers and retailers. After logging in, the supplier or retailer will be able to access information relevant to their business, such as current orders outstanding and any product lines that might be of interest.

Knowledge summary

- A website can help to achieve a wide range of business aims and objectives.

- An effective online presence enhances the ability of a business to communicate with its customers and suppliers.

quick**questions**

1 Explain how a business in the music industry such as EMI might use these online facilities to increase profits:
- downloadable music formats such as MP3
- using cookies to personalise web pages for individual customers
- a log-in page for retailers

2 Identify and explain three ways in which a new DVD/video film rental store might use an online presence to support its business aims and objectives.

data**interpretation**
Kids Casuals

Nicola Dickenson started Kids Casuals as a sole trader in 2001. The business retails clothing for children such as T-shirts, sweat shirts, tote bags, caps, hats and socks. Nicola originally purchased stock from three different distributors and then sold the products at craft shows, fairs and parent and toddler groups. Because Nicola did not have a store, her business operated on a seasonal basis and she made very few sales between January and April.

In an attempt to increase sales at the beginning of the calendar year, Nicola put together a mailing list of previous customers. At the time, Kids Casuals did not a have catalogue, so Nicola sent each customer a brochure from T-Time – one of her suppliers – along with a covering letter. T-Time's brochure listed its website and, rather than gaining business, Nicola lost a large number of her customers when they went directly to the T-Time website to buy online. Nicola realised that she would need a website in order to attract new customers.

Source: Adapted from an Opportunity Wales case study

A Explain why it was important for Nicola to establish an online presence for Kids Casuals.

B Identify three objectives for Kids Casuals' online presence. Explain their importance and suggest ways that Nicola might monitor their achievement.

C Visit and explore the Kids Casuals website (www.kidscasuals.co.uk). List the ways in which Kids Casuals has established an effective online presence.

clothes for kids

HOME | ORDER | PRICES | E-MAIL | TERMS & CONDITIONS

Pink + Glitter   Farming   Transport & Skateboard   Dinosaurs   Caps, Bags & Socks

T-shirts and sweat shirts for kids with designs ranging from fairies to tractors, rabbits to horses, and cartoon animals.

Choose your design and colour and you can have it personalised with your childs name.

Acccesories for children include socks, tote-bags and hats.

HOME | ORDER | PRICES | E-MAIL | TERMS & CONDITIONS

Topic 2 Communicating with the customer online

Setting the scene: constructing a business website

Amazon seems to have done a good job in establishing an online presence – it has designed an effective website. The company has thought carefully about how its website is organised. Any business that wants to construct a website needs to consider what information the site should contain and how it should be organised. In general, a business website should have several sections.

Homepage – this is the main page of the website, the first page you see after entering the web address in the web browser.

About us – this section should provide details about the business's history, the industrial sector it operates in, its owners and key managerial personnel.

Products and services – a business website would be useless if it didn't contain a number of structured pages detailing the range of products and customer services on offer.

FAQ – to cut down on customer e-mails and telephone calls, a frequently asked questions (FAQ) page is a must. This page will build up over time as the business gains knowledge of the questions that customers want answered.

Contact us – this page should provide ways in which customers can contact the business. It might include the business's e-mail address, postal address and telephone number. It should instruct customers to view the FAQ page before contacting the business.

Privacy – a page which is sometimes forgotten, the privacy page should explain the business's policies on how it uses customer data. This is sometimes known as the legal notice page.

Can you think of other pages that a business might want to include on its website? The best way to answer this question is to visit a range of business websites. Try to look at the websites of a variety of businesses – for example, pick a service business, a manufacturing business and a not-for-profit organisation – and note the way each website's pages are organised. Some websites you might wish to look at are www.bbc.co.uk, www.rnib.org.uk, www.cadbury.co.uk, www.bmw.com and www.edexcel.org.uk.

KEY TERMS

The **target audience** defines the types of users a website is aimed at.

Static elements are non-moving parts of a web page, such as a photograph or text.

Animated elements are moving parts of a web page, such as images or text that fades in.

Flash is software, produced by Macromedia, which enables websites to have animated elements.

Visual elements are pictures and graphics, such as product photographs or blocks of colour.

Interactive elements are parts of a web page which require the user to do something, such as enter text or click on a photograph.

Accessibility is the degree to which a website can be utilised by a wide variety of users, such as people in foreign countries or those with physical disabilities.

Communicating with the customer

A business website must communicate in ways that are accessible to the target audience. The messages must be clear and website users should be presented with the information they expect to see.

It is not just important to be accessible. If the website is going to support the business's aims and objectives, it needs to be an effective communication. Users should be able to find and access the information they are looking for. They should have the facility to respond to the messages sent by the business.

1 Expected information

French Connection UK, the fashion retailer, uses its website to engage the target audience. It provides a wide range of information to customers and potential investors. The website contains key pages setting out:

- **what the business does** – it's main activities, general sector of business activity and its history

- **what the business has to offer** – the company's range of products and customer services.

s t o p a n d **t h i n k**

Do you think the French Connection website provides the information you would expect to find from a fashion retailer? Make a checklist of the information you would expect to find and then visit the website at www.fcuk.com. Does the website pass your information test?

The French Connection website contains information on the company's:

- legal format – French Connection is a plc

- type of business – fashion retailer

- target market – 14 to 18-year-old females

- sector – retail sector

- products – fashion accessories to casual clothes.

Most retail websites will contain the same type of information. Indeed, any business website will be expected to present this type of information.

2 Effective communication

Considering its target audience, French Connection's messages are being communicated by its website in an effective way. The website makes extensive use of an internet technology called Flash. Developed by the software company Macromedia, Flash introduces animated elements to web pages. It enables companies to design websites in which text, pictures and other objects fade in and out or move around the page. This is intended to create interest in the content of the website, encouraging users to return and spend more time on it.

s t o p a n d **t h i n k**

French Connection's main website (www.fcuk.com) is almost entirely Flash based. However, the company has a separate online sales website (www.fcukbuymail.com).

At the time of writing, this online sales website was static and didn't use Flash. Why do you think French Connection designed its main site to appear animated and entertaining while presenting its online sales site in a more traditional and static way?

The use of Flash web pages is not appropriate in all circumstances. Some users feel that Flash pages are simply too flashy! They feel that information should be presented in clear and static ways. A business needs to have a feel for which style is most likely to appeal to its target audience.

How information is presented depends largely on the target audience. A business needs to understand why users are viewing the website. What are they looking for and how would they like to read and engage with the information?

To communicate effectively through a website, businesses need to consider:

- **Visual elements of a web page**
  Pictures, blocks of colour and animated images all help to direct and focus the user's eyes on key information. However, if the web page is too cluttered and makes excessive use of graphical images, then people will quickly move on to a competitor's website.

- **Interactive elements of a web page**
  Users should be very clear about how they can respond to messages. They should be left in no doubt about how they can purchase goods, get additional information or assistance, and complain. Good websites will present these interactive elements in clear ways (see Figure 4.4).

- **Accessibility of a web page**
  A business's website should be available 24 hours a day. Customers should be able to find answers to questions and order products whenever they want. If the website is targeting an international audience, then different language versions should be available. Websites should be accessible to users with poor eyesight. The Royal National Institute of the Blind (RNIB) provides advice on how websites can be made more accessible. The RNIB design rules hold true for people of all abilities – it is simply good design advice.

stop and **think**

Visit the RNIB's website (www.rnib.org.uk) and look at its advice on making websites accessible. Make a list of five things you should consider when designing a website which is accessible to people with sight impairment. Reflect on how your list is good advice for developing any website.

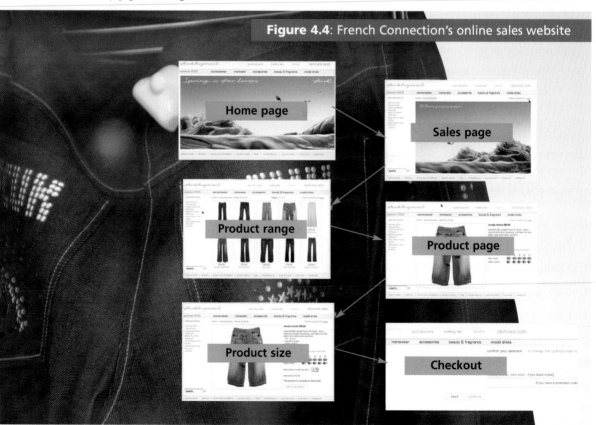

Figure 4.4: French Connection's online sales website

Home page

Sales page

Product range

Product page

Product size

Checkout

Knowledge summary

- All websites should contain a core set of essential web pages.

- A business website needs to explain what the business does and what the business has to offer.

- Effective communication is a vital aspect of any website. Web designers should take into account the visual and interactive elements of the website as well as its accessibility.

quick**questions**

1 Identify and describe three key pages that should be included in a website for a national chain of cinemas.

2 Explain how a sportswear retailer might use animated elements within its website.

3 A restaurant is planning to launch a website. The restaurant is in a rural area away from main travel routes. It charges high prices for quality food. Describe the information that might be included on:
- the homepage
- the "about us" page
- the "contact us" page.

data**interpretation**
Health Leads UK: improving a website

Health Leads UK was founded in 1997 by John and Christine Doyle. The business specialises in mail-order sales of health supplements and vitamins. In the autumn of 2001, it was decided that the business needed to improve its sales from e-commerce. To do this, the company decided to redesign its website which was not performing to expectation or potential, introducing new features and improving the site's visual elements. The new website was completed and fully operational by February 2002.

Since replacing the old site, Health Leads UK's overall company revenues have gone up substantially, with income from e-commerce now contributing nearly 30 per cent of overall sales. The internet has also proved to be a far more cost-effective means of marketing than traditional channels.

Source: adapted from an Opportunity Wales case study.

A Explain why an online presence would be essential for a business specialising in mail-order sales of health supplements and vitamins.

B Describe two ways in which the redevelopment of the Health Leads UK website might have improved the performance of the business.

C Visit the Health Leads UK website (www.healthleadsuk.com). Investigate the various sections of the website and identify four ways in which the website is designed to ensure effective communication through its use of visual and interactive elements.

D Suggest three ways in which you think the website's communication could be improved. Justify your answers.

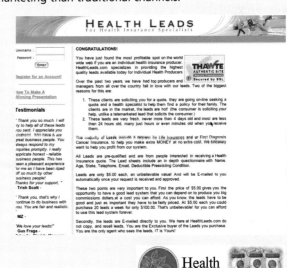

Setting the scene: Boo and the future of dotcoms

Towards the end of the 1990s a number of new online businesses, or dotcoms, entered the market. One dotcom was Boo, a fashion retailer that made extensive use of Flash technology to enhance the user's shopping experience. A flash animated character called Miss Boo helped visitors to the Boo website as they browsed and, hopefully, purchased products.

Boo spent millions on its website and new offices. Unfortunately, in 2000, Boo closed. It simply failed to get enough customers and could not cover its costs. The following is an extract from a BBC web article at the time.

Source: adapted from news.bbc.co.uk, 18 May 2000

In 2000, Boo wasn't the only company in trouble – a number of dotcoms were also facing financial problems. Try using the internet to find other examples of failed online businesses. You could try putting the words "dotcom failure" into a search engine. (The BBC news site is a good place to state: visit www.news.bbc.co.uk.) How recent are most of the stories about dotcom failures?

Now search for stories about the success of online businesses. Can you find any evidence that online companies have learned from the mistakes made by dotcoms in the late 1990s?

The future of dotcoms

Selling on the web is not much different from doing business 20 years ago. Companies have to focus on customer service, staff retention and good marketing. It is not important whether a dotcom is first to market, but whether it can keep up with growing customer demand.

A recent study suggests that, during the past year, 28 per cent of all attempted online purchases failed. Firms that cannot deliver –either because their website is poorly designed or because their distribution system is not up to scratch – are bound to fail.

KEY TERMS

E-tailers are retailers who partly, or entirely, sell online.

A **dotcom** is a start-up business whose main activities are carried out online.

Distribution systems are the means by which products are physically distributed from the supplier to the customer.

Internet connection speed is the rate at which a user can download data from the internet. With a fast internet connection speed, a user will find it much easier to access online information.

Internal stakeholders are people who are directly involved with the activities of a business, such as employees and owners.

External stakeholders are people and organisations that have an indirect interest in the activities of a business, such as customers, suppliers and competitors.

Web links direct users to other parts of a website or a different website. Clicking on a link causes the web browser to display the linked web page.

The impact of business websites

Having an online presence does not guarantee business success. Boo's website was innovative and engaging, but it relied on the user having a fast internet connection speed. While it did persuade some users to purchase products, many others were put off by how long the site's pages took to load.

Unless a business plans its online presence it will face problems. Any business needs to think about the impact its website will have on:

- **external stakeholders** – customers, suppliers and competitors

- **internal stakeholders** – owners and employees.

1 External stakeholders

An effective website will impact on external stakeholders in various ways. Customers and suppliers have much to gain from an effective website. The consequences for competitors are less beneficial as an effective website is one way a business can achieve a competitive advantage. Let's look at the impact on each of the three main groups of external stakeholders in more detail.

Customers

An effective website provides clear information about the range of products available. It makes it easy for customers to find products and makes online purchasing a simple and safe process. Some companies even offer products to online customers at lower prices than those available in stores.

Ideally, items purchased online should be delivered directly to the customer within a reasonable time – for example, two to three days – and the website should offer appropriate customer service such as a helpdesk or advice line. However, customers who continue to use the business's traditional outlets – such as a high street store – should still be provided with the same level of customer service.

Suppliers

An effective website should improve communication between a business and its suppliers, making it easier for them to supply products to the business. As a good website might generate additional customer orders, suppliers might also expect to increase their sales to the business to fulfil those orders. However, suppliers might need to improve delivery response times to meet online customer expectations.

Competitors

Competitors will also be affected by an effective website, although in less positive ways. They might begin to lose customers and their profits could fall. In response, they might be forced to establish an online presence or improve their current website.

Competitors might adopt other methods to counter the impact of a rival's website and to try and hold on to their customers. They might, for example, consider new ways of marketing their products, perhaps through strategies like price cuts, multi-buy offers and improved guarantees.

2 Internal stakeholders

An effective website will also benefit the internal stakeholders of a business – the owners, managers and employees.

If it contributes to increased profits then the business owners clearly benefit. Individuals who have invested in the business should receive a greater return on their investment. If the business is a public limited company (plc), its share price might increase and its shareholders might receive larger dividends.

Managers will also gain rewards from being seen to introduce and run an effective website. It will allow them to expand the business and to target a wider geographical market. They should also hopefully see a career benefit from the success of the website, perhaps in terms of increased salaries, improved job security and better chances for promotion.

Employees play an essential part in setting up an effective website. However, as Figure 4.5 shows (see page 166), establishing an online presence can change (or augment) the duties of business departments. These new duties might require employees to acquire new skills – some staff might see this as a threat; others might welcome the challenge. Introducing an online presence requires the business to identify and deal with any potential skills shortages by training staff and/or employing new, suitably qualified, staff.

Topic 3 Dotcoms ups and downs

Figure 4.5: How a website impacts on business departments

Sales for example, processing online orders.

Human resources for example, helping to maintain the About Us web page.

Finance for example, producing reports on how the website has affected sales.

Customer care for example, helping to produce a Frequently Asked Questions web page.

FAQ

stop and think

Figure 4.5 sets out some of the ways in which an online presence can add additional business functions. Identify and describe four additional ways in which a website might alter or introduce new duties within business departments. For each new duty, think about the new skills that might be required.

The importance of updating websites

A website, however effective, is likely to damage a business if it is not updated. A website should be regularly updated to ensure that the information it contains is accurate and relevant.

Some information needs to be updated on a regular basis:

- **product details and prices** – products must be accurately described and quoted prices should be in line with current pricing policies
- **frequently asked questions** – the FAQ pages should be updated by adding new questions and issues as they arise

- **news** – any pages containing news about the business should be updated to maintain accuracy, keep the website looking fresh and ensure that the business benefits from any positive publicity such as favourable reviews of its products

- **financial information** – websites which have pages on the business's financial position, such as balance sheets and share prices, should be updated to ensure that they contain the most recent data

- **links to other websites** – these links should still work and point to the intended web page, thereby avoiding any possible complaints from users of the business website and the owners of the linked websites.

In general, a business should ensure that any information which is no longer true or relevant is removed from the site. At the same time, the website should be updated to ensure that it continues to meet the needs of users, some of whom might be new and have quite different needs and expectations from regular users of the site.

stop and think

What other information might a business need to update on its website? Identify and explain four possible consequences to a business if it fails to update its website.

166

Unit 4 Investigating electronic business

Knowledge summary

- An effective website can enhance customer and supplier experiences, helping both to increase sales and to reduce costs.

- Well trained, experienced and enthusiastic employees are an essential part of an effective website.

- To be truly effective, a business website needs to be regularly updated.

1 Visit a successful e-tailer's website, such as Amazon (amazon.co.uk) or the movies, music and games site www.play.com, and identify four ways in which the website is designed to have a positive impact on customers.

2 When establishing an online presence, a business may need to retrain existing staff or appoint new staff to tackle potential skill shortages. Draw up a table listing the advantages and disadvantages of retraining existing staff.

3 Explain why it would be important for a DVD movie e-tailer, such as www.play.com, to update its website on a regular basis. In answering this question, briefly consider these issues:
- accuracy
- relevance
- competitiveness.

data **interpretation**
The importance of customer service

The following news story illustrates the problems experienced by faced by a customer – Paul Sissons – when purchasing a product from Boo in 2000.

A Describe two problems faced by Paul Sissons when trying to buy some shoes from Boo.

B Explain two changes Boo could have made to avoid these problems.

C Choose an e-tailer and research how the business attempts to ensure good customer service. Using this research, produce a five minute presentation describing how the your chosen e-tailer ensures good customer service.

Source: adapted from www.news.bbc.co.uk, 18 May 2000

Trouble with Boo

Paul Sissons' experiences with Boo.com perhaps give some indication of why the company failed.

After spending some time browsing the site, which Paul said was badly laid out and slow, he settled on a pair of DC trainers costing £75. He keyed in his credit card number, clicked the confirmation button and immediately received e-mail confirmation or his order.

Another e-mail followed to say the shoes had been despatched, and Paul received the delivery within three days of ordering. However, when Paul opened the parcel, he was disappointed: "They were the wrong design, the wrong colour and the wrong size. In fact, they were boots, rather than shoes."

He telephoned Boo's helpline and explained the problem. "The woman was very polite but I had to convince her they were the wrong pair. She kept asking me: 'Are you sure they're not the right ones?'" The operator told Paul that a straight swap was not possible. Instead he had to return his boots, wait 10 days for his money to be reimbursed and then make his order again.

There were further problems when Paul phoned the courier to arrange for his boots to be picked up. When asked about some details on the original delivery form, he realised the wording was only in German. "I had to go through line-by-line with the operator, who was translating for me."

After returning the boots, Paul had to wait not 10 days but three weeks for his £75 to be reimbursed. The money finally arrived on the day Boo went into liquidation.

boo hoo

Going online: the cost implications

Setting the scene: XEL Web Design Manchester

XEL Web Design Manchester is a web design business. The company's website provides advice to potential business customers on choosing a web designer.

HOME   E-Commerce   Web Designing   Web Development   Partnership   Skill Set   Website Promotion   Testimonials

el Online
.com

PORTFOLIO   PROFILE   CONTACT US   ENQUIRY

OUR SERVICES
- ECOMMERCE
- WEB DESIGNING
- WEBSITE DEVELOPMENT

BEGINNERS GUIDE
- WEB DESIGN ➤
- SEO ➤

SPECIAL OFFERS
- Click here for Offers ➤

Choosing a web design company

The differences in prices charged by web design businesses are extreme. They can range from a few hundred pounds for a simple website to a few thousand pounds for larger more complex websites with features such as easily updated product databases and search engines, animated product demonstrations, secure online payments, and audio and video enhancements

Finding a web design business can be difficult. When you find one, make sure it is reliable. Check out a list of websites that the business has worked on and look closely at its own website.

Look for a web design business that doesn't charge for a consultation. Some businesses will try to charge a fee just to discuss your web design requirements, others will try to do business over the telephone, while others will offer a free initial consultation but then build further consultations into the price of the contract. XEL Web Design Manchester believes in completely free consultation with no obligations.

[Home ·Portfoilo ·Profile ·Contact Us ·Enquiry ·ECommerce ·Web Designing ·Web Development ·Partnership ·Skill Set ·Website Promotions]

All Rights reserved @2003. **xelonline.com**, A Web Design Company in the UK

Source: adapted from www.webdesign-manchester.com

This advice highlights some of the problems of choosing a web design business. Consider how XEL Web Design Manchester is trying to distinguish itself from other web design businesses

KEY TERMS

Computer hardware is the physical parts of a computer, such as the hard drive, processor chip, monitor and modem.

Computer software is the programs required by a computer to perform specific tasks, such as web browsing and word processing.

Internet service providers (ISP) rent connections to the internet. ISP charges vary depending on the quality and speed of internet connection offered.

Web servers are computers which are permanently connected to the internet and which store the websites of business (and individual) customers. The web server responds to user requests to view pages of the website.

Web hosts rent out space on a web server. Most users will use a web host to make their website available to the world.

Online databases are remote stores of data accessed by a web browser. For example, a business might place its catalogue (containing price and product information) in an database, enabling potential customers to browse and shop online.

Secure online payment systems enable users to purchase products online using their credit or debit cards without revealing financial details to unauthorised people.

Web design businesses develop and design websites for business customers.

The cost implications of an online presence

When establishing an online presence, a business must consider all the costs. These include the costs of:

- software and hardware
- web design and consultation
- employment, training and support.

1 Software and hardware costs

Figure 4.6 (*see page* 170) sets out the software, hardware and associated services needed for a business website. Costs can be kept to a minimum if the business produces the website itself and uses inexpensive software, a competitive ISP and web host.

Taking this do-it-yourself (DIY) route could reduce the short-term costs of establishing an online presence. A DIY approach might allow a business to set up a website for as little as £100 (assuming the business already has computers). Annual ISP and hosting costs could be under £350.

However, this calculation ignores the cost of the labour time needed to design and maintain the website. Some businesses may think they have employees who are willing to build and maintain the website; unfortunately, these employees are sometimes unskilled, enthusiastic amateurs.

stop and think

Look through the software and hardware requirements in Figure 4.6. Why do you think some business websites are superior to others?

2 Web design and consultation

The possible long-term consequences of a DIY approach can be costly: a poorly designed and maintained website can frustrate customers and damage the reputation of a business. Certainly if a business wants to produce a complex e-commerce site, with secure online payment systems and efficient online product databases, it would usually be advised to work with an experienced web designer.

For these reasons, many businesses choose to use web design companies such as XEL Web Design Manchester. While these firms can be expensive, they employ professional web designers who have high-level graphic design and programming skills.

Many web design businesses provide an initial consultation service to establish the requirements of the website. An effective and efficient website is then built by using the information gained from the consultation. Charges for these consultations can vary: some companies bury these charges within the fixed fee for designing the site, others charge for consultation on an hourly basis, with fees of £60 an hour being fairly typical.

stop and think

The Department of Trade and Industry offers a wide range of detailed advice to businesses on establishing an online presence. Visit the DTI best practice site (www.dti.gov.uk/bestpractice) and download the document on building an e-commerce website (or similar document if the site has been updated). Use this document to consider the advantages and disadvantages of a business taking a DIY approach to developing its website.

3 Employment, training and support costs

Any business establishing an online presence will have to consider human resource issues. It needs to:

- identify specific employees to work with the new e-business systems – for example, it needs to decide which staff will be responsible for working with the online product database
- train existing personnel and/or recruit new staff – for example, it might send staff on Fireworks and Flash training courses or advertise for a graphic designer
- identify and implement the maintenance requirements of the online presence – for example, by deciding which staff will be responsible for minor updates to the website.

These ongoing costs can quickly mount up and often represent a major proportion of the running cost of a website. In addition, a business should always budget for long-term support costs. At some point, a business is likely to want to redesign or completely refresh its website or to carry out major updates.

Requirement	Purpose	Examples	Stop & think
Web design software	To help design and construct the pages of the website.	Dreamweaver (www.macromedia.com) Net Objects Fusion (www.netobjects.com)	Why might a business choose a web design program which is easy to use, but might not provide as many design options?
Graphic design software	To produce and edit the website's graphical elements. This type of software can be very complicated and requires the user to have significant design skills.	Photoshop (www.adobe.co.uk) Fireworks and Flash (www.macromedia.com)	Why might it be important for a business to have graphical elements within the website?
Computer system	To build access and maintain the website. Needs to be able to access the internet, preferably through broadband.	Hewlett-Packard computer system (www.hp.co.uk)	Why might a business need a fast internet connection?
Internet service provider (ISP)	To enable the business to connect to the internet.	Firenet (www.firenet.uk.net)	What factors might affect a business's choice of ISP?
Web address	To enable customers to contact the website. An annual or biannual fee is charged for registering the address. If slow to register, a business could find that the address has already been taken.	www.websitesthatsuck.com	Why might the choice of web address be important to a business?
Web host	To store the business website and make it available on the internet.	1&1 (www.onenandone.co.uk)	What questions might a business need to ask before choosing a web host?

Knowledge summary

- The basic software and hardware set-up costs of a business website can be inexpensive.

- A DIY approach to establishing an online presence can cause considerable long-term costs if the website poorly designed and implemented.

- Web design businesses can help to ensure a successful online presence by using their technical expertise and experience to design and implement effective websites.

- Long-term employment costs result from establishing an online presence. However, these are likely to be outweighed by efficiency savings and additional sales revenues if the website is effective.

quick questions

1 Identify and describe three short-term and three long-term costs of establishing a business website.

2 Explain how a small business could set up a basic e-commerce system using a website and an e-mail address.

3 Explain why a large business might prefer to develop, host and maintain its website rather than use outside agencies.

data interpretation
Investigating the cost of launching a website

In November 2004, GSWebDesign offered three standard web design packages as well as a service to refurbish an existing website.

A Explain two possible reasons for the differences in the price of the three design packages offered by GSWebDesign.

B Explain which package (basic, advanced or eshop) would be most suitable for:
- a mobile hairdresser
- a business selling car parts to owners of second-hand cars.

C Using a business idea of your own choice, research the cost of establishing a website designed to increase the profits of the business. Produce a table itemising these costs:
- start-up costs: software, hardware and web design costs (assume that you do not own a computer or any relevant software)
- running costs: ISP, hosting and employee costs (costing your own time if you choose to be a sole trader).

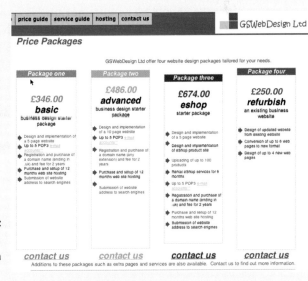

Source: www.gswebdesign.co.uk

Topic 5 Going online: design issues

Setting the scene: websites that suck

Websites that suck (www.websitesthatsuck.com) promotes good web design by providing examples of bad web design!

Vincent Flanders'
Web Pages That Suck

Showing Sucky Design Since 1996

Examples of Bad Design

Daily Sucker -- Current Examples of Bad Design

The Biggest Web Design Mistakes of 2004

Mystery Meat Navigation

Original WPTS circa 1996-98

Stupid Versions of the Home Page

Fixing Your Bad Design

Speeches / Videos

Buy my book "Son of Web Pages That Suck" -- **From** ~ $2.79 up

Mystery meat navigation

Mystery Meat is a term American kids are first exposed to in high school. At lunch there's always this one meat selection that isn't readily identifiable and it's often disguised by a layer of thick gravy. The dish became known as mystery meat because you're not sure what kind of meat you're eating and high school kids love to come up with suggestions.

Now there's a new style of confusing website navigation that is becoming popular: it's based on JavaScript rollovers and it's just like mystery meat! Mystery meat navigation (MMN) confuses people because you have to find the navigational system and then move your mouse over each image to discover where it will take you. If the user doesn't realise that MMN is being used, they can be left staring at the web page with no idea what to do next (apart from visiting a different website).

Web design is not about art, it's about making money or providing information. To make money, you don't want to design a site that might confuse someone. You want your visitors to quickly find what they're looking for and then write you a cheque.

Navigating a website should be no different to any other form of navigation: it needs to be user friendly. Imagine driving down the motorway and being faced with a set of blank road signs that wait for you to get very near them before they reveal any information – they would not be much use!

Although it is essential for a website to have a clear system of navigation, there are some circumstances when web designers might use JavaScript rollovers. Can you think of any situations when this technique might be effective and appropriate?

Visit www.websitesthatsuck.com and make a list of the some of the mistakes made by web designers. Rank these mistakes in order of how damaging they might be to the effectiveness of a website.

Source: www.websitesthatsuck.com

Effective web design

Designing an effective website is both a creative and a disciplined activity: designers need to construct an engaging experience that hooks the target customer, but they also need to produce a series of connected web pages that can be easily navigated and understood. Ultimately if a website doesn't achieve any of its aims and objectives, then it is ineffective.

To provide a structure to the design process, designers talk about the form and function of a product. A website is just like any other product, and the concepts of form and function help to ensure that a website achieves its aims and objectives.

Figure 4.7 illustrates these concepts of form and function. It uses a Nokia mobile phone, as an example, to show how considerations of form and function apply to any product.

Unit 4 Investigating electronic business

Target customers are the type of users – defined, say, by age, sex and income levels – that a website is aimed at.

Navigation concerns how the user moves from page to page within a website. Accurate navigation is essential and usually achieved through the use of menus and hyperlinks, and a clear user interface.

Hyperlinks are text or images on a web page which, when clicked, will cause the browser to display a related web page or specific place within the current page.

User interface is the components of a website that allow users to navigate and access information.

Menus are lists of options, displayed as text or images, which users click on to navigate through a site. Clear menus are an essential part of an effective website.

Hierarchical structure is one way of organising a website, in which the home page is at the top level with links to several other pages at lower levels.

JavaScript is a programming language which allows web designers to produce various animated effects.

JavaScript rollover is a feature which allows the position of the user's mouse on the screen to causes an effect, such as revealing hidden words or images.

The form of a website

When developing a website, designers need to consider several different aspects of form.

- The **layout** of each web page – the extent to which each page looks fresh and engaging; the arrangement of blocks of colour, images and text.

- The **user interface** – the accessibility and logic of menus and other navigation systems; the use of JavaScript and Flash elements.

- The **font styles** and colour schemes used – the impression given by the font styles and range of colours used within the site.

- The **use of images and sound** – the extent to which pictures, video and music files are deployed create an appropriate atmosphere.

It is essential to design a consistent look and feel for the pages of a website. This should balance the various aspects of form to appeal to the target customer. Good web design relies on restraint and a limited use of gimmicks: less is always better!

Web pages that make extensive use of images, sound and animated user interfaces are called media-rich. Media-rich pages can be engaging, but they can also be slow to load and can confuse the target user.

stop and think

Visit Nokia's website at www.nokia.com. Look at Nokia's range of mobile phones and try out some of the interactive demonstrations. Think about how the web designers have considered form and function when designing the site.

173

Topic 5 Going online: design issues

Figure 4.7: The Nokia 6260 mobile phone – form and function

	Definitions	Features
Form	The appearance of the product: how engaging and/or easy it is to use; the quality of its construction.	■ The size and weight of the phone. The materials used for the case ■ The quality of the display number of colours and detail of displayed graphics ■ The location and size of the key pad clam shell construction
Function	What the product does: the range of tasks performed and how well the product performs these tasks.	■ The phone book facilities. How easy it is to find and dial a phone number? ■ The ability to browse the internet. The speed of the connection and the ease with which you can browse websites ■ The ability to connect to a computer. Can you synchronise diary appointments with Microsoft Outlook?

The function of a website

A website should be functionally able: that is, it should perform the tasks expected of it. In general this requires that it fulfils several criteria.

- Navigation is logical and allows users to get back to the home page, or navigate to other pages, wherever they are in the website.

- All navigation links work – clicking on menus and other navigational devices (such as a hyperlink) should take the user to the expected page.

- Each web page loads within an acceptable time, even for users with slow internet connections. An acceptable time is usually be between 30 and 60 seconds using a slow internet connection.

- Information is provided in bite-sized chunks. Web pages with excessive amounts of text should be avoided. Users should not have to scroll down the web page too far to find information. Hyperlinks are useful where this can't be avoided – to link to positions within the page – but it is better to split a long page into two or more shorter pages.

It is essential to map out the structure of a website before constructing it. By sketching out the hierarchical structure of the site (see Figure 4.8), web designers can ensure good navigation and anticipate the number of distinct web pages it requires.

stop and think

Visit an e-commerce website, such as www.mp3players.co.uk or www.amazon.co.uk, and identify the features of the site which show a good consideration of function.

quick questions

1 Identify four features of bad form in a website you regularly use.

2 Sketch out a possible hierarchical structure for a fan club website (for example, a site for fans of a football team or a band).

3 Explain one reason why good web design depends on form and function reinforcing each other.

Figure 4.8: Website hierarchical structure

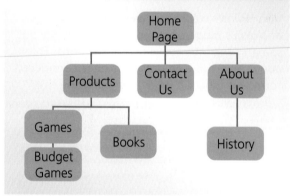

stop and think

How do you think the form of a website might change according to the characteristics of the target customers? Visit a range of websites which target different types of customers to get a feel for how the form of the websites change. For example, look at these web pages within the BBC website that are designed for different age groups:

- www.bbc.co.uk/cbeebies/

- www.bbc.co.uk/totp/

- news.bbc.co.uk/sport/

Unit 4 Investigating electronic business

Knowledge summary

- Web design needs careful consideration of form and function, given the aims and objectives of the website and needs of its target users.

- Form requires that the web designer considers layout, the user interface, fonts styles, colour schemes, and the use of images and sound.

- Function requires that the web designer sketches out the hierarchical structure of the site and ensures that web pages are not too lengthy or slow to load.

- Good web design happens when form and function reinforce each other. Bad web design happens when form and function are in conflict.

data interpretation
The colour wheel

Too many websites show a very poor sense of colour – the pages look washed out (leaving the user distinctly bored) or the colours clash (leaving the user with a headache). The colour wheel is a simple device for choosing an effective colour scheme.

Complementary colours are colours chosen at opposite ends of the wheel, such as yellow and violet. Choose these colours to produce websites with a distinctive look.

Analogous colours are those chosen in the same area of the wheel, such as blue, blue violet and blue green. Choose these colours to project a harmonious atmosphere.

Triad colours are triangular sets of colours, such as red, blue and yellow, forming a perfect triangle on the wheel. Triad colours establish a sense of balance.

For example the BBC news website (news.bbc.co.uk) uses a triad scheme but also with some analogous colours. It also uses lots of white space. The overall effect is fresh but also assured and calm. It seems appropriate for a well-respected news agency.

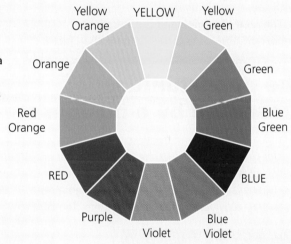

A Describe the differences between the complementary, analogous and triad colour schemes.

B Explain which colour scheme (complementary, analogous or triad) might be appropriate for each of these organisations' websites:
- Greenpeace, a pressure group whose aim is to protect the environment
- Cancer Research UK, a charity that develops treatments for cancer-related illnesses
- Toys R Us, a company retailing a range of children's toys.

C Visit at least five websites of your choice and record their use of colour in a table. Your table should have these headings:
- Website
- Probable target customers
- Type of colour scheme used
- Impression given by the colour scheme
- Overall comments

Use the completed table to justify which of the websites you feel makes the best use of colour.

Setting the scene: on-demand business

On-demand business is a phrase used by IBM, the large multinational computer manufacturer and software developer. On-demand business requires the use of the latest internet technologies to support joined-up thinking throughout an organisation. Employees access shared information systems and the business works closely with key suppliers and major customers.

In 2004, IBM ran a series of television adverts using the on-demand business slogan. The adverts depicted business executives in situations that required instant access to information and where they needed to respond to changing circumstances "on demand". Of course, the adverts showed that IBM's computers – networked by the latest technologies – helped the business executives deal with these problems.

The idea of on-demand business is an important one – it is certainly more than just a strapline to sell IBM products. It is saying that the opportunities available for a business with an online presence can be realised if its business systems are integrated and accessible to key stakeholders. In other words, the business should become one big system capable of responding to the needs of customers, employees and suppliers.

Too often, large organisations have internal communication problems – individual employees are placed in awkward situations where they simply don't know, or can't access, key information required to solve customer and supplier problems. By becoming an on-demand business, the corporate image of large businesses could be significantly improved.

An on-demand business approach could improve the corporate image of many businesses. Can you explain how it might improve the image of banks and supermarkets?

The opportunities presented by e-business

IBM's idea of on-demand business is a vision of what e-business could look like in the future. The current reality is that most businesses, even very large firms, have business systems that are not fully integrated across their activities and key stakeholders. The cost of the technology needed to achieve full integration is high, the technical expertise required is considerable and many businesses worry that the short-term costs could outweigh the long-term benefits.

However, though on-demand business has yet to be fully realised, many businesses currently make use of internet technologies to obtain two broad benefits:

KEY TERMS

A business's **corporate image** is the public's perceptions and impressions of the business, as a result of any interaction with the business and the way it presents itself.

Front-end systems are those business systems that are visible to customers, such as an online catalogue.

Back-end systems are those systems that deal with the internal processes of a business, such as delivering products to a customer.

Integrated business systems reduce the number of separate systems within a business to increase efficiency and reduce errors. An integrated system would deal with both front-end and back-end systems.

Payment bureau services provide online secure payment services to businesses. A business which uses a payment bureau service such as WorldPay does not need to have an internet merchant service and a payment service provider, making e-commerce easier to set up.

Internet merchant service (IMS) is an agreement with a bank that allows a business to collect money from its customers' bank accounts.

Payment service providers receive customers' credit and debit card details from an e-commerce website and process the transactions through associated IMS banks.

Personalised marketing is specifically targeted at the needs of an individual consumer rather than a broad group of consumers. For example, a company might make an offer to an individual based on that person's past purchases.

- improved business systems – which help, for example, to improve the way in which products are delivered to customers

- enhanced communication – which helps, for example, to target specific customer needs.

1 Improved business systems

The use of internet technologies can help to improve business processes. In particular, they can be used to provide online payment and ordering systems.

Payment systems

Secure payment systems ensure that transactions are safe – that no unauthorised person can view the details of the credit or debit card being used and possibly use that information for fraudulent transactions. By ensuring that their websites have secure payment systems, businesses can entice more customers to purchase online.

Secure payment systems can range from externally provided payment bureau services to sophisticated in-house systems. If a business decides to develop an in-house system, it will need to have an internet merchant service (IMS) and a payment service provider (PSP). In general, a small or medium-sized business would use a payment bureau service such as Netbanx or WorldPay. However, even many large established businesses prefer to use payment bureau services rather than develop their own in-house system.

	Intermediate e-commerce site	**Sophisticated e-commerce site**
Facilities	These will vary from package to package, but you can expect catalogue management, enhanced order processing, encryption for secure ordering, and a broader range of design templates. Others will offer a degree of back-end systems integration: that is, they will connect to your product database and accounts systems streamlining the order process and keeping the website up to date. This software should be more straightforward to use.	The range of options is huge and limited only by your budget and your ability to maintain the site. Intelligent cross-selling features can select and promote related products. Personalised pages can recognise previous visitors and display content that they are most interested in. Back-end systems can be integrated to trigger order confirmations, and to automatically dispatch goods and replenish stocks.
Costs	Something like Actinic and EROL will offer all of the above features for around £600. If you have a broadband connection, you will be able to receive orders in real time and update your website automatically. Broadband costs from upwards of £15 a month. Some ISPs offer a web hosting and software package all-in-one from about £1000.	At this level of sophistication, you will certainly need professional assistance from a development company to scope your technical requirements and build a website that integrates your existing systems. You may also want the services of a professional design agency. To custom design and build a sophisticated e-commerce website will cost well over £10,000.
Pros	Full e-commerce and payments functionality. Professional-looking design. Value-added features like account information, customer references and mechanisms to alert customers when goods are available.	Cutting-edge design and functionality. Site can be built to integrate with your existing systems. Provides a rich, interactive shopping experience for your customers.
Cons	Products such as technical equipment that require sophisticated options or user configuration may be too complex for this type of off-the-shelf system.	Takes longer to create than buying off-the-shelf and bespoke software can lock you into one service provider. Cost can be prohibitive for smaller businesses.

Figure 4.9: Developing online ordering systems

Source: adapted from DTI

The Department of Trade and Industry (DTI) has a website that provides advice to businesses on choosing a secure online payment system. You can visit this site at www.electronic-payments.co.uk.

Ordering systems

Online catalogues present a great opportunity for businesses to promote their products to customers. However, these catalogues must be easy to use and support accurate transactions. Various software products allow smaller businesses to develop their ordering systems. Bigger businesses might develop their own in-house solutions. Figure 4.9 sets out some of the options available to businesses that are planning to develop e-commerce websites.

The use of online catalogues has great potential for increasing the efficiency of a business's ordering systems: stock levels can be updated in real-time and reports can be produced identifying best selling items. An integrated online ordering system would also link the online catalogue system (the front end) to a delivery and shipping system (the back end). This would allow customers to track the progress of their orders and improve communication with suppliers.

> # stopandthink
>
> Using Figure 4.9, consider why a business might decide to opt for a sophisticated rather than an intermediate online ordering system?
>
> Visit the websites of Actinic (www.actinic.com) and EROL (www.erol.co.uk). How easy do you think it would be for a small business to add an online catalogue to its website?

2 Enhanced communication

The internet makes it much easier for a business to address a global audience. Websites also help a business to develop its corporate image through the use of latest news or press release web pages. However, the most significant opportunity created by internet technologies is that it provides businesses with the ability to enhance direct communication with key stakeholders. By using some of the technologies described below, a business can personalise the messages it sends to a wider range of stakeholders and encourage rapid feedback.

Wireless networks

Wireless technology makes it possible to reach employees, suppliers and customers in a wide range of locations. Devices, such as portable computers, fitted with wireless receivers do not need to be physically connected to a telephone line in order to connect to the internet. More business organisations are investing in solutions like the BlackBerry, which enables employees on the road to send and receive business e-mails and browse the internet.

Extranets

Extranets allow key business partners, such as suppliers, to access internal business systems. An extranet is an extension of a business's internal network of computers and allows trusted suppliers, and other key external stakeholders, secure access to business data. Extranets are one way a business can integrate its systems with those of its suppliers.

Dynamic web pages

Dynamic web pages use online databases to deliver user-specific information and support personalised marketing. The user is probably not aware of this, but the contents of the web page will alter depending on which user is viewing the page. Amazon UK uses this technology to offer specific products to individuals depending on the user's past purchases and browsing habits within the website. The web server knows which user is browsing the site because the user has to log in to the website or because the web server previously saved a cookie on the user's computer.

> # stopandthink
>
> Could e-mail be used for personalised marketing? Why might a marketing campaign based on e-mail be ineffective?

Knowledge summary

- The real benefits of e-business come from the integration of business systems.

- Although most businesses are unlikely to adopt a fully integrated approach to e-business, they can use internet technologies to improve the efficiency of their current systems and enhance communication with key external stakeholders.

- A business can add e-commerce systems to their existing websites by using a payment bureau service or by developing an in-house solution in partnership with an internet merchant service and a payment service provider.

- Wireless networks, extranets and dynamic web pages all help a business to enhance its communication with key stakeholders.

quick questions

1 Sketch out a design for an online catalogue web page, or a series of linked web pages, which illustrates the range of products offered by an e-tailer selling sports shoes.

2 Explain how the BlackBerry, or similar device, would be useful for teachers and students on a school or college trip. (Visit www.blackberry.com for more details about this device.)

3 Explain how dynamic web pages might be used by:
- a website dedicated to a particular music group
- a supermarket's online shopping website
- an online newspaper/magazine.

data interpretation
EROL e-commerce software

EROL (standing for electronic retail online) is a UK software company that produces e-commerce packages for small to medium-sized businesses (SMEs). The illustration shows the company's home page.

A Considering EROL's target audience, explain three reasons why this is an effective home page.

B The owner of a store retailing a range of young children's clothes – providing outfits for babies to children under five – wants to establish an e-commerce website. The owner has a website but it has no e-commerce facilities. The owner has some IT abilities but would need training to use e-commerce software.

Estimate the cost of setting up e-commerce facilities, including the cost of training (visit www.erol.co.uk) and payment bureau services (visit www.worldpay.co.uk). State any assumptions you have made in reaching your cost estimate.

Setting the scene: phishing for money

This is an extract from an e-mail received on 14 September 2004. The person receiving the e-mail did not have an account at SunTrust Internet Banking.

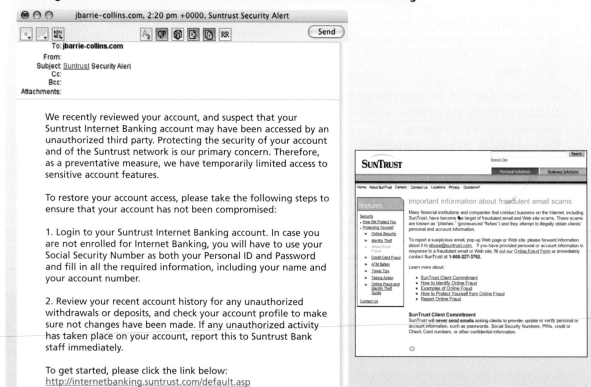

The e-mail is an example of an internet threat called phishing. The web link at the bottom of the e-mail took the user to a website that looks like SunTrust's site but was actually been set up by a criminal who used the site to try and collect customer account details. This web link, as with others that engage in phishing, was deactivated a few hours after the e-mail was sent to potential victims.

SunTrust is aware of this and other similar phishing threats. It is making every effort to protect its customers from phishing scams. There is a section of its website warning the bank's customers about phishing and other e-mail scams.

If the phishing e-mail had been sent to a person with a SunTrust account, do you think they might be tricked into following the web link? Search the internet for phishing – for example by using Google (www.google.co.uk). Is phishing a serious threat to security on the internet?

Possible threats to an online presence

The internet can be an enormously useful business tool. It can transform the activities of some companies and become the principal way in which they do business.

Given this potential – and to make the most of the opportunity – it is vital that online businesses protect themselves from two broad threats:

- internet threats – for example, not reacting to current phishing scams

- legal threats – for example, non-compliance with the Data Protection Act.

Phishing is an attempt to trick a user into providing confidential information to an unauthorised person through e-mail or a false web page. Phishing is a contraction of the words password harvesting fishing.

Viruses and **worms** are small programs attached to a standard computer file (such as a word processing document). A virus, or worm, attempts to copy and spread itself to other files and computers. Some viruses and worms are harmless, while others can delete valuable data and disable a computer.

Trojans and **spyware** are programs that collect and/or transmit information from a computer without the user's knowledge or consent. For example, a key logger spyware program transmits a user's keyboard input over the internet to a criminal's computer. The criminal is usually looking for confidential information such as online banking passwords and account numbers.

Crackers are criminals who gain unauthorised access to a computer, usually to corrupt or steal data. Crackers will try to gain access to a user's computer over the internet.

Hackers are enthusiastic or skilled computer programmers who try to access computer systems and networks for which they have no authorisation. They have no criminal intentions but would benefit from getting out more often!

Firewalls are hardware and/or software systems designed to protect a user's computer from crackers, trojans and spyware by blocking suspicious internet communication.

Copyright is the legal protection accorded to ideas created by an individual or organisation. There is copyright in newspaper articles, business trademarks and brand-related materials.

1 Internet threats

The internet is part of our daily lives. It is, therefore, hardly surprising that it has also become a target for criminal and malicious activities. Figure 4.10 summarises some of the main internet threats and suggest ways in which businesses can protect themselves.

Any business that establishes an online presence must take these threats seriously. If an online business does not establish proper internet security routines – by, for example, using anti-virus software and a firewall – then it is leaving the door open for criminals to steal valuable information and vandalise the business's information systems.

Figure 4.10: Internet threats

Threat	Nature of threat	Possible protection
Phishing	A business affected by phishing scams can lose customer confidence and its corporate image can be damaged.	Businesses should monitor e-mail activity. Customers should be warned about current phishing scams with the business providing both e-mail and website support.
Viruses and worms	Vital business information could be lost and customers' computers infected by the virus or worm.	Businesses should ensure that all files and e-mails sent and received over the internet are scanned for viruses and worms. Anti-virus software should be kept up to date with frequent updates.
Crackers, trojans and spyware	Sensitive business information could be stolen, such as customer account details. Bad publicity could result as the business's computer system might be reported as being insecure.	Businesses should use a firewall to guard against crackers attempting to access valuable and sensitive data. The business should regularly scan computer hard drives for trojans and spyware. Employees should only visit trusted websites and should be discouraged from using business computers for private reasons.

2 Legal threats

All businesses must observe a wide range of legal requirements designed to protect employees, suppliers, consumers and other stakeholders. Online businesses – like any other business – need to meet these requirements but they also need to consider the particular legal issues that can arise from having an online presence. These issues are summarised in Figure 4.11.

The Data Protection Act 1998 (DPA) is of considerable importance to online businesses that undertake e-commerce. By trading online, a business is likely to collect a range of personal data on its customers, and it must ensure that in handling and storing this data it complies with the Data Protection Act. Figure 4.12 summarises the eight key principles of the DPA.

online businesses must also ensure that their websites are accessible to people with disabilities. Failure to comply could leave a business open to prosecution under the Disability Discrimination Act (see www.disability.gov.uk for more details).

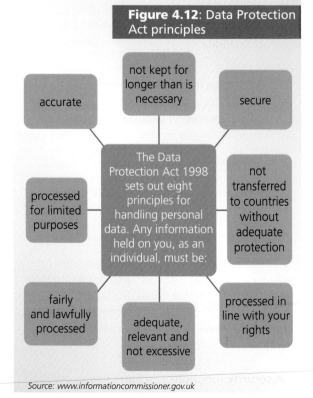

Figure 4.12: Data Protection Act principles

The Data Protection Act 1998 sets out eight principles for handling personal data. Any information held on you, as an individual, must be:

- accurate
- not kept for longer than is necessary
- secure
- not transferred to countries without adequate protection
- processed in line with your rights
- adequate, relevant and not excessive
- fairly and lawfully processed
- processed for limited purposes

Source: www.informationcommissioner.gov.uk

Figure 4.11: Legal issues that can impact on online businesses

Domain names
Before an on line business chooses its domain name, it should check that this does not use a registered trademark of another business.

Terms & Conditions
Customers need to be informed of their rights, especially when selling outside of the UK or the EU.

Distance selling
Customers have additional rights when buying certain products through the internet such as electrical equipment.

Copyright
On line businesses need to protect the content of their web sites and also ensure that they do not copy other business's web site content.

Tax implications
The tax paid by a customer depends partly on the location of the business' s web server and partly on the nationality of the customer.

Data protection
If the business collects user data through its website, then it must comply with the Data Protection Act 1998.

Knowledge summary

- Online business needs to protect itself from online threats by establishing internet security routines.

- All businesses need to establish clear guidelines for employees regarding the use of e-mail and the internet.

- A range of legal issues need to be considered before establishing an online presence, especially if this involves e-commerce.

- It is essential that online businesses provide clear information on their websites detailing how personal information is stored and used.

quick questions

1 Explain two reasons why an online business should take steps to protect itself from internet threats.

2 Explain why a business should carry out research before it chooses and registers a domain name.

3 Explain two ways in which a business could improve the accessibility of its website for people with impaired vision.

data interpretation
Maintaining internet security

Bank moves to close web loophole

A security loophole at a bank has allowed easy access to sensitive credit card information.

The Morgan Stanley website allowed users to access account details after entering just the first digit of a credit card number. The shortcut would only work if the account holder had set up their internet browser to automatically save passwords – a feature called autocomplete.

Autocomplete allows computer users to shortcut security checks by saving data such as user IDs and passwords. However, the autocomplete system should not work on secure financial sites, according to guidelines issued by the Association for Payment Clearing Services (Apacs), the body that oversees the banking payments system.

When told of the loophole, technical staff at Morgan Stanley immediately fixed the problem.

Source: adapted from www.news.bbc.co.uk, 9 November 2004

A Describe the internet security threat described in the BBC article.

B The autocomplete facility of an internet browser is switched on or off by the user. Discuss whether Morgan Stanley was at fault for the security loophole if its customers chose to switch on the autocomplete facility.

C Produce a five-minute presentation on the possible threats to a business of establishing an online presence. You should focus on a specific type of business, such as a package holiday business. Your presentation should consider either internet threats or legal threats, and should focus on four key points.

Designing your own business website

Setting the scene: Surge

Surge is the radio station of Southampton University. It has won several awards, including an award for its website (www.surge.soton.ac.uk).

On the Surge website, the images used for navigation links are simple and clear. Each has a single word describing its function. Users can quickly select the page or feature they want by clicking on one of these images.

Some of the functions of the site are:

- a sound stream so that users can listen to the radio station over the internet

- web and e-mail features for requesting particular tracks

- information about events organised or reported by the radio station

- news aimed at the target audience – the students at Southampton University.

Surge's website would seem to be helping to meet the needs and wants of its target audience. Its website is simple but effective, and fulfils its likely purpose – to entertain and inform.

Identify three features of Surge Radio's home page that illustrate good design. Explain why you think these features illustrate good design. (Remember the ideas about form and function covered in Topic 5.)

KEY TERMS

Streaming is playing sound or video in real time as it is downloaded over the internet. A plug-in to a web browser receives and plays the data. Video streams work best when the user has a broadband internet connection.

Plug-ins are programs which add to the functionality of another program. For example, Real Network's Real Player plug-in allows an internet browser to receive and play audio and video streams.

The **layout** is the way in which text and images are placed on a page, such as the number of columns of text, where pictures are placed and the use of white space.

White space, the gaps in a page layout without any content, is just the web page background.

Functionality is a way of referring to what the web page does – that is, the range of dynamic and interactive elements on the web page.

File compression is a technique used to reduce the amount of space taken up by a computer file. File compression is an essential technique for reducing internet download times.

Planning a website

Considerable planning needs to take place before a website can be made available to the public. Figure 4.13 shows the design steps that could help to ensure the development of an effective website. These issues are not always clear at the outset: for example, a web designer may have to draw on various sources of information to try and understand the needs and wants of the target audience.

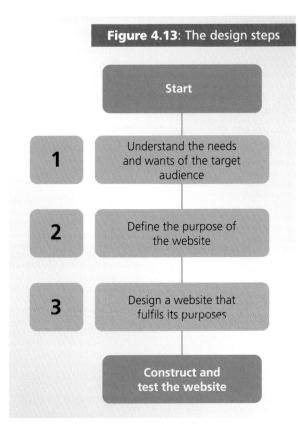

Figure 4.13: The design steps

Start

1 — Understand the needs and wants of the target audience

2 — Define the purpose of the website

3 — Design a website that fulfils its purposes

Construct and test the website

1 Needs and wants

Successful businesses understand the needs and wants of their customers. In the same way, the designer of a successful website understands the needs and wants of the target audience – the intended users of the website. Figure 4.14 summarises three general needs and wants important to users.

It would be wrong to assume that all target users of a website have the same needs and wants. Website designers should carry out research before defining the purposes of their websites.

2 Defining the purposes

> ### stop and think
>
> Make a list of what you would expect from your school or college's website. Compare your list with other students. Do they have different expectations or is it clear what the website should offer? Do you think the designers of the current website took the needs and wants of students into account?

Websites can fulfil a variety of purposes. They can be:

- educational – educating the user through a series of structured web pages and interactive elements

- promotional – interesting the user in an organisation's goods and services

- informative – increasing the user's awareness and understanding of issues and/or products

- commercial – supporting financial transactions, such as a user buying a product online

- recreational – entertaining, amusing and engaging the user.

Web designers should have very clear purposes for the websites they develop. These purposes will have been set after considering the needs and wants of the target audience.

It is sensible to have a small number of purposes when developing a new website. Each page in the website should have a very specific purpose and the number of pages should be kept to the absolute minimum required.

Figure 4.14: Needs and wants of users

Need or want	Example
Information	Users might need information on current products. They might want information on future product developments.
Products	Users might need 24-hour access to services. They might want to download free products.
Entertainment	Users might need to be entertained before being prepared to investigate the website. They might also want to be amused.

3 Designing the website

Topic 5 looked at design issues and introduced the ideas of form and function. These ideas should be applied when designing both the hierarchical structure of the website – that is, the number of pages and how they link together (see Figure 4.8) – and the layout, content and functionality of each page.

Given the purposes of the website, and the purpose of each page within it, the web designer will use a variety of design techniques to meet the needs of the target audience. Figure 4.15 illustrates some of these design techniques.

Many commercial websites will also include promotional elements within their web pages, such as advertising banners and graphics promoting products. However, advertising banners are often large images and can take time to download. This increase in download time can irritate users and could stop them visiting a website. Advertising banners are a useful promotional tool but they should be used sparingly.

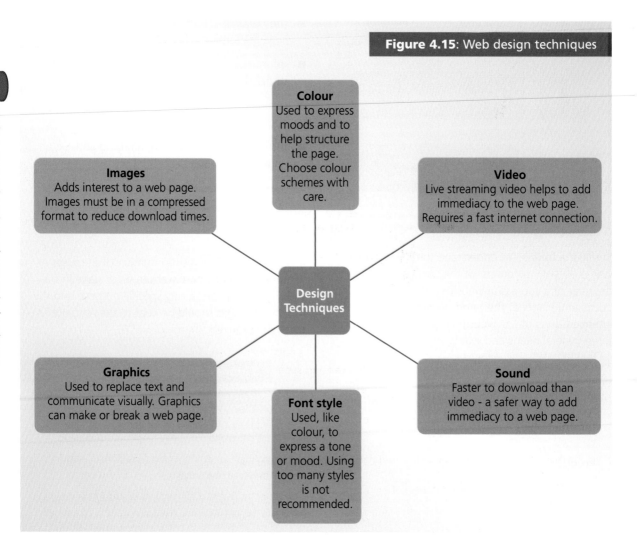

Figure 4.15: Web design techniques

Colour
Used to express moods and to help structure the page. Choose colour schemes with care.

Images
Adds interest to a web page. Images must be in a compressed format to reduce download times.

Video
Live streaming video helps to add immediacy to the web page. Requires a fast internet connection.

Design Techniques

Graphics
Used to replace text and communicate visually. Graphics can make or break a web page.

Font style
Used, like colour, to express a tone or mood. Using too many styles is not recommended.

Sound
Faster to download than video - a safer way to add immediacy to a web page.

Knowledge summary

■ Developing a website requires researching the needs and wants of the target audience, defining the purposes of the website based on these needs and wants, and designing a website that fulfils these purposes.

■ Website designers can use a range of design techniques, but these techniques should be used sparingly.

■ The hierarchical structure of a website and the design of each web page should have only one objective in mind: to fulfil the purpose of the website.

quick questions

1 List the likely needs and wants of the following users:
– 14–16-year-old fans of a music group, see for example www.destinyschild.com
– 10–14-year-old fans of the Harry Potter films, see www.harrypotter.com
– 16–18-year-old students researching higher education courses, see for example www.kingston.ac.uk

2 Describe the likely purposes of a website designed to meet the needs and wants of one of the groups of users featured in question 1.

3 These are four different font styles.

Arial: Looks like this.

Comic Sans MS: Looks like this.

Times New Roman: Looks like this.

Brush Script: Looks like this.

Rank the font styles in order of:
– how easy they are read
– how interesting they are.

data interpretation
Promoting a sponsored event

Websites are often used to promote sponsored events aimed at raising funds for charities. These websites have three main purposes:

■ to provide information about the charity and the nature of the sponsored event

■ to explain how to take part in the event or to sponsor individuals taking part in the event

■ to report the actual event and to record the amount of funds raised.

Your school or college has decided to hold two events to raise funds for Cancer Research UK:

■ a sponsored five-a-side football tournament all players have to be dressed as a character from *South Park* or *The Simpsons* cartoon series

■ a sponsored three-legged five-kilometre race.

You have been asked to design a five-page website for the sponsored events.

A Identify the main purposes of the website.

B Sketch out the hierarchical structure of the website.

C Sketch the layout of each page within the website, explaining your choice of design techniques and the purpose of each page.

Producing and launching your own business website

Setting the scene: HTML and WYSIWYG

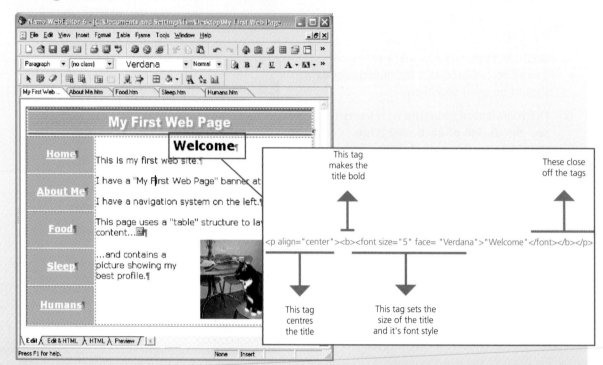

Web pages are written in HTML. This consists of markers or tags that are placed around the text to be displayed in the browser. For example, the line of HTML code shown here sets the font style, size and position of the word "Welcome" that is displayed as the title of the webpage.

Without a knowledge of HTML it used to be very difficult to produce a website. However, with the arrival of WYSIWYG web authoring programs, graphic designers with no understanding of HTML can produce complex websites. Graphic designers are now able to use their design skills to create sophisticated and appealing websites.

Namo WebEditor (www.namo.com) is a typical WYSIWIG web authoring program and it has been used here to create "My First Web Page". When in Edit mode, the program functions like a word processor. This lets the designer concentrate on the content and layout of the web page: as the content is laid out, the program writes the HTML code for you.

Web authoring was a difficult task in the early days of the internet. Why do you think the arrival of WYSIWYG web authoring programs was such an important event?

Producing a new website

When using a WYSIWYG web authoring program to create a website, a graphic designer can:

- use tables to layout the content of each web page

- use hyperlinks to create a navigation system between web pages.

1 Using tables to lay out content

Word processing programs, such as Microsoft Word, let you create tables to produce forms and other business documents. Similarly, most WYSIWYG web authoring programs also allow you to use tables to create home pages. For example, the home page illustrated in Setting the scene (above) was laid out with the help of the table.

Figure 4.16 shows a schematic version of the table used to create this home page. The table originally had six rows and two columns. This was then modified by merging some of the cells. Merging cells is achieved by selecting the cells you want to turn into a single cell and choosing the Merge Cells option. (Some programs will use the word "join" rather than "merge" to describe this function, but it achieves the same effect).

Once a table is created, the designer can hide it by making its borders invisible. This can be done by giving the borders the same colour as the page or by switching the borders off. Switching a border off is achieved by setting the border thickness to zero!

The designer completes the web page by placing text, graphics and other types of web content into the cells. Using this technique, it is possible to create an effective web page in a short space of time. Visit the BBC website to see an effective use of table layouts (www.bbc.co.uk) and note the different layouts the BBC achieves by using tables.

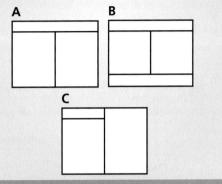
2 Using hyperlinks to navigate

The website illustrated in Setting the scene (*see page* 188) uses a simple but effective navigation system. This was created by using five cells in a table layout. Each cell was given a coloured background, and a one or two-word description of the linked web page was then entered into the cells – Home, About Me, Food, etc. A hyperlink was then attached to each cell. This is an HTML instruction that turns a graphic or piece of text into an active link to another web page.

To set up a hyperlink in a WYSIWYG web authoring program, select the text or graphic and choose the Hyperlink option. Then enter the web page the user should be taken to when they click on the hyperlink.

Figure 4.16: A schematic web authoring layout table

Banner graphic placed here	
	Text and picture placed here

Navigation buttons placed in left hand table cells

Launching a new website

Figure 4.17 illustrates the steps that need to be taken when launching a new website.

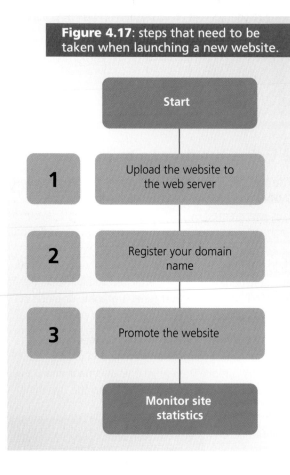

Figure 4.17: steps that need to be taken when launching a new website.

Start

1 — Upload the website to the web server

2 — Register your domain name

3 — Promote the website

Monitor site statistics

Step 1

The completed website is transferred, or uploaded, from the business computer to the web server. The web server is permanently connected to the internet and able to serve users who log on to the website using their browsers.

Step 2

If a business does not register a domain name (such as www.amazon.co.uk), or link the website to an existing domain name, users will not be able to visit the website as it will not have an address. All domain name registrations must go through registered authorities. In the UK, the main domain name registration authority is Nominet (www.nominet.org.uk). It registers all .uk domain names – including all sites that have .org.uk, .co.uk and .net.uk suffixes. However, individual businesses do not deal directly with Nominet: a business's web host or internet service provider will register domain names with Nominet for a fee.

Step 3

The website should be submitted to various search engines. Banner advertisements, on other websites, could also be used to promote the site. However, this can be counterproductive as banner advertising can irritate users. The new web address should be included on promotional materials (such as business cards and company stationery) and the site could be promoted through publicity events reported by news media.

Live websites should be constantly monitored to review the number of visitors, the most frequently visited pages and to identify problem pages. Pages will sometimes fail to load in users' browsers and these events must be monitored and corrected.

Knowledge summary

- HTML is used to construct web pages and WYSIWYG web authoring programs allow web designers to produce websites without having to understand HTML.

- Tables are an efficient way to structure the layout of web pages.

- Website navigation systems rely on the use of hyperlinks.

- Domain names are the addresses of the world wide web and must be registered with appropriate authorities, such as Nominet for .uk names.

quick questions

1 How would these HTML tags display the word "Welcome" in a browser?
`<p align="left"><i><font size="3" face="Arial">Welcome</font></i></p>`

2 Why should every page in a website have, at the very least, the following hyperlinks:
– Home page link?
– Contact Us page link?

3 When choosing the domain name for a website, when would these types be appropriate: .co.uk; .com; .org.uk; .biz?

data interpretation
The most hated advertising techniques

Research carried out by Yahoo! and eBay has found that web users are irritated by advertising that:

- pops up in a separate window
- takes time to load
- tries to trick you into clicking on it
- covers up what you are trying to see
- floats around the screen
- automatically plays sound.

People often have strong reactions to advertising. One user, referring to an advert that automatically started playing audio, wrote: "If anything could be worse than pop-ups, this is it. I hate this ad. Hate, hate, hate."

Not many adverts are actively loved by users, but some advertising techniques do have a positive impact on the user experience. Users were particularly pleased with adverts that clearly:

- indicate what will happen if people click on them
- relate to what people are doing online
- identify themselves as advertisements
- present information about what they are advertising
- provide additional information without having to leave the page.

These design elements are tightly connected to traditional web usability guidelines: make the users' options clear, speak plainly and provide the information users want.

Source: www.uscit.com

A Explain three reasons why web users are irritated by advertising on websites.

B Explain why advertising is likely to be accepted by web users if it "makes the users' options clear, speaks plainly and provides the information users want".

C Research e-commerce websites, such as eBay and Amazon, to identify two examples of:
- bad advertising, likely to irritate the user
- good advertising, likely to be accepted by the user.

Justify your choice of examples.

Business in practice: comparing two websites

Kids Casuals

Kids Casuals is a retailer of children's clothes. Established in July 2001, the business owned by Nicola Dickenson, a sole trader. As we saw in the data interpretation exercise in Topic 1 (*see page 159*), Kids Casuals is an example of how a simple website can establish an effective online presence.

Background to the business

Kids Casuals retails a range of children's clothing, including t-shirts, sweatshirts, bags, caps and socks.

The business was originally named Little Dragons Children's Funwear. Unfortunately the domain names www.littledragons.co.uk and www.littledragons.com had already been registered, so Nicola Dickenson decided to change the business's name.

Before establishing an online presence, the business achieved most of its sales at major agricultural shows, craft shows and seasonal fairs in Wales and Ireland. As a result, the business made no sales in the five months of each trading year during which there were no craft shows, fairs or other retailing opportunities and outlets.

Nicola Dickenson attempted to generate year-round sales by establishing a mail order business. She sent out a mailshot to customers, but as Kids Casuals did not have a printed brochure, Nicola enclosed a copy of one of her supplier's brochures. This brochure promoted the supplier's own website and some of

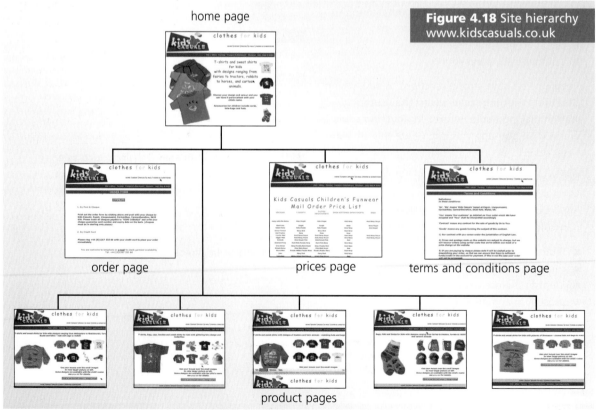

home page

order page

prices page

terms and conditions page

product pages

Figure 4.18 Site hierarchy www.kidscasuals.co.uk

clothes for kids

kids CASUALS

HOME | ORDER | PRICES | E-MAIL | TERMS & CONDITIONS

Pink + Glitter Farming Transport & Skateboard Discovaus Caps, Bags & Socks

ORDER FORM

Click to Print

| | | Your Name: | Name to send to if different: |
| | | Your Address: | Delivery Address if different |

1. By Post & Cheque

Print out the order form by clicking above a... Kids Casuals, Esgair, Llanpumsaint, Carmar... 6JU. Please make all cheques payable to "K... cheque guarantee card number and expiry ... must be in sterling only please)

2. By Credit Card

Please ring +44 [0]1267 253 86 with your ... immediately.

You are welcome to telephone or **e-mail**
Tel: +44 [0]1267

Daytime telephone no:

Your e-mail address

Design & Childs Name if Required	Garment Type	Age	Colour	Qty.	Price Total Add £2.00 if child's name added

	Total Goods
	Standard P&P
	UK & NI £1.50
	Eire €2.00
	Price Total

Nicola's clients began to buy online direct from the supplier instead of through Kids Casuals. The loss of customers led Nicola to realise that she needed to develop an internet presence to remain competitive.

Purpose of the online presence

As a sole trader with no previous business experience of using e-mail or the internet, Nicola Dickenson believed that it would be too risky to try and establish a full online retailing system. Instead, she wanted an online presence that could generate mail order sales during the five months of each trading year when there are no shows or fairs to attend. Nicola also wanted to ensure that she had the potential to compete with rival businesses that already had an online presence.

To achieve an online presence, Nicola:

- purchased a computer and a multi-function printer/scanner

- established 24/7 (24 hours a day, 7 days a week) internet access with an ISP

- paid a web designer to develop a brochure style website with a basic online order form

- registered two web addresses – www.kidscasuals.co.uk and www.kidscasuals.com

- set up a dedicated e-mail address sales@kidscasuals.co.uk to receive online mail order enquiries.

Features of the online presence

The Kids Casuals' website uses a traditional hierarchical structure. It deliberately limits itself to the pages required to generate mail order sales – the stated purpose of Kids Casuals' online presence. Therefore, in addition to pages displaying the business's product range, there are separate pages containing an order form, price details, and Kid Casuals' terms and conditions.

The colour scheme used by the website is striking. It draws on the colours present in the Kids Casuals' logo. The graphic design is clean and simple and the product pages make use of roll-over effects: when users place their mouse pointers over a small image of a product, a larger image appears. This is a simple but effective way of illustrating the business's products.

The order page contains a form (see left) which allows the users to type in the details of his or her order. A button on this order page allows the user to print out the web page. This printout can then be posted to Kids Casuals. Alternatively, the customer can telephone Kids Casuals and purchase products using a credit card.

Security issues

As the Kids Casuals' website does not have online purchasing facilities, the site does not need to be secure. However, Nicola Dickenson receives e-mails from current and potential customers and needs to ensure that her business computer is protected from online threats such as viruses and worms.

Shortly after Nicola purchased her computer, it exhibited a number of problems. An investigation by her local e-commerce adviser revealed that several viruses and a worm had infected the PC in the space of just two to three weeks. Kaspersky Anti-Virus was pre-installed on the PC, but Nicola did not realise that the anti-virus files needed updating. Just after starting to use her new computer, a major new worm had appeared (now known as MSBlaster) and, through exploiting weaknesses in the Microsoft XP operating system, had spread very rapidly via the internet. (At the time, this was the fastest spreading worm ever to affect the internet and its users.)

Nicola's e-commerce adviser rectified her computer security problems by:

- activating the firewall included in the Windows XP operating system

- updating the Windows operating system from the Microsoft website

- updating the Kaspersky anti-virus files and running the anti-virus program to clean the machine

- setting up automatic updates to the anti-virus files and setting up an automated regular anti-virus scan.

Source: some material for this case study has been sourced and adapted from Opportunity Wales (www.opportunitywales.co.uk).

Chips

Chips retails video games and accessories for personal computers (PCs) and games consoles. It was started in the mid-1980s during the birth of the video games industry. Chips is a private limited company, with several retail outlets and an award-winning website (www.chipsworld.co.uk).

Background

Chips retails a range of games and accessories for personal computers and games consoles, including Microsoft Xbox, Nintendo Game Cube and Sony PlayStation 2.

Chips has 25 retail outlets (as at January 2005), with seven company-owned stores and 18 franchised stores. The location of Chips' retail outlets are shown on the map. Further details of the company's stores can be found at www.chipsworld.co.uk/chiloc.asp.

Purpose of the online presence

Chips' website aims to provide:

■ safe and accessible e-commerce services enabling consumers to purchase video games and accessories

■ financial, marketing and operations information for anyone interested in setting up a Chips franchise outlet

■ promotional information about Chips, such as news and press releases.

In general, the website would seem to be designed to support the growth of the company by:

■ increasing sales of video games and accessories

■ increasing the number of franchised stores.

Features of the online presence

As the website has two main purposes, it is split into two separate structures: online sales and franchisee information.

Online sales

This section of the website uses a black background for all its pages. The black background helps to emphasise the video games that are illustrated on many of the pages. Green and red colours, contained in the Chips' logo, are used for key information: red for game titles and green for product prices.

The user can personalise the home page to focus on the games console format that is of most interest – by choosing from Game Cube, PC, PlayStation 2 and Xbox. A full search facility allows users to quickly find a desired product by typing in the name of a game.

This search can be restricted to a particular platform; so, for example, a search can be restricted to PlayStation games only.

The website does not have a simple hierarchical structure – unlike the Kids Casuals' website – but incorporates a technology called "active server pages" or "asp". Active server web pages are indicated by the use of a ".asp" extension rather than the usual ".htm" – compare, for example, www.chipsworld.co.uk/pccdgam.asp with www.kidscasuals.com/order.htm.

The website connects to a database that stores a list of available products, together with their description, prices and current availability. When a user selects a particular game, the website passes a product code to the database which then returns (or serves up) the details about the product back to the web page. The web page then displays the information (see example for *Half Life 2* above).

Active server pages allow Chips to quickly update its e-commerce website. Instead of altering individual web pages, an employee simply updates the product database. This is a much faster process and can be carried out by employees with no knowledge of HTML or website construction.

Franchisee information

The franchise section of the website also uses active server page technology. As well as giving information about setting up a Chips franchise, it contains an updated list of press releases and case studies about current Chips franchisees.

This section of the Chips website uses a white page background for all of its pages. All main headings are in green, while links to pages are in red.

Any potential franchisee interested in setting up a Chips franchise would find this section of the website accessible and informative. It contains (as at January 2005) 14 case studies on individual franchisees and numerous press releases outlining the development of the Chips business.

Security issues

As an e-commerce website, Chips ensures that the online sales section of its website is secure – so all financial transactions are carried out using secure web pages. In addition, Chips' website promotes the fact that it has two additional safety features.

It is a member of Shop Safe. This is an online shopping directory (www.shopsafe.co.uk) that only lists secure retail websites.

It uses the VeriSign security service which validates the fact that Chips uses a secure server for its financial transactions. This guards against any phishing activity and reassures users that they can safely use the website to purchase goods from Chips. The Chips secure server verification is shown in the panel below.

activities

1 Compare the Kids Casuals' and Chips' websites in terms of:
 – purpose
 – features
 – security issues

2 For each business, explain how its website might help to achieve its aims and objectives. You may need to visit each website to confirm your ideas.

3 For each business, outline and justify two ways in which its website could be improved to support the achievement of the business's aims and objectives. When choosing your improvements, consider both the form and function of each website.

CHOICE IS AN ESSENTIAL PART OF SOCIETY. Businesses offer customers choice and if they get their products and service right, they will attract trade. But if they get it wrong, dissatisfied customers will exercise their right to choose and take their business to competitors.

It is vital, therefore, that a business understands its customers and what they need and want. A business must constantly monitor and review its policies and procedures so that it can retain its existing customers as well as attract new customers. In short, a business must get its customer service right.

Customer service is making sure everything works for the customer. It means offering the right product at the right time, delivering efficient and incident-free service, providing a safe and clean environment, and giving excellent after-sales care.

This unit examines the importance of the customer. It gives examples of how different businesses respond to customer needs, monitor their service to customers and aim to achieve continuous improvement in customer service. It also examines the influence of the law on business activity and its impact on customers.

Investigating customer service

Introducing customer service

Setting the scene: a Smart approach to customer service

The essence of a successful business is an ability to respond to and meet customer expectations. Whatever the type of business, the focus of all business activities should be on the end customer. It is vital, therefore, that any business understands who its customers are, what their needs and desires are and what the customer is prepared to pay for products or services.

Businesses must constantly monitor and review their products and services to attract new customers and maintain customer loyalty. Loyal customers not only return to make further purchases but, importantly, they are an effective source of free word-of-mouth advertising – satisfied customers are likely tell everyone they know about great products and exceptional service. Equally, dissatisfied customers are not just lost customers but people who tell everyone they know that they couldn't recommend the business's products and services.

Mercedes-Benz has a long history of producing cars for the luxury end of the market. The company currently produces twelve models with one hundred and ninety-six variants, ranging in price from £13,000 to £142,000. Mercedes-Benz's luxury cars are produced to high design and technical specifications and customers have come to expect equally high-quality customer care.

Mercedes-Benz has traditionally only catered for the luxury end of the market. However, in 1998, following extensive market research, Mercedes-Benz launched a product to appeal to the needs of a different segment of the market. The Smart car is small, neat fuel efficient and easy to park. With prices staring at £7,955, it appeals to those would not choose, or could not afford, any of Mercedes-Benz luxury cars, while still offering Mercedes-Benz's high-quality design and technical excellence.

Mercedes-Benz has listened to the desires expressed by their customers to produce a more environmentally friendly car to suit a city lifestyle. The Smart car is almost entirely recyclable, it meets the stringent gas emission standards set by the European Union and its fuel consumption is low. The Smart car has become a status symbol in Europe for the young, upwardly mobile and environmentally friendly city dweller.

KEY TERMS

Customers can be internal or external to a business:

External customers are people or organisations that buy goods or services from a business.

Internal customers are the business's staff. Employees are internal customers in the sense that they need products and services from other staff within the business to carry out their functions.

Customer service is the process of identifying and putting the level of service in place to ensure customer satisfaction.

Customer expectations are the purchaser's wants and needs, usually expressed in terms of value, product features, customer service and after-sales care.

A business ensures **customer loyalty** by providing high quality, value-for-money products along with effective customer service.

What is customer service?

Customer service is the process of identifying and putting in place the level of service to ensure customer satisfaction. It is about making sure everything works for the customer by offering the right product to the right person at the right time in the right place. Good customer service is safe, efficient and incident free.

Successful businesses know their customers and are able to provide for their desires and needs, sometimes even anticipating what those desires and needs will be. Planning is at the heart of good customer service and businesses must organise themselves effectively to ensure a high level of customer care.

Looking after customers is important, both to gain their custom and to keep it. We live in a society that offers a great deal of choice and the level of customer service can be critical to determining where customers will spend their money. A reputation for offering good customer service will attract new customers, as well as keeping a business's existing ones. Providing poor service means risking losing customers to the business to your competitors.

What this unit covers

This unit looks at how businesses respond to customer needs and how they monitor and review the service they offer in order to implement continuous improvements. It also considers how business activity – and its impacts on customers – is regulated by law.

Businesses and customers

The unit starts by examining the importance of customer service in a variety of businesses. It explores the wide variety of customers any business has and how the business meets the different needs and expectations of those customers.

Effective customer service

This section considers the features involved in delivering good customer service. For example, it looks at the importance of staff appearance and helpfulness, the layout and accessibility of premises, and provision of quality products and services that offer added value.

Keeping customers

It is important to maintain and improve the quality of customer service both to attract new customers and keep existing customers. This section looks at codes of practice, customer service charters, loyalty schemes and discounts.

Customer service legislation

Key concepts in current UK and EU legislation and their implications are explored in the context of customer service and safe working environments.

GO TO the accompanying CD-ROM. Choose Unit 5 from the main menu. This will take you to an interactive game about providing good customer care. It is better to try this game once you have read Unit 5 Topics 1, 3, 4, 5, 6 and 8.

The importance of customer service

Setting the scene: bad service

Jayne has one hour for lunch. It's her birthday and she has many things to do. She needs to visit the newsagent, buy some cakes, collect her party dress from the dry cleaners and find out the times of the trains so that she can pick her Mum up from the station.

She phones train enquiries before she goes into town. Ten minutes pass and she has not been put through to an operator. She decides to try later.

In the newsagents, the magazine she wants is not available. She decides instead to buy a book, but the queue at the till is very long and she is kept waiting.

Eventually, she goes to the supermarket to buy some cakes for her friends at work. She picks up a packet of her favourites, but while she is waiting to pay at the checkout she realises that the cakes are past their sell-by date. She decides to leave it and to go to the bakery on the way back to work.

She is running late by now and does not have time to collect her dry cleaning. She is cross because the dry cleaners closes at 5pm and she doesn't finish work until half past.

What went wrong? How could the different businesses that Jayne was relying on have

improved their services so that she could have achieved everything she wanted to in her lunch break?

The customer base

Customers are the lifeblood of any business. Every customer demands a certain standard of care and service. In order to survive and compete successfully, businesses need to strive for high standards of customer service. This might mean:

- making sure that customers are safe

- improving the service on offer to customers

- improving the quality of products and services

- making sure that customers are not kept waiting

- demonstrating good after-sales care.

When you think of customers, you might get a mental picture of shoppers – of people buying goods and services in retail outlets – but it is important to appreciate that all organisations have customers. In some industries, such as management consultancy, a business's customers are other businesses – and these business clients, like shoppers, will demand good service. In health care, providing a good service to the "customer" is an essential part of the role of doctors, dentists, clinics and hospitals. In the public sector, local authorities, the police, the ambulance service and the fire service are all monitored to make sure that their services are efficient and meet the needs of the public.

All customers expect a quality product or service that is cost effective, safe, available and reliable. Businesses that operate in a competitive market, such as the car industry or supermarket the sector, need to monitor constantly how well they are meeting their customers' needs. Businesses that operate in the public sector are also increasingly expected to perform well for their customers. All businesses are finding that customers has become much more demanding. They expect a high level of service and care, whether it is when having a tooth filled at the dentist or when buying groceries at the supermarket.

Customers can be young or old, disabled or able bodied, come from different cultures or religions and have different tastes and preferences.

Why customer service matters

We live in a society that puts choice at its heart. Competition law (Unit 1, *see page* 48) prevents businesses from operating as a monopoly; a business therefore has to contend with rival competitors that aim to attract its customers. It is essential for a business to always have one eye on the competition in order that it can aim higher and be one step ahead in the quest to satisfy its customers and attract new ones away from its competitors.

One way to keep customers satisfied is by never taking them for granted. IBM, the computer services multinational, offers this advice:

"Every customer contact is an opportunity to increase the value of your customer asset, building loyalty, retention and profitability."

Marks & Spencer is an example of what can happen if a business does start to take its customers for granted. For years, the Marks & Spencer brand was quintessentially practical and stood for good quality. Customers could rely on Marks & Spencer: its products had a standard of quality and its stores were in every large town in the country. However, the company, to its detriment, took its eye off the ball and did not recognise the need to change in order to meet the needs of a new and more demanding generation of customers. Other brands began win market share from Mark & Spencer and the sales and reputation of a truly great British institution began to decline.

The directors have had to take a serious look at the core business to assess what it is that customers genuinely want and to understand how they can find a new niche market. They realised that competitors were exploiting the fact that many customers perceive the Marks & Spencer brand as old fashioned and boring. For example, British Homes Stores has been able to attract some of Marks & Spencer's customers by refocusing its own brand image and improving the goods it sell. As a result of the internal management review and in response to the greater competition, Marks & Spencer has made some far-reaching changes in an effort to win back its customer base and attract new customers.

stopandthink

Foxall's is a small independent electrical retailer that operates from a high street location in a Shropshire market town. It competes well with the multinational electrical retailers, such as Comet and Currys, that have stores in nearby out-of-town shopping centres.
Foxall's owners are evaluating their business's customer service. They are trying to find answers to several key questions.

■ How good are we at creating the right atmosphere for our customers?

■ What else can we do to improve our service or product?

■ How can the business increase sales or revenue?

■ Do we know our customer base?

■ How can we attract a different kind of customer?

■ Are we getting the message across?

If Foxall's rivals – the large superstores – asked these questions, would you expect them to come up with the same answers?

Understanding customer needs and expectations

Understanding what customers need is an important part of ensuring that a business can provide services and products that will deliver customer satisfaction and build (and retain) customer loyalty. A business needs to:

■ find out what people choose to buy

■ find out the profile of its customer base – such as their age, sex, income and culture

■ change its operations in order to sell to the needs of the customer.

The aim of understanding customer needs – of researching ways of improving customer service – is to enable a business to meet customer expectations. TK Maxx is a success story because it sells designer clothes at ridiculous prices. The stores are basic and the rails are packed with an array of different styles, colours and labels. It is a matter of luck whether you can find something to suit or something that is a genuine bargain. It's a hit and miss experience, and requires time and patience. But it clearly appeals to many customers. Bargain hunters are prepared to take on this challenge and do not worry too much that the clothes, shoes and other goods are not arranged carefully and orderly.

TK Maxx shows that customer service is a matter of degree. The store may not have all the ingredients of "good" service, but it has clearly found a niche in the market. And for those it doesn't suit, there is a department store or designer boutique a few doors away that will provide an opportunity to look at the latest models carefully laid out in colour, size and style at much higher prices.

The TK Maxx story also illustrates another feature of customer service: that customers have different expectations about service depending on where they shop, what they are shopping for and how much they intend to spend.

stop and think

Consider these contrasting customer scenarios:

You want a car:

■ you look to buy a brand new car from a luxury car showroom

■ you search for a second-hand car advertised for private sale in the newspaper.

You want a new computer:

■ you ask a local retailer to provide you with a new system

■ you go to PC World to buy one off the shelf.
You want some new trainers:

■ you look to buy a pair of trainers from a market stall

■ you consider spending £150 on designer trainers from a leading sports retailer.

You want a short break abroad:

■ you arrange to travel to New York first class with British Airways

■ you book a cheap flight to Prague with easyJet.

What would be your expectations about the different levels of customer service that would (or should) be offered in each of these situations?

Knowledge summary

- A business that understands its customers' needs and expectations is more likely to succeed.

- A business must keep an eye on the competition and respond accordingly in order to ensure that its customers do not go elsewhere.

- All customers expect products and services at a quality that meets (or exceeds) their needs, and delivered with a level of customer service that is honest, convenient and reliable.

quick questions

1 Choose a business where you have recently been a customer. Think carefully about the kind of service you received. Was it poor, satisfactory, good or excellent? Did you leave feeling happy or dissatisfied? Draft a letter to the businesses outlining why you were pleased or unhappy with the service that you received.

2 Businesses that are selling the same or very similar products and services often exist quite successfully side by side. Explain why two very similar businesses might both be able to attract enough customers to survive?

3 Explain why the expectations of customers might differ in relation to the type of product or service they want to buy?

data interpretation
Achieving best practice

The Department of Trade and Industry (DTI) offers advice and guidance on achieving best practice in business.

On the section of the website devoted to customer service, it offers advice about how a business can hold on to its best customers. It provides case studies which show how some businesses are keeping their customers happy and boosting their profits.

Visit the DTI website and follow the links to advice for businesses about customer service. The customer service homepage is: www.dti.gov.uk/bestpractice/sales/cust-service

A Extract some of the advice the DTI are giving to businesses.

B Examine and state how the advice might be useful to a business you are investigating.

C Write a memo explaining to a business owner how the DTI might be a source of help about effective customer service.

Identifying the customer

Setting the scene: putting customers first

Kwik-Fit, the car exhaust, tyres and brakes specialists, and Travis Perkins, one of Britain's leading building and plumbing merchants, are two companies that extol the virtues of customer service.

This is how Kwik-Fit sums up its philosophy:

"At Kwik-Fit the most important person is the customer, and it must be the aim of us all to give 100 per cent satisfaction, 100 per cent of the time. Our continued success depends on the loyalty of our customers. We are committed to a policy of offering them the best value for money with a fast, courteous and professional service. We offer the highest quality products and guarantees.

"We at Kwik-Fit recognise that our people are our most valuable asset. The Kwik-Fit people in our centres are the all-important contact with the customers and they are the key to our success."

Travis Perkins focuses its attention on the customer by engaging its staff on stated key performance indicators that aim to improve the service to the customer. In 2003, the company launched excel, an integrated customer service programme across all its branches, As Travis Perkins' managing director explained:

"Excel is all about each and every one of us making a difference by working together to provide customers with a quality of service that outstrips their expectations."

Both Kwik-fit and Travis Perkins have realised that there is a direct link between the people that work within the business and the people who use the business's products or services.

Can you think of any businesses that you have come into contact with that demonstrate real care for their customers and are genuinely concerned that they get it right each time?

KEY TERMS

A business's **internal customers** are its staff. Employees are internal customers in the sense that they need products and services from other staff within the business or from the business's suppliers to carry out their tasks.

External customers are the people or organisations that buy goods and services from a business. Some businesses' external customers are exclusively other businesses, some businesses trade exclusively with the general public and some have a mix of business and individual customers.

Suppliers are businesses that supply goods and services to other businesses rather than to the general public. Suppliers, like any business, must provide good customer service if they want to be successful.

The **supply chain** is the network of companies involved in bringing a product to the market, from suppliers of raw materials and components, through manufacturers and processors, to wholesalers and retailers. There are many things that can go wrong along the supply chain.

Internal customers

It is not just the people or organisations to whom a business sells its products that are customers, the people who work in the business are also customers. The staff that directly serve a business's customers rely on the services provided by other parts of the business (or a business's suppliers) to carry out their functions.

If a business has bad internal service, then it almost always follows that it will supply bad external customer service. For example, the serving staff in a restaurant are internal customers of the kitchen – if the kitchen fails to deliver well-cooked dishes promptly, then the servers cannot provide good service to diners however hard they work, and the restaurant is providing bad customer service.

It is important for a business to satisfy the needs and expectations of its internal customers, because these internal staff require good service if they are ultimately to satisfy the needs of external customers. This can be a complicated task. Take Travis Perkins, the company featured in setting the scene opposite, as an example. The staff that directly serve Travis Perkins' customers rely on everything being in place to carry out their work. They are internal customers of the warehouse and procurement staff, who ensure that outlets are stocked with timber, building materials, plumbing equipment, doors and windows. They also need to have computer systems, stationery, furniture, heating and lighting. Travis Perkins would not be able to operate without back office staff and the businesses that supply the materials and products it sells on to its customers.

All people who work inside a business are reliant on each other – their fellow workers, the people they report to and the staff for whom they have management responsibility. Working together in teams is an important part of creating the right atmosphere so that an internal customer to be able to provide an effective service or produce a quality product.

Another way of ensuring that staff give of their best is to treat them well, and make sure that they are safe, healthy and happy. It is the business's people that will shape its success. Shop assistants, service staff and telephone operators all need to feel part of the business they work for; if they feel valued by their employer, they are more likely to be motivated to provide a good service.

The staff that have direct contact with a business's external customers play a particularly vital role; if an employee offers poor service to a customer, it can create a lasting impression and the business risks losing that customer and it damages the service the business aims to provide.

All staff, all internal customers, need to understand their role and how they contribute to the business's aims and objectives. This includes managers, supervisors and their subordinates, frontline staff as well as temporary staff and consultants.

- **Managers** needs to communicate the aims and objectives of the business to their staff. They must have a clear understanding of what the business is trying to achieve and provide subordinates with the opportunity to deliver.

- **Departments and functions** need to work together to ensure that the activities of the business are conducted satisfactorily.

- **Individuals** need to know the aims and objectives of the business, have a good understanding of the product or service they are selling and the level of service they are expected to give to the customer and to their colleagues.

- **Temporary staff and consultants** need to have as clear an understanding of what is expected of them as the business's full-time employees.

Everyone in the business should have training to make sure they are able to perform their duties satisfactorily and provide a good service to the customer.

Case study: Blue Circle Cement

Blue Circle Cement developed a system of team working as part of its drive to increase the company's competitiveness in the marketplace. The business had been losing money because of high costs and low productivity. Workers had low self esteem and low morale.

The change to team working was supported by multiskilling the workforce. By working in

teams to get the job done, workers were encouraged to be co-operative and helpful, and a new ethos of participation was born.

This led to a much more motivated workforce, much higher productivity and reduced costs. This in turn helped to provide a competitive service and an improvement to the fortunes of the business.

External customers

Any business must understand its customers and work tirelessly to make sure that it offers the products and services that customers want.

Understanding what customers want and expect is crucial if a business is to attract customers in the first place, retain those customers and continue to attract new ones. The mobile phone industry is a good example of how an industry must constantly strive to find ways of keeping its existing customers and attract new business. What kind of features might attract an elderly person to use a mobile phone? What kind of phone might encourage a parent to buy it for a young child? New features such as the ability to take photographs or use the internet are attractive to some and a waste of time for others.

There are many issues to take into consideration here for a business. Each business is different and each customer is different. Figure 5.1 shows some different customer groups and summarises some of their needs and expectations. **As an exercise, choose a business such as Vodafone, Sony or BMW and recreate the table, explaining the needs and expectations of each customer group for your chosen business.**

There are many examples of businesses that are hugely successful because they have recognised a group of customers who have specific needs and expectations, and have produced the right product range to match what they want.

- Top Shop found a niche market in selling well-designed cheap goods to young people who want something new to wear every time they go out.

- Saga Holidays has a niche market in providing holidays for people over 50 who have time on their hands and a disposable income.

- The Smart car has succeeded as a perfect second car in the city: it is cheap to buy, economical to run and very stylish. Who do you think might be a typical customer of the Smart car?

Figure 5.1: Customer needs and expectations

Customer profile	Needs and expectations
Young people aged 16–21	This market is attracted by exciting designer goods such as mobile phones with new features, DVD players, iPods, the latest clothes, shoes and music. Disposable and cheap items that will last as long as the fashion trend. A first holiday abroad should be exciting and action packed.
Children aged 5–12	Businesses that cater for children need to know about the parents' needs and expectations. Even at this age some children are very fashion conscious, clothes need to be trendy but practical, toys need to be safe but follow the latest trend. Parents want holidays where there is plenty to occupy children.
Young couples with two incomes and no children	Money to spend on luxury items such as cars, holidays and electrical goods. Quality and status matter and the brand may be an important factor in the choices made. Designer chic for the home, in what to wear, in what to eat, in where to go.
Retired couples with a good pension	Quality and durability, style and reliability are what this group of customers might expect. Familiar and trusted brands to replace items when they fail. Cars that are economical and safe, holidays that offer variety and interesting sites to see, cruises that provide the ultimate in accessible entertainment.
Single adults living in the city	Working and living in the city, this group might look for good public transport, excellent restaurants and easy access to the shops. A flat or an apartment furnished for good looks and practicality. A car might not be essential but taxis and hire firms would be.
Families living the rural life	Local markets for good, cheap food, an excellent local butcher, baker and delicatessen. Electrical goods and furniture would need to be practical and last a long time, standing up against the rigours of growing children. A car would need to be large to fit in the bikes, or the shopping or grandma.

Knowledge summary

- All businesses must know the needs and expectations of their customers and work hard to match what the customer wants.

- Internal customers are as important to a business as external customers, and a business must satisfy the needs of internal customers if it is to provide a good service to external customers.

- Customers come in all shapes and sizes and their particular needs and expectations may vary at different times in their lives.

quick**questions**

1 Write down 10 expectations that you might have of your first employer when you start work.

2 Think of the needs of different members of your immediate and extended family. Identify the different businesses or services that individual members of your family might use to buy:
- a holiday
- a new pair of shoes or boots
- a meal out
- a car
- a computer.

3 Choose two different businesses and explain how they try to attract different groups of people to buy their goods and services.

data**interpretation**
Customer Service Perceptions

Customer Service Perceptions is a company that helps its business clients improve their customer service. Using techniques such as mystery shopping, it obtains information that assists businesses in evaluating their level of customer service. Find out more about the services offered by Customer Service Perceptions by visiting its website on www.csperceptions.com.

A Give examples of how Customer Service Perceptions helps businesses to monitor the service they provide to different kinds of customers.

B What kind of services do Customer Service Perceptions offer to businesses who want to look at how well their employees and their suppliers are performing?

C Write a letter to the owner of a business you are investigating to explain how an organisation such as Customer Service Perceptions might help to develop an insight into how well they serve different customer groups.

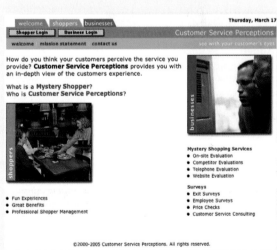

Meeting customer expectations

Setting the scene: delivering service improvements

Good customer service gets noticed: first and foremost by customers but also by rival businesses and by industry bodies. Here is an extract from a press release announcing an award for improvements of a bus service in the West Midlands.

What kind of service do you expect when you travel by public transport? How could your local public transport providers improve the level of service they offer their customers?

Press notice source: www.arriva.co.uk

Arriva wins bus award

Telford and Wrekin Borough Council, Staffordshire County Council and Arriva Midlands have been named winners in the national marketing award for local authority and joint initiatives category at the Bus Industry Awards 2004.

The partnership was nominated for its work on Ruraline 481 - recently named the fastest growing bus route in the UK with an increase of patronage of 68 per cent year on year.

The significant increase in the numbers using the service was achieved by efforts to make the route more attractive to customers, improvements to bus priority measures and infrastructure, complemented with marketing initiatives ensuring that more potential customers were made aware of the benefits of choosing the bus.

Keith Myatt, communications and publicity manager of Arriva Midlands, said: "This award recognises that local authorities and bus operators working together can achieve great improvements to services.

"We are delighted that this partnership's work in making real, measurable differences to our customers' travelling experiences has been recognised by such a prestigious award - as well as increasing the number of people choosing to travel by Ruraline 481."

KEY TERMS

Added value is the difference between the costs of the materials to make a product or provide a service and the price for which it is sold. In other words, it is the value added by the business.

A product's **unique selling point** is a characteristic that makes it distinctive or different from other similar products.

stop and think

What kind of service would you expect if you:

- look for an expensive outfit from a small exclusive shop

- buy vegetables from a market trader

- use a cash machine in the high street

- order a CD or DVD player from a catalogue.

What do customers expect?

There are limits to what a business can do in relation to how well it can respond to the needs and expectations of customers just as there are limits as to the level of service an individual customer can expect from the business. A garage offering fuel on a self-service basis expects the majority of customers to serve themselves. It would be reasonable for a customer with a disability to ask for help; it would be unreasonable for a perfectly able-bodied person to ask for help simply because he or she was too lazy to get out of the car.

Businesses recognise that customers can make a choice between different levels of service, and they pitch services to meet different needs and expectations. For example, the quality of the whole package offered by Ryanair and other budget airlines does not necessarily match the quality we might associate with a flight on, say, British Airways.

Although budget airlines don't compromise on service features that relate directly to the health and safety of passengers and crew, they have found a ready market for a no-frills airline service.

The question that all airlines must ask themselves is what is the acceptable level of service that will ensure that customers will keep coming back. Ryanair's flights are cheap but its in-flight service is basic. Ryanair makes its money by filling its planes and packing as many flights into the day as possible. If you prefer a more luxurious flying experience, it is available but at a cost. British Airways aims to add value in order to attract customers who want to travel in a more stylish fashion.

Figure 5.2: Airline punctuality	
Airline	Punctuality (%)
Ryanair	92.4
Air France	86.5
SAS	86.0
Easyjet	83.5
Lufthansa	82.3
Alitalia	80.6
Austrian	76.7
British Airways	72.0

Note: Punctuality measured by percentage of flights arriving within 15 minutes of schedule

Source: Ryanair.com

Managing customer expectations

Businesses do not just have contact with customers at the point of sale. If they are to manage and meet customer expectations fully, they must pay attention to the impression that they make on customers before during and after the sale.

1 Before the sale

In all markets, customers have a wide choice of businesses that are competing for their trade. In exercising that choice, customers are very influenced by the way that businesses market themselves in order to attract their custom. In this pre-transactional phase, it is important that a business sends out the right signals to attract customers.

In Topic 2, you saw how customers can have different needs. Their expectations and demands will vary just as much. Both new and existing customers will require information about products to help them decide what to purchase. Customers may also need information about opening hours, car parking, disabled access, availability, payment methods and credit terms.

Ideally a business needs to have some unique selling points (USP) that will offer the customer something more than its competitors. This could be a faster service, a cheaper deal, a luxurious experience, more space or some unique product features such as longer lasting, disposable and durable.

2 During the sale

Once a customer has chosen to make a transaction, the service the business offers is critical. First impressions count; and if anything goes wrong, a bad impression will linger for a very long time. Read this next case study and ask yourself how the store could have avoided losing Tom's business.

Case study:
Getting it wrong – Tom's story

Tom went into a leading computer sales store. He had won a £1000 in a competition and he wanted to buy a laptop to take to university. He looked at different machines. They varied in price from £700 to £1500, and Tom wanted help to work out the best buy. He stood around trying to look as if he needed help and hoping that someone would approach. Finally, he went to the customer services desk. The assistant at the desk was on the phone. He waited again for several minutes. The assistant eventually put the phone down and apologised for keeping Tom waiting. He explained that he needed help and Tom was directed to another assistant at the far end of the store. By the time Tom had walked to where he had been directed, there was no one there. Exasperated, he walked out of the store and went round the corner to a competitor.

Effective transactional customer service requires staff:

■ to be able to listen and respond to the customer efficiently and effectively

■ to know about the business's products and be able to answer queries and questions

■ to be able to smooth over any problems that might arise and offer reassurances

■ to be polite and happy to help.

The customer needs to be able to:

■ see the items for sale and that they are in good condition

■ feel safe and be able to move around freely

■ seek help and advice quickly and efficiently

■ know whether they can take purchases away on the day or have to order them

■ pay for items quickly using a choice of payment methods.

stopandthink

Discuss the kind of expectations you might have when you make a transaction in these different situations:

■ you are visiting the cinema to see a very popular film

■ you want to buy a desk and chair for your bedroom

■ you are buying a new pair of trainers

■ you are booking some tickets for a concert on the internet.

3 After the sale

Post-transactional service is also important. What happens if something goes wrong? Can customers get their money back, replace a faulty item or is there an adequate repair service?

The right or appropriate level of post-transactional service will depend on the product. It is unlikely that customers would expect (or receive) the same after-care service when buying second-hand washing machines than when buying brand new models. If you buy a cheap watch, radio or calculator, you could probably expect little by way of an after-sales service. If you buy similar but expensive products, they would probably come with a guarantee and would be worth mending at least for a while.

Some products are not returnable. Customers who get "treated" to the holiday from hell cannot return the product: all they can do is try to get some apology and financial compensation from the holiday company. Some experiences are subjective: a customer might think a meal is disappointing, the owner of the restaurant might take a different view. The only redress the customer has is to tell others of his or her misfortune and never go to the restaurant again.

stopandthink

What would you expect to receive in terms of after-sales care if you have bought a new car. Visit the Renault website at www.renault.co.uk to find out about its after-sales care.

Knowledge summary

- The level of customer service is often determined by the nature and quality of the product being offered.

- Businesses operate in competitive marketplaces and often look for a unique selling point to raise expectations and attract customers

- Customer expectations need to be met and managed before any sale takes place, during the selling process and after the sale.

quick**questions**

1 Give two examples of how the behaviour of a member of staff working in a supermarket might help it to meet the expectations of a customer.

2 Explain why it is so important for a business to understand the needs and expectations of its customers.

3 Crazy Horse is a new restaurant selling fast food. The business wants to open in your town. What kind of services would you like to see it offer?

data**interpretation**
On-line supermarkets

More and more businesses are selling their goods and services online. Some of the large supermarkets offer this service. Most of the high street supermarkets have online stores at which you can buy groceries.

You can see the type of services many supermarkets now provide for online customers by visiting these sites:

- www.asda.com

- www.sainsburys.co.uk

- www.safeway.co.uk

- www.tesco.co.uk.

Not all supermarkets have gone down this route. In November 2004, Morrisons managing director John Dowd said: "Morrisons believes the majority of shoppers are not interested in buying groceries online, despite rival supermarket chains ploughing millions into e-commerce. The group will stick to a tried-and-tested formula to boost its market share."

A Discuss whether you think Morrisons is right to stick to its tried and tested formula of customer service?

B Visit the websites of the major supermarkets that offer an online service and assess their strengths and weaknesses.

C Examine the possible pitfalls for a business in trying to create a positive customer service experience on an online service. How might the supermarkets avoid these pitfalls?

Features of effective customer service

Setting the scene: planning for good customer service

Good customer service does not just happen, it requires research and some imagination to understand customer needs and expectation and some planning to put ideas into practice.

Imagine you are setting up your own business. Maybe you want to run a café or a sandwich bar, or perhaps you want to set up a car repair and maintenance service, a hairdressing salon or a valeting business.

Identify five aspects of customer service that will be important to ensuring the success of your chosen business. Justify your choices, with explanations of how your plans should ensure that customers will keep coming back.

Effective customer service

The first three topics in this unit have stressed the importance of customer service and the need for all businesses to understand their customers, and to strive to meet their needs and expectations. Now, we start to look at how businesses can implement effective customer service in practice. Figure 5.3 shows the three components of effective customer service – people, place and product – and this topic looks at each of these features in turn.

1 People

A business's employees are a vital component in ensuring good customer service. Employees need to be well informed, efficient and motivated.

Though a business may have many different job functions and roles, its employees can be divided into two broad categories:

■ staff who come face to face with customers

■ staff who work behind the scenes to ensure that those who serve the customer directly are able to provide an efficient service.

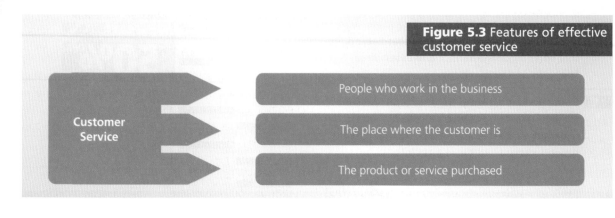

Figure 5.3 Features of effective customer service

Customer Service

People who work in the business

The place where the customer is

The product or service purchased

A computer services firm in London has recently changed its recruitment policy and will no longer take on people who smoke. It has had a smoking ban in the office for a number of years, but employees could stand outside and smoke during their breaks. The smell of smoke lingered, and smokers' clothes would continue to smell long after the last puff of the cigarette. The directors felt that people who smoked were less efficient and did not give the right impression to customers.

Is this a drastic move or common sense? In what ways do businesses that you know actively seek to improve and regulate the appearance, health and well-being of their staff to make a good impression on customers?

Businesses may have different expectations of individuals who have direct contact with customers and those that work behind the scenes, but ultimately it is the diligence of all staff that will ensure a high quality of service at the point of sale. However, it is a very true adage that first impressions count, which perhaps puts an additional onus on employees that deal directly with customers. The way staff dress, the gestures and body language they project and their general health and well-being all play there part in creating a good or poor impression on customers.

Do you wear a uniform at school? Does it make a difference to the way you think and act? Discuss the pros and cons of wearing a uniform for work, from the point of view of, first, the employees and, second, the business.

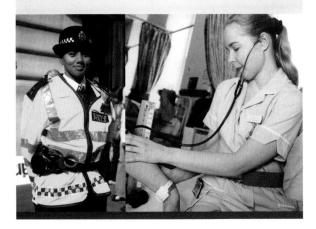

High street banks such as HSBC, Barclays, Lloyds and National Westminster all stipulate that their staff wear uniforms. This creates a corporate identity that is easy to recognise by the customer. Supermarkets and some large department stores also have adopted this policy.

Similarly nurses, armed forces personnel and the police can be easily identified by their uniform. Their rank and status is clearly defined by subtle differences in the colour or style of the uniform. Surgeons, car mechanics and butchers also have a kind of uniform that is determined by the respective demands of their jobs: they need working clothes that are safe, hygienic and practical.

Motivating people to want to provide a good service is clearly crucial. Why should an employee who earns a small fixed weekly wage work tirelessly and selflessly to make money for the owners or shareholders of a business? MacDonald's has an employee of the month award and gives stars that employees can wear on their uniforms to recognise and celebrate good customer service. Staff at Waterstone's are encouraged to read extensively in order that they can recommend and discuss the books on sale.

It is important to give staff the right equipment, and tools are important. Consider just one example, the checkout tills used in stores. New technology has transformed the kind of tills used by retailers, however a system failure can have catastrophic effects and leave any business in a mess. What happens if the scanner can't read the bar code, or won't read the details of a customer's credit or debit card.

Prompt service is vital is situations where customers' time is at a premium. Having lunch in a restaurant is a pleasure but it can turn into a very stressful experience for customers if they are still waiting for their food or the bill when it is time to go back to work. The restaurant team need to be very organised in order to ensure that the service is prompt and reliable as well as enjoyable.

2 Place

The environment is an essential part of the customer experience. It must be fundamentally safe, accessible and be fit for purpose. If you are looking to buy a new outfit, you will want to see different goods on display and have a warm and private place to try things on. The size and the price of the clothes should be clearly marked, and there should be a choice of different garments to try.

Big department stores like Debenhams or John Lewis need to be well organised; the goods need to be laid out so that they are accessible, attractive and available for the customer to view. There needs to be sufficient stock so that the customer has a choice. There needs to be different sizes or styles, a choice of colours or materials, high-quality expensive versions and cheaper more basic versions. The goods must be clean and good quality. A business may not be able to sell products if they become damaged or dirty.

Employees who work for WH Smith are encouraged in training sessions to be vigilant when they are working in the company's shops to ensure that items are brought from the stock room to replace those that have been sold. Shelves and display stands are kept tidy and items are displayed so that they don't become damaged or dirty. Any item that is damaged or dirty is quickly removed and replaced.

Keeping track of stock is an important part of customer service. It is not a good idea for any business to have too much stock in storage, but it is essential that it does not run out so that it finds it cannot fulfil a customer's order. A fine juggling act is necessary to get the balance right between having too much and too little stock. A restaurant has to make educated guesses about which dishes its customers are likely to order. Food only lasts a short while and if the restaurant gets its estimates wrong, it may have to throw away food that has gone past its consume-by date. A manufacturer of white electrical goods has to make sure that it has sufficient parts to make the finished items. If it has too many parts in stock, it is tying up working capital in material and storage costs; but if stocks run too low, the manufacturer risks production

delays and may not be able to make prompt delivery to customers.

Businesses also need to pay attention to their online environments as well as their physical environments. Consumers are increasingly using the internet to buy goods and services, such as holidays, food, books, clothes, financial services and music. A website needs to be just as accessible and easy to manoeuvre around as a shop or an office.

3 Product

The best quality customer service and the most prestigious premises in the world will be of little use, if a business's products are poor or fail to meet customer needs. The new Selfridges in Birmingham is a magnificent building – from the outside it looks like a chrome armadillo – and inside there are four floors packed with designer goods all laid out to entice the customer. This new store has to compete with a number of other department stores. Therefore, Selfridges must offer more than just a splendid façade outside and high-quality customer service inside. The goods must be different and stylish and prices must be competitive.

The variety and quality of products for sale and the service provided by the business has to meet the expectations of the customer. The Selfridges building in Birmingham promises a unique experience, and its products and services must not disappoint. Selfridges aims to meet this challenge by offering some unique and different products as well as providing a range of services that are designed to add to the customer experience, such as a Japanese Sushi bar and French style café.

Customers needs also have to be meet after they have purchased a product. They need to be reassured that if the product does not meet their expectations, there will be an after-sales care service. A customer is likely to expect a damaged item or unwanted gift to be replaced or money refunded without any fuss. A repair service or spare parts service should be well organised and efficient.

Knowledge summary

- To provide effective customer service, a business needs to train and motivate the staff who come into direct and indirect contact with customers.

- A business also needs to ensure a welcoming place or environment to serve customers, as well as provide products that meet customer needs.

- A business needs to identify and put in place the human and physical resources that will ensure effective customer service.

quick questions

1 Write down four ways that an employee working in a restaurant might provide an effective service to customers.

2 Analyse the consequences for a retail business that advertises a best selling product and then runs out of stock.

3 Why is it important to motivate staff through using reward systems that offer more than just a wage or a salary?

data interpretation
Selfridges

Selfridges has four stores in the UK: one in London's Oxford Street, one in Birmingham and two in Manchester, in Trafford and in Exchange Square.

You can visit each of these stores online at Selfridges website (www.selfridges.co.uk). Through the website, you can find details of goods and in-store services, as well as company information about Selfridges including details of vacancies and the rewards package it offers staff.

A Describe what Selfridges offers for the shoppers that visit its stores.

B Explain the different features of customer service that are available in Selfridges stores.

C What does Selfridges offer that adds value to its service to customers?

215

Topic 4 Features of effective customer service

Setting the scene: NatWest Bank

NatWest ran an advertising campaign in 2004 that featured the bank's promise to maintain a personal local branch service. Pitched at both existing as well as potential new customers, the campaign aimed to differentiate NatWest from its competitors.

NatWest, like the other high street banks, offers many different services to personal and business customers. Like its competitors, it offers online services. However, NatWest's campaign argued that it is maintaining the continuity of local branch banking in contrast to the centralised and remote call centre system adopted by many of its competitors.

Would you choose Nat West because of its promise of a more personalised banking service? Visit the websites of the main high street banks and compare how effectively each communicates its services to personal and business customers.

Visit different banks to find out about opening an account. Do you find them customer friendly? Can you talk to a member of staff directly, rather than speaking to someone behind a screen? What leaflets and brochures are available? Do they give you the kind of information you would need to open an account?

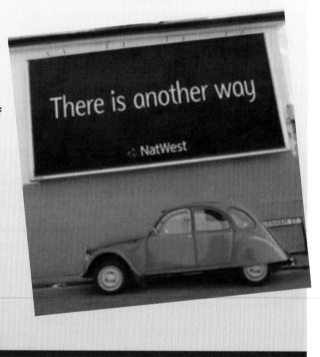

Effective communication

All businesses recognise the importance of finding efficient and trouble free ways of communicating with customers. They also need to ensure that there is efficient communication within businesses. Good communication is a key part of delivering effective customer service.

1 Communicating with customers

Effective communication is fundamental to customer satisfaction. Every aspect of the way a business operates depends on how well it communicates with its customers.

Communication is a two-way process. It is not sufficient for a business to focus on how it communicates with its customers, it also needs to think about how its customers can communicate with its staff. Too often, customers feel completely frustrated and let down by being unable to communicate with businesses. Let's look at some examples of what can go wrong.

■ You want to know how much money is in your account. You ring the phone number on your cheque book. After 10 minutes of waiting and listening to bad music you give up.

■ You want your new cooker delivered to your home. The shop has given you a date and assured you that the delivery will be made in the morning. You take the morning off work, but the cooker does not arrive. When you phone the shop, it has no record of the delivery details. You now have to arrange another date and take more time off work.

■ Your new DVD player comes complete with a set of instructions, but they are not written in English. When you telephone for help, the customer helpline is constantly engaged.

- You have found a pair of jeans that you really like on the rail, but you there is no price tag on the clothing. There are no assistants available to tell you the price.

- You've had a disastrous holiday. The brochure's description of the hotel – its proximity of the beach, its swimming pool, its high-quality food – did not match your experience. You have written a letter of complaint to the holiday company, but three weeks later you not received a reply.

Figure 5.4 shows some of the many different ways to communicate with customers. The most effective medium in any given situation will depend on:

- the message

- how quickly the message needs to be received

- what the message is actually saying

- who the message is intended for.

The medium that is used must be appropriate and effective in order that the message is received and properly understood. Effective customer service depends on the business's staff making the right decisions about the kind of communication medium to use in a variety of different situations. In each situation, staff need to consider what is the most effective way to communicate the message.

Each method of communication has advantages and disadvantages and there needs to be a careful calculation when making the decision about the best way to get the message across. Figure 5.5 shows the advantages and disadvantages of four communication methods. Consider some other methods (apart from these four): what are the advantages and disadvantages of using them in different situations?

Whatever method a business uses, it is important that its communications are accurate. Any letters sent to customers must be neat and accurate. Goods for sale must have complete and accurate labelling. Leaflets, brochures, websites and other promotional material should be error free, give the right information and be up to date. To achieve accuracy, businesses need good internal communications (so that staff are fully informed about products and procedures), the ability to choose the right medium to convey their messages and an understanding of the communication process.

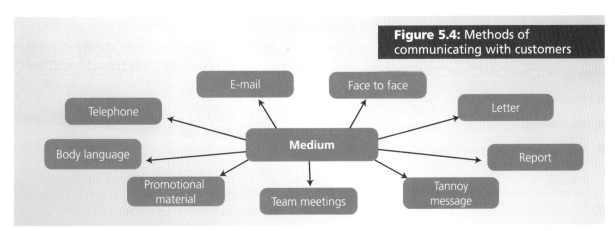

Figure 5.4: Methods of communicating with customers

Figure 5.5: Advantages and disadvantages of four means of communication

Medium	Advantages	Disadvantages
Body language	Smiling, giving eye contact, being responsive can have a positive effect on customers	Poor unresponsive body language is catching and will infect customers
Telephone	Quick and easy means of passing on information	Message may not be received by the right person, can be busy or people are not available
Website	Promotional material and information can reach many people	Customers may not have web access, the design must be right to attract the customer to buy
E-mail	Quick and simple means of sending and receiving information	Recipient may not read and act upon the message

Look at these scenarios. Some involve customer-to-business communications, other business-to-customer communication. In each case, state which method of communication might be most appropriate and explain also what might go wrong.

- A customer has seen a pair of shoes she likes but cannot find a pair in her size shoes. The shoe shop assistant needs to let her know if they are available in another branch.

- A customer has made an online booking for a flight. The airline needs to send confirmation of all the details to the customer.

- A very unhappy customer has made a complaint and wants to see the manager. The manager needs to decide how to respond.

- A small fault has been detected in a new make of car. The manufacturer needs to inform all customers who have this model, so that they can book their cars in to have the fault remedied.

- The local tourist information office wants to promote the town as an attraction to a wider audience in Europe.

- A new small business wants to promote its car cleaning service to potential customers.

- A retail manager wants to tell all staff in the store's network of branches to offer a 50 per cent discount on a select range of goods.

Communication is a two-way process and it is important to appreciate that the message that the sender intends to convey may not be what the receiver "hears". Indeed, there may be many barriers to the message being conveyed accurately. These include:

- the receiver misunderstands the message

- the message is given to the wrong person

- the message is passed on by a series of people and its meaning or content gets changed along the way

- the receiver of the message does not pass it on to the intended recipient

- the message is received but not acted upon.

2 Communicating within a business

Successful customer service is not simply about treating customers properly at the point of sale. Creating the right atmosphere and environment to ensure that a customer's experience is trouble free will only happen if everyone inside the business is working together.

Everyone in the business needs to look carefully at how effectively they carry out their work. Paying attention to detail is critical in creating a quality service that will meet customers' expectations. Staff need to fully informed about the business's products,

policies and procedures. This requires good internal communications – indeed internal communication is as important as external communications with customers – and, as with external communications, businesses have a choice of ways of communication with their staff. Figure 5.6 shows some methods that can be used for internal and external communications.

Many businesses have suggestion boxes or meetings – often called quality circles – which invite employees to suggest improvements in customer service. The baby clothes section in a large department store was moved to the ground floor instead of the first floor, as a result of suggestions by employees who were responding to complaints from young mums. Staff of a large ceramic tile retailer listened to customers and suggested that a café be provided in its showroom. Directors at French Connection responded to a profit warning by asking the company's employees in the branches around the country for their views on why fewer customers were choosing the FCUK brand.

Inside the business	With the external customer
Formal meetings	Leaflets, fliers and posters
Group and one-to-one discussions	Radio, television and newspaper advertising
Telephone, video and audio	Websites
Letters and memos	Labelling
Faxes and emails	Catalogues and brochures
Staff reports and appraisals	Letters and postcards
Customer surveys	Surveys and questionnaires
Financial reports	Face to face
Records and files of information	Telephone and call centres
Video conferencing	Receipts and invoices
Internal websites (intranets)	E-mail

stop and think

Communicating effectively in different situations requires good interpersonal skills. These skills are critical to good customer service:

- the ability to listen
- the ability to sympathise and reassure
- the ability to deal with conflict and difficult situations
- the ability to admit that you are in the wrong
- the ability to have original ideas and communicate suggestions for improvement
- the ability to work as a member of a team
- the ability to be able to solve a problem and justify your decision.

Give an example of how each of these skills might be used to create the right atmosphere for good customer service practice. (There is more about interpersonal skills in Topic 6.)

Knowledge summary

- **Communication is a vitally important part of effective customer service, both inside the business and when communicating with external customers**

- **Effective communication requires that messages are accurately conveyed by the sender, and that they are "heard" and respond to by the receiver.**

- **Communication is a two-way process, and it is important that businesses listen to their customers.**

- **Poor communication can prevent a business from functioning effectively.**

quick questions

1. Explain some of the advantages and disadvantages of using e-mail as a means of communication.

2. Explain why it is essential that employees are consulted about how improvements might be made to customer service?

3. Explain the consequences of poor communication on the ability of a well-known business, such as a supermarket, a bank or a car manufacturer, to succeed.

Customer service skills

Setting the scene: working in customer service

The Institute of Customer Service (ICS) is an independent professional body that aims to lead customer service performance and professionalism. This is what the ICS website says about working in customer service.

Customer service jobs are many and varied, and found in most organisations. Sometimes, they carry a job title which uses the words customer service, such as customer service assistant or customer service manager; sometimes there is no explicit mention of customer service in the job title, such as receptionist or travel agent clerk, but nevertheless customer service is what the job is mainly about.

What skills do you need to work in customer service? Excellent customer service is provided by people who are good with people. You need to be able to communicate with customers in differing ways according to their needs, to work consistently and reliably to meet customer expectations and to help to resolve any problems customers may have.

You also need to have a good knowledge of your organisation's products and services, and the systems used to deliver these to customers. Above all, you need to be someone who gets real satisfaction from a job well done and seeing a customer well satisfied.

Have a look in a local newspaper at advertisements for jobs in customer service. What skills are they asking for? Do you believe you have the skills for the job?

Adapted from www.instituteofcustomerservice.com

Presenting the right image

Delivering efficient and effective customer service has much to do with presenting the right image and having staff with the skills that create a positive atmosphere so that customers are helped and encouraged to make transactions.

Asda appreciates the importance of having highly skilled staff in its stores. Its approach is to explain and provide some training in customer service to new employees when they first join the company and then offer training at regular intervals as employees build their careers at Asda. In this way, as Figure 5.7 illustrates, Asda employees have the opportunity to climb a ladder of skills – from induction training through specialist training and further development – that constantly reinforces the importance of providing effective customer service at all times.

Figure 5.7: Asda's ladder of skills

Further development identifying when new skills might be learned or existing skills further developed

Continuous learning developing skills on the job

Specialist training training on equipment perhaps or specific product knowledge

Departmental training specific policies and procedures pertinent to different departments

Induction a period of time for training when the employee first joins the company

All Asda employees are provided with specific and ongoing training to ensure that they are constantly aware of the importance of customer service skills in making the shopping experience for their customers a positive one.

Type of communication	Skills needed by sender	Skills needed by receiver
Verbal communication	Being able to speak and be understood effectively and accurately	Being able to listen and interpret the needs of others
Written communication	Being able to write legibly, using good grammar, accurate spelling and convey meaning	Being able to read and interpret information
Non-verbal communication	Being able to use body language to convey feelings and meaning effectively	Being able to read and interpret others' body language accurately

Interpersonal skills

The first, and most important, skill is the ability to be able to communicate effectively. We communicate in a variety of ways, each requiring a different range of skills. Figure 5.8 shows the most common methods of communicating, and the skills deployed in each case.

Non-verbal communication – or body language – is a powerful tool in the quest for effective customer service. It is important to understand some of the messages you may be unintentionally sending with your body language.

- We turn our bodies and not just our heads towards something that we are interested in.

- We will stand closer to people we know well.

- We will believe someone more readily who makes direct eye contact.

- We display haste or a need to get away, if we tap our feet, drum our fingers or check the clock too often.

- We stand or sit up straight if we are confident.

- We hunch our shoulders or look down or away if we are depressed or fed up.

- We display an interest in someone if we nod at appropriate times or we lean towards them when they are speaking.

- We tend to fold arms or put them across ourselves if we are not sure of the situation.

- We rub our chins or put our arms across the back of the neck if we are not telling the whole truth.

So how can you put some of this into practice when dealing with customers? First, approach customers positively to find out their needs. Never assume that you know what a customer wants, so ask questions to check you have understood the customer's needs.

Second, try and build a good relationship with the customer. Display confidence by giving accurate and precise information, but don't be over confident – admit to what you don't know and be prepared to explain when you cannot meet the customer's request.

Third, remember to concentrate on non-verbal as well as verbal communication signals, and be prepared to try different communication methods to make sure you are successfully dealing with the customer

stopandthink

Try to assess your own interpersonal skills. Can you:

- deal with people effectively?

- be patient with someone who is being difficult?

- express yourself well?

- be tactful even when you disagree with someone?

- see things from another's point of view?

- be enthusiastic about helping someone out?

- understand what someone else is feeling?

Make a list of your strengths and weaknesses in dealing with people. Share your list with a friend or class mate. Do they agree with your self-assessment?

stopandthink

What other tell-tale non verbal signals do you observe in people?

Non-verbal interpersonal skills can seem less tangible but they are just as important in the quest for a high standard of customer service. There are three areas which you might need to consider.

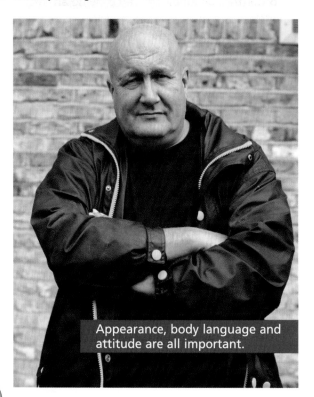

Appearance, body language and attitude are all important.

Attitude

Have a positive attitude to your work and to your organisation's customers – people can quickly detect indifference or contempt. Try to be honest, punctual, thorough in your duties and maintain high standards of work.

Appearance

Appearance matters – people do judge books by their covers! Maintain a smart and clean appearance by wearing suitable clothing, keep clothes, hair and nails clean, refrain from wearing inappropriate jewellery or make-up, and conform to a uniform if this is required.

Personality

Customers may want you to deal with their problems, but they don't want to burdened by your problems. Ideally, customer service staff should be even tempered, cheerful and not prone to moods and tantrums. They should be able to see things from different points of view, be prepared to give advice and be able to admit to sometimes being in the wrong. One other aspect of personality that helps establish a good working environment is a good sense of humour.

These are skills that cannot really be taught. However, as people become more experienced at work, many are able to develop these interpersonal skills even if some managed to keep them well hidden at school.

Product knowledge

It really will be a waste if employees have good interpersonal skills but no real knowledge of the business and the products it sells. It is the duty of the employer to make sure that information about the business is communicated effectively to employees.

Employees need to have sound understanding of their business's products and services. They need to understand the computer and manual systems that help to provide the right information to the customer. If you go into a large computer superstore, such as PC World, to buy a product, you want to be assured that an assistant has the relevant knowledge to guide your choice. You want knowledge not educated (or uneducated) guesses. So it is also an important customer service skill to be able to say: "I don't know, but I know someone who does." Referring a customer to a colleague is not defeat, it is good practice.

Some businesses have mission statements or clearly advertised aims and objectives, and it is important that the employee can relate to these when they are dealing with customers. John Lewis's mission statement is Never Knowingly Undersold. Hopefully staff at John Lewis have been briefed and trained on how to respond if a customer comes up and says: "I bought this in the store a few days ago for £50, and it's on sale at the shop down the road for just £35."

Reaping the benefits

Employees with good customer service skills will have the confidence and motivation to deal with all kinds of customers. They will be able to deal with problems but, in providing good service, they should encounter fewer problems because most customers should be completely satisfied with the service they receive. Those that are not will be reassured that their problem will be dealt with quickly and satisfactorily.

Good customer service is a classic win-win situation. The customer clearly benefits and satisfied customers are likely to remain loyal. They will also tell others of their experience, thereby helping to attract new customers to the business. So the business and the employees both benefit. The employees gain greater job satisfaction in doing a job well and share some of the rewards of being part of a successful business such as, job security, pay rises and bonuses.

Knowledge summary

- The most important skills customer service employees needs at work are interpersonal and communication skills.

- As well as needing good communication skills, customer service staff need to have the right attitude and appearance, and a welcoming personality.

- You can find out more about the skills needed for customer service positions by carefully reading the person specification for relevant job vacancies.

quick questions

1 What organisational skills are essential in order that an employee can provide an effective service to the customer?

2 Explain why an employee with poor verbal communication skills could have a detrimental effect on a business's ability to provide effective customer service.

3 What are the consequences for a business if it does not employ staff which have good customer service skills?

data interpretation
Royal Bank of Scotland

The Royal Bank of Scotland advertises job vacancies online. This is an example of one customer service vacancy that appeared on the bank's website.

RBS
The Royal Bank of Scotland Group

Home | Privacy policy | Terms of use

You are here: Home >

- About RBS
- Manufacturing
- Locations
- Working with us
- Benefits
- Training
- Meet our people
- Job search
- www.rbs.com

JOIN US

Telephone Customer Service Officer

You'll know who we are so we'll keep the introductions short. Royal Bank of Scotland is no ordinary business. We help over 20 million customers make more of their finances.

We currently have a number of full-time and part-time vacancies on a variety of shift patterns. You'll be working in a small team speaking to a wide range of new and existing customers. It will be up to you to accurately identify customers' needs so they are offered suitable products and excellent customer service. This involves:

- Ensuring a first-class quality service is provided to customers at all times whether calls are inbound or outbound.

- Maintaining an excellent level of product knowledge.

- Resolving customer queries and complaints.

Whilst experience in sales or service environment is desirable, your personal qualities are really what counts. We're looking for people who enjoy building relationships over the phone and who ensure our customers receive the professional level of service they deserve. You should have:

- Clear and effective communication skills.

- Strong customer service orientation.

- Be self-motivated with ability to work as part of a team.

Click www.join-us-at-rbs.co.uk to apply online.

A What kind of experience and activities might you be able to draw on in order to put together a CV or a letter of application for this telephone customer service post?

B What would constitute good customer service in a bank such as the Royal Bank of Scotland?

C What are the benefits to the bank of having employees who are highly skilled in customer service?

Monitoring customer service

Setting the scene: Nectar cards

Nectar is a loyalty card system used by the supermarket chain Sainsbury as well as other businesses such as BP, Debenhams and Vodaphone.

Nectar provides Sainsbury with a wealth of information about its customers' shopping habits. The Nectar card provides vital data about customers' spending power, their age, their buying habits and where they live. Sainsbury can use the Nectar card to monitor what customers buy and when.

However, there is important information that a loyalty card does not give Sainsbury. It provides no information on the times when customers:

- were kept waiting
- discovered that the goods they wanted were out of stock
- bought products that were poor quality or had been damaged
- found it difficult to find their way around the stores.

High-profile businesses such as Sainsbury's need to use a variety of methods to find out if their customers are getting good service and if they are sufficiently satisfied to remain loyal to the company.

Make a list of different methods that Sainsbury (and some of the other companies involved in the Nectar card scheme) might use to find out about whether customers are satisfied with the service they receive.

Keeping customers happy

As has been stressed throughout this unit, communication is the key to good customer service. A well-managed business will have well-defined and very effective communication systems in place to monitor and maintain the service it offers to customers. Systems need to be in place to:

- provide information about products and services
- ensure effective and efficient procedures at the point of sale
- display accurate price information and details of any discounts and special offers
- manage product distribution and delivery systems
- maintain health and safety in the work and customer environments
- manage stock systems and ensure sufficient stock is available to customer needs
- allow staff to record issues relating to customer satisfaction or dissatisfaction.

If they are to work well, these communication systems should be subject to regular reviews. It is not sufficient simply to ask staff about the systems; they may have learnt to work around any flaws in the systems even if they are resulting in poor customer service. These

KEY TERMS

British Standards Institute sets standards for industry to follow in a number of different areas such as quality, environmental awareness and product safety.

ISO 9001 is awarded when a business can demonstrate quality assurance in design, development, production, installation and service. This is an updated version of the original ISO 9000 standard.

Quality circles are small groups of workers in the same area of production or service who meet to discuss where improvements might be made.

Customer charters set out the standards that a customer can expect from the business. It is meant as a guide for both the internal and external customer.

Mystery shoppers are people employed by a business to go shopping and to give feedback on the service they receive.

reviews need to reflect any issues that might impact on customer service and produce recommendations about how the systems can be changed to deliver improved customer service.

Communicating to the staff that a system has changed is fundamental if the service is to improve. It may be necessary to review the training and development needs of staff if systems are changed or enhanced. Ongoing staff training and development will increase their ability to deliver improved services to customers.

stop and think

Have you ever been asked to fill in a questionnaire about the quality of the service you have received? Have you ever had to complain to a business about a faulty product or a poor service?

If you have, think about how the businesses might have dealt with the information you gave them. Do you ever think about how a business uses information in order to try to improve its service to you, the customer?

Monitoring customer service

The setting the scene that introduced this topic showed that although loyalty card schemes, such as Sainsbury's Nectar programme and Tesco's clubcard scheme, allow businesses to collect useful information about the buying habits of its customers, they are not much help in assessing whether customers are satisfied with the service they receive. To ensure that the service offered is of a sufficiently high standard, businesses must collect information about both customers' needs and expectations and, crucially, their views and opinions on the service they actually receive.

A good way to do this is to ask the customer to complete a survey or questionnaire about their experience of the service. Many large hotel chains, such as Quality Hotels, Holiday Inn and Novotel, put questionnaires in each room for guests to complete at the end of their stay. Of course, many customers see this as a chore or simply ignore the questionnaires completely, so some hotels offer incentives to encourage guests to respond, such as entry to a prize draw with free meals, hotel rooms or weekend breaks for the winners.

Businesses can learn much from customer surveys and questionnaires, but they need to assess carefully the reliability and usefulness of information that is collected. Only a fraction of customers may respond to a survey, and they be a totally unrepresentative group. Some businesses commission market research companies to conduct surveys on their behalf. Though costly, this helps to ensure that businesses receive independent and representative information on customers' views about their services.

Another method of monitoring the service provided to customers is to create quality circles. As we discussed in Topic 5 (see page 216), quality circles enable groups of employees who work in direct contact with customers or close to the manufacturing process to get together to discuss ideas about how quality improvements might be made. Quality circles aim to

Case study: Brother

Brother is a electronics and manufacturing company that makes printers, fax machines and other goods. Its customers include major stores and businesses like PC World, Staples, Viking Direct and Maplin Electronics as well as a host of smaller electrical and computer retailers.

Brother wants to sell printers that are reliable and durable. It needs to make sure that each printer meets the expectation of both retailers (Brother's direct customers) and consumers (who buy Brother products in the retail outlets). Brother has adopted the ISO 9001 standard in order that it can aim for a very high level of quality and provide a good level of service for its customers.

You can find out more about the services offered by Brother on its website www.brother.co.uk. To find out more about its achievement of the ISO 9001 standard, look at the information on Brother's UK business which you can find under the "about us" menu.

engage the enthusiasm and experience of employees who actually understand clearly what is happening on the ground.

Another way of drawing on employee knowledge, though in a less formal way, is the suggestion scheme. This encourages employees to offer solutions to improve the performance of the business and to enhance service to customers. Suggestion schemes often offer rewards or incentives for employees who come up with practical, beneficial proposals.

Targets and standards

Organisations often use targets as a way of monitoring and measuring customer service. Hospitals monitor customer service by measuring their performance against a series of targets, such as length of waiting lists, waiting time in outpatient's, response time when an ambulance is called. Rail companies display punctuality figures from month to month so that the travelling public can see whether trains are, in fact, becoming more punctual.

Many businesses use the ISO 9001 standard in order to monitor and maintain high levels of quality. The ISO 9001 standard is an internationally recognised standard for quality which looks at a business's entire operations, including standards of quality in the manufacturing process (if the business is a manufacturer), the delivery of maintenance and repair, the ordering process, operational controls and customer liaison procedures.

Customer codes and charters

Many businesses have introduced customer codes or customer charters. These set out – to both internal and external customers – the level of service that customers should expect to receive. The Royal Mail has a customer charter that members of the public can see in any post office around the country. In magistrate's and crown courts, there are codes of practices displayed for visitors, victims and offenders.

In the public sector, the government has set up the Charter Mark scheme. This is a national standard of customer service excellence, designed to help public sector organisations such as schools, the police, local authorities and museums to improve their performance and to "put the customer first".

Public sector organisations that have achieved the Charter Mark have found that it offers a number of benefits. It helps to:

- increase customer focus
- improve consultation with internal and external customers
- improve staff morale
- develop better internal processes
- develop more effective service delivery
- improve complaints handling
- deliver more cost-effective services.

Many private sector businesses also have published codes of practice that set out what customers can expect in terms of service. These codes provide a set of procedures for employees to follow in their dealings with customers. For example, Interflora – the network of florist shops – has a clearly defined code of practice. Interflora's mission statement states that it aims to be the first choice for customers by:

- recognising and responding to our customers' changing needs
- providing a seamless service to our customers
- leading our industry in innovation and design
- continual improvement in quality, service, processes and costs
- enabling our employees and associates to give their best.

Interflora has a rigorous system of quality control. Once it has accepted a florist to join the Interflora network, that florist's shop, product quality and performance standards are monitored on a regular basis by a team of territory managers. This team conducts an ongoing programme of mystery shopping and regular assessments.

stop and think

Find out more about the services offered by Interflora by visiting its website at www.interflora.co.uk. Find a florist that displays the Interflora logo and one that does not. Compare their products and services.

 Interflora the flower experts

Knowledge summary

- In order to retain a competitive edge and keep customers happy, it is important to monitor and maintain high levels of customer service.

- There are several ways of monitoring customer service, including questionnaires, measuring performance against targets, quality circles and suggestion schemes.

- Many organisations implement formal quality standards, such as ISO 9001 and, in the public sector, the Charter Mark initiative.

- Some businesses publish codes of practice and customer charters. These state the level of customer service they aim to achieve and the service standards that customers should expect to receive.

- Businesses need to assess carefully whether the information collected about customer service is reliable and representative before taking decisions to change their procedures.

quick**questions**

1 State three ways in which a small retail business might monitor the service it is providing to its customers.

2 Explain the advantages to a business of working towards a customer charter or code of practice.

3 Explain different ways in which staff in a business might be encouraged to say how the service to the customer might be improved.

data**interpretation**
Mystery shoppers

Increasingly businesses are using a monitoring process called mystery shopping to find out their customer service.

Mystery shoppers are employed by a research company to use the target business's services. They report back on their experience and the quality of customer service that they experienced, providing valuable information that the research company can feed back to the business.

Performance in People is one of many organisations that offer a mystery shopper service to its business clients. Visit the company's website at www.performanceinpeople.co.uk. Find out about mystery shopping by clicking on the menu selection for mystery shopper.

A Suggest two different businesses that might choose this mystery shopper service to monitor their customer service. Give reasons for your choices.

B Explain the advantages and disadvantages of using mystery shoppers as a means of monitoring and enhancing customer service.

Improving customer service

Setting the scene: The Everyman Theatre

The Everyman Theatre in Cheltenham stages around 400 shows a year, selling around 200,000 tickets.

To be successful, the theatre is aware that it must attract new customers and make sure established customers keep coming back. In order to do this, the theatre has invested in systems to help it identify and target specific customers and improve customer satisfaction.

The theatre managers asked themselves a number of questions to determine how they could maintain their existing customer base and attract new customers.

Just how well do they know their existing customers?

■ Have customers' needs changed over time?

■ How often do existing customers use the theatre?

How good is customer service?

■ Have staff the right information to give to customers when they make an enquiry?

■ Are customers kept waiting when they make contact?

■ How are complaints dealt with?

■ Are there acceptable response times to complaints or queries for information?

■ Are customers generally satisfied with the service they receive?

■ Is the customer retention rate good?

■ Are customers loyal?

■ How often do customers recommend the theatre to others?

How good are sales?

■ Are we happy with the amount of revenue we receive from each customer?

■ Are we spending enough or too much on marketing to attract customers?

■ How successful are our marketing campaigns?

How good is communication?

■ Do all members of staff communicate effectively?

■ Is there enough communication between the different functions of the theatre?

■ Do members of staff spot opportunities and pinpoint weaknesses?

■ Do all members of staff pass on information about customer needs?

These questions are taken from Understanding your Customers, a Department of Trade and Industry (DTI) pamphlet. To find out how managers at The Everyman Theatre answered these questions, and how they acted upon the answers, visit the DTI website www.dti.gov.uk/bestpractice. You will need to click on "case studies", then click on "customer services" listed under sales and marketing, and scroll down to find The Everyman Theatre case study which you can download in pdf and plain text formats.

The need to improve customer service

All businesses will occasionally have customers who are unhappy with the service they have received. They need to take their complaints seriously, as unhappy customers may quickly become customers of rival businesses. Here are three examples of some typical problems that can occur.

■ A traveller using a rail company, such as Virgin or Great Western, who can't get accurate advice on train times and ticket prices is going to be very frustrated – next time she might travel by car.

■ A customer who has bought a gift for a relative that turned out to be unsuitable is unlikely to use the store again if he cannot exchange the item or get a refund.

■ If you arrive home from shopping at a department store and find that the goods you have bought are faulty or damaged, you are unlikely to recommend that store to your friends.

Most businesses have some complaints procedure that they will follow in order to rectify the situation. The complaints system may be formalised, setting out clear procedures for staff to follow, or informal,

requiring staff to react to each problem as it arises. The best businesses don't just deal with complaints, they analyse the problem and make changes to practices and procedures to improve the service for all customers.

In earlier topics in this unit, you learned about some of the features and systems needed to deliver effective customer service. So how do businesses go about building on their existing customer service arrangements. This topic reviews four strategies used by business to improve customer service:

■ seeking continuous improvement

■ empowering employees

■ acting on feedback

■ exploiting new technology.

1 Continuous improvement

A system of continuous improvement will help the business to eliminate poor quality and raise customer service standards. Figure 5.9 illustrates the process of continuous improvement. A business must commit to making improvements: it needs to plan, take action and review the improvements continuously, and then make commitments to take further steps to develop an even better quality service.

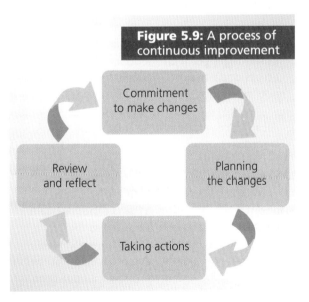

Figure 5.9: A process of continuous improvement

Commitment to make changes

Planning the changes

Taking actions

Review and reflect

2 Empowering employees

Employees should have a clear understanding of their role in achieving a high level of customer service. Each employee needs to have a good understanding of how the business operates and how each function is interdependent. Without this understanding, employee may not be much help at all – indeed, they may be part of the problem, not part of the solution.

Many businesses recognise that there is a direct link between the motivation and well-being of employees and the satisfaction of customers. Asda changed the way it recruited staff and concentrated on offering new staff a better work-life balance. By allowing employees to work shorter hours, with more part-time options and with greater flexibility, Asda has improved the way staff view their jobs, generating a positive attitude to the business and ultimately to the customers.

Case study: John Heathcote Limited

John Heathcote is a textile manufacturer that employs 450 people. The owners were aware that a lack of communication between different departments in the business were contributing to inferior products, late deliveries and a lack of motivation among staff. The business wanted to empower staff, to allow them to take more decisions about how the business was organised in order to create a better quality service for customers.

The company began by promoting a new culture of co-operation and inter-departmental communication. A consultative committee of staff and managers was set up as the main point of feedback. Staff worked across departmental barriers to share ideas and work together to face challenges.

All staff now take part in a business awareness programme. This includes a training programme of in-house presentations and cross-departmental tours. This allows staff to understand and care about how their work affects other departments and overall business performance. As a result of these changes, customer complaints have reduced by 50 per cent, well above the company's 33 per cent initial target.

Improvements have been made in product quality and the time it takes to produce goods, allowing Heathcote to deliver the products in good time so that retailers have sufficient stock to meet customer demand.

3 Acting on feedback

Information is the key to effective strategies for improving customer service. In his book Thriving On Chaos, the management guru Tom Peters suggests to business owners that they should treat each customer complaint as a jewel. His advice is to welcome complaints and encourage feedback. This leads to an opportunity to improve services and avoid repetition of the problem.

Feedback about poor customer service, whether it is via a direct complaint from a customer or received from the results of a survey, is valuable in developing effective strategies for improving the situation. Businesses can benefit greatly by acting on the feedback it receives and choosing suitable and effective means of improving services.

There are many issues that might be highlighted as a result of the positive monitoring of customer service. The important point to is to take appropriate action. This might include strategies as varied as:

- improving product labels so that the customer can see at a glance the price and size

- providing a map that clearly directs the customer to places they might want to visit

- improving procedures at the till so that customers do not have to queue

- developing better telephone answering systems so that customers are not kept waiting

- improving website designs so that customer can find what they need quickly and easily

- building closer relationships with suppliers to ensure products are delivered on time

- developing better systems to ensure that products are fit for purpose and in good condition

- improving delivery services so that customers are less inconvenienced

- reducing the burden of paperwork by simplifying the forms that customers have to complete.

4 Exploiting new technology

New technology can be used to enhance customer service. Businesses have invested in better communication systems, much improved database management, and use of the internet and e-mail to offer a much faster response time to customer enquiries, orders, communications and complaints.

Taylor Walton is a Sheffield-based firm of solicitors with four offices and 260 employees. Problems with their telephone system meant that calls would sometimes be missed. The partners decided to change their telephone system – a missed call can be missed business, as well as a great inconvenience for existing clients. The new system uses an electronic voice to greet callers, asking them for the name of the person or department they wish to speak to before connecting them. All calls are recorded and no calls are missed. The automated service has allowed the company to improve its customer service and reduce its receptionist costs.

Using new technology to improve customer service can benefit most businesses. However, systems need to be properly implemented. It is essential to make sure that staff are trained to use new systems and procedures. The changes must be monitored to ensure that the customer has benefited. New technology, effective working practices, good communication and staff training all work hand in hand in the quest for improved customer service.

Knowledge summary

■ Improvements in customer service can be achieved through changes to working practices, improved and effective communication with staff and customers, and a programme of customer service training for all employees.

■ Other strategies for improving customer service including empowering employees, acting on feedback and exploiting new technology.

■ Some businesses adopt a policy of continuous improvement, involving commitment to change, planning, action and review.

quick questions

1 Explain why customer service might improve as a result of a business providing a better work-life balance for staff.

2 Explain the business consequences of not making changes to customer service procedures in response to problems and complaints.

3 Examine the implications of introducing new technology into a business. Think about the positive impact on customer service and any negative aspects that might arise

data interpretation
Tesco's customer question times

Tesco dedicates a section of its website for customer services. One of the services offered is customer question times. This facility allows customers to ask questions about the business.

Visit the Tesco website at www.tesco.com/customerservice. Look at "frequently asked questions" to find out the kinds of issues that Tesco needs to address as a result of customers' questions. Tesco also holds customer question times all over the country. These are held so that "you can tell us about your shopping experience at Tesco".

A Why is improved customer service so important for a retailer such as Tesco?

B Suggest how Tesco can improve its service to the customer based on some of the frequently asked questions.

C Evaluate what might happen to Tesco as a leading retailer if it does not effectively monitor and continuously improve its service to customers.

Customer service legislation

Setting the scene: protecting the customer

There are many different laws regulating trade and business. These laws provide consumers with protection from misleading and unfair business practices, and they provide a legal context and framework for customer service.

There are several government agencies that play various roles in implementing competition law and monitoring the conduct of businesses to make sure that they trade within the law and operate fairly. Two of the most important are the Office of Fair Trading and the Trading Standards Institute.

Learn more about the Office of Fair Trading by visiting its website at www.oft.gov.uk. By following the links to consumer information, you can find the range of advice it offers to consumers. Two of OFT brochures are illustrated here – there are many more.

Again, you can learn about the Trading Standards Institute from its website at www.tradingstandards.gov.uk. By following the links, you can find the type of advice provided for consumers and businesses.

Laws that impact on customer service

Competition and consumer legislation aims to protect businesses, customers and employees. It protects businesses by setting out rules and regulations that allow fair competition. Laws such as the Restrictive Practices Act, the Fair Trading Act and the Competition Act ensure that there is competition in markets and they prohibit any business from obtaining, and potentially abusing, a monopoly position. Customers also have legal rights which both protect them and act as a guide for businesses.

There are other constraints imposed on business, both by trade organisations and as a result of other ethical considerations that are not enforceable by law. The external constraints impacting on businesses – from the wider political, economic, social and legal environment in which they operate – were discussed in Unit 1. This topic focuses in more detail on some of the legislation that impacts on customer service.

1 Contracts of sale

If a business agrees to sell goods or services to a customer, it has entered into a legally-binding contract. Sometimes the terms of the contract of sale are implied rather than explicitly stated. For example, if you purchase a television or a new PC you expect it to work, and the law protects your right to expect the product to work. There does not need to be an explicit contract between the retailer and you (the purchaser) to this effect.

Contract law can be very complicated, and the law is sometimes difficult to interpret. A business that is found to be in breach of contract law will be fined and it undoubtedly risks losing customers if it has to resort to the law to settle a dispute.

Many businesses actually offer more rights to customers than are strictly required within the law.

James Beatties, a large chain of department stores in the Midlands, displays a message to customers throughout its stores: shop with confidence. Any goods can be returned within a month of purchase (or beyond in some cases) and a full money back guarantee is offered. Beatties do not have to do this by law, but it believes it is a part of offering good service to its customers.

There are a number of acts that set the legal framework for contracts of sale. The Sale of Goods Act 1979 and 1995 states that:

- goods must be as described
- goods must be of satisfactory quality in relation to the price that has been paid and the description and age of the goods
- goods must be fit for the purpose for which they are intended.

The Supply of Goods and Services Act 1982 covers services such as repair and maintenance. It protects customers against poor workmanship, overcharging and unreliability of service. The act states that work should be carried out:

- for a reasonable charge and within a reasonable time
- with reasonable care and skill
- using satisfactory materials.

2 Consumer protection

The Consumer Protection Act provides further safeguards for customers by giving legal protection against unsafe and potentially dangerous goods. Under the act, businesses must also be truthful about the price of goods and services. The Trading Standards Institute monitors business to ensure they are complying with the legislation.

The Consumer Protection Act in a nutshell:

- prohibits the supply of goods that are unsafe
- provides for the safety and protection of consumers
- provides powers for seizing and forfeiture, and powers to suspend the sale of suspected unsafe goods
- requires businesses to publish notices warning of unsafe goods previously supplied
- provides for liability for damage caused by defective products
- prohibits misleading price indications.

Sometimes goods are recalled because it has been discovered by the manufacturer that they are unsafe or unfit for purpose. The Consumer Protection Act explains the right way to give notice to customers in these situations.

stop and think

OFT gets fairer deal from Land of Leather

Furniture company Land of Leather has agreed to give consumers a fairer deal following action by the OFT. The OFT had received complaints about the use of unfair terms in Land of Leather's contracts, delay in delivery of goods, goods being supplied that were not of satisfactory quality and misleading advertising offering interest-free credit.

The OFT has approached Land of Leather and the company has agreed to put in place a number of measures to comply with the legislation. Land of Leather has signed undertakings that it will no longer use the unfair terms and will not breach certain terms implied by the Sale of Goods Act 1979.

Christine Wade, OFT consumer reg-

ulation enforcement director, said: "Consumers have a right to expect goods to be of satisfactory quality and delivered on time, for advertising to be accurate and not to have their legal rights undermined by unfair terms. Where companies breach consumer legislation we will take action to protect consumers."

This extract is taken from a press release issued on the Office of Fair Trading website on 19 August 2004. You can read the full article by following the links to the 2004 press releases on www.oft.gov.uk.

Do you think you know your rights sufficiently that you could have argued if you were asked to sign up to some of the practices described in the extract? Why is it important for a business such as Land of Leather to make sure it stays within the law?

stopandthink

The BBC Watchdog website (www.bbc.co.uk/watchdog) provides information about all product recalls over the preceding six months. Over the years, the site has listed products as diverse such as:

■ television stands

■ potato wedges

■ garden furniture

■ toddler's harness and reins

■ cheesecake

■ biscuits

This is a small sample of a very long list. Choose one of the products currently listed as recalled on the Watchdog website – go to the homepage and click on the link to product recalls.

Investigate further the nature of the problem that caused the product you selected to be recalled. Discuss the implications to the business that makes or sells the product. Discuss the implications for any consumers that are not aware that the product has been recalled.

3 Trade descriptions

Another important piece of consumer protection legislation is the Trade Description Act. This protects consumers against false and misleading descriptions of goods. If you go into your local supermarket and choose to buy free range eggs, then the eggs in the carton should be free range. A handbag that is described as leather on the label cannot simply resemble leather, it must be made of leather and not some plastic substitute.

Many goods and services are complex and consumers may not be aware that the description of the goods they are buying does not necessarily accurately describe what they may be purchasing. The Office of Fair Trading investigates cases of potentially misleading product descriptions. For example, it has investigated the claims made by some companies about healthcare products that they offer for sale on the internet.

4 Consumer credit

The Consumer Credit Act 1974 protected the rights of consumers buying goods or services using credit. Updated in 2005, the new Consumer Credit Act 2005 strengthens the protection for consumers against unfair credit terms and excessive interest rates. The legislation sets rules for any business providing credit card services, hire purchase agreements and loan deals. It therefore affects many retail businesses that offer their customers credit terms.

The consumer credit legislation ensures that all credit agreements have to be in writing, and the customer must be a given a copy of the agreement. Customers entering into credit agreements when they are buying goods have a statutory cooling-off period, which gives them some days in which they can change their minds and return the goods without obligation.

5 European regulations

The European Union seeks greater co-operation between member countries and works to harmonise laws so that businesses can operate throughout Europe on a level playing field. The EU issues directives or rules that all member states must use to develop their laws and regulations. Businesses in the UK are expected to abide by EU rules and directives.

In terms of consumer protection, the European Union's Health and Consumer Protection Directorate has three main areas of activity that impact on the way businesses can operate as well as providing consumers with further protection. These are:

■ food safety – from farm to fork

■ public health

■ consumer affairs – covering non-food consumer products and services.

In December 2004, a new EU forum was set up to look closely at consumer affairs in order to develop a toolkit for better law making. This covers an investigation into many aspects of non-food consumer products and services.

stopandthink

The European Union is encouraging young people to become more aware as consumers. It has published The European Consumer Diary, a free resource aimed at 16–18-year-old students. Have you got a copy? Find out more from www.generation-europe.org.

Implications for business

Businesses must be aware of their obligations under the law. They must ensure that their goods and services comply with general safety requirements. They must ensure that everyone on business premises is safe. They must also make sure that what they offer the customer is accurately described and that any claims made about products are true.

If a business does not comply, goods can be seized and destroyed, and companies can be fined. This has a dramatic impact on the reputation of the business and can have a long-term negative effect on sales, profitability and reputation.

A well-run business that stays within the law, protecting both its staff and its customers, will retain a level of trust and respect. Staff will be motivated and able to work in a risk-free environment, and customers will feel confident that they are buying goods or services that are safe and fit for purpose.

The law impacting on customer service has been strengthened in recent years to meet greater public concern about consumer protection and health and safety. This has a great many implications for business. All businesses face:

- higher costs in meeting safety standards

- pressure to improve quality control to ensure accuracy, safety and zero defect

- demands from increasingly well-informed consumers

- challenges to ensure that staff are well informed and trained.

Knowledge summary

- **Competition law and consumer protection legislation gives legal rights to customers.**

- **Consumer protection law can increase business costs while at the same time create consumer demand for improved quality and performance standards.**

quick**questions**

1 Explain how consumers are protected by the law of contract.

2 Examine some of the ways a food retailing business such as Tesco might be affected by current consumer protection legislation.

3 How might the EU affect the way UK businesses operate?

data**interpretation**
Advice services

Many different organisations advise both consumers and businesses on the detail and potential impact of consumer protection and competition law. Look at the websites of these six organisations that give information and advice on consumer protection law:

- **Citizens Advice Bureau – www.citizensadvice.org.uk**
- **Trading Standards Institute – www.tradingstandards.gov.uk**
- **Office of Fair Trading – www.oft.gov.uk**
- **National Federation of Consumer Groups www.nfcg.org.uk**
- **BBC Watchdog programme- www.bbc.co.uk/watchdog**
- **Consumer World – www.consumerworld.org**

A List services each of these organisations can offer to businesses and consumers.

B Choose one aspect of the law, such as misleading pricing, and produce a fact sheet advising consumers about their rights.

C Evaluate the services offered by two of the websites for a business that is looking for help.

Business in practice: Royal Mail Group

Royal Mail Group is a public limited company wholly owned by the government. Annual sales exceed £8 billion and the business employs around 200,000 employees.

Royal Mail Group has three main brands:

- Royal Mail serves both individual and business customers. It collects, sorts and delivers mail to the UK's 27 million addresses and provides business mail services to help companies communicate with their customers and market their businesses.

- Parcelforce Worldwide collects, sorts and delivers parcels, mainly for business customers.

- Post Office Ltd – operating under the Post Office brand – has a network of 15,000 Post Office branches and offers around 170 products and services. Customers can buy stamps, send mail, collect benefits, pay bills, make cash withdrawals and buy from a range of financial and commercial services such as foreign currency, home, car and travel insurance, unsecured loans, and a home telephone service. Some 94 per cent of people in the UK live within a mile of a Post Office.

The Royal Mail business saw a turnaround in fortunes in the early part of the 2000s. In 2002, Royal Mail – then known as Consignia – was losing £1 million a day. Two years later, operational and service improvements turned this loss into a profit of more than £1 million per day. In the first half of the 2004/5 financial year, Royal Mail made a £217 million profit on its operations.

External customers

Everyone is a customer of the Royal Mail Group. Everyone receives or posts letters and packages from time to time. It is probably a service we take for granted.

Post Office branches are the point of call to post letters, parcels and cards, to obtain a passport form or tax a car. Post Office staff can give information about a wide range of government initiatives and will change sterling into foreign currency without making a commission charge.

Businesses are also customers, with nearly 90 per cent of the mail posted being from businesses. Many businesses use direct mail as part of their marketing strategies and Royal Mail has a service to give help and advise on how to make the best of this form of advertising. Many business and financial documents have to be sent using the post. Business customers also take advantage of the Parcelforce Worldwide express delivery service.

	Quarter 2 2004/5	target	Quarter 1 2004/5	3 month change	Quarter 2 2001/2	3 year change
First class	92.1%	92.5%	88.3%	up 3.8%	90.7%	up 1.4%
Second class	98.6%	98.5%	98.0%	up 0.6%	98.5%	up 0.1%

Figure 5.10: Service improvements in postal services

Internal customers

Royal Mail Group employs around 200,000 people. The group has introduced changes in working practices in recent years, but has made significant increases in pay and offered better conditions. The new improved Royal Mail – a business in which targets are being met and the reputation and integrity of the service is growing – has produced a more motivated and happier workforce.

Customer service expectations

Customers expect letters and parcels to arrive on time and undamaged. When people need to use the post office to tax their car or collect child benefit, they do not want to queue for too long. If customers are wheelchair-bound or otherwise disabled, they need to know they can still use the Post Office. If customers want information about a postcode, or the cost of sending a letter to Africa, or the best way to send a parcel, they want to know that the information is accurate.

The Royal Mail knows that customer expectations are changing. By introducing online services, guaranteed delivery times and computerised systems to make

waiting times shorter, Royal Mail is trying to maintain and improve the quality of service to its customers.

Service improvements

Royal Mail has had to reinvent its business to meet the changing needs of customers and to offset increasing competition. Royal Mail's goal is "to be the world's leading postal service". The government has set targets, but the Royal Mail's initiatives to improve performance has meant that in many cases targets have been met and exceeded.

Modernisation is the key to operational change and to improving customer service. There have been worries that some changes might impact on the most vulnerable members of society.

For example, the the Department of Work and Pensions has asked people who collect benefits from the Post Office branches to opt to have their money paid directly into a bank account. This impacts on the Post Office because fewer people are visiting branches to collect benefits. Post Office Ltd is seeking to replace this business and generate revenue by offering new services to its customers, such as banking facilities, foreign exchange and financial services.

Another important change was the introduction of a single postal delivery to every household in the UK. This replaced a system in which most parts of the UK had two deliveries a day. This change has enabled the Royal Mail Group to improve the wages and hours for its postmen and women.

Improvements have also been made to ensure the integrity of the service. All new recruits are now vetted to ensure that any who attempted to conceal past convictions are prevented from joining the company.

Parcelforce Worldwide is also responding to the needs of its customers. It now focuses on express services guaranteeing delivery within a timeframe. It has restructured and cut its losses, and was on target to break even by the end of the 2004/5 financial year.

People issues

Royal Mail believes that increasing profitability is about improving service and efficiency, and that this is linked to the dedication and commitment of the staff in the business. Increasing quality of service to customers is the number one priority for Royal Mail, and investing in people was seen by directors of Royal Mail as essential if they were to provide an improved service for customers.

In 2002, pay for postal workers was low and they worked a six-day week. Royal Mail had one of the worst strike records in the country. Customers were suffering the loss of nearly 30 million letters a year and the first class letter delivery performance was poor.

Postmen and women now work a five-day week, with national basic pay of around £300 a week. A ground-breaking pay deal increased pay by 14.5 per cent. The amount of mail lost has been halved, with 99.92 per cent arriving safely at its destination. By 2005, the business was on target to achieve more than £400 million profit on operations, with employees set to receive a "share in success" payment of at least £800.

The company has also openly tackled bullying and harassment issues that had caused some problems.

Harmony within the workforce will hopefully be reflected in the service to customers.

In the spring of 2004, there were 20,000 temporary employees. By autumn 2004, this was reduced to 2,500. A pool of experienced, trained temps has been established to ensure people are available when there is a short-term need for extra workers. Training has also been improved and new recruits are assigned a mentor to help them pick up the job more quickly.

Monitoring customer satisfaction

Postwatch (www.postwatch.co.uk) is the consumer watchdog and Postcomm (www.postcomm.gov.uk) is the postal services regulator. Both bodies monitor the performance of the Royal Mail. They carry out regular surveys to record the satisfaction levels of customers.

Postwatch and Postcomm commissioned a survey of customer experiences at Post Office branches in October 2004. The survey used mystery shoppers to sample services at 302 urban branches. The survey looked at:

■ exterior and interior presentation of offices

■ information available on products and services

■ staff performance when dealing with customers

■ accuracy, quality and completeness of information.

The main conclusions of this Postwatch survey were that:

■ staff were seen to be polite, calm and efficient, but they were not always well informed and sometimes did not give the correct advice

■ wheelchair access was not universal

■ one in five mystery shoppers had to wait in queues for more than five minutes before being served. Post Office Ltd serves 29 million customers a week with the large majority being served within five minutes

■ of a sample survey of packages sent first class, 71 per cent of mail arrived the next day and 22 per cent of packages were left unattended at the recipient's house.

Royal Mail and the law

The Royal Mail is highly regulated. The government sets targets and these are reviewed on a regular basis. Service standards are carefully monitored and regulated by Postwatch and Postcomm. Prices for services are also carefully controlled. Royal Mail would like to have more autonomy in the way it sets prices for its products so that it can compete more vigorously with its rivals.

The business has to adhere to consumer legislation and must not make claims about its services if these cannot be met. Customers must be safe and there should be access for those with disabilities.

The challenge

In 2004, Adam Crozier, chief executive of Royal Mail, said: "The progress we have made in improving both our service and profitability supports our vision to be demonstrably the best and most trusted mail company in the world

"We are determined to consistently provide the highest quality, dependable mail services, and that includes innovative products for all our customers as well as the one-price-goes-anywhere universal service to the UK's 27 million addresses.

"The challenge now is to make a commercial return that's acceptable to our shareholders and, above all, which allows us to make the investments we need in both our people in improving quality further."

Websites

www.royalmailgroup.com

www.royalmail.com

www.parcelforce.com

www.postoffice.co.uk

activities

1 Who are Royal Mail's customers?

2 What are the expectations of Royal Mail's different customers?

3 Describe some of the ways in which the Royal Mail has set out to improve its services to the customer.

4 Explain how changes that the Royal Mail has made to improve customer service meet customer needs and expectations.

5 Evaluate the services of one of Royal Mail's three core businesses, considering the strengths and weaknesses and how it might improve.

6 Explain how Royal Mail reviews and analyses its service to customers.

UNIT 3 INTRODUCED THE FOUR Ps OF THE marketing mix: product, price, promotion and place. This unit looks in greater depth at promotion. Promotion is a vital part of marketing. It allows a business to communicate the benefits of its products to potential customers.

Promotion is just one element of the marketing mix. The best promotional campaign in the world will not rescue a business offering the wrong product in the wrong place at the wrong price. However, a brilliant combination of price, product and place is useless unless an effective promotional campaign communicates these potential benefits to the target audience.

This unit helps you to understand:

- how promotion is used by businesses to influence buyer behaviour
- the variety of promotional media available to businesses
- the relative advantages and disadvantages of different media
- the constraints affecting promotional activities
- how promotional campaigns are planned and evaluated.

Investigating promotion

Setting the scene: effective communication

In Unit 5, you learned how good communication is a vital part of customer service (*see page* 216). It is also a key element in promotion. A promotional activity must be able to communicate clearly with the target audience.

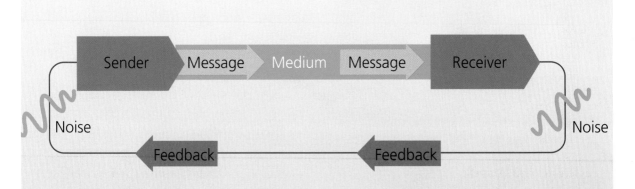

Figure 6.1: The communication process

Figure 6.1 illustrates the key components of the communication process.

Sender – the individual, group or organisation wanting to communicate ideas and information about the product.

Message – the use of text, images, sounds, etc. to convey ideas and information about the product.

Medium – the platform used to deliver the message, such as television, radio magazines and the internet.

Receiver – the individual, group or organisation the message is intended for. The receiver interprets the message and attempts to understand its meaning.

Feedback – the receiver's response to the message. This could be made using a variety of different media or might simply be an action (including ignoring the message!)

Noise – anything that gets in the way of the receiver understanding the sender's true message.

KEY TERMS

Promotional tools are the promotional activities available to a business when promoting its products. They include advertising, sales promotion and sponsorship.

Promotional campaigns use a mix of tools to try to achieve specific objectives. For example, a campaign might use television advertising and direct mail leaflets to increase the number of people subscribing to a digital TV service.

Target audience defines the group of people that the promotional activity or campaign is designed to reach. It might be defined by characteristics such as age, sex, income levels and location; for example, 20–30-year-old males earning over £20,000 and living in the Midlands.

Media is the platform used to deliver the promotional activity, such as cinema, leaflets and web pages.

Mass media is a platform that has the potential to reach large audiences, such as television and radio.

What is promotion?

Promotion is one element of the marketing mix (Unit 3, *see page* 140). It communicates the benefits of products to potential and current customers. Promotion can be very general; for example, an advertising campaign about the dangers of drink-driving. However, promotion can also be very specific, such as a "buy two, get one free" sales promotion.

Promotion uses a wide range of promotional tools.

Advertising – communicating with customers through mass media, such as television, radio and newspapers; for example, a television advertisement highlighting the release of a new film.

Sales promotion – providing customers with a direct incentive to buy products; for example, an offer of a free cinema ticket when purchasing a meal in a fast food restaurant.

Personal selling – personal, face-to-face communication aimed at informing and persuading customers; for example, a salesperson in a department store providing information about a new range of cosmetics.

Public relations – favourable use of publicity communicated through mass media; for example, local newspapers reporting the opening of a new store.

Sponsorship – improving the image of a business and/or product by funding unrelated activities; for example, a business funding the kit and equipment of a local football team

stop and think

In December 2004, Burger King offered a free cinema ticket with every "kids' meal". What type of promotional activity is this?

In recent years, direct marketing has become an essential part of many businesses promotional activities. In direct marketing, a business communicates directly with specific customers. The form of communication can vary – from telephone calls to direct mail leaflets – but the intention is to develop a one-to-one relationship between the business and its individual customers.

This leaflet from Sky is a typical example of direct marketing. This direct mail leaflet contains information about Sky's digital television services and the price it charges for each service. The leaflet also contains contact details for potential customers wishing to subscribe to a service.

The leaflet has the potential to carry out two essential aspects of promotion: informing and persuading.

■ It informs readers about the technical aspects of the product – the channels available, prices charged and equipment required.

■ It attempts to persuade readers to purchase a subscription and does this by using well-known cartoon characters – The Simpsons and Nemo.

Finally, the leaflet incorporates a sales promotion technique – a free installation offer – aimed at persuading readers to buy from Sky. Do you think it is an effective promotional tool?

GO TO the accompanying CD-ROM. Choose Unit 6 from the main menu. This will take you to an interactive game about organising a promotional campaign. It is better to try this game once you have read Unit 6 Topics 3 to 6.

How promotional tools affect buyer behaviour

Setting the scene: sending the wrong message?

Communication is an essential element of any promotional activity – get the message wrong and the effects could be disastrous. This extract from an article by communications expert Jonathan Gabay provides some examples of ill-considered messages.

Explain the problems with the messages in example of communication given the article. What might have been the financial consequences for each business?

Pardon my language

Clairol introduced a hair curling iron - the Mist Stick - into Germany, only to find out that "mist" is slang for manure.

When Gerber started selling baby food in Africa it used the same packaging as in the USA. This had a picture of a beautiful baby on the label. Later, Gerber realised that African companies routinely put pictures on the label of what's inside the jar, since many people can't read.

Arcadia and Topman bosses were left red-faced after Topman brand director, David Shepherd, was interviewed by a trade magazine. David Shepherd said Topman customers only wore a suit for their first interview or their first court appearance.

Japan's second-largest tourist agency was mystified when it entered English-speaking markets and began receiving some unusual telephone calls. Upon finding out why, the owners of Kinki Nippon Tourist Co. changed the company's name.

Source: adapted from www.gabaynet.com

Communicating with buyers

The purpose of any promotional activity is to change the behaviour and attitudes of customers. This is a difficult task as people need convincing reasons to change their views and purchasing habits. However, every minute of the day people are being persuaded to purchase products as a direct or indirect result of effective promotional activities.

These promotional activities work because they consider and understand two crucial issues:

- effective communication
- influences that affect buying behaviour.

1 Effective communication

Effective communication occurs when a message being sent is understood by the person receiving it. The receiver will also know how and when to respond to the message.

KEY TERMS

Feedback is the response to a message. Feedback can use a variety of different media or may be absent if the message is not understood or does not interest the person receiving it. It may take the form of an action such as purchasing a product.

Noise is anything that gets in the way of the receiver understanding the message, such as conflicting information or an inability to believe the message.

AIDA is an acronym for Attention-Interest-Desire-Action. These are the stages an individual needs to be taken through before purchasing a product.

Buyer behaviour describes the way individuals make purchasing decisions. Buyer behaviour is affected by a complex range of influences. These can be grouped under three headings: social, psychological and personal influences.

Figure 6.1 (*see page* 242) illustrates the key elements of communication. Let's see how this communication model applies in a real situation. Alpro manufactures soya drinks, desserts and dairy free alternatives to single cream and yogurts. This advertisement for alpro soya™ appeared in the June 2004 issue of the Waitrose Food Illustrated magazine.

Look at the communication elements in Alpro's advertisement.

Sender – Alpro wants to communicate the benefits of its soya milk drink.

Message – the advertisement uses text and images to communicate the health benefits and versatility of Alpro's soya milk.

Medium – the advertisement was placed in a colour magazine published by a major supermarket chain.

Receiver – readers of the supermarket's magazine might interpret the advertisement as saying that Alpro soya™ is good for your health and can also be used for making fruit smoothies.

Feedback – readers might purchase the product, call the freephone number provided, visit Alpro's website for more information or ignore the message.

Noise – readers might be uncertain about what soya is or might believe that it is no substitute for traditional dairy products are essential for good health.

For effective communication to take place, any business needs to ensure that its promotional activities deliver messages which:

■ help to achieve business objectives

■ target the intended audience

■ are capable of being understood by the target audience

■ promote positive feedback from the target audience.

Promotional activities that do not consider the key elements of the communication process are likely to be ineffective. An advertisement might be entertaining and amusing but it will be ineffective if it attracts the wrong target audience or fails to promote positive feedback.

stop and think

Which target audience do you think is the Alpro advertisement is aimed at? Giving reasons, do you think the Alpro soya™ advertisement has the potential to communicate effectively with this target audience?

2 Buyer behaviour

In addition to communicating effectively and providing information, promotional tools attempt to affect buyer behaviour by:

■ creating and raising awareness

■ creating, enhancing and/or changing image.

In both cases, the focus is on perception. The promotional campaign aims to shape customers' perceptions of a business and its products. In other words, promotional tools are being used to influence the purchasing decisions of consumers by creating a favourable view of a business and its products.

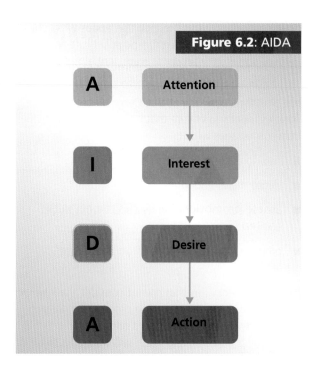

Figure 6.2: AIDA

- A — Attention
- I — Interest
- D — Desire
- A — Action

A systematic approach to altering buyer behaviour can be taken by using AIDA (see Figure 6.2). Used chiefly within advertising, AIDA is a way of thinking about the key steps an individual needs to be taken through before agreeing to buy a product. It can be applied to all promotional tools and helps when considering the timing of activities in a promotional campaign.

Making purchasing decisions is a complex process. Figure 6.3 illustrates the three main influences on buyer behaviour. It indicates that the decision to purchase a product can be a very complex one, especially if the product is expensive (such as a house) or of significant interest to a consumer (such as buying clothes to wear at a party). How many of these factors affect your purchasing decisions?

stop and think

Could an advert, such as the Alpro magazine ad, cover all stages of the AIDA process? What other promotional tools might be required?

Promotional tools, such as advertising, need to focus on some of the influences listed in Figure 6.3 if buyer behaviour is to be altered. The choice of influence depends on the product being promoted and the audience being targeted. Sometimes promotional tools will be used in emotive ways, by acting on our feelings and targeting emotions such as fear and happiness. At other times, promotional tools will be used to inform rather than persuade – to provide facts rather than appeal to our emotional identity.

A clothing business, such as French Connection UK, launching a new range of clothes would possibly focus on these aspects of buyer behaviour:

- **social** – focus on the attitudes of friends and use advertising showing groups of people with similar age and background characteristics

- **psychological** – communicate the values represented by the range and to which the buyer might aspire, such as "edgy" or "casual"

- **personal** – promote key aspects or benefits of the product likely to appeal to the target age group, such as price ranges or the style of the clothing.

When promoting a new range of fashion clothing, it is likely that the social and psychological factors will be most important; psychological factors are likely to be most dominant, because fashion is often based on an abstract idea rather than a functional product.

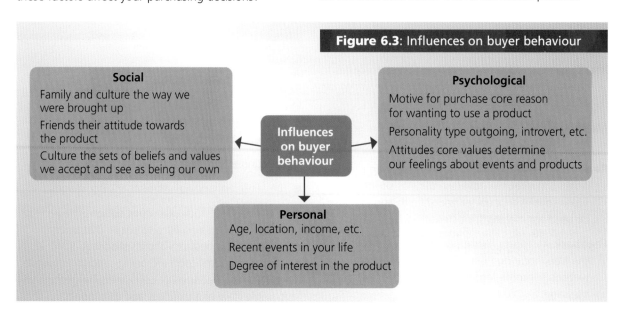

Figure 6.3: Influences on buyer behaviour

Social
Family and culture the way we were brought up
Friends their attitude towards the product
Culture the sets of beliefs and values we accept and see as being our own

Influences on buyer behaviour

Psychological
Motive for purchase core reason for wanting to use a product
Personality type outgoing, introvert, etc.
Attitudes core values determine our feelings about events and products

Personal
Age, location, income, etc.
Recent events in your life
Degree of interest in the product

Knowledge summary

- Promotional tools must communicate effectively, considering key factors such as the content of the message, the structure of the message, the medium used to deliver the message, the presence of noise detracting from the meaning and impact of the message.

- AIDA (attention-interest-desire-action) looks at the key steps an individual needs to go through before purchasing a product.

- Promotional activities alter buyer behaviour by focusing on some or all of the three main influences: social, such as attitudes of friends; psychological, such as reasons for wanting to use a product; personal, such as current level of income.

quick questions

1 Explain why effective communication would be important for these two promotional campaigns:
- a government "don't drink and drive" campaign
- a UK business introducing its products to markets in the USA.

2 Explain which stages of the AIDA process these promotional activities might be best suited to:
- buy one get one free offers
- sales staff offering advice on a store's product range.

3 Identify a product you recently bought, or had bought for you, and which was important to you, such as shoes or a mobile telephone. Use Figure 6.3 to list, in order of priority, the main factors influencing the purchase of the product.

data interpretation
Tweenagers

This is an extract of an article written by Martin Lindstrom. It is based on a study investigating children's attitudes towards famous brand names such as Nike and Sony.

A Using the article, identify three reasons why tweenagers have become an important target audience for promotional activities.

B Explain why the internet might be a more appropriate media than television for promotional activities aimed at tweenagers.

C Identify three examples of promotional activities aimed at tweenagers. Using these examples, prepare a five-minute presentation with the title: "What influences a tweenagers' buying behaviour?"

How tweenagers are taking over

Welcome to the world of tweens - children aged between 8 and 14. Almost every aspect of today's tweenager is different from what we have seen in past generations. They've grown up faster, are more connected, more direct and more informed. They have more personal power, influence and attention than any other generation before them.

No other generation has ever had as much disposable income as this one, and close to 80 per cent of all brands purchased by parents are controlled by their children.

Research shows that grammatically correct sentences in ads, on television or the internet are considered outdated. Tweens have an overwhelming preference to use the same language that they employ when texting with their friends.

New ways of communicating will most likely replace the traditional channels that we know today. It's already happening. About a third of all tweens prefer surfing the internet to watching television. And almost half would rather play a computer game than turn on a TV show.

Source: adapted from www.news.bbc.co.uk, 19 March 2003

Setting the scene: the Ability Suite

Vodafone UK, the mobile telephone services provider, sponsors Manchester United Football Club. The company became Manchester United's principal sponsor in 2000.

The deal means that Vodafone's logo and name appears on team's kit, but is also allows Vodafone to organise many other joint activities with the club. One example is the Ability Suite, which was opened at Old Trafford in April 2003 by Sir Alex Ferguson with representatives from Manchester United, Vodafone UK and Manchester United Disabled Supporters' Association (MUDSA).

Financed by both Manchester United and Vodafone UK, the suite is a focus point and match day facility for disabled fans. It contains a wide range of assistive technology along with specially designed facilities to enhance the match day experience.

At the launch, David Gill, group managing director of Manchester United plc said: "The Ability Suite is the first of its kind in the Premiership, a unique facility for all our disabled supporters from the visually impaired to the hard of hearing. It's important to make all our fans feel part of the club, with Vodafone's help the Ability Suite has done just that."

Gavin Darby, chief executive officer of Vodafone UK, added: "We are more than just a name on United's shirt. It's a partnership. Vodafone wanted to help Manchester United ensure that all fans of the club are given the best access and facilities. The room is a physical illustration of Vodafone's commitment to make a positive difference to the world around us."

Why do you think that contributing towards the finance of the Ability Suite might be an effective promotional activity for Vodafone? Why might Manchester United have been a suitable organisation for Vodafone to sponsor?

Source: www.vodafone.co.uk

KEY TERMS

Sponsorship involves the support of an event, individual or organisation by a business in return for the prominent display of the business's name or brands.

Public relations (PR) is a coordinated effort to ensure that key stakeholders, such as customers, employees and suppliers, adopt and maintain a positive view of a business.

Advertising is a paid form of non-personal communication transmitted through mass media.

Sponsorship and PR

One of the purposes of promotion is to raise a business's profile – to increase awareness and create a positive image of the business and its products. Sponsorship and public relations are often used for this purpose.

Sponsorship can be in the form of a financial grant, such as a £1000 donation given to a local performing arts group in return for some acknowledgement in the art group's publicity or programmes. It can also be

Figure 6.4: Sport sponsorship

Year	1997	1998	1999	2000	2001	2002	2003
Expenditure (£ millions)	322	353	377	401	421	429	411
Number of sponsors	995	969	1172	859	698	656	516

Source: Marketing Pocket Book 2005

in the form of other types of material support, such as providing free sports equipment. Many forms of entertainment now receive sponsorship of some form. In particular, artistic and sporting events are often sponsored by major corporations.

Figure 6.4 shows the financial value of sports sponsorship by corporations and the number of businesses providing this sponsorship. The table indicates that although the total value of sports sponsorship has been increasing (at least up to 2002), the number of corporations carrying out this sponsorship declined from a peak in 1999. What might this table say about the effectiveness of sponsorship as a promotional tool for corporations?

Figure 6.5 illustrates the top five business sectors taking part in sports sponsorship in 2003, measured by the number of involvements. Why are these types of businesses more likely to sponsor sports events?

Many sole traders, partnerships and small private limited companies also provide sponsorship of some form. Combined with public relations, sponsorship can raise the profile of a business and establish favourable connections between a business and the sponsored event or activity.

Public relations activities make use of the mass media to get publicity and to communicate positive news stories about the business's activities. For example, Vodafone would have received publicity about its

stop and think

Flora pro.active, a healthy low-fat spread manufactured by Unilever, sponsors the London Marathon. Explain two benefits Unilever might receive from sponsoring the London Marathon.

involvement in Manchester United's Ability Suite in local newspapers and regional media as well as on the football club's website. This publicity would be obtained at no direct cost to Vodafone.

Public relations activities which are single events, such as the opening of Manchester United's Ability Suite, are referred to as PR events. Sustained activities, combining several events over a period of time, are referred to as PR campaigns. Figure 6.6 illustrates the types of publicity that can be used by a business when carrying out a PR event or running a PR campaign. You might consider how celebrities like David Beckham uses these types of activities to further their careers and maintain their public profile.

Figure 6.5: Top five corporate sponsors of sport

Sector	Number of involvements
Finance – insurance	92
Hotel and travel	49
Sports goods	47
Automotive	40
Drinks: beer	38

Source: Marketing Pocket Book 2005

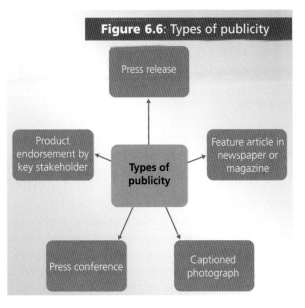

Figure 6.6: Types of publicity

Press release

Product endorsement by key stakeholder

Types of publicity

Feature article in newspaper or magazine

Press conference

Captioned photograph

249

Topic 2 Sponsorship, public relations and advertising

Advertising

Advertising is undoubtedly the main form of promotion that we encounter. Advertising is all around us – on television and radio, in magazines and newspapers, on billboards and bus shelters and, increasingly, through the internet.

The primary purpose of advertising is to inform and persuade current or potential customers. It attempts to take individuals through the AIDA process (*see* *page* 246). Figure 6.7 illustrates some specific uses of advertising.

Let's look at the typical structure of a printed advertisement. We'll use as an example this Vodafone advert for a new generation mobile phone.

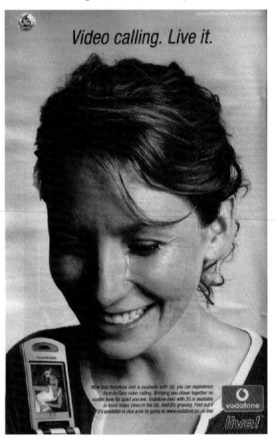

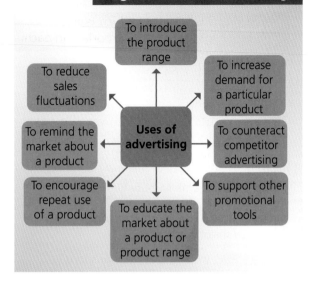

Figure 6.7: Uses of advertising

Signature

Most adverts carry a recognisable logo and or text identifying the business. This signature should be distinctive and easily recognisable. This advert carries the Vodafone logo and the brand name – "live!"

Illustration

The visual elements of the advertisement could either provide additional detail about the product or act as an emotive, persuasive element of the message. Vodafone's advertisement has both a picture of the product and also an emotive picture of someone using the product.

Headline

The headline is the first text noticed by the reader. The headline needs to convey the main message as quickly as possible. Most readers will ignore the rest of the advert unless the headline appeals to them.

Body copy

The body copy carries the main message of the advertisement. The body copy might attempt to inform or persuade the reader. It might use AIDA to structure its message. In this example, the body copy ends by suggesting an action – to visit the Vodafone website.

Knowledge summary

■ Sponsorship and public relations are used to develop the relationship between a business and its target markets by creating positive messages about the business and its products

■ Advertising can be used to achieve a variety of objectives. It is a key element of the promotional mix and attempts to deliver informative and persuasive messages about the business and its products.

■ Adverts require a structure if they are to successfully communicate their message. The ideas of headline, body copy, signature and illustration help to define the structure of an advert.

quick**questions**

1 Using Figure 6.6, explain which type of publicity might be most appropriate in each of these cases:
- a car manufacturer sponsors a major charity and wants to publicise its involvement
- a cosmetics manufacturer wants to raise the profile of one of its skin care products
- a band wants to publicise its new CD and UK tour
- a school wants to publicise some excellent examination results.

2 Outline the headline, body copy and possible illustrations for each of these advertisements:
- a leaflet, to be distributed in a shopping centre, advertising the opening of a new health and fitness centre
- a half-page advert, to be placed in a local newspaper, promoting a "closing down" sale at an electrical goods retail outlet
- a full-page colour magazine advert warning of the dangers of smoking cigarettes.

data**interpretation**
McDonald's Salads Plus

The BBC News online magazine has a regular Ad Breakdown feature which reviews advertising campaigns, identifying key features of advertisements and analysing the thinking behind them. Here are extracts of its review of McDonald's 2004 campaign for its Salads Plus range.

The brief: Attract people who would never eat a Big Mac and large fries.

What's going on: After a rundown of the menu, including Caesar salads, Quorn, yoghurt, "or even a crunchy apple", the voiceover says: "These girls are also new in McDonald's. Impatient Sophie, sensible Charlotte, and… Joanna, who's always late! New food – new people, Salads Plus."

Reasons: Recently the company recorded the first loss in its history, possibly due to a trend for dieting. So salads were introduced, designed to be "contemporary and relevant", ideal for appealing to "ladies who lunch" and to mums taking their children for a Happy Meal. The tactic seems to be working. In April 2004 the company reported a 56 per cent increase in first quarter profits – in spite of newspaper reports that a crispy chicken Caesar salad has more calories (when served with dressing and croutons) than a Big Mac.

Media: Initially a television campaign, McDonald's is now focusing its efforts on putting these adverts in women's magazines, on websites and on the radio. One of the advertisements, placed in a women's health magazine, reads: "Aromatherapist Anna is typical of the new breed of customer attracted to McDonald's… Anna hates football, but loves Thierry Henry. She hates alcohol but loves bars… She hates her job but loves her boss."

Adapted from: www.news.bbc.co.uk 19 May 2004

A Describe the likely purpose of the McDonald's Salad Plus advertising campaign.

B Explain three possible reasons why the television advert used three female characters described as "impatient Sophie", "sensible Charlotte" and "Joanna, who's always late".

C Do you think the magazine version of the Salad Plus advertisement adopted the same approach as the televised version? Justify your answer.

D Selecting an advert of your choice, prepare a short presentation which outlines the structure of the advert, explains why the advert is structured in this way, and evaluates the likely effectiveness of the advert.

Topic 3 Direct marketing and sales promotion

Setting the scene: direct mail or junk mail?

Direct mail is often referred to as junk mail. Many individuals regard direct mail as being unwanted, or unsolicited, mail. So why do businesses send direct mail? Read this BBC news story.

Why do you think businesses are increasingly using direct mail, even though many householders describe it as junk mail? Why would businesses be willing to pay for information about the location, lifestyles and activities of UK citizens?

Source: adapted from news.bbc.co.uk, 9 June 2004

Rogue mail

The nation's letterboxes are under siege. Last year more than 10 billion items of junk mail dropped through British letter boxes.

Goldfish, a direct bank, is trying to sign people up for its branded credit card through a direct mail campaign. Its research shows an almost 10 per cent take up. For Goldfish, sending out millions of glossy pamphlets is an expensive but worthwhile activity. In fact, even a 0.1 per cent take up can justify a direct mail campaign.

Pam Jackson of Goldfish speaks for many companies when she says:

"Because Goldfish is a direct bank, we don't have a very big high street presence. It's very important for us to talk directly with our customers and our potential customers. So, direct mail is a very important channel for us to reach customers on a very personalised one-to-one basis."

Goldfish, like other direct marketers, claims it targets its mail shots at people who are likely to want them. It has all sorts of information about our past purchasing decisions – there are some companies who specialise in collecting details about you through your lifestyle and activities.

KEY TERMS

Direct marketing involves delivering promotional material directly to the target audience. Direct marketing tools include direct mail, door-to-door selling and telemarketing.

Telemarketing involves contacting the target audience by telephone. This can include the use of short text messages via mobile telephones.

Sales promotion are direct financial inducements or promises of added value that encourage the purchase of a product. Examples of sales promotions include the use of coupons and free samples.

Point-of sale materials are any physical items used to enhance the display of a product within a retail outlet or to provide additional information about the product. For example, some companies arrange with retailers to install purpose-built in-store display shelves or computerised interactive displays featuring their products.

1 Direct marketing

Direct marketing is becoming one of the main promotional activities used by businesses. Many businesses use direct marketing to adopt a more immediate approach to promotion. It allows a focused, one-to-one communication with the target audience. The use of direct marketing techniques can save money for a business and increase the likely effectiveness of a business's promotional activities.

Traditionally, direct marketing uses two tools:

■ direct mail – printed advertising materials delivered to current and potential customers

■ mail order – printed catalogues delivered to current and potential customers.

In both cases, it is vital that the business has accurate, relevant and up-to-date mailing lists containing the addresses of suitable recipients. If a business uses out of date, or inappropriate lists, then its direct marketing campaign is likely to be ineffective and potentially damaging.

stop and think

What information might a business already have which could help it to develop its own mailing lists? Would these mailing lists be accurate, relevant and up-to-date?

Visit the Royal Mail website (www.royalmail.com) and click on the "direct mail" option to see how businesses can purchase mailing lists.

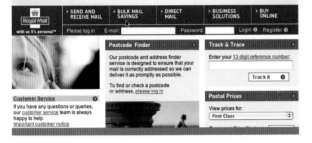

Today, direct marketing has moved away from total reliance on direct mail and mail order. As Figure 6.8 illustrates, there are a wide range of promotional tools and media that can be used for direct marketing.

Figure 6.8: Direct marketing tools

In terms of the AIDA process, introduced in Topic 1, direct marketing can assist in raising product awareness and establishing a willingness to investigate purchasing a product. However, direct marketing is likely to be most effective when aimed at an individual who is already interested in the product – it is best at working on the desire and action steps of the AIDA process. This is another reason why accurate, relevant and up-to-date mailing lists are vital.

Telemarketing and direct response television advertising are two direct marketing tools that have increased in significance in recent years. This is because:

■ modern telephone call centres are now capable of handling many calls

■ global telecommunication networks allow call centres to be located in countries with lower wage rates than the UK – which helps to drive down the costs of the operation

■ cable and satellite television technology allows businesses to communicate directly with viewers – for example, by advertising and selling products on shopping channel programmes.

The widespread use of the internet also opens up new ways for businesses to establish direct communications with customers:

■ e-mail is an inexpensive direct marketing tool and is effective if the business is careful in its sourcing and use of e-mail address lists

■ websites can now adapt their content to the past purchasing and browsing habits of the user, opening up the possibility of direct web marketing.

However, despite the greater use of new technologies, direct mail continues to be a significant component of direct marketing activities. Figure 6.9 shows that expenditure on direct mail steadily increased between 1993 and 2003.

Figure 6.9: Direct mail expenditure

	Expenditure, £m		
	Production costs	Postage costs	Total costs
1993	555	352	907
1994	646	404	1,050
1995	673	462	1,135
1996	904	500	1,404
1997	1,039	596	1,635
1998	939	726	1,666
1999	1,062	814	1,876
2000	1,180	869	2,049
2001	1,308	921	2,228
2002	1,399	979	2,378
2003	1,412	1,019	2,431

Source: Marketing Pocket Book 2005

2 Sales promotion

Sales promotion acts directly on buyer behaviour by offering a financial incentive for the buyer to purchase the product. It is a simple and direct form of promotion. Figure 6.10 illustrates the variety of sales promotion techniques that can be used by businesses. How many of these techniques have you experienced? Did any work, by encouraging you to buy the product being promoted?

Figure 6.10: Sales promotion techniques

Competition

Coupons and money refund

Demonstration *showing use of a product*

Free samples

Sales promotion techniques

Frequent user incentive *the more you purchase the more you save*

Point-of-sale material *an illustration showing the benefits of using the product*

Price-off offers

Loyalty cards *discounts for continuing to use product*

In terms of the AIDA process, sales promotion helps to confirm a purchasing decision – in other words, it helps to complete the action step of AIDA. In itself, sales promotion is unlikely to turn a disinterested individual into a customer. However, in competitive markets in which several businesses are apparently offering very similar products, the effective use of sales promotion techniques can help to "win" a sale.

One of the most common forms of sales promotion are coupons – offering discounts or money refunds when presented at all (or selected) retail outlets that sell the product being promoted. As Figure 6.11 shows, about 10 per cent of all coupons distributed actually get redeemed by customers. Figure 6.11 also shows that the vast majority of coupons now get distributed by direct mail; however, coupons can be distributed in a variety of ways, including:

■ inserts placed in newspapers and magazines – known as free-standing inserts or FSIs

■ direct mail and leaflet drops

■ printed advertisements

■ within retail outlets.

Figure 6.11: Distribution and redemption of coupons

1999	2003
4.7 billion coupons were distributed.	5.9 billion coupons were distributed.
Of these, 487 million were redeemed by customers – that is, about 10 per cent of coupons issued were used.	Of these, 524 million were redeemed by customers – that is, about 9 per cent of coupons issued were used.
Of the 487 million coupons redeemed, 37.7 per cent were distributed to individuals by direct mail and 24.6 per cent in retail outlets.	Of the 524 million coupons redeemed, 75.8 per cent were distributed to individuals by direct mail and 2.8 per cent in retail outlets.

Source: Marketing Pocket Book 2005

Price-off offers are an obvious way to provide a direct incentive to purchase. However, this type of sales promotion should be used with care as:

■ customers might purchase the product without the discount and so revenue is lost

■ the image of the product might be damaged if it appears to be constantly on offer.

Sales promotion techniques are also used to persuade retailers to purchase a supplier's products. In general, free merchandise and point-of-sale materials are often used to encourage a retailer to take on a particular product or product range. For example, a supplier might offer the retailer 10 per cent off the invoice or an attractive in-store stand to display the products, if the retailer agrees to stock the supplier's products.

stop and think

Supermarkets, such as Tesco and Sainsbury, heavily promote their loyalty cards which provide customers with various financial benefits depending on the amount of their spending in the supermarkets' stores. What factors might a supermarket take into account when deciding on the size of these financial benefits?

Knowledge summary

■ Direct marketing has evolved from its mail catalogue origins to include a wide range of tools.

■ Direct marketing is most effective when targeting the desire and action stages of the AIDA process.

■ Direct mail has established itself as the most widely used direct marketing tool, but its effectiveness relies heavily on the accuracy and relevance of the mailing lists used.

■ Sales promotion is the most direct promotional tool employed by businesses and operates by offering the buyer a financial incentive to purchase the product.

■ Sales promotion targets the action stage of the AIDA process.

quick questions

1 Explain how the AIDA process (*see page* 246) might help a door-to-door salesperson achieve a sale.

2 Look at the sales promotion techniques in Figure 6.10. How might these techniques be used by:
- a supermarket
- a cinema
- a mobile phone manufacturer, such as Nokia?

3 How might a supermarket use its loyalty card to improve its direct marketing activities?

data interpretation
Designing a coupon

This is an extract from a guidance leaflet produced by the Institute of Sales Promotion on how to design an effective coupon.

A Using the information in the leaflet, identify four features any coupon must clearly state in order to avoid potential problems. In each case, explain the possible consequences if the feature is omitted from the coupon.

B Design a coupon promoting the sale of DVDs at Blitz Entertainment, a retail outlet that sells music, games and films. The coupon should include a closing date (make this one month after the day you tackle this task), a value (say £5 off the next purchase of a Top 20 chart film in DVD format), and state where it can be redeemed (make it only redeemable at Blitz Entertainment, 10 High Street, Newtown ZZ1 1AA).

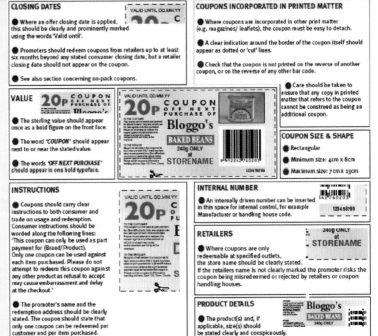

If possible, use a suitable computer software package to produce the coupon. Which methods would you use to distribute the coupon. Justify your choices.

Source: Institute of Sales Promotion

Promotional media: print

Setting the scene: POW!

Posters On Wheels (POW) claims to be the UK's mobile billboard advertising specialists. This is how the company sells the benefits of mobile billboards.

Imagine an advertising medium that will attract a customer's eye just by the way it looks. Then imagine coupling this medium with your stunning creative/message and running rings around your competitors. That's what mobile advertising is all about – it's a unique way of delivering your message directly to your target market.

POW mobiles' unique and unusual appearance demands attention and each have in-built personal address systems and stadium quality loud speakers. They are also equipped with bright lights for early morning and night time use.

On the road, the medium is a moving billboard. Stationary, it continues to broadcast your message. The result is media exposure close to 100 per cent of the time

You can find out more about mobile billboards by visiting Posters On Wheels' website at www.postersonwheels.com. Why might a mobile billboard be an effective promotional medium? Apart from the cost of hiring the vehicle and driver, what other costs might be involved in producing a mobile billboard advertisement?

KEY TERMS

Graphic designers are skilled in producing artwork and using desktop publishing and graphic design programs. Graphic designers will have received professional training. Having a graphic design program on your computer does not make you a graphic designer.

Desktop publishing programs enable graphic designers to layout a printed page ready for sending to a professional printing business. The most commonly used desktop publishing packages are QuarkXPress and Adobe InDesign.

Graphic design imaging programs enable graphic designers to produce images which can be imported into a desktop publishing program or sent to a professional printing business. Commonly used imaging programs are Adobe Illustrator, Adobe Photoshop and Macromedia Freehand.

Drafts are initial versions of a document. A **proof** represents the finished version of a document. The perfect proof represents the final version of the document.

1 Print production requirements

Posters On Wheels offers an interesting platform for displaying printed media. However, the company does not provide a design service – the customer must supply the poster design in an electronic format, either on disc or uploaded to the Posters On Wheels website. The website (www.postersonwheels.com) details the requirements of any electronic file sent to Posters On Wheels. It also provides templates – blank documents – which can be opened by computer design software such as:

- QuarkXPress and Adobe InDesign (desktop publishing programs)

- Adobe Illustrator, Adobe Photoshop and Macromedia Freehand (graphic design imaging programs).

Any business wishing to produce printed promotional material – whether designing a leaflet, newspaper or billboard advertisement – needs to follow the steps set out Figure 6.12.

Step 1 – identifying design requirements. Often work must be submitted using particular software and/or templates; if colour printing is being used, additional design requirements will be stipulated.

Step 2 – producing first drafts. This work can be done in-house, by the business, or can be completed by a design agency. A design agency should be used if the business has no staff with graphic design qualifications and experience.

Steps 3 and **4** – producing subsequent drafts and final proofs. Why do you think it might be important to produce several drafts and proofs before sending work to a printer? It is the responsibility of the business to check and approve the final proof for accuracy before it is printed.

Figure 6.12: Print design steps

- Complete rough outline of the promotional material
- **1** Identify the design requirements of the agency printing your promotional material
- **2** Use compatible software and appropriate templates to produce a draft copy of the promotional material
- **3** Check the draft copy for content accuracy and visual appearance. Produce a proof version
- **4** Check the initial proof version for errors to produce a perfect proof
- Perfect proof delivered to the advertisor or printer

Topic 4 Promotional media: print

2 Costs

Print costs vary considerably. The cost of any print job will depend on several factors.

The use of colour

Black and white is less expensive than full colour, but the price gap – between black and white and full colour work – has fallen in recent years and will continue to decline as colour printing technology improves.

The size of the print run

The larger the print run (that is, the number of copies printed), the cheaper the unit cost. In other words, the cost of printing each leaflet falls as you print more of them. Figure 6.13 shows the costs of printing various quantities of an A4 full colour leaflet.

Figure 6.13: Costs of printing a two-sided, A4, full-colour leaflet

Quantity	Total cost	Unit cost
1,000	£154.00	£0.15
5,000	£219.00	£0.04
10,000	£338.00	£0.03
50,000	£1,112.00	£0.02

Note: Trade prices from Imex Print, as at 30 January 2005, based on print using lowest weight paper

The size of the printed promotional material

The cost of a 48 sheet billboard will obviously be much higher than an A4 leaflet.

The use of design and/or advertising agencies

Costs can be reduced considerably if the design work is carried out in-house by the business itself. However, the quality and effectiveness of the finished promotional material is likely to suffer unless the business employs professional graphic design and marketing specialists.

3 Benefits and limitations

A business needs to consider not just the costs of printing any promotional material but also the costs of distributing that material to its target audience. It can distribute materials itself, through direct mail or by putting leaflets through the letterboxes of houses in the local area. It can pay another company to distribute its promotional materials; for example, by buying advertising space in a newspaper or magazine.

Figure 6.14 illustrates the different media available for printed promotional materials. A vital factor is the coverage and frequency of the printed promotional material.

■ Coverage is measured by the proportion of the target audience that views the promotional material; for example, the number of people within the targeted age group who buy a particular magazine compared with the total population in that targeted age group.

stop and think

Newspapers and magazines base their advertising rates on their circulation – the size of readership and their demographic profile – and on the size and position of the individual advert. They calculate the cost of an advert by the amount of column inches or column centimetres it occupies. For example, if the column centimetre rate is £10, then an advert which is 5 cm in height and two columns wide will cost £200 (= 5 x 2 x £10).

Visit the websites of local and national newspaper, such as the *Eastern Daily Press* (www.edp24.co.uk) and *The Guardian* (www.guardian.co.uk) and research their advertising rates. How much more expensive is it to advertise nationally?

ARCHANT}NORFOLK

rates

October 2004

- Frequency is the number of times the promotional material might be viewed; for example, the number of times an advert is carried by a daily newspaper each week.

Ideally, to produce a useful cost indicator, the total cost of the printed promotional material – including design, print, distribution and (any) advertising fees – should be divided by the number of people viewing the material. For example, hiring Posters On Wheels to drive around a city centre during peak shopping times might incur a high total cost, but the coverage and impact could be significantly higher than distributing leaflets on local housing estates.

The wider the coverage and the greater the frequency, the greater the possible impact of any promotional material. However, wide coverage and high frequency comes at a price, driving up the total cost of producing and distributing the promotional material. The final choice of print media depends on the business's objectives and the amount of money allocated to the promotion campaign. Figure 6.15 summarises the key benefits and limitations of some print media.

stop and think

What might be the benefits and limitations of using leaflets:

- handed out in a town centre
- delivered by hand to peoples' houses
- delivered by direct mail?

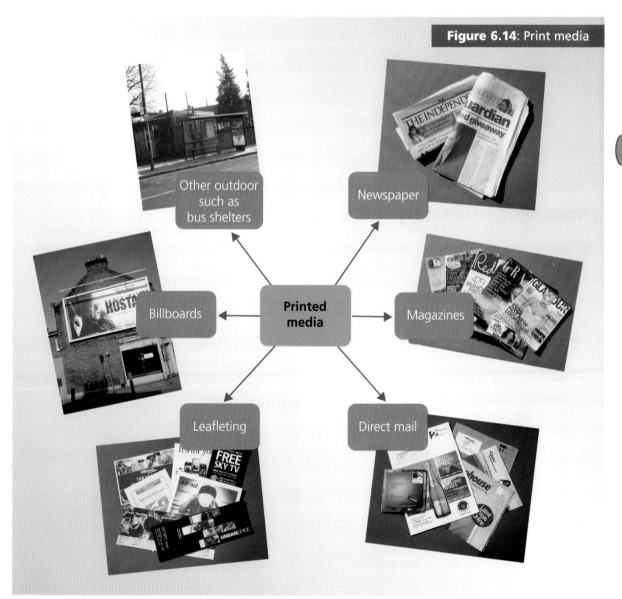

Figure 6.14: Print media

Other outdoor such as bus shelters

Newspaper

Billboards

Printed media

Magazines

Leafleting

Direct mail

Printed media	Benefits	Limitations
Newspapers	Many people read newspapers. Can define the type of person reading the newspaper – by age, income group, etc. Adverts can be placed without too much notice, say one to two weeks. Published daily or weekly.	Discarded very quickly. Limited printing capabilities – quality of graphics can suffer and limit the design of the advertisement.
Magazines	Easy to identify the readership of magazines, especially with specialist publications. Good printing capabilities with high-quality graphics. Kept for long periods resulting in repeated exposure.	High initial advertising costs compared to other printed media. As most are monthly publications, advance notice needed when placing an advertisement. Could be kept for too long and resulting in out-of-date promotional messages.
Billboards and other outdoor methods such as bus shelters	Low cost given repeated viewing. Can be located close to where target market lives, works or travels. Always displaying the message.	Message can't be complicated as only a few seconds devoted by the reader. Doesn't often gain full attention. Can't easily control who views the message.

Knowledge summary

■ While printed promotional materials can be produced in-house, businesses must take care to ensure the accuracy and quality of the final proof.

■ The accuracy and quality of printed promotional media can be improved by employing a professional design agency

■ The true cost of printed promotional media is determined by the design costs, the printing costs and the distribution costs.

■ Advertising rates are based on a publication's coverage, as well as the size and frequency of the particular advert.

■ The choice of printed media depends on the objectives of the promotion campaign and the size of the budget.

quick questions

1 Explain in each case whether a sole trader, with word processing skills, who operates a mail order business should design these promotional materials in-house or use a design agency:
 – a leaflet, without any graphics, which announces a new product range
 – an ad placed in a national newspaper
 – a brochure detailing the product range to be sent to customers with their order.

2 Calculate the cost of these newspaper ads:
 – three column width and 9 cm depth, £12.50 per column centimetre
 – four column width and 14 cm depth, £82 per column centimetre.

3 Explain why a full-colour magazine advertisement placed in a specialist magazine might be more cost effective than a black and white advertisement placed in a national tabloid.

Advertising in newspapers

Figures 6.16 and 6.17 present data about the advertising expenditure with different print media sectors and the readership profiles and advertising rates of selected national newspapers. Use this data to complete the tasks.

Figure 6.16: Press advertising expenditure (£ millions)

	2000	2001	2002	2003
National newspapers	2,252	2,062	1,933	1,902
Regional newspapers	2,762	2,834	2,874	2,986
Consumer magazines	750	779	785	784
Business & professional magazines	1,270	1,202	1,088	1,048
Directories (such as Yellow Pages)	868	959	990	1,029
Total advertising expenditure	7,902	7,836	7,670	7,749
Of which: press production costs	702	669	643	634

Source: Marketing Pocket Book 2005

Figure 6.17: Readership profiles and advertising rates (2003)

	Readership ('000s)	ABC1 (see note 1)	SCC (see note 2)
The Sun	8,824	36	173
Daily Mirror	4,785	39	122
Daily Express	2,045	61	97
Daily Telegraph	2,208	86	104
The Times	1,729	88	66
The Guardian	1,272	88	42
Financial Times	465	96	102

Note 1:   Figures in this column show percentage of readers who have professional or skilled employment
Note 2:   Figures in this column show the single column centimetre advertising rates to the nearest £
Source: Marketing Pocket Book 2005

A Using Figure 6.16, compare the expenditure on advertising in national and regional newspapers between 2000 and 2003.

B Which two forms of press advertising show the biggest increase in advertising expenditure? Explain your answer.

C Explain three factors which might cause advertising expenditure to increase.

D Using Figure 6.17, explain how and why the following factors help to determine the advertising rate (SCC) charged by national daily newspapers:
  – readership (the average number of people who read each edition of the newspaper)
  – ABC1 percentage (the percentage of readers who are in professional or skilled employment).

Promotional media: audio and moving image

Setting the scene: Access all areas

Virgin Radio, the national radio broadcaster, offers an advertising service to businesses. This service is called Virgin Radio Access All Areas and examples of campaigns developed by the service can be found on Virgin Radio website (www.virginradio.co.uk/sales/accessallareas). This is an example of a campaign to promote Tic Tacs for Ferrero UK Ltd.

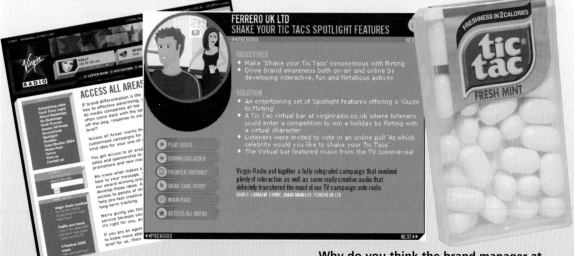

Source: Virgin Radio

Why do you think the brand manager at Ferrero was pleased with Virgin Radio's Tic Tac campaign?

1 Production requirements

Virgin Radio appears to develop close relationships with its clients when developing and implementing advertising campaigns. The Tic Tac campaign used a variety of techniques to mirror the television campaign based on the "shake your Tic Tacs" strapline:

■ entertaining features and storylines, such as a guide to flirting

■ links with new media – an interactive page on Virgin Radio's website

■ an online poll – which celebrity would you most like to share your Tic Tacs with?

Campaigns using audio and moving images require careful planning. As with print media, a systematic approach to planning and executing any campaign is essential. This is certainly the case when producing moving image promotional media, such as television or cinema advertisements.

The variety and level of skills required to produce audio and moving images are demanding. In general, all audio and visual work will be carried out by

KEY TERMS

Strapline is a phrase, usually occurring at the end of audio or moving image promotional material, that summarises the benefits of the product or helps to define the product's image. For example, the strapline for Gillette razors is: Gillette – the best a man can get. Straplines help to deliver the main message and are effective when they agree with the target audience's psychological reasons for purchasing the product.

Scripts are the words (including all text and dialogue) used in audio and moving image promotional materials.

Storyboards set out the sequence of images/events in films and videos.

An audio or moving image product moves through various stages during the editing process. A **rough cut** characterises the initial stages, while the **final cut** represents the finished product.

specialist agencies. Any organisation producing audio and moving image promotions needs to undertake the work in several stages.

- A rough outline of the promotion should be produced. This needs to take into account the objectives of the campaign and to determine what messages need to be conveyed, and what characters and events might be involved.

- A script (audio) and storyboard (moving image) should be produced. These are used to direct the production of the soundtrack and/or moving image.

- The audio or moving image piece needs to be recorded and edited. A rough cut, or draft version, is reviewed by the customer. A final cut is then produced.

- The final cut is stored using an appropriate format, such as DVD, web server, digital audio tape, film and video tape.

- The finished product is distributed to appropriate locations, such as particular radio stations, television channels and cinemas, and/or uploaded to websites. Broadcasting time slots, if required, should have been booked in advance.

stop and think

Iceni Productions produces corporate television, video and web content. This extract from Iceni's website (www.iceni.tv) describes some of the advantages of moving image material.

Video is a very effective way of communicating the benefits of your product or service. It can be shown at a conference, on a plasma screen in a shopping centre, on your stand at an exhibition, mailed directly to your clients on tape or disc, streamed on your website or emailed to your prospective clients in a video mail.

How might the arrival of DVD, broadband internet connections and wider access to large format video display units increase the use of audio and moving images in promotional activities?

2 Costs

The cost of producing and using promotional material using audio and/or moving images depends on several factors.

The quality of the final production

High-quality radio, television and cinema advertising is much more expensive to produce than material intended for more limited distribution across the internet or on a video display unit in a supermarket. Production standards are much higher for television and cinema advertising, and the editing and image processing costs are also higher.

The running time

As the running time of the material increase, so will the final cost of production. These costs can escalate and it's vital that the production has clear targets regarding content and duration.

The delivery method

Advertising rates depend on the platforms being used. The internet presents an almost costless platform (if a company runs material on its own website) and, in comparison, advertising on television can seem very expensive. Distributing material on DVD can be relatively inexpensive and is an attractive option, even when taking into account original production (filming) costs.

Timing and location

Advertising on radio or television at peak viewing times inevitably costs more than running adverts off-peak as campaigns can reach much larger audiences. Similarly, showing advertisements in busy, inner city cinemas is more expensive than running a campaign in rural cinemas.

stop and think

In January 2005, Northern Films was offering companies a DVD deal. For £10,000, Northern Films would produce a corporate DVD lasting between 10 and 20 minutes, handling script, production, editing, graphics, etc. Clients would receive 1000 copies of the finished DVD. What factors would determine whether £10,000 was cost effective?

3 Benefits and limitations

Figure 6.18 illustrates the different media available for audio and moving image promotional materials. As with printed promotional materials, the true cost of a particular method depends on its coverage and frequency.

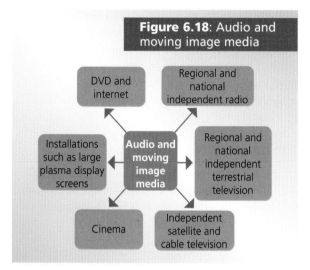

Figure 6.18: Audio and moving image media

Although it is possible to produce audio and moving image materials inexpensively and distribute them at virtually no cost across the internet, the coverage (the percentage of the target audience viewing the website) and the frequency (the number of times the website is viewed) may be low. Television and radio advertising offers the potential to reach much wider audiences (most mainstream television channels and radio stations have good coverage), but at a price – this advertising is expensive.

For television and radio advertising, it is sensible to think in terms of the cost per 1000 viewers and in terms of 30, 15 or five second adverts. In this way, true comparisons can be made. Figure 6.19 shows the average cost per 1000 potential adult viewers, of a 30-second advertising slot using different UK television channels.

Figure 6.19: The cost of television advertising (2003)

Channel	30 second equivalent per 1000 viewers
ITV	£6.86
Channel 4	£6.96
Channel 5	£4.09
GMTV	£3.75
Satellite	£3.99

Source: Marketing Pocket Book 2005

Coverage (or reach) data for television channels is available from Barb (the Broadcasters' Audience Research Board, visit www.barb.co.uk for more details. Rajar (Radio Joint Audience Research Limited, www.rajar.co.uk) performs a similar function for radio. The Advertising Association (www.adassoc.org.uk) provides detailed information on how to assess the true cost of radio and television advertising. Figure 6.20 summarises the key benefits and limitations of radio and television media.

If promotional budgets are limited, the use of radio, cinema and television advertising might be prohibitively expensive. The high initial production costs alone will rule out cinema and television advertising for many businesses.

Figure 6.20: Benefits and limitations of radio and television media

Method	Benefits	Limitations
Radio	Accessible by target audience at home or travelling – highly mobile. Relatively low cost compared to television and cinema – a 30-second slot on a national station might cost around £1500 for a peak listening time slot. Message can be quickly modified. Plenty of regional stations.	Obviously limited to audio messages only. Prestige of the medium has declined. Attention span of listener is limited – people listen to the radio and do other things at the same time. Once the audio message has been played, it's gone – message does not persist.
Television	Reaches a very large audience. High initial cost, but low cost per viewer. Benefits from using both sound and vision – some adverts can be highly memorable. High prestige. Regional television stations afford some selectivity of audience. Stations also have some age group and income level selectivity – compare, say, Channel 4 to ITV.	High initial cost. As with radio, a "perishable" message. Audience size can fluctuate. Space extremely limited during peak viewing times. Increasing use of videos and other recording technologies means that viewers can skip advertisements. Viewers can also switch channels during the advertising breaks.

Knowledge summary

■ The production of audio and moving image promotional materials cannot usually be done in-house

■ The true cost of audio and moving image promotional media is determined by the quality and duration of the final product, the delivery method used (such as cinema, television or DVD) and the timing and location of advertising slots.

■ There are benefits and limitations to each method of delivering audio and moving image promotional material. The limited size of promotional budgets might rule out cinema and television advertising for many businesses.

quick questions

1 Explain why most businesses would need to employ outside agencies to produce their audio and moving image promotional materials.

2 What might be the peak viewing/listening times for:
– radio
– cinema
– television?

3 Explain how a sports equipment retail outlet might use in-store audio and moving image promotional materials.

data interpretation
Advertising on ITV

Television advertising is a commodity, and the cost is dependent upon the number of advertisers wishing to purchase commercial airtime at any one time. Prices are related to demand as supply is fixed at an average of seven minutes commercial airtime per hour.

The cost of advertising on television varies by the length of the commercial. Airtime is sold in multiples of 10 seconds and the most popular time length is 30 seconds. The longest time length is usually 90 seconds, longer time lengths are often called infomercials. Price also varies by time of day reflecting the size and type of audience delivered by programmes.

Daytime:	06:00-17:29
Early Peak:	17:30-19:29
Late Peak:	19:30-23:00
Night Time:	23:01-05:59

The cost of advertising on television varies by month reflecting demand. January, February, March and August are often cheaper than the heavily demanded periods of pre-Easter, pre-summer and pre-Christmas. Cost also varies by region reflecting size of population and relative demand. London, as the capital region, is the most highly demanded and therefore, the most expensive.

Source: www.itvsales.com

A Explain four factors that affect the price of an advertising on ITV.

B Produce a report comparing the cost of placing 10 30-second advertisements, including at least three at peak times, on two regions' ITV channels during one week. You can find this information by visiting the regional ITV websites; for example, for the Anglia region visit www.angliatv.com. Present your findings using tables and charts where appropriate.

Promotional media: ambient and new media

Setting the scene: AdsOnCars

AdsOnCars is an ambient media company. Its core service, as you might guess from its name, is to place promotional material on cars.

According to the AdsOnCars website, it offers business customers the chance to cover the company vehicles with their unique business messages or images, in an innovative, exciting and cost-effective way, using safe, state-of-the-art technology.

The high-tech vinyl used by AdsOnCars is, according to the company, picture-quality, safely removable (professionally), guaranteed and long-lasting (up to five years). It helps protect the vehicle from rust and everyday damage, and is approved by major leasing companies.

AdsOnCars claim that this form of ambient advertising has many advantages:

■ holds the power of a mass advertising medium, delivering millions of impressions on busy roads and in densely populated areas

■ has the ability to reach motorway, suburban and retail audiences, often the sole advertising medium permitted

■ is a high-impact, highly visible medium with exceptional head-turning capability

■ creates a buzz of excitement which associates your company with a fun feel-good factor

■ is ideal for short-term campaigns, frequent brand changes as well as having long-term visibility

■ is extremely cost-effective.

What do you think is state of the art about the technology used by AdsOnCars? Why might AdsOnCars promotional media be extremely cost effective?

Source: www.adsoncars.com

KEY TERMS

Ambient media delivers promotional activities in unusual or non-traditional locations such as posters on supermarket floors, adverts on packaging and tickets.

New media uses the latest methods of communication. Currently, this includes e-mail, text messaging and web pages.

Web server is a computer that provides information to users' computers when they browse a business's website. The web server can be located within the business or managed by a specialist web hosting business.

1 Ambient media

AdsOnCars use of modern printing technology is an example of ambient media. Ambient media refers to any promotional message delivered in an unusual way. Types of ambient media include:

■ two-dimensional "floor" posters in retail outlets, messages on shopping trolleys and packaging

■ product placement in films and television programmes, for example Audi's concept car appears in the movie I, Robot

■ promotional messages printed on the back of till receipts, stickers, the bottom of drinks glasses and other unusual places.

Ambient media uses a variety of production techniques. You have already looked at the steps required when producing printed, audio and moving image media (topics 4 and 5). Most ambient media uses the same range of production techniques.

The cost of ambient media will vary according to the volume of production and the nature of the technology employed. This can be as simple as placing stickers on objects. However, it can also require the use of more expensive technology. For example, AdsOnCars uses high-tech vinyl materials and Figure 6.21 sets of the cost of the company's basic services.

Figure 6.21: Prices for wrapping a vehicle		
Vehicle size	**Full car wrap (minimum price)**	**Roof only (minimum price)**
Small car	£1,100	£300
Medium car	£1,500	£300
Large car or van	£1,900	£300

Note :Prices are per car and exclusive of VAT. For multiple wraps of the same design, the price per car will decrease. Prices include production and fitting of wrap subject to receipt of full artwork in correct format.

Source:AdsOnCars website, as at 27 January 2005

As with all promotional media, businesses needs to assess the production costs of any particular ambient medium against the frequency and coverage it offers. In the case of AdsOnCars, the cost per 1000 potential viewers could be very low. a strikingly wrapped car could make a real impact.

stopandthink

What additional costs might a business have to meet when wrapping a vehicle? How might the unit cost change as more vehicles are wrapped in the same design? What might be the production requirements of this media?

2 New media

New media refers to the use of the latest modes of communication, such as web-based, e-mail and mobile telephone technologies.

Web-based technologies

The science fiction movie *Minority Report*, released in 2002, featured interactive video advertising screens. These video screens, located in public places and shopping centres, had the ability to identify individuals and address them by name.

Today, e-commerce websites can perform a similar, if less spectacular, trick by using small files, or cookies, stored on our computers (see Unit 4, Topic 1). The technology works as follows:

- when you visit a website your cookie file is read and your identity is revealed – this only works if you have previously used the website

- the website uses this information to communicate with the central web server, drawing down a profile of your buying behaviour

- the web server then can deliver specific promotional messages – for example, on Amazon's website it does this with the message "we have recommendations for you").

Web servers also record the particular web pages that users browse or click through. Promotional materials appearing on web pages, or as separate pop-up windows, encourage you to click on them to get more information; the web server then records these events for later analysis.

This analysis helps to build a profile of our interests and browsing habits. In turn, businesses can use this information to improve their online promotional activities and their understanding of buyer behaviour. Double Click is a business that specialises in this type of analysis and technology. Find out more by visiting the company's website at www.doubleclick.com.

E-mail and mobile telephone technologies

E-mail and mobile telephone text messaging can provide very accurate channels of communication. Businesses can purchase lists of e-mail addresses covering a particular target group; for example, lists of individuals within a certain age and income group and who are known to have bought particular products in the past. These lists can be used to bulk e-mail carefully designed promotional messages to individuals who (if the company has got the profiling right) should be interested in the offer.

This success of this strategy depends on the accuracy of the e-mail address list – if it is inaccurate, or too general, then the promotion campaign will be ineffective. To counteract this problem, many businesses use opt-in lists. These e-mail lists are comprised of users who have actively agreed (or opted-in) to receive further e-mail communications.

Bulk text messaging is also being used by businesses to send promotional messages to target audiences. Given the use of text messaging by tweenagers, teenagers and young adults, this is likely to be an effective medium for products targeted at these age groups. The arrival of 3G networks also makes it possible to use picture messaging.

Delivering e-mails and text messages to your target audience is not particularly expensive, see Figure 6.22 for a guide to the cost of sending bulk text messages. However, it can be expensive to rent or purchase accurate e-mail and telephone lists. In addition, bulk e-mails suffer from the same "junk mail" problem as direct mail. Text messages lack any real visual impact, but this limitation can be overcome by using picture messaging.

stop and think

What might be the benefits and limitations of these new media:

- e-mail
- text messaging?

stop and think

Visit an e-commerce website, such as www.play.com, and identify the ways in which new media is used to promote the business. Do you think the website makes good use of new media in its promotional activities?

The production requirements and cost of new media varies according to the scale of the operation and particular technologies used. It is virtually costless for a business to place promotional messages on its own existing website – the website has already been established and promotional graphics for web pages are not difficult to produce. However, it does cost time and money to establish a website (see Unit 4 for details) as well as to gain the skills and technologies needed to target website users with specific promotional messages.

Figure 6.22: The cost of bulk texting

Volume of texts	Cost per message
1–999	£0.060
1,000–4,999	£0.055
5,000–9,999	£0.052
10,000–24,999	£0.050
25,000–49,999	£0.048
50,000–99,999	£0.046
100,000–149,999	£0.044
150,000–249,999	£0.042
250,000–499,999	£0.039
500,000–1,000,000	£0.038

Note: Prices, exclusive of VAT, as at 27 January 2005

Source: www.zimepl.com

Knowledge summary

■ Ambient media uses non-traditional locations to deliver its message and relies on this innovative approach to make its impact.

■ The cost of ambient media varies considerably and depends on the production techniques used.

■ New media refers to any media that uses the latest forms of communication, such as web-based, e-mail and mobile telephone technologies.

■ The cost of new media can be low if a business has an established website and uses e-mail within its day-to-day business activities.

1 Suggest possible ambient media for each of these promotional objectives:
  – a school or college trying to reduce the number of students smoking cigarettes
  – a record company raising awareness of a new band
  – a local authority encouraging recycling of domestic waste
  – a charity, such as Oxfam, wanting to increase donations.

2 Explain how a fashion retailer could make use of bulk e-mail and/or text messages in these situations:
  – opening a new store
  – introducing a new fashion line
  – announcing a sale.

data**interpretation**
TV-style ads arrive on the web

Internet users may have to get used to watching television advertisements between web pages, if trials currently under way on high profile websites are successful. The new video advertisements are being tested on 15 websites over the next five weeks.

They are the result of collaboration between online advertising developers, Unicast, and software giant, Microsoft. Unicast's Video Commercial is a full screen online video format that plays a 2MB, 30 second, broadcast quality video, regardless of connection speed.

Unicast describes its new online format as "a giant leap forward" and believes that it will offer a more effective advertising medium. Consequently, businesses will be willing to pay much higher prices to advertise on websites using this new format. This could reduce the overall number of advertisements on websites, such as banner and pop-up advertisements, as websites make more money from fewer advertisements.

However, some experts feel that these new advertisements will be too intrusive. Individuals browsing a website want to move easily from one web page to the next. Having this flow interrupted by a 30-second advertisement, even if it you can stop it playing, is likely to irritate people.

Source: adapted from news.bbc.co.uk, 3 February 2004

A Explain two reasons why Unicast's new online video format might be described as "a giant leap forward".

B Explain two reasons why this new format might be ineffective.

C Discuss whether online video is likely to be an effective promotional medium.

Regulation and legislation

Setting the scene: Tuxedo Paint System

A promotion for the Tuxedo Paint System on a shopping television channel was the subject of a complaint by a viewer. As part of its investigation into the case, the Advertising Standards Authority set out these facts about the broadcast. (Note, a tuxedo is a black suit, usually worn by men at formal occasions.)

A teleshopping broadcast for the Tuxedo Paint System showed the product being used to paint walls by a man wearing a tuxedo. The broadcast included these claims:

> now there's a painting system so easy to use, so clean to use, you could paint in a tuxedo

> a revolutionary system that doesn't need a tray and never splashes paint

> just the right amount of paint, just the right flow to paint up to 100 square feet evenly, cleanly, stroke after stroke without reloading – no tray, no spray, no bending over.

A product called Spin Clean was included in the offer. A demonstration showed it being used to clean paint brushes, which were also included in the offer. The advertising claimed: "Forget that

messy clean up and save those expensive brushes. Just snap your brush into spin clean and spin it clean in 30 seconds, every bristle as good as new right down to the stalk."

A presenter dipped a paint brush in white paint, used the Spin Clean to clean it and then wiped it on the shirt and dinner jacket of the other presenter. The clothes remained spotlessly clean and the presenter said: "Nice black tuxedo with white paint. Would you believe this? I mean it's amazing."

A presenter said the paint brushes were "the last paint brushes you will ever need to buy" and said the Spin Clean was "the item that was in the Millennium Dome that won the Millennium Award".

Make a list of points the viewer might have made when making the complaint about this promotional activity to the Advertising Standards Authority.

Source: ASA broadcast advertising adjudications, 19 January 2005

Regulating promotional activities

Since November 2004, the Advertising Standards Authority (ASA) has been the "one-stop shop" for all complaints regarding promotional activities. The ASA regulates a broad range of promotional activities and is keen to demonstrate its ability to cope with new media as and when it is used by businesses.

The ASA investigates complaints about:

- the content of advertisements, including newspaper and magazine ads, television, radio and cinema commercials, posters, SMS, MMS and e-mail ads, leaflets, brochures, direct mailings, and internet banner and pop-up ads

- the administration of sales promotions (short-term offers, prize promotions, etc.)

- the non-receipt of mail order goods and sales promotion offers or refunds

- the use of personal data for direct marketing purposes, specifically complaints about companies sending direct marketing to people who have already requested not to be sent it.

KEY TERMS

The **Advertising Standards Authority (ASA)** is responsible for regulating broadcast and non-broadcast advertising.

Advertising codes are documents published by the ASA defining acceptable advertising practices.

The ASA publishes a series of advertising codes detailing the grounds on which a consumer, or business competitor, can make a complaint. These advertising codes are extensive. All businesses must carry out their promotional activities within both the letter and spirit of the codes – in other words, businesses must not contravene any of the codes and they must not seem to be trying to avoid them. Ignorance of these codes is no defence.

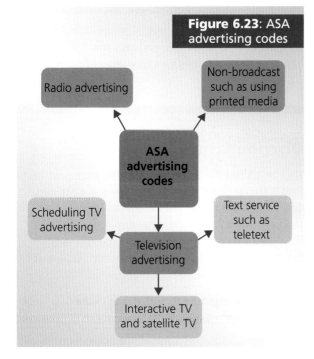

Figure 6.23: ASA advertising codes

Figure 6.23 illustrates the scope of the main codes published by the ASA. These are all available for free download from the ASA's website (www.asa.org.uk). While it is impossible to summarise the content of these codes, these principles, taken from *The British code of advertising, sales promotion and direct marketing* (the ASA's non-broadcasting advertising code), provide a good general introduction:

- all marketing communications should be legal, decent, honest and truthful

- all marketing communications should be prepared with a sense of responsibility to consumers and to society

- all marketing communications should respect the principles of fair competition generally accepted in business

- no marketing communication should bring advertising into disrepute.

The ASA's ruling on the Tuxedo Paint System complaint is summarised in the panel below. What this shows is that the ASA does not automatically take

stopand**think**

How many of these general principles might have been broken by the Tuxedo Paint System television promotion? Visit the ASA's website to view the code for television advertising. This can be found at www.asa.org.uk. Would you have complained about the Tuxedo Paint System promotion?

the side of the individual making the complaint – it is impartial and reaches judgements on the basis of evidence. In this particular case, the problem was that the business had not provided sufficient documentary evidence to back up its claims about the product's performance. It wasn't that the business had lied about the paint system, simply that insufficient evidence or substantiation was provided for viewers.

To summarise, when producing promotional materials a business must make sure that the message:

- is true

- can be supported by impartial evidence

- is not likely to offend

- does not break any laws.

ASA Tuxedo Paint System adjudication: Complaint upheld

The teleshopping channel successfully defended its claims that the paint brushes would last a lifetime as the product came with a lifetime guarantee. It also stated that no trick photography had been used whilst filming the promotion. Furthermore, the company provided documentary evidence of a Millennium Award – a Millennium Products Design Council certificate.

However, the company: "…did not have documentary evidence to support the other claims made in the broadcast. We did not consider that demonstrations alone were enough to substantiate the claims made [...] We therefore found the advertising in breach of Rules 5.1 (Misleadingness) and 5.2.2 (Claims – implications) of the CAP (Broadcast) Television Advertising Standards Code. The advertisement must not be shown again unless satisfactory evidence is provided to support the claims made."

Legislation affecting promotional activities

As well as taking care not to infringe the ASA code, businesses must also ensure that their promotional activities do not contravene relevant UK and European legislation. There are three main areas of legislation that businesses must take into account when constructing and implementing their promotional activities. These are:

- trades description regulations
- consumer protection laws
- anti-discrimination legislation.

These laws help to define what is meant by "legal, decent, honest and truthful". The scope and impact of legislation that impacts on businesses was covered in Unit 1 (in particular, *see pages* 36–47), but let's recap some of the most important points that relate to promotional activity.

Trade Descriptions Act

It is illegal to falsely describe a product or the benefits it provides; for example, it would not be lawful to advertise a motor car claiming that the vehicle is so safe you could "walk away without a scratch" after an accident. You can get information about the Trade Descriptions Act from www.tradingstandards.gov.uk.

Knowledge summary

- The Advertising Standards Authority regulates all advertising in the United Kingdom.
- The ASA's advertising codes detail the grounds on which people can complain about the content of an advertisement.
- One of the main principles of the ASA's codes is that all advertising (marketing communications) should be legal, decent, honest and truthful.
- Promotional activities must comply with UK legislation, such as the Trade Descriptions Act, the Consumer Protection Act and laws protecting groups and individuals against discrimination.

Consumer Protection Act

it is illegal to provide misleading or false information about the price of a product; for example, it would not be lawful for a sales promotion to claim that a product is now available at a 50 per cent reduction in price if, in fact, the product had never been sold to the public at the original price.

stop and think

Think of four other possible promotional activities that could contravene the Trades Descriptions Act and/or Consumer Protection Act.

Discrimination

Legislation relating to discrimination is extensive. In Unit 1 (*see* topics 6 and 9) you looked at how these acts protect the rights of employees. These regulations also protect the general rights of groups within society. In terms of promotional activities, legislation relating to discrimination stops businesses using promotional messages that discriminate against specific groups, including:

- women (discriminating by sex)
- people who classify their ethnic origin as Afro-Caribbean (discriminating by race)
- people who have impaired vision or hearing (discriminating by disability).

quick questions

1 Explain why these promotional activities might fail to comply with ASA's advertising codes:
  - an advertisement for a slimming product claiming guaranteed weight loss
  - a text message promoting an alcoholic drink
  - an individual receiving direct mail
  - a sales promotion stating "We've managed to source these products from a well-known manufacturer that has unfortunately gone out of business. This is a one time offer – never to be repeated! Take advantage of massive discounts of at least 50 per cent!"

These historical adverts appear on the ASA website (www.asa.co.uk).

(source: www.asa.co.uk):

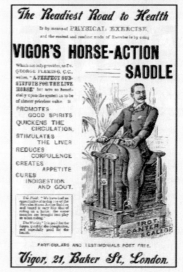

A Study the advertisements shown here. For each advertisement in turn, explain specifically why people might have felt it was not legal, decent, honest or truthful.

B Collect two half-page or full-page printed advertisements. Discuss how the ASA's advertising codes and UK legislation might have altered the design and content of each one.

Topic 8

Voluntary codes and ethical considerations

Setting the scene: self-regulation in the direct marketing industry

The Direct Marketing Authority is an independent body established by the
Direct Marketing Association (UK) Ltd (the DMA) in 1997 to ensure the direct
marketing industry continues to maintain and continually raise its standards.

The authority investigates any complaints made by consumers and other businesses against DMA member companies. It decides if there has been any breach of the DMA's code of practice, and makes adjudication as appropriate. Complaints against non-member companies that have applied for membership of the DMA will be assessed as well.

The Direct Marketing Authority is essential to the effectiveness and credibility of self-regulation within the direct marketing industry. It has the responsibility for monitoring compliance with the DMA's code of practice by all DMA members and provides an annual report on its activity and effectiveness to the Director General of Fair Trading.

The DMA's code of practice for direct marketing sets out standards of ethical conduct and best practice that must be followed by all members of the Direct Marketing Association. The DMA's compliance manager works with member companies to ensure that they are aware of both their responsibilities under the code and other best practice initiatives.

The Direct Marketing Authority is funded independently of the Direct Marketing Association, through a levy paid by members of the industry on advertising and direct mailings.

Why do you think a business, working in the direct marketing industry, would want to become a member of the DMA

when this requires compliance with the DMA's codes of practice as well as payment of an annual fee?

Visit the DMA's membership site to investigate the cost and benefits of membership www.dmamembership.org.uk. Members of the Direct Marketing Association display a logo on their printed materials and websites. Why is a logo important for voluntary associations such as the DMA?

Source: Direct Marketing Association (www.dma.org.uk)

KEY TERMS

Best practice is the most effective and efficient method of achieving any objective or task.

Ethics are sets of beliefs that define what society considers as acceptable behaviour.

Voluntary codes are sets of agreed work practices adopted by members of an association. Membership of the association is not compulsory.

Benefits	Costs
Individuals using the services of an association member can feel more confident that the business will do a good job and will operate fairly.	Non-members benefit from the improvements in the image of the industry – that is, member businesses indirectly help out non-members.
Businesses will feel that they are not wasting money and opportunities by over-regulating their activities.	Membership fees can be a significant cost for small businesses.
Members receive support and guidance from the association, often in the form of legal advice that provides clear guidelines on meeting UK legislation.	Members activities are constrained by the voluntary codes, while non-members continue to carry out "bad practice".
The image and performance of the industry improves and external government regulation is less likely.	

Voluntary codes

The Advertising Standards Authority provides a set of advertising codes that must be met by all businesses engaged in promotional activities covered by these codes. However, as the Direct Marketing Association illustrates, industry bodies will often develop their own voluntary codes. These voluntary codes can lead to changes in the ASA's codes and UK legislation, because:

- either, they are very good codes and should be adopted by all businesses in the industry and not just members of the particular self-regulating association

- or, they are poor codes and illustrate the need for enforcement by the government or an industry group appointed by the government.

Figure 6.24 sets out benefits and costs of being a member of an association that has voluntary codes.

stopandthink

The Outdoor Advertising Association of Great Britain (OAA) is another trade organisation that provides guidelines on best practice. The panel (above) shows some of the standards that OAA members are required to meet.

How might the outdoor advertising industry – the companies that own and operate billboards – benefit from members of the OAA complying with these standards? In particular, what are the benefits of points 3.1.2 to 3.1.6?

The Direct Marketing Association (which we featured at the start of this topic) provides considerable best practice guidance on direct marketing activities. This guidance sets out the standards expected from DMA members. The advice covers:

- catalogue and home shopping

- collecting and using data for direct marketing

- e-mail marketing

- use of inserts

- interactive television advertising

- promotions and prize draws.

3 STANDARDS OF BEST PRACTICE

3.1   Maintenance of Plant

3.1   Members are responsible for any questions which may arise in relation to the Town & Country Planning (Control of Advertisements) Regulations in respect of their plant.

3.1.2   All advertising structures should be maintained in a good state of repair, be regularly painted, and kept reasonably clean.

3.1.3   All advertising panels should be numbered and should display the names of the contractors who have control over them.

3.1.4   All posting should be carried out with due care and attention so as to ensure that every poster is displayed in the manner intended and in due time.

3.1.5   Any posters found to be damaged or defaced should be replaced as soon as is practical.

3.1.6   Any forecourts, gardens or other land within the precincts of poster panels, and any fences erected by the contractor as part of a display, should be maintained in a good condition.

3.1.7   No advertisement should be erected which would materially obscure the view of another member's advertisement under contract. In case of doubt the other members should be consulted before the advertisement is erected.

Ethical considerations

Ethics are the codes of behaviour. We all have views about what constitutes acceptable behaviour, and these collectively shape ideas about what society as a whole regards as ethical behaviour. Ethical standards evolve and change as a society develops. In 19th century Britain, for example, child labour was considered acceptable. Today we would find it very hard to accept that a 10-year-old child should work long hours in a dark, dangerous and airless workshop. Yet many of us do not consider this a problem if a developing country, such as Thailand, uses child labour in its factories.

In 2003, Barnardo's – a charity which aims to protect the interests of children – ran a controversial newspaper advertising campaign to raise awareness of child poverty. The advertisements showed a series of powerful images: one had a computer-generated photograph of a baby with a cockroach crawling out of his mouth, others showed a syringe and a meths

stop and think

Should ethical standards dictate the content of promotional activities? How can a business producing a promotional activity know whether it has breached ethical standards?

Visit the ASA's website to search for adjudications on Barnardo's and other controversial advertising campaigns (such as Benetton campaigns). In what ways were the campaigns seen as being unethical?

bottle in the mouths of baby girls. The aim was to show that not all children were born with a silver spoon in their mouths,

The Barnardo's campaign generated 475 complaints to the Advertising Standards Agency, the most complaints it received for a single promotional campaign in 2003. The ASA ruled that the advertisements were considered to be too disturbing for general viewing and the campaign was halted. It was accepted that Barnardo's intentions were reasonable – it was a worthy cause and the adverts were extremely effective in demonstrating the plight of many babies and children – yet the ASA still found that its campaign was considered ethically unacceptable.

When constructing promotional activities, businesses should conform to current ethical standards. The ASA will, in any case, probably insist that the promotional materials be modified if they breach current ethical standards – that is, if they fail the "decency" test in "legal, decent, honest and truthful". Many advertising campaigns are withdrawn because they are judged to have breached ethical standards. Paradoxically, these advertisements are often effective at delivering their intended message.

Knowledge summary

- Many industry associations, such as the Direct Marketing Association, have voluntary codes of practice that are designed to improve the quality of promotional activities in line with, and beyond, the standards required by regulatory authorities and UK law.

- Members of industry associations, such as the Outdoor Advertising Association of Great Britain, benefit from the support and guidance provided by these bodies. Customers are reassured and members are clearer about the standards they need to maintain.

- Ethical standards affect the content of promotional activities by defining what the ASA, and the general public, consider decent.

quick questions

1 Do voluntary codes maintain the standards of promotional activities? Explain your answer.

2 Think of a televised or printed advert you have seen that either offended you or someone in your family
- what caused you or your family member to take offence?
- was this an essential part of the advertisement?
- how might you have modified the advertisement so as to remove its offensive nature but still retain its core message?

data interpretation
Cadbury Prize Draw

This web page (below) is taken from Cadbury PLC's website. In order to enter Cadbury's free prize draw, visitors to the website need to register. This involves entering their contact details and completing a short questionnaire.

Source: www.cadburymilk.co.uk

A Explain the benefits to Cadbury of running free prize draws.

B Download the Best Practice Guidelines for the Promotion of Prize Draws from the DMA's website (www.dma.org.uk/content/Pro-BestPractice.asp)

Produce a five minute presentation on:
How the DMA guidelines on the promotion of prize draws help to ensure the effectiveness of this type of promotional activity.

Games & Prizes > Free Prize Draw

Free Prize Draw!

Win 2 Seats to see "The King and I" on 27th April, at the Alhambra Theatre, Bradford

This new production of THE KING AND I is a heart-warming story set to one of the most unforgettable scores ever written, which includes Shall We Dance?, and Getting To Know You.

This week you could win 2 Seats to this event at the Alhambra Theatre, Bradford at 7.30pm on 27th April 2005 simply by entering our Free Prize Draw.

To take part in the weekly Free Prize Draw you'll need to register with us and then log in again each week using the button below.

Click here to **return to the main 2 Seats Competition**

Assessing a promotional campaign

Setting the scene: Independent Direct Marketing

Independent Direct Marketing Ltd (IDM) provides a wide range of direct marketing services. One of the company's services is the sale of mailing lists which it sources from businesses that rent out their lists of customers to IDM. By law, these businesses can only pass on the details of customers that have opted to receive additional communications.

Figure 6.25: Some mailing lists available from Independent Direct Marketing

Business providing the mailing list	Details of the business and its customers
CD WOW www4.cd-wow.com	Offering chart music at low prices, products include CDs, DVDs, games and electrical appliances. Customers are aged 18–35 years, 45 per cent female/55 per cent male, credit card approved.
Olan Mills Photography www.olanmills.co.uk	Buyers of beauty make-overs and photography portrait plans for young families. Typical customers are mainly women, with young children aged 0-4.
Forbidden Planet www.scifiwarehouse.com	Mail order responders from Sci-fi Warehouse, the UK's largest sci-fi and entertainment mail order company. Typical customers are men aged 18-45 years.
Hawkin's Bazaarnwww.hawkin.com	Buyers and enquirers of unusual and innovative gifts, toys and curiosities. Predominantly ABC1 females aged 35–54, with children at home.
Chums www.chums.co.uk	Cash-with-order purchasers of footwear, both male and female, advertised in the national daily and Sunday press. Some 62 per cent are male, aged 45 plus.

Note: As at February 2005

Source: Independent Direct Marketing (www.idmltd.co.uk)

Figure 6.25 shows some of the mailing lists that could be bought from Independent Direct Marketing. Why is the information provided in the table important to someone buying a mailing list from the company?

KEY TERMS

Promotional campaigns use a mix of tools to try to achieve specific objectives. For example, a campaign might use television advertising and direct mail leaflets to increase the number of people subscribing to a digital TV service

Promotional mix is the combination of promotional tools and activities used within a promotional campaign.

Planning and assessing promotional campaigns

Promotional campaigns rely on accurate information about their target audiences. Getting accurate data about the target audience is essential. If a campaign's promotional messages are delivered to the wrong audience, the campaign will not achieve its objectives. The campaign budget will have been wasted.

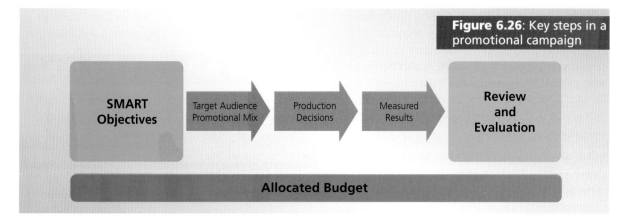

Figure 6.26: Key steps in a promotional campaign

SMART Objectives → Target Audience Promotional Mix → Production Decisions → Measured Results → Review and Evaluation

Allocated Budget

However, this is not the only way in which a promotional campaign can go wrong. Figure 6.26 illustrates the key steps that should be taken when planning, implementing and evaluating a promotional campaign.

As Figure 6.26 suggests, there are five stages to planning, implementing and evaluating a promotional campaign.

■ **Define the campaign's SMART objectives**. Every promotional campaign must be based on a set of specific, measurable, achievable, relevant and timely objectives (see Topic 2 in Unit 3).

■ **Identify the target audience and select the promotional mix**. The campaign should define the audience that the promotional activities are aimed at; for example, by age group, lifestyle, etc. The promotional activities, which make up the promotional mix, should take the target audience through the AIDA steps of attention, interest, desire and action (see Topics 1, 2 and 3 in this unit).

■ **Make realistic decisions on how the promotional materials will be produced**. The media used to deliver the campaign must be appropriate for the target audience and the components of the promotional mix (see Topics 4, 5 and 6 in this unit).

■ **Collect data to measure the results of the campaign**. Key data should be collected during and after the campaign. This data should measure the achievement of the campaign's SMART objectives.

■ **Review and evaluate the campaign**. The campaign could be reviewed during its operation in order to fine tune the delivery and content. After the campaign has finished, and all relevant data has been collected, the campaign should be evaluated using the measured results to assess whether it achieved its SMART objectives.

However, underpinning all these stages is a clear imperative – always work within the allocated budget. The size of the budget will partly determine the SMART objectives, target audience, promotional mix, product decisions and the range of data used to measure the success of the campaign.

stop and think

How might the size of a promotional campaign's budget affect the choice of promotional tools and media?

1 SMART objectives

The promotional campaign should be based on SMART objectives and these objectives should take into account the amount of money allocated to the campaign. If the budget is small – say £1000 – then the objectives will have to be limited in scope. Nevertheless, even with a small budget, these objectives should be capable of being monitored. They should be SMART; for example, a business might aim to increase the awareness of a product by at least 20 per cent.

With larger budgets come higher expectations. If a business is prepared to allocate a relatively large budget to a promotional campaign, then the objectives will certainly have to be SMART and will probably need to stipulate some significant goals such as "to increase the percentage of 21–26 year old male customers signing up to an online dating agency by 10 per cent in the first week of the campaign and by 30 per cent at the end of the campaign".

2 Target audience

A promotional campaign's SMART objectives should refer to the target audience. The target audience forms the heart of any promotional campaign.

A business (and its marketing agency) needs to understand the key personal, social and psychological factors influencing the buyer behaviour of the target audience (see Topic 1 in this unit). It also needs to understand the target audience's use of media; for example, how does the target audience engage with mass media such as cinema, television, radio and newspapers?

By defining the target audience carefully, and using an understanding of the audience's buyer behaviour and media preferences, a business can select the promotional tools to use. For example, by knowing what makes the target audience tick, a business will be able to decide whether price promotions will be more effective than loyalty cards.

3 Production decisions

The types of promotional media used by a campaign depend largely on the target audience's pattern of media use. For example, it would not be appropriate to use new media if the target audience makes little use of the internet.

The choice of promotional media also depends on the size of the allocated budget and the expertise and capabilities within the business. Given a generous budget, outside agencies should be used to produce and deliver most promotional materials. In other situations, a mixture of in-house and agency solutions will have to be used.

In-house resources can be used for promotional activities that do not incur significant production costs and/or require expertise beyond that held by current employees. For example, in-house staff could organise the printing and distribution of small quantities of a simple black and white A4 leaflet, the production a press release or the handling of a simple PR event.

External agencies should be used for more complex activities requiring specialist equipment and expertise.

4 Collecting and reviewing data

Relevant data should be collected to assess the effectiveness of each promotional activity and the campaign as a whole. This needs careful planning and a research plan should be constructed that:

- lists the type of information needed to assess the achievement of the campaign's objectives – for example, changes in audience attitude towards a product, measured on a five-point scale, after viewing a televised advertisement

- identifies how the information will be collected – for example, interview a sample of the target audience before and after the advertisement is broadcast to record any changes in attitudes

- identifies how the collected data will be analysed – for example, comparing the averages of customer attitudes to the product before and after viewing the televised advertisement.

When all the data has been collected and analysed, a final evaluation should take place. Judgements should be made, based on the collected data, about whether the campaign achieved its objectives. Did the campaign work or were significant mistakes made and opportunities lost? What can be improved in any future campaigns?

Figure 6.27: Readership of television listing magazines

Magazine	Circulation	Readership profiles				
		Men %	15-34 %	35-54 %	55+ over %	ABC1 %
Radio Times	1,157,701	49	27	33	40	74
TV Quick	405,935	36	42	38	20	43
TV Times	548,141	46	37	29	34	46
What's on TV	1,660,231	38	47	32	21	40

Source: Marketing Pocket Book 2005

Knowledge summary

- A promotional campaign cannot be assessed if it does not have a set of SMART objectives.

- Relevant data should be collected during and after the campaign. The data should be analysed to assess whether the campaign has met its objectives.

quick questions

1 What is a SMART objective? Why is it very important for a promotional campaign to have SMART objectives?

2 Why might a very large allocated budget be just as much a problem as a small one?

3 Why is understanding the buyer behaviour of the target audience an essential part of an effective promotional campaign?

data interpretation
Carlton Screen Advertising

In order to demonstrate the effectiveness of cinema advertising, Carlton Screen Advertising frequently carries out audience surveys. This assessment of a Dr Pepper campaign was taken from Carlton Screen Advertising's website. The campaign's objective was "to increase awareness of, and likelihood to try, Dr Pepper amongst the key 15–24 target audience".

Results

- Recall at the cinema was above average. A huge 85 per cent of cinema goers could recall seeing the advert compared to 63 per cent of non-cinema goers.

- Depth of communication amongst cinema goers was far higher than that of control sample – those seeing the ad on the big screen were able to recall over four different aspects, compared to under two mentions for the average television viewer.

- Over half of cinema goers spontaneously recalled the advert's strapline – What's the worst that could happen? – compared to a quarter of non-cinema goers. Cinema goers were also more likely to find it funny and enjoy watching the advert.

Figure 6.28: Impact of Dr Pepper campaign

Spontaneous descriptions of ad	Cinema goers	Non-cinema goers
Boy picked up his date	75%	20%
Girl comes downstairs	52%	15%
Dad and boy wrestled	50%	11%
Mention of date/prom	76%	20%
Mention of offering – Dr Pepper & strapline	46%	15%
Average number of mentions	4.28	1.69

Source: www.carltonscreen.com

A Explain how Carlton might have collected this data.

B Does the data demonstrate the effectiveness of cinema advertising? Justify your answer.

C Discuss how a business could assess the effectiveness of a printed advertisement before launching it in a colour magazine with a nationwide distribution.

Topic 10 Business in practice: the Get On campaign

Background to the campaign

The Department for Education and Skills (DfES) is the government body responsible for all aspects of education, training and learning. The DfES is keen to promote the idea of life-long learning – that learning should not end after we finish our time in formal education at 16 or 18.

Through its Skills for Life initiative, the DfES is working with key stakeholders (such as colleges and employers) to improve adult literacy and numeracy.

For many adults lacking basic numeracy and literacy skills – for example, those with an inability to read or write – the thought of "going back to school" is terrifying. Through fear and embarrassment, adults lacking basic skills have traditionally never spoken about their problem: they struggle in silence.

The Get On campaign's main aim is to encourage this target market to take that first step – to pick up the telephone and call the Get On hotline.

Understanding the target audience

The Get On campaign's target audience are those adults who lack basic literacy and numeracy skills. At a public relations event held in August 2003, a government education minister said:

"Millions of adults in the UK do not have the skills of an average 11-year-old. This lack of basic skills affects many areas of their lives – from how much they get paid, to being unable to help their children with homework. Many people with poor basic skills will see their own children or other young people getting their GCSEs later this week – something they feel they could never achieve themselves. Tackling the problem of adult basic skills is a key priority for the government and we are determined to help 1.5 million adults improve their reading, writing and maths by 2007."

The 2004/5 Get On campaign made very effective use of this advertising signature:

The gremlin theme has become a distinctive feature of recent Get On campaigns. Stuart Barnes, from the advertising agency St Luke's, explains the reasoning behind the gremlin theme:

The Get On campaign to promote awareness and take-up of adult basic skills learning opportunities was the result of careful research by St Luke's. The research showed that people with poor reading, writing, spelling or numbers skills felt that it was their own personal issue which only they could fix and only when they felt it was right for them. They couldn't be told or even encouraged to learn, either by advertising, by an organisation, and often not by friends or family

Nearly everyone we spoke to with poor literacy or numeracy had the same emotional response. They felt very frustrated with themselves when they were unable to complete tasks they thought they should be capable of. They were scared of being found out and were afraid of the severe impact on their self confidence that would result. This is where the idea of the Gremlins came from

The Gremlin personifies this emotional response as a third party. It appears when you are confronted with a task involving reading, writing or numbers. The Gremlin is the thing which stops you being able to do things – it undermines your confidence, it mocks your mistakes and always threatens to embarrass you.

Additional research carried out by St Luke's showed that people with poor literacy or numeracy skills do not see it as a problem as long as they can adopt coping strategies to get through everyday activities. The lack of literacy and numeracy skills did not make them any less of a person and did not impact on their social and family lives.

St Luke's concluded that both humour and fear would be essential parts of any advertising campaign capable of breaking through the barriers put up by people with poor literacy and numeracy skills: humour to get the attention and interest of the person; fear to generate desire and action.

Get rid of your gremlins and get on 0800 100 900

Promotional tools

This is the script for a 40-second television advertisement produced by St Luke's for the Get On campaign.

Note: super means superimposition and refers to the telephone number and Get On logo – the signature of the advert – that were displayed on screen at the end of the advertisement.

Open on a man sat at a table in a factory rest area. In front of him on the table we see a large envelope, which he's looking at slightly anxiously.

After a short while, we suddenly see a gremlin appear from behind the table.

GREMLIN: OH NO, NO, NO, WE DON'T WANT TO OPEN THAT. WE'LL JUST BE DISAPPOINTED.

We then see the gremlin and the man sat on some steps together.

GREMLIN: LET'S FACE IT, YOUR ENGLISH IS ABOUT AS GOOD MY TAP DANCING.

We then see the man and the gremlin in the washroom, the guy splashes his face with water while the gremlin files his nails.

GREMLIN: I TOLD YOU YOU'D NEVER PASS THAT COURSE. YOU KNOW WHAT PEOPLE CALL YOU BEHIND YOUR BACK?

We see the man walk through the corridor, gremlin following.

GREMLIN: IT'S FAILURE, FAILURE, LOOK AT YOU, YOU'RE A FAILURE!

We see the man pick up the envelope and start to open it. We see the gremlin fold his arms in annoyance.

GREMLIN: GO ON THEN. SEE IF I CARE.

As the man looks at the contents of the envelope, we see the gremlin look at himself and realise that he's shrivelling and shrinking. As he does so, he speaks in an ever higher pitch of voice until he's really tiny.

GREMLIN: URGHH. NOT THE QUALIFICATION. I HATE QUALIFICATIONS.

We then see the man accidentally tread on the tiny gremlin. The confident man puts up his feet on the table. On the sole of one of his shoes we see a squashed tiny gremlin.

GREMLIN: I'LL BE BACK. THIS ISN'T THE LAST YOU'VE HEARD FROM ME!

Cut to the man using the side of the table to scrape the gremlin off his shoe. As the gremlin lands in a wastepaper bin we here a small thud.

VOICE OVER: GET RID OF YOUR GREMLIN. CALL 0800 100 900.

SUPER: 0800 100 900 and Get On logo.

GREMLIN: I WANT MY MUMMY!

In addition to advertising, the Get On campaign has used several other promotional tools including

- **public relations exercises** – for example, the campaign has used celebrities such as Phil Tufnell to publicise the campaign

- **direct mail** targeting key stakeholders and raising awareness of the campaign

- **personal selling** through encouraging key personnel in contact with the target audience to deliver the message – these front-line personnel include GPs, health visitors, counsellors, prison officers, probation officers, immigration officers, Jobcentre Plus personal advisers and social service staff.

New drive against learning gremlins

The Department for Education and Skills says the latest figures show that since the Get On campaign began two years ago, some 320,000 people have gained a reading, writing or maths qualification, and millions more have started courses. A new series of adverts will build on the previous theme of the campaign and feature people being tormented by a little gremlin - their embarrassment over a lack of basic literacy or numeracy skills.

Among those in the new campaign is former cricketer and *I'm A Celebrity Get Me Out of Here* winner Phil Tufnell. "When I was growing up all I thought about was cricket, so it's fair to say I wasn't too hot at things like spelling," he says. "But just because you missed out on a chance to learn first time around, doesn't mean you can't go back into learning and knock your own gremlins for six."

Source: news.bbc.co.uk, 18 August 2003

Promotional media

A wide range of promotional media has been used by the Get On campaign. This perfect proof for a printed advertisement (see below) shows a continuation of the "get rid of your gremlin" theme. While focusing more on humour than fear, it reinforces the main message delivered by the televised adverts.

Radio advertisements have also been broadcast and they used the same combination of humour and fear. You can listen and view radio and television advertisements by visiting the campaign's promotional website at www.dfes.gov.uk/get-on and clicking on the download menu button.

The campaign also makes use of various ambient and new media in the form of:

- balloons – white, with blue Get On logo and 0800 100 900

- postcards – three different gremlin designs, with top tips and space for local details

- gremlin masks – available in both paper and plastic

- beer mats – gremlin branded on the front with the 0800 100 900 on the back

- posters – available in A2 and A3, the smaller posters have space for local information

- bookmarks – gremlin branded with the 0800 100 900

- notepads – yellow pads with the Get On logo and 0800 100 900

- stickers – single gremlin window stickers and smaller sets of Get On and gremlin stickers

- scratch cards – types available workplace, sports, personal finance, family learning

- Get On pencils – white pencils with the Get On logo and 0800 100 900

- CD-ROMs – electronic copies of the templates and pictures

- video – motivational video designed to engage potential learners.

Finally, key stakeholders (such as schools and colleges) can download templates of posters and logos, along with clip art, to help them to put together their own printed promotional materials. Here are some examples of the clip art available for download.

Results and review

According to Stuart Barnes, from St Luke's advertising agency, the campaign has been successful.

The Gremlin campaign is very direct, and sometimes feels quite disturbing. But, possibly because the idea came about through discussion with non-learners, we've found that, although some providers feel uncomfortable, people with basic skills problems respond well to the message.

They appreciate the campaign's empathy with the difficult emotions they have to deal with on a daily basis, and are able to start talking more openly about getting rid of their own gremlins. The response to the advertising we have had so far speaks for itself. It made lots of people pick up the phone and make the first move towards a better life.

Susan Pember, the Director of Skills for Life, also feels that the campaign has been a success.

The campaign has generated excellent levels of awareness, from 73 per cent recognition rate amongst the target audience in year one to a current rate of 84 per cent (91 per cent peak during March 2003). Basic skills are on the nation's agenda, and the stigma attached to the issue has reduced. The majority of our target audience now know that there is help available and 65 per cent feel there is no need to be embarrassed when asking for help.

It is estimated that around 26 per cent of the adults who have called 0800 100 900 over the last three years have gone into learning as a direct result of speaking to an adviser and watching the Get On

video. Additionally, research shows that up to six times as many adults may have taken some form of action to improve their skills as a result of the advertising (such as contacting a local college) without directly responding to the national campaign helpline.

In the publication, *Get On Campaign – Promotions and Communications Strategy*, Susan Pember goes on to say that the 2004/5 advertising campaign will be evaluated through pre and post-advertising tracking research before and after each burst of advertising. This will test awareness and recall of advertising, impact and effectiveness of the advertising message. There will be a PR evaluation to monitor messages within the media.

In addition, caller follow-up research will be conducted with respondents to the advertising, who have called the campaign learning advice line. This will evaluate what action the potential learner has taken since receiving the fulfilment video/DVD, as well as the quality of the call handling service and the fulfilment pack itself. Finally, the DfES will commission a media buying review to assess how cost efficiently the media was bought.

The last word

The Get On campaign appears to have been a successful one and plans to adapt its promotional activities as its objectives change. A strange combination of fear and humour appears to have worked wonders.

Source: Case study material and direct quotes from www.dfes.gov.uk/get-on

activities

1. Explain how the following factors might influence the willingness of the target market to take part in Get On literacy and numeracy courses:
   - social factors
   - psychological factors
   - personal factors.

2. Explain how and why the promotional campaign used the following promotional tools:
   - public relations
   - ambient media
   - advertising.

3. Using the evidence in this case study, evaluate the effectiveness of the Get On promotional campaign.

4. Using the clipart available from the Get On campaign website, produce an A4 poster that could be used to promote basic literacy and numeracy course run by your school or college. Justify the content and layout of the poster.

THE GOVERNMENT HAS RECOGNISED the importance of enterprise to the future well-being of the UK economy. It has taken a number of steps to promote enterprise.

For example, the government has created Enterprise Agencies in some regions of the UK with the intention of fostering enterprising behaviour among individuals and businesses. Scottish Enterprise aims to "help new businesses get underway as well as supporting and developing existing businesses".

Selected schools throughout the country have been granted special business and enterprise status. This means that these subjects are given particular emphasis in the school's curriculum and additional resources are made available to the school to improve and enhance the teaching of these subjects. The objective is to encourage greater enterprise amongst future generations.

This unit introduces the linked concepts of enterprise and entrepreneurship. The material is organised into four broad topics.
- launching a business
- appointing its officials
- monitoring the performance of the company
- winding up a company.

Investigating enterprise

Introducing enterprise

Setting the scene: an enterprising country?

Enterprising countries encourage entrepreneurs and support the creation of small businesses. People are supported in their attempts to use their ideas, skills and expertise to create new businesses. Governments support enterprise because it provides economic benefits: by setting up businesses, entrepreneurs and others are provided with employment and the production of the businesses adds value to the economy. The new ideas that entrepreneurs bring can create work for suppliers and other related businesses.

Recent research suggests that the UK government has enjoyed some success in creating an enterprising culture. The government has financed training for potential entrepreneurs and also offers a range of grants to assist newly established businesses. As Figure 7.1 shows, more UK people have tried to start their own business than in any other country apart from the USA.

The survey by Global Entrepreneurship Monitor showed an increasing degree of entrepreneurial activity in the UK. In 2003, 6.4 per cent of UK citizens surveyed said they had tried to start their own business compared with a figure of 5.2 per cent for the previous year.

One of the UK's best known entrepreneurs is Richard Branson. He established Virgin Records after leaving school at 16. His first major success was with Mike Oldfield and he later signed the Sex Pistols to the company, both contributing to the rapid growth of the business. Since then, Branson has launched the transatlantic airline Virgin Atlantic as well as budget airlines in Australia and Europe.

His Virgin empire also includes businesses in a variety of diverse sectors including mobile phones, trains, personal finance and clothing. Branson's entrepreneurial flair has created thousands of jobs in the UK and has contributed millions of pounds to the government in tax revenue.

Branson's personal wealth is estimated to exceed £1000 million, although his fortune has fluctuated over the years.

Figure 7.1: People thinking of starting a business

Country	Budding entrepreneurs (see note)
USA	12.0%
UK	6.4%
Germany	5.2%
Italy	3.2%
Japan	2.8%
France	1.4%

Note: Percentage of people who have considered setting up a business in the past 42 months
Source: Global Entrepreneurship Monitor survey, 2004

KEY TERMS

Enterprise is the activity in which people risk their money in establishing and running a business.

Innovation is the process of introducing novel ideas to develop new products or new methods of production.

Company is a general term for any incorporated business. Companies are business organisations in which a number of individuals contribute to the capital of a business in return for shares in the business.

Limited liability is a privilege that restricts financial responsibility of the owners of a business to the amount they have invested, or agreed to invest.

Profit is the surplus of revenues over costs.

What is enterprise?

Enterprise refers to the activity in which people risk their money in establishing and running a business. It is also common to call a business an enterprise. Individuals who have a business idea can try to put their ideas into practice by raising capital and starting the business. This process is called innovation.

People starting a business (who are called entrepreneurs) usually have to put some of their money into the business. This is a risky option because it is not uncommon for entrepreneurs to lose their money. However if the business is successful, they receive a reward in the form of profit.

Entrepreneurs with business proposals need to assess the commercial viability of their ideas. Once the entrepreneur has come up with an idea, he or she will need to consider:

■ will my idea provide a saleable good or service

■ will people want to buy this good or service

■ how much profit might I make

■ does the level of profit I might make mean that the risk is worthwhile?

The challenge for entrepreneurs is to organise the factors of production – land, labour and capital – in a productive and effective manner to deliver a product or service which people want to buy.

Entrepreneurs have certain personal qualities if they are to be successful in establishing and expanding a business. They must be prepared to work hard, to be determined and creative. They need confidence and the ability to plan ahead. They need a vision or aim and to be able to communicate this to other people: to investors, suppliers, employees and, perhaps most importantly, customers.

What this unit covers?

This unit introduces the linked concepts of enterprise and entrepreneurship. It does this by leading students through the process of setting up, running and closing down a business.

Launching a business

This outlines how to form a company, the documents and legal procedures that are necessary to set up a business and the planning process. It also focuses on the application of entrepreneurial skills in assessing markets, using creativity and business judgment to consider external factors such as market forces.

Appointing its officials

Companies are legally recognised bodies and need officials to run them. This section sets out the key job roles within a business, the duties and responsibilities they entail as well as the importance of team working to the success of companies.

Monitoring business performance

Entrepreneurial behaviour is not simply about establishing a business in a burst of creativity. It also includes checking on the performance of all aspects of the business once it is operational.

Winding up a company

This final element of the unit considers the planning that is necessary before winding up a company as well the documentation and actions that are part of the process. It also examines the effects that winding up can have on key stakeholders such as employees and shareholders.

GO TO the accompanying CD-ROM. Choose Unit 7 from the main menu. This will take you to an interactive game about running your won business. This game requires you to have some knowledge of all the units in this book that you have so far studied. However, it may be particularly helpful if you read Topics 5 and 6 of Unit 7 before playing this game.

Topic 1 — Planning a new enterprise

Setting the scene: James Dyson succeeds at the 5,127th attempt

James Dyson, the man who invented the "bagless" vacuum cleaner, showed enormous determination in turning his idea into a commercial success. In 1978, he noticed how vacuum cleaner bags clogged with dust and he determined to resolve the problem. It took five years and 5,127 prototypes before his G Force Dual Cyclone had become a product that was saleable.

Dyson then sought a business to produce his product under licence. It was two years before a Japanese company took up the idea. The vacuum cleaner became a huge success in Japan and sold for a premium price. This generated enough profit to provide the finance for Dyson to start manufacturing in the UK.

His first cleaner, the DC01, became the fastest selling vacuum cleaner ever in the UK. Not satisfied with this, he carried on his research and introduced the Root Cyclone vacuum cleaner and later the Dyson DC06 robot, which cleans automatically without human intervention.

Dyson's vacuum cleaners, characterised by their bold colours, have achieved sales in excess of £3,500 million globally. The Dyson company has achieved sales of over £3,000 million worldwide, with profits in excess of £40 million in 2003.

James Dyson is the company's chairman and sole shareholder and, with an estimated fortune of £700 million, he is one of Britain's richest men.

The idea

Ideas can result in new businesses, as the case of James Dyson demonstrates. Many ideas are also generated by existing businesses and can lead to new product ranges. For example, in 2003 Apple introduced the iPod which gave a new lease of life to the computer and technology company. Dyson's cleaner and Apple's iPod are both examples of innovation, where businesses have turned good ideas into products that are wanted by consumers.

So how are these ideas generated? Some, of course, as in the case of James Dyson are the result of an inventor working alone and developing an idea. Other good ideas are the result of expensive research by a team of employees. For example, Viagra, the anti-impotence drug was the result of 10 years research and development by Pfizer. Though the research was costly, it turned out to be worthwhile – by 2004 the company's sales exceeded £1,500 million.

When an entrepreneur or business has to decide whether or not to attempt to turn an idea into a business proposition, there are a number of factors to take into account.

KEY TERMS

Market research is the systematic collection and analysis of data to enable a business to make better marketing decisions.

Prototypes are sample products to see if the ideas and design work in practice.

A **business plan** is a detailed statement setting out the proposals for a new business or describing the ways in which an existing business will be developed.

A **mission statement** is a brief outline of the overall purpose of a business.

Estimating demand

Innovation depends on more than a good idea. Unless consumers want to buy the product, the idea will not lead to commercial success. In June 2004 Oscar-winning director Sam Mendes opened a play in London's West End. This was his first venture in the theatre. Two weeks later *Fuddy Meers* closed due to poor ticket sales. It is vital for businesses to research customers, using the market research techniques discussed in Unit 3 (*see page* 126) to establish that sufficient demand exists for a product before launching a business venture.

Developing prototypes

A prototype is a sample product manufactured to see if the business idea will work in practice as well as theory. Boeing, the aircraft manufacturer, used to produce wooden prototypes of its aircraft to ensure that they could be assembled successfully and to iron out any design errors. Since 2000 the company has used software to simulate this process. One of Britain's most famous inventors, Sir Clive Sinclair, also produces prototypes of his latest ideas before attempting to sell them. Developing prototypes should result in better quality products and more satisfied customers.

stopandthink

In 2004, Sir Clive Sinclair launched his A-bike. This bicycle, which weighs just 5.4 Kg and folds into a bag, is aimed at city dwellers. The A-bike, priced at £170, went on sale in the UK, US, Singapore and Japan.

Sir Clive is a talented inventor. Why might many of his previous ideas (a small electrical car, the C5 and an electrical bicycle) have failed to be commercial successes?

Costs, resources and timescale

For any new entrepreneur, finance can be an insurmountable hurdle. To start a business often requires considerable expenditure on market research, premises, machinery and vehicles, staff, promotion, raw materials and staff. Considerable costs can be incurred before the business starts trading and earning any income. A business can therefore face serious cash flow difficulties when trying to put an idea into practice. This is one reason why James Dyson initially had his vacuum cleaner produced under licence. He licensed a Japanese company to manufacture and sell his cleaners, and received a fee for each sale.

stopandthink

In 2001, entrepreneur Damaris Evans launched a company making lingerie for women. Her newly established business makes expensive, high fashion garments selling for over £100 per item. What resources would Damaris have needed before starting manufacturing? How might she have raised the capital needed to start her business?

The environment

Increasing concern about damage to the environment has influenced many business decisions, including the development of new products. In 2004, two Tyneside students invented a cigarette that will wash away in the rain in a few minutes. Traditional cigarette butts can take up to 12 years to rot away. No cigarette manufacturers have shown any interest in the idea so far. Toyota has received praise and awards for its new car, the Prius, which uses a combination of a petrol engine and an electric motor to deliver environmentally friendly transport.

The planning process

Unit 2 covered the process of drawing up a business plan in detail. Any entrepreneur who wants to maximise the chances of business success and who needs to raise external finance will need to draw up a business plan. You should look back at pages 62–65 to remind yourself of the main elements and features of a business plan.

The starting point for many entrepreneurs is to draw up a mission statement. This is a simple statement of the general purpose of a business. This can provide a sense of direction to the business; major decisions should be taken with the aim of fulfilling the mission statement. Consider, for example, the Christian Charity Oasis Trust, which was formed to provide help to young people in South London. Its mission statement – raising young people's belief in the future – helps the charity's managers to decide which projects to support.

Financial planning

An entrepreneur will face a number of financial issues when launching a business. Again, financial planning is covered in detail in Unit 2 and it may be necessary for you to review pages 58–105 to support your study of this topic. However, it is worth emphasising three aspects of financial planning which are particularly crucial when setting up a new business.

Raising capital

An entrepreneur may need funds to purchase vehicles and machinery, to lease premises and to pay for market research and advertising. This may amount to a substantial sum. Entrepreneurs normally invest some of their own money into their businesses and then seek further financial support from friends, family and banks. Drawing up a business plan, including full detail on finance, will be vital to persuade others to invest into an enterprise.

Managing cash

About 80 per cent of new enterprises fail within the first five years of trading. A prime cause of business failure is mismanagement of cash. New businesses have to pay out large amounts of money before they start to receive any revenue. This can result in a shortage of cash and an inability to pay bills as they are due. This forces many small firms to cease trading. Planning cash flows, forecasting periods of shortage and preparing plans to overcome these tough times are an essential element of financial planning.

Aiming for a profit

Although many businesses fail because of shortage of cash, the aim of most businesses is to make a profit. This requires a business to generate more revenue than costs over some period of trading. An important element of financial planning is to estimate future costs and revenues (based on market research) to see

whether the business is likely to make a profit. It is not unusual for new businesses to make a loss (the Channel Tunnel was opened in 1994 and has yet to record a profit). However, investors want to see evidence that a profit is anticipated within a reasonable period of time.

Health and safety

Entrepreneurs have to take account of a range of legislation when launching a business. One important area of legislation relates to health and safety. Any business employing people has a duty to its staff. It must "ensure, so far as is reasonably practicable, their health, safety and welfare at work". An entrepreneur might be required to:

- display a written safety policy (if the business has more than five employees)

- provide free safety equipment and clothing

- operate a safe working environment (for example, avoiding the use of hazardous machinery).

In the UK, the Health and Safety Executive regulates and oversees the implementation of health and safety in the workplace in the UK. The executive was set up under the Health and Safety Act 1974, which is the main legislation that governs health and safety in the workplace.

stopand**think**

Perween Warsi is a rising entrepreneur. She has built up a family business supplying ready-made meals to UK supermarkets and pubs. Her business employs 1,400 people in four factories in the north of England. Why is health & safety an important issue for Perween Warsi?

Knowledge summary

- Planning is an essential element of the process of launching a new enterprise.

- Business success does not simply depend upon a good idea. It is important that the new business delivers product that consumers want to buy.

- In launching a new business, entrepreneurs have to take into account many factors including environmental issues, health and safety and the need to develop and test prototypes.

- Financial planning is a key activity in developing a new business and must encompass cash and profit issues.

quick questions

1. Explain three benefits that an entrepreneur might receive as a result of carrying out thorough financial planning before starting a business.

2. Why is market research an essential activity for entrepreneurs?

3. Explain why a business should spend time and money producing prototypes.

data interpretation
Finance South West

A multi-million pound fund to help entrepreneurs in Devon set up in business was launched in 2005. The fund, called Finance South West, will draw on a funding pool of European money.

The fund will provide loans from £5,000 to £1 million through a range of financial options tailored to the needs of individual businesses. Successful applicants in Devon are offered the chance to meet a business mentor to help make sure their businesses prosper.

There is also a reward scheme offering reduced interest charges for businesses that achieve their business plan. The fund has been set up with £8.88 million from the European Objective Two programme and £9.52 million from Barclays Bank.

Source: adapted from www.bbc.co.uk, 3 February 2005

A Why might Barclays Bank have decided to take part in the Finance South West scheme?

B The fund offers financial support and business advice. Assess which of the two might be most important to an entrepreneur starting a business for the first time.

C Discuss the main factors that might lead to a new business established by an entrepreneur failing.

Topic 1 Planning a new enterprise

Setting the scene: off-the shelf companies

One way to start a company is to buy a ready-made company. These "off-the-shelf" companies can be bought from businesses that offer this specialist service. Using this method, it is possible to start a company for less than £100.

The business selling the "off-the-shelf" company will do everything necessary to set it up as a legal entity, including preparing all the necessary documentation and helping with the choice of a company name, and many provide a free website for those choosing to trade online. This extract describes some of the services offered by @UK PLC

Source: www.uk-plc.net/companyformation/index.htm

uk PLC Company Formations *online* FROM JUST £24.99 FREE COMPANY NAME CHECK SERVICE! CHECK AVAILABILITY ▶

You can now form a new company online, usually within three hours. It takes just minutes to check the availability of your company name, enter your details, and submit a registration.

@UK PLC are much more than just the leading company formation agent, we have a network of @Advisors that can help you get your company up and trading online with an effective ecommerce website that earns you money. We provide the complete personal service, company formation, domain names, website, ecommerce, accountancy and phones at great prices so that you can focus on making your business profitable.

Your company formation includes a website and a listing in the @UK PLC Business Directory. Our directory is used by over 1000 portals and is a great way of getting your newly formed company in front of as many customers as possible. With @UK PLC, company formation is just the start of your journey.

With the Premier package, costing £89.50, we supply:

Electronic memorandum and articles of association
Electronic certificate of incorporation
Printed certificate of incorporation
Company Seal and Register
Six bound copies of memorandum and articles
Free website worth £24+ VAT

Note: Price includes UK delivery only.

KEY TERMS

A **company** is any business that is incorporated.

Shareholders are the owners of a company.

Directors are senior managers within a business who are elected by shareholders at an annual general meeting to the company's board of directors.

Shares are documents that give their owners part ownership of a company and certain other rights such as a vote at annual general meetings.

A **memorandum of association** is a document that sets out a company's purpose in trading, the amount of capital it plans to raise and its registered name and address.

The **articles of association** state the internal arrangements under which a company is to operate.

Starting the company

Any entrepreneur setting up a company needs to consider a number of basic issues. These include the company structure, name, ownership and management.

1 Types of companies

Companies are formed when a group of individuals contribute capital in return for ownership of shares in a business. In the UK, there are two main types of company.

- Public limited companies are expensive to create. They can sell their shares on the stock exchange. They are distinguished by the letters *plc* after the company name.

- Private limited companies are subject to less regulation and have the term *Ltd* after their name.

Public limited companies tend to be much larger than private limited companies. Most businesses start out as private limited companies – sometimes converting to public limited company status when they need to raise more capital for expansion – and, for this reason, we shall focus on private limited companies in this topic.

One of the major benefits a private limited company offers to its owners (shareholders) is limited liability. Limited liability restricts the financial responsibility of shareholders in the event of the company failing and incurring large debts. This can be done in one of two ways.

- Private company limited by shares. This restricts shareholders' liability to the amount they have invested plus any shares they have agreed to buy but have not yet purchased.

- Private company limited by guarantee. Shareholders' liability is limited to the amount they have agreed to contribute to the company's assets.

2 Company name

An entrepreneur is unable to choose any name they want for their company. Anyone forming a company has to check and clear the proposed name of the business with Companies House.

Companies House is the official organisation that keeps records of all companies in the UK and oversees the formation, operation and closure (called winding up) of companies. In general, there are three restrictions when selecting a company name:

- it is not possible to use the same name as another company

- names likely to cause offence are not allowed

- the use of some terms, such as council and authority, is monitored.

Companies House restricts the use of words such as "council" and "authority" in a business because it is deemed to imply representative or authoritative status. This would not be allowed unless it was deemed appropriate.

stopand**think**

Nelson Mandela's foundation has warned companies to stop using his name as part of their business name. About 200 firms have sprung up with names like Nelson Mandela Panel Beaters and Nelson Mandela Fine Art, which have no connections with the man. Does this matter? Should it be controlled by the law?

IMPI

- HOME
- SUPPORT
- SUPPORT DATABASE
- IMPI FORUM
- SECURITY
- NEWS
- HISTORY
- MORE INFORMATION
- ASK FOR APPLICATION

First comes the trader, then the missionary, then the red soldier.

King Cetshwayo kaMpande 1879

3 Shares and shareholders

Shareholders are the owners of a company. A share represents part ownership of a company as well as giving shareholders voting rights. Under the Companies Act, at least two, but not more than 50, members can hold shares within a private limited company and these must be "desirable individuals" stipulated in the company's memorandum of association.

Private limited companies face other rules relating to their shares:

- they cannot be advertised freely for sale (in newspapers, for example)

- shares cannot be sold on the stock exchange

- any shareholder wishing to sell shares must obtain permission of the directors

- shares and debentures cannot be offered to the general public.

There are no restrictions on the minimum and maximum numbers of shares a new private limited company should issue and sell. However, many companies typically start by issuing 1000 shares.

4 Directors, meetings and voting

Directors are senior managers within a business. They are elected by shareholders at an annual general meeting to the company's board of directors. Directors are part of the company's most senior decision-making body – the board of directors. Anyone can be a director of a company unless they are registered as bankrupt or they have previously been disqualified from being a company director. There are no age limits on directors in England and Wales.

Many private limited companies hold annual general meetings (AGMs) at which shareholders have the opportunity to vote on major decisions. This is not, however, a legal requirement for private limited companies. All shareholders have the right to receive notice of company meetings, to attend these meetings and to vote as appropriate.

Voting power at company meetings is based on the number of shares held by shareholders. If a group of shareholders that holds more than 50 per cent of the company's shares vote in a particular way, then its views will prevail.

s t o p a n d t h i n k

Why is a private limited company a popular form of organisation for family businesses?

Company documents

The formation of a company requires the completion of two major documents.

1 Memorandum of association

All companies must have a memorandum of association. This states:

■ the company's name,

■ the address of the registered office of the company

■ its objectives – the stated object of a company may simply be to carry on business as a general commercial company

■ the company's share capital.

2 Articles of association

The articles of association set the rules for the running of the company's internal affairs. The articles state:

■ the rights of shareholders

■ the names and powers of directors

■ the rules governing company meetings, such as the annual general meeting (AGM).

Anyone a new company also needs to complete to further documents:

■ Form 10 – giving details of the directors and the business's registered address

■ Form 12 – a declaration of compliance with all legal requirements relating to the formation of a company.

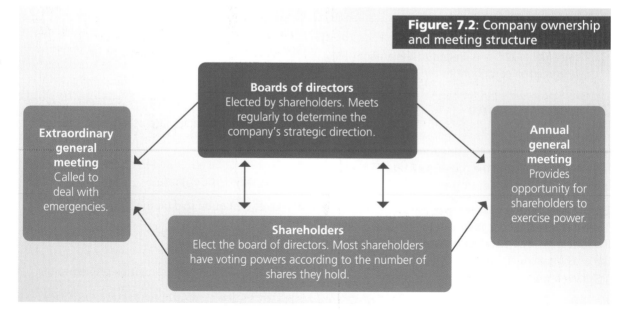

Figure: 7.2: Company ownership and meeting structure

Boards of directors
Elected by shareholders. Meets regularly to determine the company's strategic direction.

Extraordinary general meeting
Called to deal with emergencies.

Annual general meeting
Provides opportunity for shareholders to exercise power.

Shareholders
Elect the board of directors. Most shareholders have voting powers according to the number of shares they hold.

The Registrar of Companies oversees the registration or formation procedure for companies. Once the Registrar of Companies has received the memorandum of association and the articles of association and is satisfied that all legal requirements have been met, a certificate of incorporation will be issued. This certificate allows a company to start trading. It is an offence for a company to start trading or borrowing money until the certificate has been granted.

Once formed, a private limited company has a separate legal entity from its owners, the shareholders. A company is responsible for its debts, can sue and can be sued. For example, in 2004 a former employee of Honeywell sued the company because he believed that his body was contaminated by uranium while he worked for the business. The company was the legal party in this action – not Honeywell's shareholders.

Knowledge summary

- **Shareholders own companies, directors take day-to-day decisions and control its strategic direction.**

- **Companies offer shareholders the benefit of limited liability and have an independent legal existence.**

- **To form a company it is necessary to send a memorandum of association and a certificate of incorporation to the registrar of companies.**

- **A company is not permitted to commence trading until the Registrar of Companies has issued a certificate of incorporation.**

stop and think

Which of the company's stakeholders might be interested in the information in, respectively, the memorandum of association and the articles of association.

quick questions

1 Outline the three restrictions that apply to the selection of a company name.

2 Explain the benefits that owners of a company receive from limited liability.

3 Outline the role of Companies House in forming a new company.

data interpretation
Companies House

Companies House is the organisation responsible for forming, monitoring and winding up companies in the UK. This exercise requires you to use the information available on Companies House website to answer a series of questions about forming a company.

To start, go to the Companies House website (www.companieshouse.gov.uk) and research the pages on company formation.

A Who can form a company? What is a registered address?

B What is (a) Premium Service and (b) Electronic Filing Service?

C Draw up a list of forms that you would have to complete and the information that you would need to provide to form a company. Decide whether you would form your own company from scratch or buy one "off-the-shelf".

External issues and new enterprises

Setting the scene: more business starts ups

Government statistics show that the number of new businesses starting in the UK is rising substantially. As Figure 7.3 shows, there has been a steady increase in the number of company start ups and incorporations.

Figure 7.3: Company start ups						
	1998/9	1999/0	2000/1	2001/2	2002/3	2003/4
Number of company start ups	218,000	225,000	236,000	225,000	322,000	394,000
Average number of companies in the UK	1,233,000	1,319,000	1,406,000	1,464,000	1,555,000	1,752,000
Start ups as a % of existing companies	17.68	17.05	16.78	15.36	20.70	22.48
Percentage growth in the economy	2.8	2.3	1.3	2.2	3.2	3.2

Source: Office for National Statistics and Companies House

There could be several reasons for this growth, both in the overall number of businesses and in new business start ups. Improving economic prospects give entrepreneurs more confidence, and the increasing level of government support for entrepreneurship in the UK over recent years could also be a factor.

The growth has not been uniform across all business sectors. According to government statistics, the majority of company registrations are in business services (accountants, business consultants, for example) as well as construction and the hotel and leisure sectors. There has been an increase in the numbers of new restaurant companies, possibly trying to benefit from increasing disposable incomes.

Over the same time, there has been a decline in the numbers of agriculture and manufacturing businesses. Why do you think few companies being formed to carry out manufacturing activities?

Different types of businesses

Companies can operate in very different sectors of the economy. Consider these three, contrasting business sectors.

Manufacturing

Manufacturers make goods rather than supply a services. Newly established companies might manufacture relatively inexpensive and simple products such as pottery, garden furniture and candles. Setting up a company to manufacture products can be expensive because the enterprise might require industrial premises, vehicles, machinery, equipment and a substantial amount of raw material. The capital required to do this on a large scale may not be available to many entrepreneurs.

Services

The number of companies supplying services in the UK has risen substantially in recent years. The capital required to set up service businesses is relatively low and rising consumer disposable incomes and changing lifestyles have fuelled demand for cleaners, therapists, gardeners, decorators and personal trainers.

Business services

The overall growth in businesses has generated an increase in demand for a range of business services. As a result there has been an increase in the number of companies supplying business services such as accountancy and auditing, IT installation and maintenance (including website services), and management consultancy.

Opportunities, risks and growth potential

The business world offers many opportunities for entrepreneurs to develop an idea and to turn it into a commercially viable product. Opportunities and the potential for business growth are created in many ways.

Changes in the law

In 2004, the European Union passed legislation making businesses responsible for the clean-up costs of any pollution they cause. This has already created work for environmental protection consultancies that are able to advise firms on the scope of the new environmental legislation as well as the policies and procedures that can introduce to minimise the risk of pollution.

Similarly new UK legislation enacted in 2005 placed a responsibility on businesses to make their goods and services accessible to disabled people. The Disability Discrimination Act (Unit 1, *see page* 36) has created work for business consultants and builders alike. Many shops have had to build ramps or install lifts to ensure the disabled can reach all parts of the building.

Technological change

James Dyson founded his business manufacturing vacuum cleaners on his invention of a "bag less" machine with a stronger suction. The development of the internet has had a major impact on businesses offering a host of opportunities. Even small businesses have been able to sell products through this medium.

stop and think

Devon entrepreneurs Jason Nickels and Steve Waters gave up well paid jobs in IT to become chilli farmers. They grow about 80 varieties on their south Devon farm and also dry and pickle their products for sale worldwide. Not surprisingly, given their backgrounds, online sales are important to them. Discuss why technological advances may have been so influential in the careers of Jason and Steve.

Rising incomes

In the late 1990s and the first half of the 2000s, the UK economy showed strong growth. Incomes in the UK have been rising at about 3 per cent per annum in real terms. As a result, people are purchasing goods and, especially, services that they would not have been previously able to afford. This has created opportunities for businesses to supply products to people who are relatively cash rich. Businesses in the service sector, such as restaurants, hotels, airlines and fitness centres, have all benefited from steadily rising disposable income.

Social change

The ways in which people live their lives are changing. While disposable incomes are rising and many are becoming cash rich, they are also becoming time poor. For example, it is increasingly common for couples with children to both have full-time jobs. This has created opportunities for businesses offering a range of time-saving services, such as house cleaning, childminding services and even dog walking.

stop and think

Increasing numbers of people in the UK are living alone. Between 1991 and 2001 there was a 23 per cent increase in the number of single person households. What business opportunities might this offer?

Government support

The government offers some financial support as well as a range of advice services to help new businesses over the risky initial period and to increase their chances of survival and growth. Business grants vary over time and need careful research. A good starting point is Business Link (www.businesslink.gov.uk). Grants are available to support innovation, training and income support in the early stages of managing the business.

Improving infrastructure

Some developments, such as the extension of broadband internet services to most parts of the UK, have assisted businesses in growing. High speed access to the internet has assisted researchers, writers, accountants and others who work from home.

Risks

The UK's enterprise economy also poses risks for businesses. As Figure 7.4 highlights, there has been a significant increase in the numbers of companies that ceased trading. In part, of course, this rise in the number of company closures merely reflects the fact that there are more companies in the UK than 10 years ago. The increased number of companies means that most businesses face greater competition.

Figure 7.4: Company closures	
Year	Number of companies ceasing trading
1998/9	119,000
1999/0	134,000
2000/1	155,000
2001/2	163,000
2002/3	180,000
2003/4	182,000

Source: Companies House

However, there are other causes for company closures. Businesses that aim to take advantage of consumer trends – for example, there was a relatively brief fashion for executives to employ personal trainers to provide advice on fitness – can experience a sudden decline in sales if tastes and fashions change. Similarly, businesses that flourish when incomes are steadily rising – restaurants are an obvious, example – may see sales fall if the economy suffers a downturn. Note also that although the

Restaurant trade may suffer in an economic downturn

internet provides multiple opportunities, it also poses a threat in that rival businesses can use it too.

Newly established companies are also very vulnerable. They do not have previously accumulated profits to fall back on it sales decline. Furthermore, they are often short of cash and frequently experience difficulties in paying bills as they fall due.

Other factors also pose risks and may limit the ability of new businesses to flourish and grow.

■ **Fluctuations in economic activity**. Over time the level of income in the economy can fluctuate. This process is known as the business cycle. Businesses such as airlines and restaurants are highly susceptible in a recession when income levels may fall. A recession can have a serious negative impact on many business's sales and may threaten their survival.

■ **Increasing competition**. The expansion of the European Union to encompass 25 states in 2004 opened up the UK economy to competition from many overseas businesses. Some of the new European Union member states benefit from very low wages and businesses based in these countries are able to provide goods and services at very competitive prices.

Market forces

The UK economy is a free market economy. This means that there is relatively little intervention by the government to influence prices or to regulate the quantities and types of goods and services supplied by businesses. This can benefit businesses in that they are free to avail themselves of any opportunities that may exist, to supply a wide range of products and to charge whatever prices they choose. However, there are also risks associated with free market economies. The relative absence of government intervention means that businesses receive no support if demand falls and no compensation of companies are unable to survive.

Knowledge summary

- Recent figures show an increasing number of company start ups in the UK. Most new companies provide services, either direct to consumers or by supplying services to other businesses.

- The UK economy provides many opportunities for entrepreneurs. Rising incomes and technological developments have created many new business opportunities.

- The risks of entrepreneurship are ever present. Increasing numbers of companies have succumbed to fierce competition and changing patterns of consumer demand.

quick questions

1 Why are increasing numbers of companies providing services to other businesses?

2 Give three major risks facing a newly established restaurant selling meals made exclusively from organic ingredients.

3 What do you consider to be the most important reason behind the increase in the number of company start ups in the UK over the last few years? You should explain your decision.

data interpretation
Business support

There are a range of organisations that offer advice and guidance to entrepreneurs establishing and managing small businesses. However, finding the best sources of support for "your" business can be tricky. To assist in this process Business Link provides help in identifying the best sources of advice for any given business.

Go to the Business Link website (www.businesslink.org.uk). Click on "Finance and grants"; and then click on "Grants and support schemes" in the menu marked "Find" in the right-hand column. It takes you to this page.

A Find out the details of your local Business Link office and investigate three ways in which they might assist you in starting up a business.

B Using Business Link's Business Support Directory (see web page above), fill in the details in "Method 2" for a business you propose to start. Investigate the results of this exercise.

C Choose the best two sources of information and support. Which of the two was the most valuable? Why?

Company officers: roles and responsibilities

Setting the scene: Eurotunnel's board thrown from office

In 2004, rebel shareholders of Eurotunnel, the company that runs the Channel Tunnel, succeeded in a campaign to overthrown the company's board of directors. This unusual demonstration of shareholder power showed that a company's senior officers and its board of directors are subject to ultimate control by the company's shareholders.

Over 150 million people have travelled through the Channel Tunnel on Eurotunnel's passenger shuttle service since it opened in 1994. Eurotunnel is the market leader for cross-Channel travel – the choice of 2.3 million motorists and 1.3 million truckers in 2003. Despite this volume of traffic, rail passenger numbers are below forecast numbers.

The company's financial position has always been weak due to the enormous loans it took out to build the tunnel. Eurotunnel's management team has never managed to reduce the company's huge debts and its crippling interest payments on these loans. In 2004, Eurotunnel's financial crisis deepened as its revenues fell due to rising competition from budget airlines.

This led to angry scenes at that year's AGM in Paris, where more than 5,000 shareholders made their protest felt. When outgoing chief executive Richard Shirrefs attempted to speak to the AGM, he was booed by the audience.

The rebels, many of whom have seen value of their investments fall by 90 per cent, wanted a new management team to cut the firm's £6,400 million debt. At the AGM, the rebel shareholders won a vote not to renew the board seats of the chairman and chief executive, paving the way for new company officers and a new management team.

KEY TERMS

The **board of directors** is a company's most senior decision-making body which is elected by shareholders to manage this enterprise

Directors are senior managers within a business who are elected by shareholders at an annual general meeting to the company's board of directors.

A **chairman (or chairperson)** takes responsibility achieving the company's strategic objectives and runs the meetings of the board of directors.

Company secretary is the senior administrative officer of the company, usually with a law qualification and responsible for the company's legal affairs.

Auditors are qualified accountants who carry out an independent check on the company's accounts.

Key roles in a company

For a company to function efficiently and legally a number of key roles must be carried out.

1 Chairman (or chairperson)

The simplest description of the role of the chairman is that he or she organises and runs the company's board of directors. A chairman may also establish and monitor the company's strategy.

A chairman must have:

- experience of a broad range of management such as finance, marketing and production
- the skills necessary to run the directors' meetings, ensuring discussions are relevant and that clear decisions are taken
- good communication skills
- good judgement and decision-making skills
- possibly formal qualifications, such as an accountancy qualification.

2 Managing director

In larger companies and plcs, the title of managing director is increasingly being replaced by the US term chief executive officer, usually called by its abbreviation CEO. The managing director has overall responsibility for the company's operations and for implementing the agreed corporate strategy. The managing director is answerable to the chairman, the board of directors and ultimately the shareholders. In some companies, the posts of chairman and CEO are combined, although this does not accord with best practice guidelines as it concentrates too much power in the hands of one person.

A managing director or CEO is likely to need similar qualifications and skills to the chairman, but many CEOs have established the businesses that they run and possess other important skills such as determination, creativity, vision, the ability to inspire others and to provide leadership.

3 Company secretary

All companies must have at least two directors including a company secretary. The company secretary is the chief administrator for the company and has a range of responsibilities:

- maintaining company records
- sending annual returns to the Registrar of Companies or the stock exchange
- keeping records of the company's property
- ensuring that the company and its directors operate within the law
- acting as a link between shareholders and directors
- organising board and general meetings.

The recognised professional qualification for company secretaries is Associateship of the Institute of Chartered Company Secretaries and Administrators (ICSA). Company secretaries need to be able to understand complex legal and financial matters, be able to explain complex matters to non-experts, have good judgement and be competent with figures.

4 Directors

Directors are senior managers. They are elected by shareholders at an annual general meeting to a company's board of directors. Directors normally bring

stop and think

Even world famous chief executives can hit troubled times. Carly Fiorina was appointed chief executive of the US technology manufacturer Hewlett Packard in 1999. At first she received praise for her leadership but decided to resign in 2005 after the much publicised merger with Compaq was seen to be unsuccessful. Do you think a chief executive should resign if a major decision goes wrong? Justify your view.

some particular skills or expertise to the board. There are two types of directors.

- **Executive directors** – these directors are employed by the company and have significant responsibilities within the business, often for a function such as sales or finance.

- **Non-executive directors** – these director are company employees but are appointed to bring particular experience or expertise to the board. It is common for politicians to be appointed as non-executive directors because of their knowledge of some aspect of government policy. This type of director is expected to give independent advice and to look critically at the board's decisions.

Directors' qualifications and skills depend upon the wider role that they play within the business. For example, a director responsible for marketing might be expected to have qualifications from the Chartered Institute of Marketing – the professional body for those working in marketing and sales. Most directors also have substantial experience of business, but this may depend upon the size of the business.

Directors of small companies may have limited experience and few qualifications. They may have started the company or have been appointed for their flair, drive or initiative – though these skills may not be sufficient or appropriate if the company grows rapidly and becomes a large operation – and they have a significant managerial responsibility.

5 Accountants and auditors

Companies might employ their own accountants or choose to use the services of a specialist accountancy firm. Most qualified accountants have taken professional examination after completing a degree course at university. Both in-house accountants and outside accountancy firms carry out similar functions:

- accounting – keeping full accounts for the business

- taxation – calculating how much the business owes in tax and making returns to the Inland Revenue

- risk management – identifying potential risks to a business and introducing control measures to reduce business losses.

All companies are required by law to have their financial records audited. Companies must appoint independent auditors to check that their financial accounts are a true and fair record. Companies are free to choose which firm of auditors to use, and they must pay for this service, but the audit reports are supposed to be entirely independent.

The management team

Although individuals in positions such as chief executive can have an enormous influence on a company, it is the combined management team as a whole that is more influential. As with most teams, a management team needs to be a blend of contrasting individuals with complementary skills. It needs creative people, good organisers, people who are determined and people who pay attention to detail.

stop and think

Ollila Jorma has been chairman and chief executive officer of Nokia since 1992 and there has been little change in the senior management team in that period. However, in 2004 two senior managers left the company breaking up the long-established management team. What advantages might this change bring to Nokia?

Nokia, the Finnish manufacturer of mobile phones, is one of the world's most successful companies. Its senior management team has been relatively stable over a long period of time and this has been one of the factors contributing to the company's achievements. A successful management team will:

- communicate well with each other, exchanging ideas and discussing major decisions thoroughly

- review the roles carried out by each manager on a regular basis with the intention of ensuring that each team member contributes to the maximum extent over time

- ensure new team members bring new and complementary skills to the group.

Many companies use psychometric tests to assess the personalities of applicants for senior management positions in an attempt to appoint people who will fit in with the team and contribute something different.

stop and think

Do you think it is more challenging to be a director of a small business (with perhaps only one or two other directors) or of a multinational company with a large board of directors?

Knowledge summary

- A company needs officers to run the business. Key officers include the chairman, chief executive and the company secretary.

- Directors can be executive (employees of the company) or non-executive (notionally independent).

- A well-balanced, experienced and well-qualified management team is an important element in the success of a company.

quick **questions**

1 Outline the differences in roles between a company secretary and a chief executive officer.

2 Why might a company benefit from having executive and non-executive directors on its board?

3 How might the roles carried out by directors vary between a small and a large company?

data **interpretation**
Sir Christopher Gent

Sir Christopher Gent became a non-executive director at GlaxoSmithKline (GSK) in 2004 having recently retired as chief executive officer of Vodafone. In January 2005, Sir Christopher become non-executive chairman at GSK, Europe's biggest pharmaceutical company.

Vodafone became the world's biggest mobile phone operator under Sir Christopher, achieving rapid growth by taking over major rivals such as the German mobile phone network operator Mannesmann at a time when the demand for mobile phone services was increasing rapidly.

Sir Christopher became Vodafone's CEO early in 1997 and proved to be a highly entrepreneurial leader. Over a period of seven years, he transformed the company, increasing its market value from £7,500 million to £77,000 million; its share price hit 399 pence in 2000 compared with about 50p when he took over. By 2005, Vodafone operated in 29 countries with over 100 million subscribers.

Sir Christopher's pay deals caused much controversy. On retirement, his pension was worth over £650,000 a year. In his last year at Vodafone, his basic salary was nearly £3 million plus a performance-related bonus of £1.6 million.

A Explain why GlaxoSmithKline might have wanted to appoint Sir Christopher Gent as a non-executive director.

B What problems might a new CEO face when taking over a large, established and successful company such as Vodafone.

C Sir Christopher was very highly paid by Vodafone and some analysts believe that this was fair as the company's success was due to his leadership. Do you agree with this view? Explain your answer.

Topic 4 Company officers: roles and responsibilities

Monitoring performance: operations

Setting the scene: communication is key

ACAS (the Advisory Conciliation and Arbitration Service) believes a company's performance is determined by its employees and, for a company to work efficiently and perform well, it needs an effective workplace and workforce.

Performance can be improved if employees feel that they are involved in the company's future by being part of the decision-making process and if they are kept well informed. Most importantly, communication and consultation are essential to an effective workplace.

By consultation and communicating effectively, performance can be improved through:

- wasting less time, money and resources as a result of clearer understanding – which improves productivity, quality and efficiency

- better employee performance and commitment – more committed employees are likely to also show increased productivity, quality and efficiency

- increased job satisfaction leading to greater workforce motivation

- improved management decision-making in implementing change or choosing strategies.

Many other benefits may also be gained, such as lower costs and increased profits or perhaps increased customer satisfaction.

KEY TERMS

Performance indicators are set targets or quantities against which the success of an activity is measured.

Consultation is the procedure of finding out stakeholders' views and taking these into account before making a decision.

Self-assessment is the process by which individual employees reflect upon their own performance in the work place.

Household penetration is the number of households in market that are actually using a particular brand.

Market share is the percentage or proportion of the total sales in a market that is achieved by a company. It is measured in terms of volume of units sold or sales value.

Monitoring operations

No business knows how well it is performing unless it monitors its position. It needs to measure and compare its performance against some sort of performance indicator. Performance indicators can come in many forms. For example, a business cam make comparisons with:

- historical data

- their competitors

- budgeted figures

- benchmark figures.

Companies must measure their own performance and then relate it to selected performance indicators to determine whether or not they have been successful. This is a matter of judgement: for example, it may seem good if a business has improved its productivity by 20 per cent in the last year (making a historical comparison); however; if it makes a comparison with rival companies and finds that its productivity is still lower than its competitors, then how well has it performed?

Team working and motivation

Motivated employees and teams are more efficient and productive than an unmotivated workforce. Many companies, therefore, make it a priority to monitor their employee's performance, feelings and opinions. The thinking here is that if motivation starts to decline, then the company's performance may also decline as a result.

Key performance indicators in this area include labour turnover, which measures the rate at which employees leave the company, and absence rates, which measures the average number of days each employee takes as sick leave each year. They are calculated using these formulas.

$$\text{labour turnover} = \frac{\text{number of leavers per year}}{\text{average number of staff}}$$

$$\text{absence rates} = \frac{\text{number of days staff take off sick per year}}{\text{average number of staff}}$$

Obviously, the more motivated and committed a company's employees, the less likely they are to leave the business or take days off work. Many companies go to much greater lengths to measure employee performance. Some measuring productivity per employee; some regularly assess staff attitudes using self-assessment or employee opinion surveys.

Meetings

The efficient and regular dissemination of information to all levels of an organisation is paramount in achieving good levels of performance. Good communication is a two-way process and, in an inclusive business culture, employees are encouraged to take part in decision making. This aids management decision making and improves industrial relations with a workforce. It also ensures employees are aware of organisational objectives and can act appropriately to help achieve them; this increases co-ordination of effort and resources within the business.

JD Wetherspoon, plc, the national pub chain, considers employee participation invaluable. Wetherspoon employees are actively encouraged to make suggestions to their line managers. The company believes that managers can often miss good ideas that are obvious to employees, who interact with the products and customers everyday.

Meetings can take many forms from annual general meetings of shareholders to departmental, project and team meetings. The key performance indicator here is that meetings should be relevant and that employees should feel that the information they are receiving and giving is important and valued.

Wetherspoon has a regular "big meeting" strategy, bringing together the company chairman, directors, managers and employees. These meetings review company performance and consider ways to improve it. This helps improve day-to-day operations and enhance strategic plans; for example, new advertising proposals may be considered and the meeting may jointly decide which one to use.

Production and quality

The efficiency of a business can be measured by its productivity. This is a measure of how well a business is able to turn its inputs into output that it can sell. The more productive a business, the quicker and more cost effective it is at supplying goods, and this can give it a competitive edge in the marketplace. Productivity can be measured by this formula.

$$\text{productivity} = \frac{\text{output (quantity or value of output)}}{\text{inputs (labour cost + capital cost + materials)}}$$

This can be compared to a performance indicator such as industry benchmark data. Companies again may do this in more depth by considering factors such as productivity per employee. This could be compared with last year's data to see if employees are becoming more or less efficient.

$$\text{productivity per employee} = \frac{\text{output (usually in quantity)}}{\text{number of employees}}$$

Quick and cost-effective production also has to be quality production, or else consumers may not buy the company's products. Quality also needs to be measured, for high productivity is useless if output is of poor standard. Quality can be measured in many ways, but three indicators to assess performance are:

- number of defects – the number or products rejected or that need to be reworked due to faulty workmanship

- returns – the number of products returned by customers

- complaints – the number and frequency of customer complaints and whether or not they were resolved.

Achieving quality helps raise revenues – it helps to ensure greater customer satisfaction and hence more repeat business – and it reduces costs through wasting less time and resources. However, quality also comes at a price: it costs money to put in place the training, equipment and processes needed for checking and improving product quality.

Promotional campaigns

Companies also need to assess the impact of their promotional activities. This is discussed in some detail in Unit 6, Topic 9, however it is worth emphasising there are several factors to consider. First, a company needs to have clear (and well understood) objectives for any promotional campaign. Second, it then needs to measure the impact of any campaign on the company's performance against these goals.

A company may assess a promotional campaign's impact using one (or a combination of) several indicators.

- **Sales value** – has sales revenue increased as a result of the promotional campaign?

- **Sales volume** – has the promotion increased the number of units sold, indicating increased demand?

- **Market share** – has the promotion increased the company's market share (by either value or volume) for its products?

Note that increases in sales revenue or sales volume may also be a result of market growth – for example, consumers may be buying more products from every supplier – not the result of their promotion. Also note that in many markets, a firm may have to make some trade off between sales volume and sales revenue. It may, say, reduce prices (and perhaps take some drop in revenue) in order to attract increased demand.

There are other performance indicators that companies can use to measure the impact of promotional activity. Two are household penetration and product awareness.

- **Household penetration** – has the promotion increased the number of households using the product (that is, new customers) or is it simply persuading existing customers to buy more.

- **Product awareness** – has the number of potential consumers who are familiar with a product increased even if they haven't actually bought it, as this may be an indicator of potential future sales – consumers cannot buy a product if they don't know it exists.

The main consideration for any company is that advertising and promotional strategies are expensive, yet in many industries essential. Companies must be able to assess the impact of different promotional techniques so that in the future they can use promotional strategies and methods that are effective for their company.

Again it is worth noting that evaluating a promotional campaign can also be a significant cost. It can be expensive to commission market research into the effectiveness of a promotion, such as assessing consumer awareness of a product before and after a campaign.

Knowledge summary

■ Performance indicators allows a firm to compare its performance against agreed targets such as industry benchmarks.

■ Productivity measures the efficiency with which a business supplies good and services. Productivity has to be linked to quality to get a true measure of performance.

quick questions

1 Explain two ways a company can monitor the performance of its employees.

2 Why are motivated employees an important factor in improving company performance?

3 Consider the benefits and drawbacks for an organisation of monitoring quality.

data interpretation
Promoting success

The microwaveable ready meal market has been a major growth area in the UK food retail industry. In recent years, there has been particular growth in the microwave Indian and Chinese takeaway market.

To capitalise on this growth, the Golden Phoenix brand of take home Chinese meals launched a "two for one offer" campaign in July. This was supported by a television and magazine advertising campaign starting in June and continuing through July into the start of August. The last advert was set to appear on 6 August with the promotional offer ending on 12 August.

Figure 7.5 shows the sales data for all brands in this retail sector. It covers the month preceeding the campaign, as well as the three months of the Golden Phoenix campaign (June, July and early August) and the four subsequent months through to the end of the year.

Figure 7.5: Market sales of Indian and Chinese ready meals by brand

Brand name	Market sales £m'							
	May	June	July	Aug	Sept	Oct	Nov	Dec
Golden Phoenix	28	27	30	38	40	35	34	36
Oriental Blossom	12	15	16	12	12	14	17	16
Blue River	14	15	12	11	14	15	13	14
Canton Carry Outs	14	13	17	16	16	17	19	19
Supermarket own label	24	24	25	25	24	25	24	27
Others	8	8	6	8	7	8	6	9

A Explain the difference between the terms market share and market growth.

B Calculate Golden Phoenix's percentage market share for each month. (Market share equals Golden Phoenix's sales times 100 divided by total market sales). Give your answers to two decimal places. Alternatively, use a spreadsheet to display the market shares of all brands as a graph or pie chart.

C Prepare either a five-minute presentation or a short report, including any relevant data, facts and figures, explaining whether or not you think Golden Phoenix's promotional strategy was a success.

Topic 5 Monitoring performance: operations

Monitoring performance: finance

Setting the scene: interpreting financial data

The function of accounting is to provide financial information that informs stakeholders about how a particular organisation has performed over a given period. Ratio analysis is one way that interested parties can assess the financial performance of a business. Ratio analysis's main purpose is to assist in interpreting financial information and to support managers in monitoring performance by determining how far the company has achieved its objectives.

However, the results from any financial analysis mean absolutely nothing unless an organisation's objectives are also taken into consideration. Businesses have different objectives. To some extent, a business's objectives are dependent on the type and size of the business, and this must be taken into account before a judgement can be made about whether financial results are acceptable or unacceptable.

Consider, a sole trader business: a net profit of £60,000 might be considered as being quite a healthy return. But would a partnership of 10 partners be equally satisfied? To take a more extreme example, contrast the objectives of a major public limited company such as Coca-Cola with those of a small retailer such as a newsagent. Coca-Cola may have a range of objectives, including maximising profits, being the market leader in its sector and corporate growth. The newsagent is likely to have less lofty goals such as just making a profit.

So when interpreting financial accounts, it is important to consider what any organisation is trying to achieve. For example, would you consider the financial results of a hospital in the same way as a commercial business such as Lotus Cars? How might the objectives of the two organisations differ?

KEY TERMS

Ratio analysis is a method of examining financial data. It allows for more meaningful interpretation of financial data by measuring a number of aspects of a business's performance.

Profitability is a measure of a business's ability to generate more revenue from its activities than it actually costs to undertake those activities.

Liquidity is an assessment of a business's ability to meet its short-term debts. It is a measure of whether the business has enough cash available to pay bills and invoices as they come due for payment.

Profitability ratios measure the relationship between gross/net profit and sales, assets and capital employed. These are sometimes referred to as performance ratios.

Liquidity ratios investigate financial stability of the firm by examining the relationships between assets and liabilities.

Margin of safety is the amount by which a company's current output and sales exceed the level of output necessary to break even.

Monitoring finance

Businesses can undertake various forms of analysis to interpret their financial performance. There are four main forms.

Vertical analysis

Vertical analysis considers relationships between figures from the profit and loss account and the balance sheet. This analysis looks at the interdependence of one figure to another. For example, gross profit is not only affected by sales but also by the cost of sales.

Horizontal analysis

Horizontal analysis compares current financial statements with previous financial statements. This is done on an item-by-item basis to determine whether there has been any areas of significant change. For example, a company would want to know if any particular area of expenditure increased significantly from last year to this year.

Trend analysis

Trend analysis takes figures from current accounting statements and from several previous periods and maps them out (usually on a chart) in an attempt to determine any trends. For example, a company might wish to see if there had been any significant change in the level of sales over the previous three years and, furthermore, establish the relative sizes of the changes.

Ratio analysis

Ratio Analysis uses set formulas to compare and interpret financial statements. This method allows for:

- in-depth monitoring of financial performance from one period to another
- comparisons over time
- comparisons with other companies
- analysis of current financial performance.

Alongside these methods, companies will also monitor other key performance indicators such as their breakeven position and margin of safety.

1 Monitoring profitability

Profitability ratios measure the relationship between gross/net profit and sales and capital employed. They are sometimes called performance ratios. One objective of most private companies is to make a profit. However, it is not sufficient just to measure the amount of profit a company makes; analysts want to consider how that profit was made. They do this by calculating different profitability ratios.

Gross profit margin

The gross profit margin examines the relationship between the profits made on trading activities against sales. It is expressed as a percentage, using this formula.

$$\text{gross profit margin} = \frac{\text{gross profit}}{\text{sales}} \times 100$$

The higher the gross profit margin, the better the performance. A company can use the gross profit margin to compare its current results with previous years to establish if its trading position has become more or less profitable.

Gross profit margins vary considerably between different markets. For example, the gross profit percentage on luxury goods like chocolates is far higher than that on necessities like bread. So any result must be looked at in the context of the industry in which the firm operates.

Net profit margin

Net profit margin measures the relationship between the net profit and the level of sales. Again the result is expressed as a percentage, and the higher the percentage, the better the result.

$$\text{net profit margin} = \frac{\text{net profit}}{\text{sales}} \times 100$$

This ratio is used to establish whether a firm has been efficient in its operations. Comparisons with previous years' results and other companies in the same industry are made to judge relative efficiency.

Return on capital employed (ROCE)

This ratio measures the efficiency of funds invested in the business at generating profits. This is sometimes known as the primary ratio and it is considered to be one of the most important profitability ratios. Again the result is expressed as a percentage, and the higher the percentage, the better the result. A higher percentage provides owners with a greater return.

$$\text{ROCE} = \frac{\text{net profit}}{\text{capital employed} \times 100}$$

Inevitably this figure needs to be compared with previous years and with the ratios for other companies to determine if the result is satisfactory.

This result also needs to be compared with the percentage return offered by interest-bearing accounts at banks and building societies. Ideally, the ROCE should be higher than any return that could be gained by simply placing cash in interest-earning accounts. After all, would you start your own business – with all the hard work and pressure that entails – to make a return of 5 per cent, when you could invest in a savings account earning 8 per cent and work for someone else?

2 Monitoring liquidity

Liquidity is concerned with the financial stability of the organisation. All companies are concerned with cash flow and many want to know if their working capital is being managed effectively. Working capital is needed by all organisations in order to finance their day-to-day activities. Too little, and the company may not have enough cash available able to pay all its debts. Too much, and it may not be making most efficient use of its resources.

Current ratio

The current ratio examines the relationship between current assets and current liabilities and gives the liquidity position of the firm. It is expressed as a ratio.

current ratio = current assets : current liabilities

A result of 3:1 would show that a business has three times as many current assets as it has liabilities. This means that for every £1 of debt it owes, it has £3 available to pay these debts. This company is therefore in a comfortable position to pay its debts.

Convention is that an ideal current ratio should be approximately 2:1 – that is, a business should have £2 of assets for every £1 of debt. A low current ratio means a business may not be able to pay its debts. A result of 0.8:1 shows that the business only has 80p to pay every £1 it owes and is not currently in a position to be able to cover all its short-term debts.

The business must consider its current ratio alongside its cash flow forecast and current bank balances. A low current ratio result implies that the company may well experience cash flow difficulties in the future.

3 Monitoring purchases and sales

Monitoring purchases and sales can partly be done by the gross profit margin ratio, as component parts of

calculating gross profit are the cost of goods sold and sales. The gross profit margin can be improved by increasing sales revenue while keeping the cost of sales static; or by reducing cost of sales while maintaining the same level of sales revenue. In either case, the business's cost of buying goods becomes relatively cheaper compared to the price for which they sell.

The cost of purchases also has to be compared to the level of output. As output increases, we would expect more materials to be needed, and therefore purchases to rise. Therefore an increased cost of purchases is not necessarily bad, providing output has also risen in equal or greater proportion.

Variance analysis is employed in this area (Unit 2, see page 85). Variance analysis is used to compare the forecasted or budgeted figures (what a business expects to happen) with actual figures (what actually does happen). This allows a business to spot any areas where its forecasts were inaccurate. By investigating why any variances occur, a business should be able to make more accurate forecasts in future or discover areas of activity that are not operating as expected.

Of course, actual results may turn out to be better than forecast. In this situation a business can try to determine the reasons for this success, so that it can repeat it again and build on any areas of strength.

4 Monitoring breakeven

Breakeven analysis was considered in some detail in Unit 2 (see pages 92–95). One feature of breakeven analysis is the margin of safety. This can be defined as the amount by which current output and sales exceed the level of output necessary to break even. The margin of safety can be calculated by subtracting the breakeven output from the current output and dividing the answer by the current level of output. This formula can be used to calculate the margin of safety, expressed as a percentage.

$$\text{margin of safety} = \frac{(\text{current output} - \text{breakeven output})}{\text{current output}} \times 100$$

The margin of safety tells a business how much it can afford sales and demand to drop before it starts making a loss. In fluctuating markets, it is vital to assess and monitor the margin of safety regularly. If a company sees its margin of safety falling, it should be able to take remedial action to remedy the situation before it starts making a loss.

Knowledge summary

■ Financial indicators must be evaluated against an organisation's objectives.

■ Profit performance can be assessed in terms of gross profit, net profit or the return on capital employed. Figures should be compared with previous years results or industry benchmark data.

■ The current ratio analyses a business's liquidity position, and can highlight any potential cash flow problems.

■ Variance analysis can be used to compare targets with actual results so that weaknesses can be identified and remedied, and strengths built on.

quick questions

1 Explain two ways a company can monitor its performance in terms of its profitability.

2 Why is monitoring a company's liquidity important?

3 Name three basis a company can use as key performance indicators for comparing their results with.

data interpretation
Penny Talbot Foods

Penny Talbot started in business in 2002 after graduating from Warwick University with a degree in business management. Penny currently owns six frozen food wholesale outlets scattered across the north east of England.

From starting with a small-scale operation, Penny has rapidly expended her business through a shrewd series of takeovers and buyouts of other small competitors. She is currently considering further expansion, and she has identified two wholesalers in Durham and Sunderland as potential takeover targets.

Penny can only raise the finance to purchase one wholesaler. Figure 7.6 presents the financial information she has managed to obtain on the two businesses.

Figure 7.6: Financial indicators for two food wholesale businesses

	Jefferson Frozen Foods Ltd	Quickfreezers
ROCE	17%	6%
Current ratio	2.7:1	0.7:1
Sales per year	£243,000	£180,000
Net profit margin	13%	21%
Margin of Safety	14%	21%

A Calculate the net profit made by each business featured in Figure 7.6.

B Explain what is meant by the margin of safety. Why is it an important area for a business to monitor?

C Advise Penny about which of the two businesses – if either – you would recommend that she buys.

313

Topic 6 Monitoring performance: finance

Winding up a company: liquidation

Setting the scene: company liquidation

Nothing in business is guaranteed, good ideas are not always profitable and a profitable business is not necessarily one that is well managed. Businesses cease trading every year for a variety of reasons, including loss of custom and too many debts.

Companies are legal entities (Topic 2, *see page* 294). They are formed and their personality is artificially created by the submission of a memorandum of association and the articles of association to the Registrar of Companies. If these documents are in order, the company is issued with a certificate of incorporation – in effect, the company is born.

Similarly for a company to die, it has to go through an official legal process to terminate its existence. This is known as winding up and takes place using a procedure called liquidation. This can take two forms with either a court ordering a compulsory liquidation or the members of the company voting to cease trading and apply for voluntary liquidation.

A key point is to differentiate between bankruptcy and liquidation.

- **Bankruptcy** applies to private individuals. People can be forced to declare themselves bankrupt if they are unable to pay their debts and their personal assets may be seized and sold to pay off as many debts as possible.

- **Liquidation** applies to limited companies, private and public, that are ceasing to trade. Companies may be forced into liquidation if they are unable to pay their debts – if they become insolvent – but owners may decide to liquidate companies for other reasons.

This distinction is important in business. If sole traders and partnerships become insolvent – they can't meet all their business debts – then the business owners (the sole trader or the individual partners) face bankruptcy. They do not have the protection of limited liability and are responsible for meeting all of their business debts.

If a company becomes insolvent, then the business faces liquidation. However the business owners (the shareholders) have limited liability, which means in effect that they will not be liable for all of the company's debts.

Closing down trading activities

Companies go out of business for many reasons. However, in practice, companies are either forced out of business or go out of business voluntarily. Different winding procedures apply depending on whether liquidation is compulsory or voluntary.

1 Compulsory liquidation

There are two main reasons why a company can be forced into liquidation by a court:

- the company cannot pay its debts and

- the court considers it just and equitable to wind up the company.

A company is deemed to be unable to pay its debts if:

- a creditor who is owed more than £750 has served a written demand for payment on the company and three weeks later the company has neither paid the debt nor given a security for its payment

- a creditor has obtained a court judgement for payment against the company and the debt has still not been paid

- a court is satisfied that the company is insolvent and is unable to pay its outstanding debts.

The other reason for compulsory liquidation is if a court considers it just and equitable to wind up a company. This situation occurs when a court judges that it is in the best interest of justice or fairness that a company should cease trading. This usually occurs for one (or a combination) of these reasons:

- the company was formed for a fraudulent purpose

- there is a justifiable lack of confidence in the management of the company

KEY TERMS

Winding up is the process of closing down a company that is ceasing to trade.

Liquidation is the formal legal procedure for winding up a company. It can take two forms: voluntary liquidation and compulsory liquidation.

Insolvency is the term applied to a business that is unable to pay its debts as they fall due for payment.

Statement of affairs is a formal document detailing all the assets a company possesses alongside all the creditors (debts) that it owes.

- the substratum of the company has gone – this means that the main purpose for which the company was formed has either been achieved or has become impossible to achieve

- there is a deadlock in the management and the business is unable to continue as the management cannot agree and make decisions.

Compulsory liquidation occurs, therefore, because the company is being ordered to wind up its affairs as it is unable to pay its debts or has not acted in a proper manner. It is key that the businesses affairs are wound up in an organised and effective way; other businesses and individuals are owed money and this will have an effect on their income, cash flow and livelihood.

Figure 7.7 (over page) demonstrates the process and documentation used throughout a compulsory liquidation situation.

2 Voluntary liquidation

Voluntary liquidations are more frequent than compulsory liquidations. They occur when the directors and shareholders of a company voluntarily decide to cease trading. This may be because the directors and shareholders realise that the company is insolvent and cannot pay its debts.

However, many companies are wound up even when they are financially sound. This happens when the shareholders and directors decide that they no longer want to own and run the business. This mainly occurs in small family-owned private limited companies when the family that comprises the directors and the principal shareholders decides that it no longer wishes to continue trading – in effect, the family decides to retire from business – and it chooses to sell off the company's remaining assets.

Voluntary liquidation takes two forms:

- a member's voluntary winding up
- a creditor's voluntary winding up.

Member's voluntary winding up

This method is chosen when a company is financially sound – that is, the business is solvent and able to pay all its debts. In this case, the company must call an extraordinary shareholders meeting and the shareholders must vote through and issue a special resolution that the company shall be wound up. By law, this requires that 75 per cent of the members vote in favour of winding up the company.

The directors then make a declaration of solvency that states that in the directors' opinion the business will be able to pay off all its debts within the next 12 months. The directors also compile a statement of affairs and send this with the declaration to the Registrar of Companies. From the point of the commencement of the voluntary winding up, the sale or transfer of any shares is prohibited.

The company then draws up a plan detailing what commitments it has to meet and continues to trade with a view to honouring any outstanding contracts and debts until such point as all debts are paid. When this is done, the final accounts of the business (profit and loss account and balance sheet) are presented to a final meeting of shareholders, a copy of these accounts and details of the meeting are again sent to the Registrar of Companies. A note is made on the company's file and three months later the company is dissolved.

Creditor's voluntary winding up

This is similar in process to a member's voluntary winding up except that the business is being wound up because it is financially unsound – that is, it is insolvent and unable to pay all its debts. The directors have recognised this fact and acted before one of their creditors goes to court to bring a compulsory winding up order against the company.

The following steps are taken to process a creditor's voluntary winding up:

- a shareholders meeting is held and the shareholders vote and issue a special resolution that the company shall be wound up

- within 14 days, a meeting of creditors is called and the directors of the company present a statement of affairs

- the company and creditors agree to the appointment of a liquidator

- the statement of affairs, notice of the declaration and details of the liquidator are sent to the Registrar of Companies

Figure 7.7: The compulsory liquidation process .

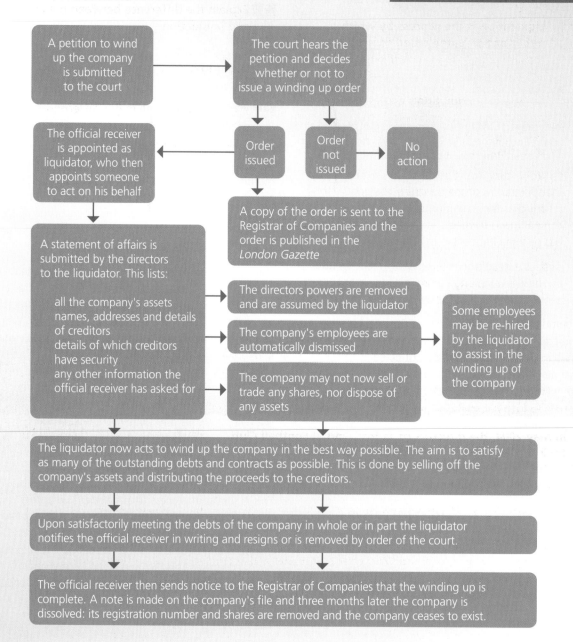

- the directors are removed and their powers are assumed by the liquidator

- the company's employees are automatically dismissed

- shares can no longer be sold or transferred.

The liquidator now acts to wind up the company in the best way possible, by satisfying as many of its outstanding debts and contracts as possible. This is done by selling off the company's assets and distributing the proceeds to the creditors. The liquidator then presents the final accounts of the business to separate shareholder and creditor meetings, sends a copy to the Registrar of Companies, and three months later the company is dissolved.

Note that the main difference between a creditor's and a member's voluntary winding up is that the control and execution of the winding up is placed in the hands of a third-party liquidator who is appointed by the creditors. In this way, the creditors are assured that the liquidator is acting in their best interests and seeking to meet as much of the debt as possible from money raised from sale of the company's assets.

Knowledge summary

- **Liquidation is the process by which public and private limited companies cease to trade and are formally wound up.**

- **Compulsory liquidation occurs when a court action is brought against a company by a creditor for non-payment of debts.**

- **Voluntary liquidation occurs when a company's owners decide that they no longer desire or are able to keep the company trading.**

- **The process of liquidation, in any form, is planned and designed to ensure that, as the company closes down, as many creditors are paid back in full or in part as possible.**

data interpretation
Troubled Telford

In May 2004, the directors of Telford United Football Club took the decision to go into liquidation after taking advice from a Birmingham firm, Moore Stephens Corporate Recovery. The club were in financial trouble ever since their former chairman's business collapsed.

Until March, Telford United was owned by Andy Shaw, who also has other business interests. His main business is a refurbishment company called Miras Contracts. Miras has contracts to refurbish hospitals and hotels across the country. As well as Miras, Shaw also owns Whitehouse Hotels, a chain of four hotels in Kegworth, Worcester, Manchester and at the Bucks Head, Telford's home ground.

Shaw's bank has demanded the repayment of loans and his businesses don't have the money to repay, so all of them have gone into receivership. Miras Contracts has ceased trading, with 400 staff laid off, while Telford United won't get any more money from Shaw. Only the future of the hotel chain is relatively secure as it is a profit-making business. It is continuing to trade.

Telford's acting chairman, Rob Cave, said there was no other choice open to them. The club was losing £16,000 a week. Creditors were owed £100,000, and if any one of them had called in their debt the club would probably go under. The sell-off of players has already began, with goalkeeper Chris McKenzie going to Chester. A creditors' meeting is being organised, once the extent of the club's debts are known.

Source: adapted from www.bbc.co.uk, 27 May 2004

A Explain what type of liquidation is occurring at Telford United.

B Outline the procedure that Telford United Football Club should follow.

C Write a letter from the board of Telford United to the club's creditors explaining what has happened and what will happen regarding any debts they are currently owed.

Winding up a company: closing down activities

Setting the scene: stakeholders at risk

A company has many groups that are involved with and interested in the business. These interest groups are known as stakeholders. They include shareholders, financiers, suppliers, directors, government, local communities, employees and customers.

When a company ceases to trade and goes into liquidation – either for voluntary or compulsory reasons – all stakeholder groups will be affected in some way. Many stakeholders will actually be owed money by the company, and so they will have a financial interest in what happens to the company's remaining assets – their own profits, income, cash flows and perhaps livelihood may be dependant on whether they will receive payment to cover what they are owed.

So creditors will be particularly concerned about how a company plans to liquidate and sell off its assets so that as much money as possible can be raised. They will be keenly interested in how any money is to be distributed to creditors and in what order this distribution takes place. Of course, many will feel the worst – because they know that many companies go into liquidation precisely because they don't have the assets to pay all their creditors.

You can see some of the effects of liquidation in shopping centres. You quite often see local retailers having closing down sales. Sometimes this is a marketing ploy, sometimes the retailer is moving to new premises and doesn't want to carry over old stock, but often a closing down sale is a sign that a company has gone into liquidation and the remaining stock is being sold off to raise money.

Identify four stakeholder groups which you think are most likely to be owed money by a company going into liquidation. Consider how these groups may be affected if they do not receive all or any of the money they are owed.

KEY TERMS

Creditors are individuals and companies to whom a business owes money.

Liquidation is the formal legal procedure for winding up a company. It can take two forms: voluntary liquidation and compulsory liquidation.

Insolvency is the term applied to a business that is unable to pay its debts as they fall due for payment.

Distribution of assets is the order in which a liquidating company must pay back its creditors.

Solvency is the term applied to a business that has sufficient assets to pay all outstanding creditors.

The role of the liquidator

The role of the liquidator is to take over a business that is going into liquidation and oversee the winding up of its affairs. The liquidator is either appointed by the Registrar of Companies or by agreement between the company's directors and its creditors.

By appointing a liquidator to take responsibility for winding up a company's activities, the law aims to ensure that the winding-up process is impartial and independent. Liquidators should not favour one party over another. It is their job to sell a company's assets and pay, as far as possible, the company's debts.

The liquidator has specific responsibilities to carry on the company's business to allow it to be wound up beneficially. This includes collecting debts owed to the company and completing any outstanding contracts for which the company will subsequently be paid. However, liquidators have the right to refuse to complete and honour contracts that they deem will be unprofitable.

In carrying out their functions, liquidators:

- make compromises with debtors to receive payment in part for contracts that will only be partially completed

- sell the company's property – this includes physical assets (premises, vehicles, machinery) as well as intangible assets (such as patents, copyrights, brand names)

- sell the company's remaining assets such as stocks of materials, components or finished goods

- pay as many classes of creditors in full as is possible with the funds raised

- make compromises with creditors for payments in part if insufficient funds are available for debts to be paid in full.

It is important, therefore, that liquidators are seen to act fairly and in the best interests of all concerned parties. In many winding up cases, some creditors may not receive all the money that they are owed, some customers may not see contracts honoured and some people involved with the company may not get any money at all. To ensure fairness, and to prevent disputes, liquidators must follow strict regulations about how a company's assets should be distributed.

Distribution of a company's assets

If a company has gone into member's voluntary liquidation, distribution of assets should not provide too much of a problem. The company's directors will make a statement declaring that the company is solvent – that is, it possesses enough total assets to pay back all creditors – and that in the process of winding up the company it will pay all debts back within the next 12 months.

The problems arise when companies go into liquidation because they are not solvent. In the case of a creditor's voluntary liquidation or a compulsory liquidation order being issued by a court, companies are being wound up because they are insolvent – that is, they do not have enough total assets to cover all the debts that they owe to various stakeholder groups.

It is in these circumstances that some creditors may not receive all of the money they are owed or, in fact, any of the money they are owed. This is because the company does not have sufficient assets of value that can turned into enough cash to pay everybody back.

The order in which creditors are paid off is laid down in the Insolvency Act 1986. Liquidators acting for companies that are winding up their activities must follow the order and provisions as stated by this act. Any money raised is used to settle the company's debts in the following order.

1 Winding up costs, expenses and charges

This covers items such as the fee (wages) of the company (or person) appointed as liquidator and any expenses that the liquidator incurs. It can seem odd that the first creditor to get paid is the liquidator, but without this provision few responsible individuals or companies would take the liquidator role as there would be little chance of being paid in many cases.

2 Preferential debts

Preferential debts are considered to be equal in status. The liquidator will try to be pay all preferential debts in full, but if there are insufficient funds at this point each separate creditor will receive an equal proportion of what is owed to them. For example, all creditors with preferential debts may be paid 70 per cent of what they are owed.

Preferential debts include:

- any sums owed to occupational or state pension schemes

- up to four months' wages per employee (if they have not been paid in the period before the company went into liquidation).

In addition, any loans secured (borrowed) by the company to previously allow them to pay any of these debts are also classed as preferential debts.

3 Creditors with secured debts

Companies secure some loans or debentures that they borrow against particular assets. For example, a bank might have loaned the company money through a mortgage secured on the company's property. In this way, creditors are trying to partially guarantee their loan by attaching them to an asset that has value. These secured debts must be met before unsecured debts, but only after preferential debts have been met.

4 Creditors with unsecured debts

Many creditors that are owed money will have loaned it to the company or supplied goods and services on credit with no security against specific assets. For example, most suppliers sell goods to companies on credit terms, expecting to be paid a specified period after delivering the goods and sending an invoice. Any suppliers offered these credit terms who had yet to be paid for their services would be creditors with unsecured debts.

Under the terms of the Enterprise Act 2002, various government debts previously regarded as preferential debts are now treated as creditors with unsecured debts. These include:

- any income tax owed by the company to the Inland Revenue for up to 12 months in arrears

- any VAT owed by the company to HM Customs and Excise for up to six months in arrears

- any national insurance contributions owed for up to 12 months in arrears

5 Any sums owed to shareholders that have not yet been paid

Remember, it is possible for a profitable business to go into liquidation. A company may have declared a dividend on its profits, and then gone into liquidation before that dividend had been paid to shareholders.

6 Distribution to owners

If there are any remaining assets left to be distributed at this point, they are now shared out between the company's shareholders according to their rights in the company's articles of association. This is usually in proportion to their individual shareholding. Frequently, after the distribution of assets to everybody else, shareholders will receive nothing.

Knowledge summary

- **A company liquidation has wide-ranging effects on a variety of stakeholder groups, from the government to the suppliers and customers of the company.**

- **The Insolvency Act 1986 and the Enterprise Act 2002 lay down the rules and strict order by which outstanding creditors should be paid.**

- **Except in the case of a member's voluntary liquidation, where the company is solvent, creditors may not receive all (or any) of the money they are owed.**

- **An independent liquidator is appointed to see that the distribution of assets is undertaken fairly and in compliance with the law.**

- **Shareholders are least likely to receive any money from the liquidation of a company. However the financial implications of liquidation can and do effect all stakeholder groups.**

stop and think

Apart from the liquidators, which two stakeholder groups are most likely to receive all or part of any monies they are owed? Which two stakeholder groups are least likely to receive any payment?

Consider the dot-com boom and bust. Several companies like Boo, the internet clothing trader, eventually went into liquidation after a relatively brief period of activity. Why is it unlikely that shareholders would receive any recompense from dot-com companies that were forced to cease trading?

quick questions

1 Name three stakeholder groups that would be affected by the liquidation of company.

2 Why is it important that an independent liquidator is appointed?

3 Explain what is meant by the term preferential creditor. In what way do they receive preference over other creditors?

data**interpretation**
Donaldson Aircraft Instrumentation Ltd

Based just outside Kidderminster and employing 387 staff, Donaldson Aircraft Instrumentation was a highly technologically advanced company making precision navigation and landing instruments for use in passenger jet aircraft. However, 2003 saw a downturn in orders for new aircraft and a corresponding downturn in orders for instrumentation.

Always a forward thinking company, Donaldson once again invested heavily in technology and research and development to compete for contracts for the new super transatlantic jets being designed by the American Boeing and the European Airbus concerns. Unfortunately, the company was unable to win any major contracts for either development and, having massively overextended the company's finances, called for a creditor's voluntary liquidation.

A statement of affairs was presented at the creditors' meeting by the liquidator. This showed that the liquidator estimated that £20,400,000 could be raised from the sale and realisation of the companies assets. However, of this sum, £8,000,000 relates to the sale of the company's factory and office buildings over which the Birmingham and Worcestershire Building Society hold security as Donaldson had taken out a £6,000,000 mortgage with the building society. Figure 7.8 details the company's other creditors.

Figure 7.8: Donaldson Aircraft Instrumentation creditors

Creditor	Amount owed	Notes
Component suppliers	£7,500,000	
Raw material suppliers	£1,200,000	
Dividends owed to shareholders	£1,600,000	
Local engineering firms	£1,720,000	For manufacture of some parts under subcontract
HM Customs and Excise	£2,000,000	Three months VAT arrears
Donaldson employees	£890,000	One month's wages
Directors	£90,000	Four month's salary
Oliver Donaldson, MD	£2,000,000	He remortgaged his home to lend the company money to pay its outstanding income tax bill to the Inland Revenue
Bank	£4,300,000	A loan for new equipment, secured against the company's assets

A Which groups would be classed as Donaldson's preferential creditors?

B Calculate which parties will receive full, part or no payment of the money they are owed.

C Draft a report to Oliver Donaldson detailing the role of the appointed liquidator, the process that the liquidator will undertake, explaining how the assets of the firm will be distributed.

Winding up a company: further implications

Setting the scene: customers at risk

It is not just the shareholders, employees and creditors of a business who may suffer if a company goes into liquidation. There are far reaching implications for many different stakeholder groups. As this article illustrates, customers also suffer.

Perform a brainstorming (mind map) exercise identifying all the different groups that would be affected by the liquidation of Global Sports Travel. As well as considering those stakeholders that have a direct involvement with the company, also think about the businesses in Ireland that might be affected if the 560 fans did not turn up.

Rugby fans let down by travel firm

Hundreds of Welsh rugby fans planning a trip to Dublin for the international may miss the match, as their travel company has gone into liquidation. Global Sports Travel Limited specialises in sporting trips and has sent thousands of supporters abroad to follow the fortunes of Wales' national rugby and soccer sides.

But now hundreds of people who have paid in full for the Ireland versus Wales Six Nations rugby game now face paying another travel operator to get them there, or missing the game altogether.

Global Sports Travel is based in Llandarcy, Neath, south Wales, and its core business is rugby international package trips. Around 560 people have paid the company at least £145 each for a trip to Ireland to see Wales's Six Nations game at Lansdowne Road in Dublin. Liquidator Grant Thornton has said arrangements have been made with another tour operator, Travel City of Cardiff, to help travellers where possible, but there will be extra costs involved. Grant Thornton has set up a helpline number for creditors to call with questions about the liquidation.

news.bbc.co.uk, 13 February 2004

KEY TERMS

Preferential creditors are paid back first under the provisions of the Insolvency Act 1986 from any money realised from the sale of a liquidated company's assets (after winding up costs have been paid).

Financiers are organisations (or individuals who are not shareholders) that loan or invest money in a company.

Stakeholders are any individuals or groups that has an interest in the financial performance of a company.

Distribution of assets is the order in which a liquidating company must pay back its creditors.

Market obsolescence occurs when the market for a particular good or service disappears due to changes in society's wants and needs.

Financial implications

The financial implications for each stakeholder group depends to some extent on the type of liquidation and the amount and value of assets held by the company being wound up, as these determine whether or not there are sufficient funds for all creditors to be paid. However, in broad terms, let's consider the implications for each group in turn.

Government

The government's interest lies in several areas. First, it may be owed money through unpaid tax. As a preferential creditor, the government should receive payment (in whole or in part) for any back taxes owing as part of the distribution of the company's assets. Second, the government has to consider that the liquidation of a company invariably leads to some unemployment as well as the loss of any future tax revenues (income tax, VAT and corporation tax). At the very least, the government may face increased expenditure commitments as the company's former employees seek support through benefit payments.

Employees

As preferential creditors, it would be hoped that employees would receive any wages owing to them (to a maximum of four months) out of the distribution. However, this will only happen if sufficient assets exist to cover these payments and the payments to the other preferential creditors as well, otherwise the employees will only receive part of any money they are owed. As well as facing an uncertain future, employees also receive no compensation – on liquidation all company employees are dismissed, they are not made redundant and so receive no compensatory payments.

Secured creditors

Secured creditors are usually financiers such as banks, building societies or debenture holders who have loaned the company money against the security of a fixed asset. Again, so long as sufficient funds exist, because of their secured creditor status, they will get some part of their debt repaid. However, they do run the risk that there may be no funds left at this point and may receive nothing.

Unsecured creditors

As each stage of the distribution of assets is completed – in line with the provision of the Insolvency Act – the probability of the next set of creditors beeing paid in full, or beeing paid anything at all, decreases. Unsecured creditors – normally the company's suppliers – face a very high risk of not receiving all the money they are owed. This could have a knock-on effect on their own businesses' stability, as it will impact upon their profitability and cash flow.

Customers

Customers who have paid deposits (or the full price) for goods or services that will never be delivered, or who are owed refunds, are also unsecured creditors. For example, consider the position of customers of Global Sports Travel who still wished to travel and see the rugby. If they had paid their travel fee upfront, do you think they had any chance of a refund?

Shareholders

Shareholders are the group that is least likely to receive anything. If any funds from the distribution are left, they would receive any unpaid dividends that they are owed, but in most cases this is very unlikely.

It is even more doubtful that shareholders would receive any money in return for their initial investment in buying shares. Once liquidation proceedings begin, trading in the shares of a company is suspended (so shareholders cannot sell them) and at the end of proceedings the company ceases to exist, so the shares are valueless. In the majority of cases, shareholders will lose all the money they have invested. This may be true even with a member's liquidation as money invested by shareholders is not classed as a creditor and so any declaration of solvency (the ability to pay their debts) does not have to take into account paying back shareholders.

All groups of creditors face a considerable wait for their money, even if they are lucky enough to be paid in full. It takes time for the liquidator to dispose of the company's assets and then distribute the funds. This will impact on, and perhaps cause difficulties for, many creditors' cash flow positions as well as causing difficulties for former employees who may have to wait months before receiving any wages that they were owed.

External factors

Companies may go into liquidation for various reasons, these are discussed in depth in Topic 7, but a key point not to be overlooked is that in many cases the reason for liquidation is not due solely to mismanagement of the business. The influence of external factors outside the control of the company's management can play a major role in tipping a business into insolvency. These external factors can be grouped under five main headings.

Social

Social trends and changes in lifestyle may affect many businesses' activities. In particular, a change in fashion or in moral values may leave some companies with few or no consumers – this is termed market obsolescence. For example, many small businesses have been forced to close because they couldn't compete against the relatively new large out-of-town shopping malls. These malls have produced a change in society's shopping habits – many consumers simply prefer them as a retail experience.

Legal

Changes in legislation can have a large impact. In the most extreme cases, the government may outlaw particular products completely, or force increases in costs through, say, new health and safety regulations or the minimum wage. This can force some firms into liquidation as they are unable to operate profitably and pay the costs need to comply with the new law.

Economic

The performance of an economy has a direct relation on how many businesses perform. Changes in the economic environment can make or break a company. Figure 7.9 summarises the impact of changes in some key economic variables.

Political

Changes in government can potentially have a large effect on businesses. The new government's political agenda will both have a direct impact on economic policy such as tax rates and those sectors of the economy under government control like transport (roads and rail), health, education and foreign policy.

Technological

A business can be successful, be the market leader, make large sustainable profits and face no cash flow problems, but what if a rival company invents a new product that makes its products obsolete? Without radical change that business will close. For example, how many companies now produce vinyl records?

Wider impacts

Company failure does not just impact on the direct stakeholders – those groups and individuals that had a financial interest in the business. It can also have wider ramifications.

The closing down of any business can have an impact on the local community in which it used to operate. Obviously, the degree of impact depends on the size of the business that closes, but local communities may be faced with increased unemployment and falling property values. In addition, other local business that provided support services – for example, by supplying cleaning or catering facilities, raw materials and subcontract work – will also be affected even if they were not owed money directly by the firm that goes into liquidation as one of their (actual or potential) clients no longer exists. In effect, the local economy is diminished by the closure.

Failed businesses also impact on the environment. This is perhaps one of the most difficult areas to quantify, but organisations that liquidate, especially from specialist industries, may not be able to find other companies that want to buy their premises or equipment, and there may not be funds to adequately dispose of potential pollutants and secure premises and industrial sites. Consider the closure of a coal mine: a derelict mine can have a major effect on the environment if it is left unused and abandoned with no pollution safeguards. In these situations, the government and local authorities are unable to order the company to clean things up as, of course, it no longer exists. The resulting environmental problems may take years to resolve.

Figure 7.9: How the economy impacts on business

Economic change	Impact on business
Rise in interest rates	Cost of borrowing and cost of paying back existing loans increases – this can make previously profitable businesses into loss-making ones. At the very least, increased repayment charges can contribute to cash flow problems. Consumers also have less disposable income and so cut back their own spending.
Rise in exchange rates	Makes the cost of export goods more expensive for foreign purchasers. This inevitably leads to a decline in demand and sales. Again, profits and cash flows of companies that rely on export markets are affected.
Increases in taxation	Increase the costs of employment and trading for businesses, as well as meaning a greater proportion of profits is paid in tax, leaving less for reinvestment or distribution to shareholders.
Recession	Increased unemployment and decreased consumer demand. Particularly effects sales of companies making luxury goods
Rising inflation	Means increased costs. Prices of raw materials rise alongside rising wage demands from employees. In many cases leads to lower profits alongside increased cash outflows.

Knowledge summary

- The financial impacts of a company liquidating are not just limited to those stakeholders directly involved with and working for the company itself.

- Many external factors can effect the operations of a company and cause it to go into liquidation despite the best efforts of its directors.

- A company closure can have knock-on effects for other firms that provided support services and can have impact on the local community.

quick questions

1 In what circumstances can a customer of a business be considered a creditor of that business?

2 Why are shareholders unlikely to receive back all the money they invested in a company that goes into liquidation?

3 Why might an increase in interest rates increase the number of company liquidations?

data interpretation
Scottish business failures soar

The number of Scottish firms going into liquidation has soared by more than 40 per cent, according to new figures. Business advisers Grant Thornton have also warned that the number of Scottish companies going into liquidation has hit a 10-year high.

The company's report said that liquidators were appointed for a total of 240 firms in Scotland. The directors of 70 firms appointed liquidators, while in the other 170 cases creditors pulled the plug. This means that more investors and banks are also under pressure to recover debts.

The hotel and catering trade was the worst affected industry, with the figures suggesting a year-on-year increase of 200 per cent. Business services were also badly hit. BBC Scotland business correspondent Hayley Millar said there was always a lag between an economic downturn and the time when individual companies were affected.

These problems may have bottomed out – but insolvency experts at Grant Thornton believe there is still cause for concern for the rest of the year. Last year, the firm warned of "early signs of growing problems within the Scottish economy" when it reported that the rate of company failure was at its highest level for nearly nine years.

Source: Adapted from news.bbc.co.uk

A What would be the main effects on the Scottish government of so many business failures?

B Explain how the liquidation of so many firms could have affected other businesses in Scotland.

C Discuss two external factors that could have contributed to the number of hotel and catering businesses going into liquidation.

Business in practice: Naturally Good

Gordon Farquhar had assembled his business plan. He was happy with and expected the bank manager to feel the same. As he sat waiting nervously in the bank's outer office waiting to speak to the manager, he ran through the major sections of his business plan in his mind.

The big idea

Edinburgh attracts thousands of tourists each year, especially during the festival in August. It has a wide range of restaurants, but Gordon had spotted a gap in the market. Nobody was providing organic meals to match the growing demand for organic foodstuffs.

Gordon did not discuss his idea with anyone. He planned to open a restaurant – to be called Naturally Good – which would:

- provide a range of organic food, wine and beer

- focus on quality of food

- have a menu, that regularly changes, of which at least half the dishes were vegetarian

- be located in a quiet area of Edinburgh, away from noisy bars and clubs

- offer a relaxing dining environment with tables far enough apart for privacy.

Gordon thought that he would open his restaurant six nights each week, closing on a Monday evening, usually the quietest of the week. This would allow him to make maximum use of his facilities. He hoped to open from 7 pm and to take last orders no later than 11 pm. This should allow him two sittings.

Pleased with these initial thoughts, Gordon had decided to investigate his idea further.

Gordon's experience and skills

Gordon is 32 and has 12 years' experience as a chef. He has worked in several leading Edinburgh restaurants. He started in a relatively junior capacity having studied catering for three years at a local college. His creative talents and complete reliability marked him out as a rising star and a series of promotions followed working in restaurants owned by other people.

Gordon's current post is as head chef at The Gaslight, probably Edinburgh's best-known restaurant. When appointed to his post, he refurbished the restaurant's dining areas and revolutionised its menus. The results were an outstanding success and The Gaslight's owners offered him a new salary package including a share of profits.

Market research

Gordon has talked to 30 friends and former work colleagues. He explained the concept of Naturally Good and sought their opinions. He has kept notes of their comments and has shown them some sample menus, which they thought were interesting and different from menus available in most other restaurants. At least 20 people thought that using all organic ingredients would be a good USP. He asked them in detail about the improvements that he might make to both the menu and his business idea and used many of the suggestions in drawing up his business plan.

Premises and resources

Gordon was determined to find a good location for his restaurant and chose a Georgian building just off Lothian Road. This had previously been a restaurant and would need minimal changes. It would, however, need decorating, refurnishing and new equipment in the kitchens.

The location is close to the castle, to many of Edinburgh's tourist attractions and to other high-quality restaurants. On enquiry a five-year lease was available and a monthly rental which he felt he could manage.

Staffing

Gordon's business plan was based on having four other staff to help him run his restaurant. He would be supported by one other chef, and Gordon was proposing to advertise for a recently qualified person who could train further. In addition, a long-standing colleague had agreed to become front-of-house manager looking after diners as they arrived as well as looking after the waiting staff and dealing with any enquiries, and Gordon was looking to recruit two waiting staff with some experience.

Gordon's father, a retired businessman – he had been a director of a clothes manufacturing company – had agreed to assist him in recruiting his staff.

Raising the capital

Gordon had always planned to open his own restaurant – this was not a spur of the moment decision. He estimated he would need £95,000 to start the business. This would be needed to buy the lease on the property, to decorate and refit his chosen premises and to pay for launch publicity. In preparation, he had saved regularly and had amassed £25,000. In addition his father had promised to invest a further £20,000 and Gordon had approached his bank for a £50,000 bank loan.

Forming a company

Gordon had decided that he and his father needed the protection of limited liability. He had decided to form a private limited company, initially issuing 1,000 shares. His father had agreed to act as company secretary, using his business experience and relevant qualifications to fill the role. In return for his investment, Gordon's father would receive 210 shares.

Gordon had researched buying a company "off the shelf" and realised that this would be a relatively inexpensive option as well as speeding up the process.

Financial planning

Gordon's restaurant would seat 25 diners at a single sitting. With two sittings, his business had the capacity for 50 diners each evening or 300 per week. Gordon felt that the average charge per head for this restaurant should be about £60 per person to allow the use of quality organic produce and to give a "quality image".

He used his experience along with his investigation into the running costs of the proposed premises to estimate his costs. He estimated fixed costs to be £5000 per month and the variable cost of an average meal to be £35. Figure 7.10 shows a cash flow forecast Gordon has prepared.

Marketing and promotion

Gordon plans to run an advertising campaign in local newspapers and on local radio. In addition, he has budgeted for a launch evening to which he intends to invite a number of Edinburgh's celebrities as well as newspaper editors.

Unit7 Investigating enterprise

Figure 7.10: Gordon's cash flow forecast

	July	August	September	October
Cash in				
Cash sales	7,200	8,900	10,700	12,000
Capital	20,000	50,000		
Total inflow	27,200	58,900	10,700	12,000
Cash Out				
Ingredients for meals	6,000	5,000	4,500	5,300
Start-up costs (eg lease)	65,000	9,500		
Beer, wine & other drinks	12,000	1,500	1,300	1,500
Wages & drawings	3,500	3 500	3,600	3,800
Other costs (eg rent)	7,500	2,000	2,500	9,500
Total outflow	79,000	21,500	11,900	20,100
Net monthly cash flow	(66,800)	(12,000)	(1,200)	(8,100)
Opening balance	25,000	(41,800)	(4,400)	(5,600)
Closing balance	(41,800)	(4,400)	(5,600)	(13,700)

Other matters

A few days before the interview with the bank manager, Gordon's father had pointed out an article in the Scotsman indicating that the rate of economic growth in Scotland had slowed noticeably in recent months and that some economists were forecasting a recession.

... and now

Gordon's thoughts were pulled back to his present situation as the bank manager opened his office door and invited him in.

activities

1 How effectively do you think that Gordon researched and planned Naturally Good? What strengths and weaknesses exist in his plan?

2 What responsibilities do you think that Gordon should take in running his restaurant? Which should be looked after by other people?

3 Discuss the ways in which Gordon might monitor the performance of his business once it starts trading. Which methods of monitoring might be the most important in this case?

4 In the event of Naturally Good not succeeding, what steps would Gordon need to take to wind up his business?

Index

Applied Business AS for Edexcel

Applied Business AS for Edexcel